ENCYCLOPEDIA OF BEAUTY AND HEALTH

Parvesh Handa

Beauty Expert

Exceptional Assistance and Contributions by

Dr. D.S. Jaspal

President, Indian Medical Association, Haryana

and

Dr. Rita Jaspal

Chairperson IMA (Haryana Unit) and Senior Gynecologist

ATLANTIC

PUBLISHERS & DISTRIBUTORS (P) LTD

Published by
ATLANTIC
PUBLISHERS & DISTRIBUTORS (P) LTD
7/22, Ansari Road, Darya Ganj,
New Delhi-110002
Phones : 2327 3880, 23275880, 23280451
Fax : +91-11-23285873
Web : www.atlanticbooks.com
E-mail : info@atlanticbooks.com

Branch Office
5, Nallathambi Street, Wallajah Road,
Chennai-600 002
Phones : +91-44-64611085, 32413319
E-mail : chennai@atlanticbooks.com

Printed in India at Nice Printing Press, A-33/3A, Site-IV, Industrial Area, Sahibabad, Ghaziabad, U.P.

PREFACE

The concept of beauty has widened during the last three decades. For achieving success in one's career, looks and guts are needed. It is seen that many men and women have the aptitude but due to lack of knowledge they are unable to get good results. The art of Indian make-up and hairstyles has no parallels. Indian faces are exotic enough and without being too ethnic they are attractive. Indian girls are smart and beautiful. They have lovely skin tone and natural look. If they are well groomed, they are as good as the best in the world.

Glamour is not out of reach if one is fully conversant with correct techniques of living and know-how about what to wear, eat and the art of make-up; one can even match the famous glamorous women in the world. A survey conducted in this regard reveals that women—whether living in metros or in small cities and towns—have a penchant for glamour, beauty and fashion, but their aspirations are not always fulfilled owing to lack of knowledge and guidance. This *Encyclopedia* has touched all vital aspects of beauty and health to make you confident, perfectly beautiful, keeping your hair and skin healthy.

I hope this book will prove to be a good friend, a useful guide and a sincere advisor not only to women, but also men suffering from disorders of skin and hair, which are curable with a little care and save them from ailments later in life. I have tried to give maximum natural remedies based on herbal formulations in this book. Such remedies were unknown to Indian women decades ago. However, awareness thereof has increased rapidly during past over two decades and today the picture is different. Beauty-conscious people themselves have rediscovered the potential hazards of synthetic products and are shifting to natural products.

I have come across several men and women who look aged in the prime of their youth due to sedentary habits, lack of certain vitamins and nutrient-rich diet and with a low level of physical fitness.

They are worried and spend hours before the mirror hiding their tired, puffy and wrinkled faces under make-up, frustrated with flab, upset with excess weight, stressed out and angry at the diets that didn't work. This book has been designed in simple and easy-to-follow language to lay out a wonderful road map for those who become victims of premature ageing and lose youth, health, beauty and confidence in themselves. I hope this book will guide those seeking rejuvenation to stay and look younger.

Planning for a baby is a pleasure and joy and on the other hand a duty and responsibility. The right knowledge provides an expectant mother a healthy and jubilant baby. Painless pregnancy is one such effort to provide handy help to pregnant women, especially those going to be mother for the first time. During pregnancy, the expectant mother should see her doctor at least once a month to get herself examined to make sure that the fetus is developing satisfactorily. Besides, she needs to do a lot herself—and this book tells all that. Various problems faced by women during pregnancy have been categorised into four parts—before conceiving, during the three stages of pregnancy, labor and when blessed with a baby—and have been described in detail.

Thanks to the amazing advances of medical science, the discomforts connected with pregnancy have become much easier to cope with, and with a little care you can make your pregnancy and life enjoyable and painless. So it is no longer time to worry about or brood over but to plan and dream.

I am highly thankful to the experts for the cooperation and assistance rendered for making this book useful to the readers, especially to those suffering from beauty and skin ailments and body diseases. I hope it will help readers to avoid, control and cure their sufferings with a little care and timely treatment. The readers should keep in mind that medical treatments described in this book are for reference only, and it is neither a medical guide nor a manual of self-treatment. No medical treatment should be taken without consultation with a qualified doctor.

Parvesh Handa

CONTENTS

SECTION 1: BEAUTY

1

ABOUT THE SKIN

TYPES OF SKIN

Skin can be divided into seven categories:

1. **Normal Skin:** has a fine texture with a supple and smooth surface. It is usually moist, neither greasy nor dry. The pores of the skin are smooth.
2. **Dry Skin:** has tendency to flake easily. It is prone to wrinkles and lines due to insufficient secretion of sebum. Dry skin is not capable to retain moisture and ages faster.
3. **Oily Skin:** is caused due to over-secretion of sebum by the oil glands and is usually prone to pimples, acne, blackheads, white-heads, spots and blemishes.
4. **Combination Skin:** has combination of both oily and dry skin. It has certain areas of the face oily and the rest dry. Usually, the forehead, nose and chin are greasy whereas the cheeks and the area around the eyes and mouth are dry. For treating and understanding skin better, the facial skin is divided into different zones such as T-Zone, C-Zone and Y-Zone. T-Zone is always greasy, Y-Zone is a normal zone and C-Zone is generally dry and sensitive and there is redness in the sensitive region.

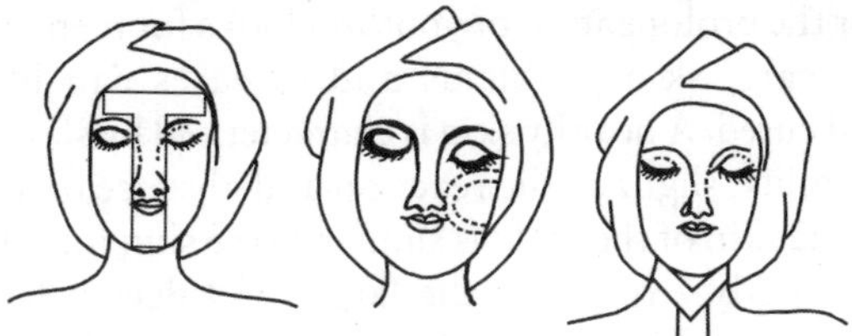

T-zone C-zone Y-zone

5. **Sensitive Skin:** has fine texture and is usually sensitive to change in the climate-Hot or Cold.
6. **Dehydrated Skin:** usually falls under the category of dry skin due to lack of moisture. It can also be aggravated by exposure to sun rays and may cause premature ageing, fine lines and wrinkles.
7. **Sallow Skin:** is a pale yellow colour skin due to deficient diet and lack of vitamin B.

HOW TO ANALYSIS THE SKIN

The selection of correct face pack and right type of make-up is made after the thorough study of the facial skin. Generally facial skin is categorized in three zones as stated above and described below:

1. **T-Zone:** comprises of the part of the forehead, nose and upper and lower lip. This area is always greasy.
2. **C-Zone:** comprises the part of the cheeks, which is usually dry and sensitive. There is redness in this sensitive part.
3. **Y-Zone:** is usually the normal area on the neck and upper part of the chest.

The skin is detected by pinching. By pinching the skin, its type can be found out. If there is redness when pinching, it means the skin is sensitive. If the redness soon disappears after pinching, it indicates, the skin is normal. If there is no redness on pinching, then the skin is dry and rough.

The skin is made-up of moisture, oil and water. If there is too much oil it shows as a shiny skin or oozes out, this means that the is only skin which would finally change into sebum. Skin with balanced amount of oil, water and moisture is normal skin. The skin lacking oil, water and moisture is a dehydrated skin.

HISTORY OF THE SKIN

The skin is the largest organ in the human body and is composed of cells which keep dying but are being renewed all the time. Skin care is essential for the prolongation of youthful looks for men and women. With a little care, skin problems and diseases can be avoided, controlled and cured. A healthy skin is characterised by slight moisture, softness, flexibility, slight acidic reaction and absence of any blemish or a disease. The skin of the scalp is similar to the skin found elsewhere on the human body, except for the larger and deeper hair follicles present on the scalp. The surface area of the skin on human body is

1.62 sq. metres in average adult male and 1.43 sq. metres in an adult female. The skin consists of three components: The Epidermis, which forms the outermost covering. The Dermis, which provides the base on which the epidermis rests. The Hypodermis, which provides the cushion under the skin.

Composition of the Skin

One inch square of skin consists of:

Cells	19,500,00
Sensory cells	19,500
Nerve endings	1300
Sweat glands	630
Pressure complexes	160
Sebaceous glands	95
Sensory nerves for the heat	78
Nerves	78
Hair muscles	65
Blood vessels	19-20
Sensory nerves for cold	13

Cells of the Skin

The whole skin is made up of cells. The cells grow and are divided into two parts and are pushed towards the surface of the skin. After some time the old cells die and are replaced by the new ones, and are pushed towards the epidermis.

Nerves

There are three types of nerves:

1. **Motor Nerves:** These are distributed to the blood vessels and are made of fibre.
2. **Sensory Nerves:** Usually react the heat, cold, touch, pressure and pain.
3. **Secretary:** These are distributed to oil and sweat glands.

Glands

Glands are a part of body that makes a special fluid, is called a gland. The dermis glands are of two types:

1. **Sebaceous glands:** These usually open into the hair follicle and secrete oil. They are found in large numbers on the face, back and scalp.
2. **Pseudoferous glands:** These glands secrete salt water, urea and other waste products on to the skin surface.

Functions of the Skin

The skin is just a covering to:

- protect the body from heat, cold, bacteria, environment and other harmful elements.
- regulate skin and temperature of the body. In case of extreme heat the skin secretes sweat resulting coolness of the body.
- respirate the skin. Skin breathe to some extent and take out unwanted gases.
- help excretion, which eliminates salt and waste products dissolved in the form of sweat.
- secretes sebum, which keeps the skin smooth and soft.
- helps hydration, resulting the skin hide moisture that keeps the skin soft and moist.
- helps absorption. The skin permits certain substances to pass through its tissues. The capacity of the skin to absorb these substances make it possible to apply products externally.
- help sensation and many nerve ending are just under the skin, which makes us aware of the heat, cold, pressure and pain. These sensations transmitted to the brain. These nerves has acid mantle, which helps the skin to fight bacteria and infection.

Structure of the Skin

The skin is the largest organ of the body and consists of the components: The Dermis, The Epidermis and Hypodermis.

The Dermis

It rests upon a thick pad and is about 10 to 30 times thicker than epidermis. It consists of collagen, elastic fibres and ground substance within which blood vessel, lymph, vessels, nerves *etc.* are embedded. The dermis may be divided into two compartment or layers:

1. **The Papillary or Super Facial Layer:** Which lies immediately beneath the epidermis and contains papillae those bring about close contact between the capillaries of dermis and cells at the epidermis.
2. **The Reticular Layer of the Dermis:** It is the deeper portion of the dermis which consists of dense connective tissues. The structure in the dermis are blood vessels, the lymph vessels, sensory nerve ending, hair follicle, sebaceous glands and sweat glands etc.

The Epidermis

It forms the outer most part of the skin and is composed, at the cells, which are called keratinocytes. The epidermis has a thickness between 0.07 mm and 0.12 mm, but in certain parts of the body *viz.* sole of the feet and palms of the hand, it is very thick ranging from 0.08 mm to 1.4 mm. The epidermis is composed of five layers of the cells as below:

1. **The basal layer:** It is a deepest single cell layer, which provide a pigment called melanin.
2. **The Prickle Cell Layer:** It is made of 3 to 7 layers of spiny cells.
3. **The Granular Cell Layer:** It is made of 2 to 3 layers of diamond shaped cells.
4. **The Clean Layer:** The cell in this layer loose their nucleus.
5. **The Horny Layer:** It has dead cells, but have the property to absorb and retain water.

Hypodermis

Beneath the dermis is highly variable tally tissue layer called hypodermis also called adipose. It varies in thickness according to the age, sex and general health of the individual and gives smoothness and contour to the body. It is absent on the eyelids and male genital organs.

Hair Follicles

These are tube like structures within which the hair (on the skin) develops and grows. The hair extends up and out onto the skin through a pore—a minute opening in the skin surface. Each hair follicle has a rich blood supply feeding the cells.

Sebaceous Glands

These are generally attached to hair follicles and produce the skin's natural lubricant—an oily substance called sebum, which provides lubrication for the skin and hair maintaining suppleness and the hair's luster. As we comb or brush our hair, the sebum is taken down its length. Brushing the hair one hundred times at night would keep hair in good condition. Use of a hair dryer, evaporates the sebum reducing its lubricating qualities. We replace lost or lacking sebum with hair conditioners.

Sweat Glands

These are also known as exocrine glands or sudoriferous glands, which are of two types: Eccrine and Apocrine. The Eccrine glands are found all over the body, but are more numerous on the palms of the hands, the soles of the feet and under the arms. Their function is to produce sweat which helps to regulate body temperature. The sweat from these glands travel to the surface of the skin via a sweat duct, which open onto a sweat pore. Aprocrine glands are found mainly in the underarm and genital area of the body and usually develop in puberty. The sweat produced from these gland is broken down by the bacteria present on the surface of the skin resulting in body odor. Arrector pili muscles are small structures attached to hair follicles. The tiny muscles contract as the body temperature drops from 36.8°C.

The Cells

The human organism is made of a vast variety of parts that vary in complexity. These include organs, tissues and cells. The cell is the basic structure from which all other body structures are made. These are the basic units of all living things, including bacteria, plants and animals. The human body is composed entirely of cells, fluid and cellular products. Cells are made up of protoplasm—a colorless, jelly like substance in which food elements such as protein, fats, carbohydrates, mineral salts and water are present. The principal parts of a cell are:

1. Cytoplasm, which contains materials necessary for the growth, reproduction and self-repair of the cell.
2. Centrosome, which also affects the reproduction of the cell. Centrosome is a small, round body in the cytoplasm.
3. Nucleosome, too, is a small spherical body, which plays an important part in the reproduction of the cell.
4. Cell membrane, which permits soluble substance to enter and leave the cell.

Growth of Cell

As long as the cell receives an adequate supply of food, oxygen and water, eliminates waste products, and is favored with proper temperature, it will continue to grow and thrive. In case these conditions do not exist and there is presence of toxins or pressure, then the growth and health of the cells are impaired. When the cells reach maturity, reproduction takes place by direct or indirect division. Direct division also known as amitosis is a simple process whereby the cells elongates, forming two separate cells. This method of reproduction rarely takes place in human tissues. Indirect division also known as mitosis is a complex process whereby a series of changes occurs in the nucleus before the cell divides in half. This method of reproduction occurs in human tissues.

Metabolism

Metabolism is a complex chemical process whereby the body cells are nourished and supplied with energy to carry on their activities. In a healthy body, the metabolic rate is kept under control by a secretion from the thyroid glands. There are two phases of metabolism:

1. **Anabolism:** It is a constructive process, which build up larger molecules from smaller ones. During this process the body stores water, food and oxygen, which are needed for cell growth and repair.
2. **Catabolism:** It is a destructive process, which breaks down larger substances or molecules into smaller ones. This process releases energy that can be stored by special molecules to be used for muscle contraction, secretion or heat production. The cells are made of protoplasm, which is a colorless, transparent, jelly-like substance consisting of nearly 70% water together with organic and inorganic substances.

Body Tissues

Tissues are composed of group of cells. Each tissue has a specific function and can be recognized by its characteristic appearance and are of five types:

1. **Connective tissue:** These serve to support, protect and bind together other tissues of the body. Fat tissues are examples of connective tissue.
2. **Muscular tissue:** These tissues contracts and moves various parts of the body.
3. **Nerve tissue:** They carry massages to and from the brain. These control and coordinate all body functions.
4. **Epithelial tissue:** It is an protective covering on body surfaces such as skin, mucous membrane, linings of heart, digestive and respiratory organs and glands.
5. **Liquid tissue:** These carry food, waste products and hormones by means of the blood and lymph.

Organs

These are structures designed to have good functions of the body. The most important body organs are:

1. The brain, which controls the body.
2. The heart, which circulates the blood.
3. The lungs, which supply oxygen to the blood and control respiratory system in the body.
4. The liver, which removes toxic products of digestion.
5. The kidney, which excrete water and other waste products.
6. The stomach and intestines help to digest the food.

Body Regions

The skeleton is divided into three main regions:

1. The scull.
2. The spine.
3. The limbs.

Respiration System

It is a controlled exchange of the gases oxygen and carbon dioxide. Cells are bathed in a fluid known as interstitial or tissue fluid. This fluid allows the interchange of substances between the cells and blood. The blood carry oxygen from the respiratory system and nutrients from the digestive system to the cells and are absorbed in five different ways such as Diffusion, Osmosis, Dissolution, Transportation of substances and Filtration.

Conditions affecting the skin

- **Abscess:** A pocket of local infection which is painful, swollen and contains a pus formation.
- **Acne Rosacea:** Redness of the nose and cheeks. These are caused by delation of minute capillaries in the skin. Papules and pustules accompany this disorder.
- **Acne Vulgaris:** Infected sebaceous glands result papules, pustules and comedones. Common infected areas include face, neck, back and chest.
- **Allergy:** Sensitivity causing the skin to react adversely which becomes red, hot and itchy.
- **Asteatosis:** Under activity of sebacous glands causing excessively dry, scaly and itchy skin.
- **Atheletes Foot:** Also known as Tinea Pedis. It is a form of ringworm resulting from a fungal infection affecting soles of the feet in between toes. It causes itchy, soggy skin which flakes and peels.

- **Bed Sores:** Also known as Decubitus Ulcer. These are painful, cracked, weeping areas of skin caused by irritation on the body. They are commonly found on buttocks, heels and elbows.
- **Blister:** A swelling caused by an accumulation of clear fluid under the skin generally caused by injury, heat, friction and reaction to an irritant substance.
- **Boil:** A bacterial infection of a sweat gland or hair follicle caused by a pore or follicle being blocked by dead skin cell and other debris. A pus formation develops which becomes a abscess on the head. A collection of boils is also known as a Carbuncle.
- **Bruise:** A discoloration in or below the skin tissue resulting from an injury. Blood leaks from damaged blood vessels into surrounding tissue.
- **Callus:** Thickening of the skin caused by abnormal pressure or friction, commonly found on the feet.
- **Cancer of skin:** Mostly associated with exposure to ultra-violet radiation from the sun.
- **Cellulites:** Spreading inflammation of skin, which becomes hot to touch, tender and shiny.
- **Cherry Spots:** These are red or purple spots, which appear on the chest and trunk. They bleed easily but harmless.
- **Chilblains:** Painful, red, blue or purple areas on the skin found on the toes and fingers as a result of poor circulation.
- **Chloasma:** Small, dark colored patches on the skin as a result of by melanocyte action being stimulated, usually caused by hormone imbalance and contraceptive pill.
- **Cold Sore:** Also known as Herpes Simplex. Generally caused by virus, which can lie dormant in the sensory nerve cells and may be activated by fever, menstruation, sunburn or extreme cold.
- **Comedone:** Also known as blackhead. The opening of pore becomes blocked with sebum, dead skin cells, sweat and dirt mostly on the center panel of face.
- **Corn:** A thick layer of the skin following repeated friction. The affected areas are toes and soles of the feet.
- **Cyst:** Small, painless lump found on the body in the sebaceous glands which are easily infected, many times on the scalp.
- **Dermatitis (Eczema):** An inflammation of the skin, causing swelling, itching and blisters. It eventually dries with scabs and crusts.

- **Ephelides:** Small, flat, irregular patches of melanin found on the face and body. These are known as Freckles.
- **Fissures:** Cracks within the epidermis, which expose the dermis.
- **Herpes Simplex:** A viral infection commonly known as a cold sore, mostly in the mouth.
- **Hirsutism:** An abnormal pattern of hair growth involving a male pattern of hair growth on the skin in women.
- **Hives:** Also known as Urticaria. A swollen area of the skin surrounded by red wheal and generally known as nettle rash.
- **Hyperidrosis:** Excessive perspiration affecting areas such as the hands, feet and underarms.
- **Hypertrichosis:** Abnormal growth of hair involving hair growth in unusual areas of the body.
- **Impetigo:** A highly contagious skin infection starting with a red spot which becomes a blister and discharge liquid. A yellow crust develops and spreads on the affected area like face, hands and nails.
- **Ingrowing Hair:** Hairs on the skin, which continue to grow below the surface of the skin.
- **Keloid:** A harmless mass of excess tissue forming in the scar of an injury, commonly in black skin.
- **Keratosis Actinic:** Hard, dry, scaly, flat, brown growths most commonly found on the exposed skin such as face and back of the hands. These usually occur in later life.
- **Lentigines:** A large, distinct freckle-like mark, slightly raised.
- **Macule:** Flat, colored area of skin, which may be lighter or darker than the surrounding skin.
- **Mature skin:** Skin looks like an ageing skin because of harsh products and exposure to extreme temperature.
- **Melanoma:** Pigmented mole usually a harmless juvenile melanoma and a malignant melanoma.
- **Milia:** Small, harmless pinhead cysts around eyes and cheeks on a dry skin.
- **Mole:** A darkened, raised skin of varying size, shape and color.
- **Monilethrix:** An irregular development of hair in the follicle on skin resulting in bead-like swellings along the hair shaft.
- **Papule:** A small raised area of unbroken skin often developing into a pustule. It is painful solid to touch.
- **Pigmented naevi:** Harmless, colored birthmark.
- **Pili-multigenmini:** Twin hair growing from the same follicle.

- **Port-wine Stain:** Flat patches of dark red staining in the skin resulting from an abnormality of the capillary blood vessels.
- **Prickly Heat:** A rash caused by excessive heat when the skin becomes red, itchy and is accompanied by inflamed or blocked sweat glands. Prickly heat is also known as Miliaria Rubra.
- **Psoriasis:** A scaly eruption of the skin. Red patches develop covered by scale, which can be itchy.
- **Pustule:** A white head spot or pimple slightly raised.
- **Ringworm:** A fungal infection of the skin, which is known as Tinea Corporis.
- **Scabies:** A highly contagious disease of the skin caused by an infestation of a mite, which burrows into the skin. It affects between the fingers, inside the wrist and soles of the feet causing itchy.
- **Scar:** A replacement tissue formed over the site of injury.
- **Seborrhea:** Over-active sebaceous glands causing oily skin with enlarged, blocked pores, comedones and pustules.
- **Sensitive skin:** A fine, pale skin, which needs extra care.
- **Shingles:** Also known as Herpes Zoaster. It is a blistered skin eruption over an area of skin by a nerve. It is a severely painful condition.
- **Skin Tag:** Tiny, loose growth of the skin, which develops on the neck or groin. It is colorless, painless and usually the disorder attack armpit and trunk at any age but most commonly in elderly women.
- **Spider Naevus:** These are small, painless, red spots with thin blood vessels usually appearing on the face, body and legs during pregnancy.
- **Strawberry Naevus:** A bright red mark varying from a small pinhead to a swollen, irregular dome-shaped mark most commonly found on head and the neck.
- **Stretch mark:** Thin lines of over-stretched skin, which are generally shiny and discoloured due to loss of elasticity in the dermis.
- **Sunburn:** Inflammation of the skin after excessive exposure to sun.
- **Tinea Pedis:** A form of ringworm resulting from fungal infection. It usually affects the soles of the feet and in-between the toes.
- **Vitiligo:** White patches of the skin caused by destruction of melanocytes and hormonal imbalance.
- **Warts:** Small, solid growth on the skin caused by virus. It is highly contagious. When they appear on the feet, are known as Veruccas.
- **Wheal:** A localised area of swelling.
- **Whitlow:** An infection of the soft pad at the tip of the fingers or thumb. It's tender to touch with pus formation.

Factors for Balancing the Skin

The skin will benefit from drinking fluid. Drink as much water as you can at room temperature to aid digestion. Food with special value for this system will help a lot. Vitamin A, C and E are essential natural anti-oxidant which provide protection to the skin. Take rich, balanced diet and fresh vegetables and fruits which will contribute to clear skin, rest is equally important for skin cells. An adult needs 6 to 8 hours of quality sleep in every 24 hours. Rest allows the skin to replenish and regenerate efficiently. Physical activity stimulates the circulation ensuring an active blood supply to the skin. Cleansing, exfoliating, stimulation, toning, applying masks for nourishing, moisturizing are important skin care routines.

Foundation of Good Skin

Family habits, breathing in fresh oxygen, relieving out carbon dioxide and waste from the body, fresh environment, a regular exercise which leads to more collagen production for improved texture, glow and moisture retention to your skin, a rich diet to food your skin, dairy products diet, sound sleep to help regenerate skin cells. Spraying face with spring water makes it dewy fresh on a hot day. Ice cold water splashed on the face in the morning increases circulation and plays miraculous effect. Estrogen hormone is an important skin regulator. A good supply of oestrogen means that skin tends to be supple, soft and healthy. Hormone Replacement Therapy (HRT) brings back glow on the skin.

Natural Moisture in the Skin

The moisture contents in the skin play important role, which govern its softness and elasticity, and is responsible for its youthful appearance. Water is constantly being lost from the skin surface, apart from what is lost through sweating and this loss is continuously being replaced from below.

There are two main factors, which reduce the loss of water from the skin—the outer horny layer or the stratum corneum and the invisible hydro-lipidic film that covers the skin surface. The overlapping dead cells of the stratum corneum make a waterproof cover forming a natural barrier against excessive water loss. This layer contains chemical substances, which is the natural moisturizing factors helping to retain water contents in the skin. Sebum is another important factor, which prevent water loss. Sebum forms a hydro-lipidic film, which hold onto the water contents. The degree of protection offered by sebum varies depending upon the skin type, it is maximum if the skin is oily. In an atmosphere with low humidity (cold windy weather or with central heating or air-conditioning), excessive exposure to sun, use of soaps and detergents reduce the ability of the skin to retain water because they damage the natural moisturizing factors and remove the oil from the hydro-lipidic film.

What is pH of the Skin?

The symbol pH is used in day-to-day language to represent the degree of acidity or alkalinity of a substance. When a solution is neither alkaline nor acidic, it is called neutral. Cosmetic manufacturers have done considerable research in order to discover and produce products whose pH is beneficial for the skin and the hair.

The pH of water, a neutral substance is 7. If the pH of a solution is less than 7, it is acidic and if the pH is more than 7, it is alkaline. The pH of a healthy normal skin is between 5.2 and 6; that it is slightly acidic. The acidic pH of the skin is due to the presence of acid in the sebum, sweat and keratin. It is necessary to maintain the acidity of skin. It is due to this only, the curd and lemon juice when applied would do wonders for your skin. This is also the reason why ordinary soaps, which are usually alkaline, have erroneously, a bad name.

Soaps and detergents generally have an alkaline pH. If, because of its formulation, the pH of a soap falls near enough to natural so as not to disturb the pH of the skin, then these soaps are called ‘pH controlled’ soaps. These pH controlled soaps are superior to ordinary soaps.

How to choose a soap?

Variety of soaps are available in market today. ‘Which soap to buy?’ People usually want to know. Here is a checklist to help you.

- **Medicated Soaps:** These are often useful by those who have spots. The medication added is an antiseptic (natural and synthetic). Ordinary soaps does a fairly good job of removing the bacteria. Medicated soaps can cause allergic reactions and are best avoided unless your doctor advises you to use them.
- pH soaps and detergents have an alkaline pH. The exact pH is usually stated on the label. Since the skin has a tremendous reserve, the pH altered by ordinary soaps is normally rapidly restored after thorough rinsing. So these pH controlled soaps are only marginally superior to ordinary soaps.

- **Moisturising Soaps:** These do not have any advantage over ordinary soaps because after rinsing all moisturising ingredients are removed.
- **Superfatted Soaps:** These contain fatty materials to prevent excessive stripping of surface oils. They also deposit a emollient film to replace some of the natural oils removed in cleansing process. These soaps can be applied on dry skins.
- **Transparent Soaps:** These soaps are costly and difficult to manufacture. They are not more effective or safer than ordinary soaps.
- **Liquid Soaps:** These soaps have no advantage over other soaps.
- **Perfumed Soaps:** These soaps contain artificial perfume, which may sometimes cause allergic reaction.

HERBAL COSMETICS

- **Herbal Deep Cleansing Milk:** Natural herbs, oils and rose water are the ingredients, which emit the properties of moisturizer, cleanser and emollient. The cleansing action includes opening of pores temporarily, removing deep-seated dirt, sebum, sweat and make-up residue.
- **Herbal Skin Toner:** Enriched with herbal extracts including aloe vera, rose water and natural moisturizers. It relieves acne, atmospheric microbes and harsh effects of sun rays by reducing pore size and tightening skin muscles.
- **Herbal Moisturizer:** Moisturizer is beneficial for all types of skin especially a dry skin. It is enriched with Vitamins A, D, E, wheat-germ oil, olive oil, turmeric extract and rose water — all these helps to retain moisture in epidermis making it soft and supple.
- **Herbal Astringent:** A refreshing preparation containing a herbal extract, camphor and mint. It is a perfect remedy for oily skin, cures acne and over secretion of sebum.
- **Herbal Cold Cream:** An herbal cold cream is usually non-sticky, non-oily that makes skin smooth and soft without leaving behind any residue. It contains Vitamin B that nourishes skin, removes wrinkles and makes skin glow youthfully. It also contains herbal extracts to provide extra smoothness and health to the skin.
- **Herbal Massage Cream:** A special herbal cream for massage with extra moisturizing properties is available. It prevents ageing and dehydration of skin and impart glow to the skin.
- **All Purpose Cream:** It prevents ageing and dehydration of skin. It has an extra moisturizing rich formula for winter care and protects

the skin against dryness, keeping it satin soft and increase blood circulation.

- **Almond Nourishing Cream:** Herbal based nourishing creams include light weight ingredients rich in source of vitamin E. Almond Nourishing cream is a perfect blend of almond, avocado oils and NMC 70 which nourishes, moisturizes and refreshes the skin.
- **Winter care lotion:** It protects the skin in winter. An extra rich moisturizer formulated with goodness of vitamin A, C and E usually present in the cucumber and wheat-germ oil provides satin smooth, youthful and radiant skin (without the sticky feel) in winter if applied regularly.
- **Sunscreen Lotion:** Usually a light weight, non-greasy lotion with two variants: SPF 5 for dark complexion and SPF 15 for fair complexion. It protect the skin and makes its texture soft, smooth and fair.
- **Calamine Lotion:** A complete make-up base, which helps lighten the skin blemishes and sunburns. Its creamy, easily absorbable formula and have antiseptic properties.
- **Natural Fairness Cream:** Herbal fairness cream helps UV (ultra violet) protection. It is a blend of useful herbs with aroma oils. It is absolute a non-greasy formula which protects the skin from the harsh UV rays of the sun.
- **Peel-of Mask:** It recharges retired and dull skin and removes premature wrinkles to revive the skin texture. Lemon peel-of mask is suitable for oily skin and Apricot and Honey peel-of mask is most suitable for normal and dry skin.
- **Rose Water:** Rose water is one of the oldest skin-fresheners. It softens coarse skin and its pores, protects the skin from irritation, heat, rashes and makes the skin to appear youthful.
- **Tulsi-neem Soap:** This type of soap is manufactured from active extract of Tulsi which is anti-bacterial and Neem which is an antiseptic. When both are mixed to multani mitti (Fuller's Earth), which is a coolant, and applied to the skin, it imparts a beautiful, spotless and glowing skin.

CARE OF THE SKIN IN DIFFERENT SEASONS

The weather such as summer, winter, rainy, hot, wind and water — all natural phenomena, excessive of which can have an adverse effect on the skin. The condition of the skin varies with the weather. During winter season, the skin becomes dry whereas in summer season, the skin generally becomes oily. The following precautions must be taken for caring skin:

Summer Care

- Wash face preferably with gel (as soap makes skin dry) at least twice a day.
- Cleanse the skin thoroughly before sleep at night.
- Apply astringent lotion on oily skin.
- Wash the skin or take bath preferably with cold water.
- Perform a home facial once a week or a saloon facial once or twice a month.

Winter Care

- Avoid using soap as far as possible. Wash the face with gel.
- Clean the face before going to bed. Remove accumulated dirt and stale make-up on the skin with cleansing milk or a lotion.
- Wash the face once a day preferably with tepid water.
- Perform a home facial once a fortnight or a facial from beauty parlour once or twice in a month depending upon the condition of skin.
- Apply a rich nourishing cream or a skin tonic followed by moisturiser at night before sleep, and also when going out in cold and dry weather. Wipe off excess cream and clean the face next morning.
- If the skin is excessively dry, apply a face cream containing vitamins. Vitamin E cream is most beneficial for the skin.

Monsoon Care

- **A three-step skin care programme:** Cleansing, toning and moisturising should be made part of daily routine.
- **Remember, even an oily skin needs a moisturiser too:** Lack of moisturiser on the skin enhances premature lines and wrinkles, and gives an impression of older age. Apply a moisturiser under the make-up.
- Moisturise the area around the eyes daily at night, wipe of excess cream after about 30 minutes to avoid puffiness around the eyes the next morning.
- Steam the face once a week if the skin is blemished and prone to wrinkles. Clean the face thoroughly before steaming to unclog the pores of the skin and remove blackheads with a blackhead extractor.

2

TAKING CARE OF YOUR SKIN

Cleansing is the first step in caring for your skin. It clears perspiration, grease, dust, stale make-up, dirt and bacteria that collect on the skin. Soap is a cleanser although not very good one when it comes to cleanse the skin especially when make-up has been used. The first step is to cleanse the skin. Face gel and water remove most of the impurities but it does not remove make-up completely. Cosmetic cleansers are made in many forms and these include cleansing cream, lotion, cleansing milk, liquefying creams, liquid cleansers, a cold cream and pads impregnated with cleansing lotions and emulsions and a cold cream. These products are designed especially for dry or oily skins. The cleanser must be massaged into the skin with a light upward and outward movement, applying especially to the creases of nose, under the chin, on the neck and ear lobes, which are most neglected areas on the face. Use cotton wool for cleaning the skin.

HOW TO CLEANSE YOUR SKIN?

A cleanser dissolves make-up, remove dirt, dust and grime from the pores. Some cleansers are slightly astringent or refreshing and these are usually intended for quick daytime cleansing before reapplying fresh make-up. The creams and emulsions are more commonly used at night when it is essential to deep-cleanse the skin to remove every trace of the make-up and grime. On the whole, almost any cleanser will do for any type of skin but generally rich creams are best for dry skins and liquefying creams or cleansing lotions are best for oily skin. There are special cleansers made for blemished skins and these tend to have a drying effect. Cleansing creams are easy to make yourself and you can try some of the cleansing creams as described below:

Cucumber Juice Cleansing Cream

Collect the ingredients such as 3 tsp Bees-wax, 4 tsp Coconut oil, 5 tsp Olive oil, 4 tsp Cucumber juice, 1 tsp Glycerine, a pinch of Borax powder and a drop of green colouring. Mix oils and wax into an enamel bowl and melt slowly on a pan of boiling water to save useful contents from burning. Simultaneously heat the cucumber juice, glycerin, colouring and borax in a separate bowl. Ensure that the borax dissolves thoroughly. When the contents of both are melted and warm, add water drop by drop to the oil stirring continuously. Now store the cream in the refrigerator.

Easy-to-make Cleansing Cream

Collect the ingredients such as ½ tablespoon bees-wax, 1 tablespoon emulsifying wax, 4 tablespoons baby oil or mineral oil, 2 tablespoons coconut oil, 2 tablespoons distilled water, ¼ tablespoon borax, 1 tablespoon witch-hazel and few drops of perfume.

Mix waxes and oils in a enamel bowl and melt slowly over a pan of boiling water. In a separate bowl, heat water and borax stirring until the borax is completely dissolved. Then add to it witch-hazel. Avoid heating for too long, otherwise it will completely evaporate. When the waxes have melted, remove both bowls from the heat and mix. When the cream begins to cool, add perfume. Beat until the mixture thickens. Use of baby oil or mineral oil does not penetrate the skin and spreads easily.

Rose Water Cleansing Cream

Collect the the following ingredients ingredients:

½ tablespoon	Bees-wax or white paraffin wax
1 tablespoon	Emulsifying Wax
4 tablespoons	Mineral oil
6 tablespoons	Rose water
½ teaspoon	Borax
Few drops	Rose oil (perfume)

Melt slowly waxes and oils on low heat. Mix to it rose water and borax, stirring continuously. Use, when cools.

Corn Oil Cleansing Cream

Collect ingredients such as 2 tablespoons vegetable lard, 2 tablespoons corn oil and 4 tablespoons sunflower oil. Melt vegetable lard and mix it to the mixture of corn oil and sun-flower oil. Stir continuously, when it cools. Mix to it a few drops of perfume. Store cream in the refrigerator.

How to Moisturize Your Skin?

All skins, even oily types, need a moisturizer but for a dry skin a moisturizer is vital. They protect the skin by combating the drying effect of cold weather, sun, hair dryers, central heating, radiant, fires, dust, fog and tinted cosmetics. Most moisturizing creams and lotions have a low oil but high moisture content. Although they supply some moisture to the skin, they work mainly by preventing evaporation of natural moisture from the skin. Moisturizers are available either in the form of cream or a lotion. Moisturiser is applied after cleansing and toning, and always before applying make-up. A thin layer of moisturizer under a face pack is also very useful for dry skin. Here are few easy-to-make simple herbal moisturisers:

Almond Oil Moisturising Cream

Collect the following ingredients:

Bees-wax	2 teapoons
Emulsifying wax	1 teaspoon
Almond oil	5 teaspoons
Lavender oil	a few drops

Melt bees-wax and emulsifying wax in a bowl over water. When melted, mix almond oil to it. In another bowl heat water so that the contents of both bowls are at the same temperature. Now slowly add water to melted waxes and oils, stirring. Remove from the heat and continue stirring. When cool, add a few drops of lavender oil.

Herb Cream for Toning the Skin

Collect the following ingredients:

Lanolin	1 tablespoon
Emulsifying wax	2 teaspoons
Bees-wax	6 tablespoons
Almond oil	6 tablespoons

Melt oil and waxes together over water bath. Teaspoons of malted wax and mix to it a teaspoon of any herb lotion or infusion. Comfrey is a healing herb ideal for sensitive or irritated skin having spots or scars. Take a handful of comfrey, liquidize it, then strain it and use.

Avocado and Almond Cream

Collect the following ingredients:

Bees wax	3 teaspoons
Emulsifying wax	3 teaspoons
Almond oil	½ cub
Avocado oil	¼ cup
Rose water	3 tablespoons

Melt waxes over a water bath. Add to it avocado and almond oil. Now mix to it heated rose water drop-by-drop, stirring constantly. Remove from heat and continue stirring till cools. Mix in it a few drops of perfume.

Sunflower Cream

Collect the following ingredients:

Lanolin	4 teaspoons
Emulsifying	2 teaspoons
Bees-wax	2 teaspoons
Sunflower oil	5 tablespoons
Water	6 tablespoons
Glycerine	2 teaspoons
Borax	½ teaspoon

Melt the waxes, oil and lanolin over water bath. Heat water, glycerine and borax in a separate bowl making sure the borax is completely dissolved. While the melted oils and waxes are still on the heat, slowly mix water to it drop by drop and continue beating until you get a whitish, thick and creamy textured rich cream.

Jasmine Moisturizing Cream

Collect the following ingredients:

Emulsifying wax	2 tablespoons
Almond or Sunflower oil	2 tablespoons
Lanolin	1 teaspoon
Borax	½ teaspoon
Witch-hazel	1 teaspoon
Glycerine	1.5 teaspoon
Water	8 tablespoons
Jasmine oil	few drops

Melt waxes, oil and lanolin together over water bath. In a separate bowl heat water, glycerine and borax to make sure the borax is completely dissolved. Mix to it witch-hazel. Now slowly add water to the oils, stirring constantly until cools. Add a few drops of jasmine oil. This non-greasy cream is suitable for normal as well as greasy skins.

Honey Moisturizing Cream

Collect the following ingredients:

Lanolin	3 tablespoons
Honey	½ tablespoon
Lecithin	1 teaspoon
Warm water	4 tablespoons
Perfume	a few drops

Heat lanolin, honey and lecithin in a bowl. Now mix to it warm water stirring constantly. You need not to refrigerate this cream.

Nourishing and Toning Preparations for Your Skin

Nourishing preparations include all oil-based or moisturizing type skin foods and tonics. Hormone creams, lotions, vitamin creams (especially vitamin E cream or capsules), serum ampoules, anti-wrinkle creams and lotions, biologically active preparations—all come into the nourishing group. What your skin needs will depend on its types and the age factor. The more dry or mature your skin is, the richer and more active product your skin needs. It is hard to generalize but on average the ordinary inexpensive skin foods will supply all that skin needs in the way of oils and lubricating ingredients throughout the 20s and 30s and possibly until the menopause. During the menopause and afterwards the supply of hormones and other vital elements produced by the body slow down, then creams and lotions containing hormones and other special extracts and serums, rich creams containing vitamins and concentrated oils may all help to provide the skin a more youthful appearance. Some of the easy-to-make recipes are given below:

Cocoa Butter Cream

Collect the following ingredients:

Cocoa butter	2 tablespoons
Emulsifying wax	2 tablespoons
Bees-wax	1 tablespoon
Sesame oil	4 tablespoons
Almond oil	1 tablespoon

When the ingredients are completely melted, remove from the heat and stir until the cream is cool. Mix a few drops of perfume. This cream leaves the skin smooth and nongreasy.

Lanolin Cream

Mix 2 tablespoons lanolin with 8 tablespoons almond oil and heat over a water bath. It is good for dry skins and neglected areas of body such as elbows, knees, feet and neck. In case the cream has to be applied on oily skin, mix 2 tablespoons rose water or ordinary soft water, in case rose water is not available.

Elder Flower Cream

Mix the following ingredients in a bowl over water bath (low heat):

3 tablespoons	Almond oil
4 tablespoons	Elderflower blossoms
2 teaspoons	Lanolin

Let it simmer together for an hour, strain and then add to it warm water slowly, stirring.

Honey Cream

Honey is very beneficial for a dry, coarse and sensitive skin. To make a nourishing cream for sallow skin, mix the following ingredients in a bowl and melt over a water bath (low heat):

3 tablespoons	Lanolin
½ tablespoon	Honey
1 teaspoon	Lecithin

Now slowly mix to it 4 tablespoons warm water, beating continuously until it cools.

Vitamin Cream

The following ingredients are required:

Bees wax	1 tablespoon
Emulsifying wax	1 tablespoon
Lanolin	1 tablespoon
Wheat-germ oil	2 tablespoons
Vitamin E capsules	1 capsule
Carrot oil	2 tablespoons
Vitamin A	1 capsule
Distilled water	6 tablespoons
Borax	½ teaspoon
Tincture of benzoin	2 drops
Organge flower oil	a few drops

Melt waxes and oils over water bath. In a separate bowl dissolve borax in warm water. Mix water to the oils and beat until it cools. Add to it tincture of benzoin and continue beating until you get a thick nourishing cream. While mixing vitamin capsules, simply prick open the capsules and add contents to the mixture.

Wheat-germ Cream

Collect the following ingredients:

1 teaspoon	Bees-wax
1 teaspoon	Emulsifying wax
5 tablespoons	Lanolin
3 tablespoons	Sesame oil
2 tablespoons	Wheat-germ oil
5 tablespoons	Distilled water
1 tablespoon	Witch-hazel
½ teaspoon	Borax
a few drops	Perfume

Melt waxes and oils over water bath. Heat water and borax and make sure that the borax has completely dissolved. Now slowly mix water to the melted oils and waxes. Stir until a thick, glossy nourishing cream is ready. Lanolin and wheat-germ oil contain Vitamin E, which is useful for all types of skin.

Vegetable Cream

Collect the following ingredients:

Bees wax	2 tablespoons
Emulsifying wax	4 tablespoons
Lanolin	3 tablespoons
Almond oil	4 tablespoons
Sesame oil	4 tablespoons
Avocado oil	2 tablespoons
Safflower oil	2 tablespoons
Sunflower oil	2 tablespoons
Water	5 tablespoons
Borax	½ teaspoon
Amber oil	a few drops

Mix and melt waxes and oils together over water bath. In a separate bowl dissolve borax in warm water. Now mix water to the oils and beat until the cream cools. It leaves no sign of grease but gives the skin a satiny sheen.

Strawberry Juice and Cream

Mix 250 gm. strawberries and 100 gm. sugar in a pan and bring to boil. Cool and boil again. Allow strawberries juice to cool and store in the refrigerator. This lotion is very useful for oily skins. Now melt 2 tablespoons each of lanolin and sunflower oil together over a water bath and mix to it strawberries juice. Remove from the heat and stir till it thickens to creamy form.

Oily Nourishing Cream

Melt the following oils and waxes over water bath (low heat):

3 tablespoons	Coconut oil
2 tablespoons	Olive oil
1 tablespoon	Almond oil
½ tablespoon	Bees-wax

In a separate bowl dissolve ½ teaspoon borax in 3 tablespoons of heated water. Mix to it melted oils slowly, stirring until a cool cream is ready.

Orange Flower Skin Tonic

Collect the following ingredients:

Bees-wax	2 teaspoons
Emulsifying wax	2 teaspoons
Almond oil	8 teaspoons
Lanolin	4 teaspoons
Coconut oil	4 teaspoons
Orange Flower Water	6 tablespoons
Tincture of benzoin	a few drops
Orange oil	a few drops

Melt waxes and oils together over very low heat and add to it hot orange flower water and drops of tincture of benzoin and orange oil, stirring continuously. Besides nourishing, this cream helps to clear lines and wrinkles.

Herbal Remedies for the Skin

Mix and shake the following ingredients in a glass jar with a tightly fitted lid:

Honey	2 tablespoons
Coriander seeds (Dhania)	2 teaspoons
Nutmeg (Jai-phal)	2 teaspoons
Cloves	1 teaspoon
Lemon peel (grated)	4 teaspoons
Orange flower water	4 teaspoons
Alcohol	8 teaspoons
Rose water	4 teaspoons

Rose Water Skin Tonic and Gypsy Rose Water

It is one of the oldest skin tonic which was discovered by an Arabian dermatologist in tenth century. To make rose water, mix rose essence in pure water and shake thoroughly. Two tablespoons of essence of roses is sufficient for 4 liter purified water.

Gypsy Rose Water

Put 2 handfuls of dark, scented rose petals into a jar containing one litre water and 200 gm. sugar. Keep the mixture for two hours, shake thoroughly; then strain and store in a cool place.

Witch-hazel Tonic

Mix 1 cup of rose water and ¼ cup witch-hazel. If your skin is over-greasy, mix equal quantity of rose water and witch-hazel.

Flower and Herb Tonic

Flower and herb water of all kinds make deliciously scented, highly effective skin tonics. Mix 2 tablespoons of dried herbs or flowers to ½ litre boiling water and cover the pan to prevent steam from being lost. Let the herb steep for a couple of hours, strain and bottle.

Marigold Skin Tonic

Marigold flowers heal skin disorders. Mix two dried or three fresh marigold flowers to ½ litre clean water. Store for 10 to 12 hours and 2 tablespoons of witch-hazel. This tonic is especially beneficial for facial skin having scars and spots.

Hollyhock Skin Tonic

Put three tablespoons of hollyhock leaves into a half pint of boiling water. Cover and simmer gently for 5 minutes. Leave for 30 minutes, then strain and it is ready for use.

Elderflower Tonic

Wash a handful of elder flowers and mix to it 6 tablespoons of boiling water. Steep overnight, and strain in the morning.

Vinegar Skin Tonic

Mix the following ingredients and leave for seven days, shaking the bottle twice daily:

Cider vinegar (or wine)	½ cup
Cloves	½ teaspoon
Lavender	1 tablespoon
Rose petals	1 tablespoon
Rose/Orange flower water	2 tablespoons

Cucumber Tonic

Wash and liquidize half-peeled cucumber. Bring the juice to boil, then simmer it for five minutes. Cool and strain and add to it one tablespoon of witch-hazel. Store the juice in a refrigerator. Mint can also be used in it. Add four tablespoons mint in the cucumber tonic.

Orange and Lemon Tonic

Put one slice of orange, half lemon and two tablespoons of castor sugar into a pan with a cup of milk. Heat the mixture to nearly boiling point. When it is cool, it is ready for use.

Apple Tree Bark Tonic

Infuse 4 tablespoons of apple tree bark in 2 cups of boiling water. Mix to it one tablespoon of sage and apply to the face. Other herbs can also be used for skin tonic, which include yarrow, camomile, resemary, parsley, tansy, mint, fennel and comfrey. The properties of these herbs are:

- Yarrow is ideal for greasy skin.
- Camomile helps eliminate wrinkles.
- Rosemary is healing and firming.
- Mint is stimulating.
- Parsley contains Vitamin C and is very useful for spotty and patchy skins.
- Tansy helps to get rid of freckles.
- Comfrey is good for clearing up spotty skins.

Milk and Almond Tonics

Collect the following ingredients:

Buttermilk or plain milk	½ cup
Elder flower water	6 tablespoons
Honey	1 tablespoon

Heat milk and elderflower water together on very low heat for about 30 minutes. Remove and let it stand for three hours and strain. Add to it honey. This recipe is very useful for a hard and itchy skin. To make almond tonic, mix 4 teaspoons each almond oil, lanolin and coconut oil. Melt 2 teaspoons each bees-wax and emulsifying wax on low heat. Mix together, stirring. Then mix to it 6 teaspoons of orange flower water and continue stirring till it becomes thick. Add to it three drops of tincture benzoin. When the mixture gets cold, store in a bottle.

Elderflower Tonic

Mix together the following ingredients in a bottle and shake thoroughly before use:

Elder flower water	3 tablespoons
Rose water	3 tablespoons
Witch-hazel	3 tablespoons
Boric acid	1 tablespoon

Cucumber Tonic

Mix the following ingredients together in a large bottle:

Elder flower water	10 tablespoons
Cucumber juice	5 tablespoons
Eau-de-cologne	4 tablespoons
Tincute of benzoin	1 tablespoon

Honey Water Astringent

Mix the following ingredients together in a airtight jar, and keep for two weeks, shaking twice daily:

Sandalwood oil	8 tablespoons
Musk or sandalwood chips	a pinch
Bergamot oil	1 teaspoon
Lavender oil	¼ teaspoon
Clove oil	1/8 teaspoon
Rose water	4 tablespoons
Orange flower water	4 tablespoons
Honey	1 tablespoon

Rosemary Water Astringent

Mix the following ingredients together in a large airtight bottle and store it for 48 to 72 hours, shaking frequently:

Rosemary	2 tablespoons
Rose water	½ cup
Alcohol or witch-hazel	¼ cup
Orange peel and pitch	¼ cup
Lemon peel and pitch	½ cup
Mint	4 sprigs

Lemon Astringent

Mix the following ingredients together in a large bottle for 24 hours, then strain and use if the skin is greasy skin:

Lemon Juice	4 tablespoons
Peppermint extract	½ teaspoon
Witch-hazel	8 tablespoons
Alcohol	2 tablespoons

Camphor Astringent

Mix the following ingredients in a large bottle:

Rose water	½ cup
Witch-hazel	½ cup
Distilled water	½ cup
Camphor spirit	1 tablespoon
Blue colouring	2 drops

Add a pinch of alum to make astringment strong. Strain and use to tighten and tone the skin.

3

LUMPS AND BUMPS OF THE SKIN

WHAT IS LESION?

Structural changes in the tissues of human body caused by injury or a disease are known as lesions, which are basically of two types: Primary and Secondary.

Primary Lesion

1. **Macule:** Small discolored spot or patch on the skin. Sometimes, it causes change in the skin color. It may be erythematous, hypo-pigmented, depigmented, hyper-pigmented or have any other color.
2. **Papule:** Small elevated pimple without fluid or developing pus. A solid raised area of skin (usually less than 5 mm. in diameter) produced by proliferation of the tissue cells.
3. **Micro-papule, Nodule and Tumor:** A papule which is 1-2 mm in size is called a Micro-papule, 5-10 mm in size papule is called a Nodule and if the size is more than one centimeter, is called a Tumor. The shape of a papule may be like an inverted cone. A papule situated at the opening of a hair follicle is called a follicular papule.
4. **Vesicle:** Small blister with clear fluid in it, beneath the epidermis. A raised lesion filled with fluid (less than 5 mm in diameter). A vesicle larger than 5 mm is called a bulla or a blister.
5. **Wheal:** Itchy, swollen spot due to mosquito or insect bites. A sudden exudation of fluid in dermis produces a flat raised area of any size.

6. **Tubercle:** Soiled lump projective above or under the surface of the skin.
7. **Tumor:** An external swelling varying in size, shape and color.
8. **Bulla:** Large blister containing watery fluid.
9. **Pustule:** A pimply looking elevation with inflamed base containing pus. It may be follicular or non-follicular.
10. **Scale:** A flake-like lesion, which represents visible shedding of the skin.
11. **Plaque:** A flat area of skin, which may be raised or depressed below the skin surface.
12. **Atrophy:** Caused by loss of tissue, which may involve the epidermis, the dermis or both.
13. **Fissure:** A crack in the skin surface, usually located in skin-fold.
14. **Blackhead (comedone):** A small papule-like lesion containing a keratinous plug—visible as a black dot at the center of the lesion, also known as blackhead.
15. **Burrow:** An irregular brownish streak.
16. **Hyper keratosis:** Thickening of the stratum corneum.

Secondary Lesions

These lesions develop in the advance stage of a skin disease which include:

1. **Crust or scab:** An accumulation of sebum and pus with epidermal material. Crusting is drying up of the exudate or a necrosed area of the skin.
2. **Excoriation:** Skin abrasion produced by scratching or scraping due to loss of skin. Scratching, often lead to the removal of the top of a lesion or the skin.
3. **Ulceration:** Mucous membrane of the body accompanied by pus. It is loss of the surface layer from a localised area of the skin.
4. **Scar:** It is usually formed after healing an injury or skin condition. An atrophic scar remains below the surface, whereas hypertrophic scar is raised above the surface.
5. **Stain:** An abnormal discoloration of skin.
6. **Lichenification:** A diffuse thickening of the skin with hyper-pigmentation and severe itching.
7. **Unbilication:** A crater-like depression on the top of a papule.

8. **Maceration:** Soddening of the skin associated with scaling or hyperkeratosis.

Combination of Lesions

These are of following types:

1. **Macule-papule:** A papule situated at the centre of a macule.
2. **Maculo-vesicle:** A vesicle situated at the centre of a macule.
3. **Maculo-squamous:** Scales present over a macule.
4. **Papulo-vesicle:** A vesicle located at the top of a papule.
5. **Papulo-pustule:** A pustule located at the top of a papule.
6. **Papulo-squamous:** A papule covered with scales.
7. **Papulo-wheal:** A papule situated over a wheal.

Types of Skin Diseases and Disorders

- **Acute:** Less violent disease.
- **A chronic:** Long duration and recurring disease.
- **An infectious:** Disease caused by pathogenic germs.
- **Contagious:** A disease communicable by contact.
- **Congenital:** A disease present since birth.
- **Seasonal:** A disease influenced by the weather.
- **Occupational:** Disease afflicted by one's occupation.
- **Parasitic:** A disease caused by a vegetable or animal parasitic.
- **Pathogenic:** Disease produced by bacteria.
- **Systemic:** Disease due to over functioning of internal glands.
- **Venereal:** Disease acquired by contact with an infected person usually during sexual intercourse.
- **Epidemic:** A disease that attacks simultaneously large number of persons.
- **Allergy:** Caused by contact with foods, cosmetics, medicines and tints resulting in itching, redness, swelling, blisters, oozing, pain, heat and scaling.

Any kind of blemish on the skin spoils the personality and charm of a man or woman. Every beauty-conscious person wants to avoid such beauty dampners. The spots and skin disorders are of various kinds. In case of any skin infection or suffering from contagious skin disorder the matter should be referred to a skin dermatologist. The skin disorders fall into four categories:

1. Disorders of the secreting apparatus.
2. Disorders relating to growths such as boils, rashes and cysts etc.
3. Inflammatory conditions.
4. Nervous and parasitic infections.

Symptoms, causes and cures of some of common skin imperfections are described here. The human body has been given a most beautiful covering—the skin. Nothing is more lovely and attractive than a glowing and healthy skin. Skin troubles often run in families. The skin has several important functions:

- Skin is the first line of defence against the germs that might enter the body. Enzymes on the surface of skin quickly destroy germ, provide the skin health and intactness. But small tears and breaks on the surface of skin may open the way to infection within the skin and in the deeper tissues as well.
- The skin has another important function. It helps to regulate body temperature. When exercising vigorously, a lot of heat is produced in the muscles. To keep the temperature of body at normal level, this heat must be removed quickly. To cool the body, large amounts of blood are rapidly sent to the skin.
- The process of perspiration is more important. Tiny sweat glands within the skin pour out surprisingly large quantities of water. The perspiration evaporates and carries of large quantity of heat and this helps to cool the body.
- When the skin is cut or damaged, it usually heals quickly. This not only seals off the loss of blood, but also closes the damaged area against the entrance of germs. The healing of a wound is one of nature's miracles. Damaged tissues are quickly removed by the white blood cells, leaving the skin clean and ready for the new tissues that will form.
- Itching on the skin is very common, and is rather unpleasant sensation, which a patient attempts to relieve by scratching. A certain amount of mild itching is normal for everyone. Only when the itching is persistent and troublesome does it become serious. Many conditions contribute to itching. These include insect bites, hives, contact dermatitis, food allergies and heat rash. Other causes are diabetes, uraemia, jaundice, pregnancy, the change of life (menopause), drug allergies and various types of nervous conditions. Persistent scratching may produce swellings in the

skin with deep scratch marks and small ulcers into which germs have found their way causing more trouble. Itching may be due to drug's reaction (use of medicines such as aspirin, phenobarbital, pencillin etc), skin ointments, allergic to certain clothes such as nylon, wool, dyes and various surface dressings in the cloth.

ITCHING SKIN

If the itching has spread over the large areas of the body, try an oatmeal bath. Mix one cup of oatmeal with two cups of cold water and pour this into a tub of water. Lie in this tub full filled with water for 15 to 20 minutes twice daily, preferably in the morning and evening. Avoid rubbing your body after having bath when drying yourself. Rubbing the body vigorously with towel will increase the irritation. Gently pat the skin and then apply some soothing medication such as calamine lotion or caladryl. If the itching is severe, try the following home recipe two to three times a day. Collect the following ingredients:

Camphor	1 gm.
Menthol	1 gm.
Calamine lotion	100 cc.

If the itching is very severe, apply Hydrocortisone Ointment twice a day, also to control itching around the rectal, genital areas and face. Consult a doctor before treatment.

Moles and Warts (Verruca Vulgaris)

Pink, brown and black, hairy or hairless swellings (also known as neoplastins) anywhere on the surface of any part of body, but usually occur on the face, fingers and trunk. Warts are benign skin tumours on any part of the body that can occur singly or in large pack. These are usually pigmented and formed as a result a defect of the melanocytes, which multiply and grow down into the dermis. The only remedy is to excise by electro-surgery or surgical diathermy under local anaesthesia by a doctor.

Warts are plain, smooth, silky, silk-coloured or brownish epidermal growths, which occur on the skin, usually on the face and outer surface of the hands, varying in size and shape. They don't have roots or runners that go down to the pores. Warts are caused by a virus—a viral infection of the skin, is common in children as

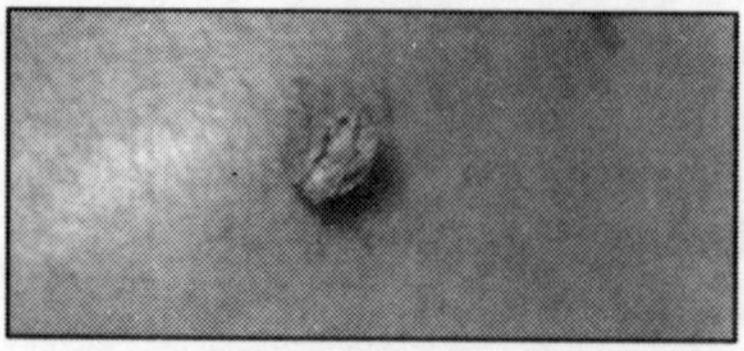
Warts on Face

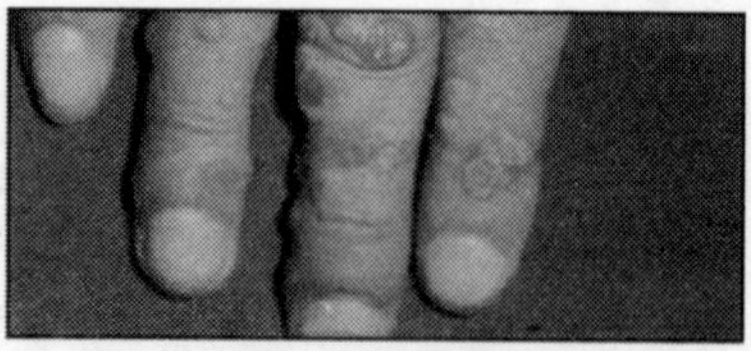
Warts on Fingers

well as adults with immune deficiency. Usually, the lesions start as skin coloured or brownish, irregular papule. 'Verruca Plana' are skin-coloured papules slightly raised from the skin surface.

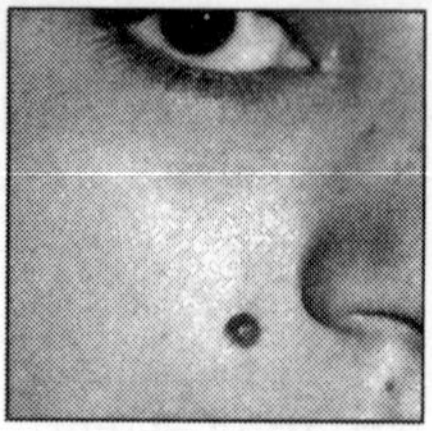
Moles

Warts are of three types: Plane Warts, Common Warts and Planter Warts, as detailed below:

1. **Plane Warts:** They are simplest of all warts usually small, smooth skin coloured or brownish lesions, which are slightly raised from the skin surface. The most commonly affected are children and youths. They usually occur on the face and outer surface of hands.
2. **Common Warts:** These are larger and firmer elevations with a rough surface. They usually occur on the hands, forearm, knees and the upper parts of the feet. People usually, develop thickening of the skin surface at the weight-bearing area in the sole.
3. **Planter Warts:** They are slightly different and normally contain blood vessels and the surface of the wart, if carefully pared, bleed because of this. These warts are simple afflictions, not a threat to life, but they can be quite troublesome and may cripple the smooth running of the day. Planter warts occur on soles and cause pain due to pressure.

GENITAL WARTS (CONDYLOMATA ACUMINATA)

Like anywhere else on the body, surface warts can also occur on the gentitalia. Genital warts are usually transmitted by sexual contact. This can occur in both sexes and are located on the moist surface of genitalia. They start as minute reddish swelling and grow into grouped lesions. They produce fungus growth on the male organ (glands) in men and on vulva in females, and around the anus both in men and women.

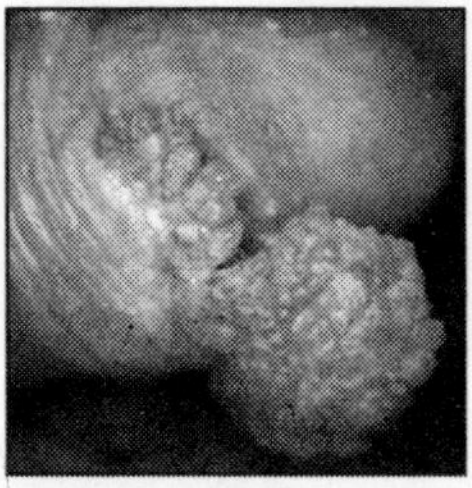

Warts on Male organ

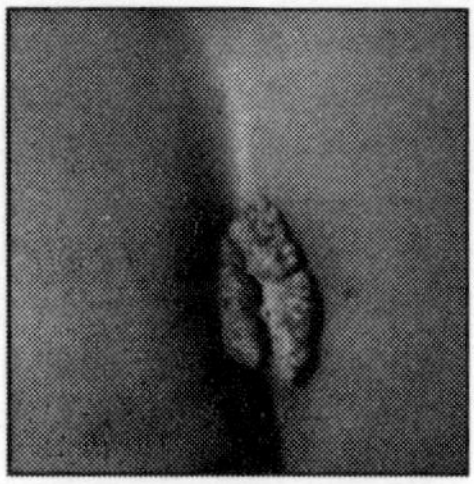

Warts around anus

Genital Warts

Blackheads and Whiteheads

These are worm-like mass of hardened sebum appearing most frequently on the face, forehead and the nose. Blackheads always accompany pimples and often occur during the teens. Whiteheads are caused by the accumulation of sebaceous matter beneath the skin. They occur on different parts on the face, neck, chest and the shoulders. Whiteheads are usually associated with the fine textured dry skin. Blackheads and whiteheads are removed with an extractor a sterilized implement, known as blackhead extractor.

Following remedies are suggested in case you suffer from frequent blackheads:

- Wash the skin three times a day with medicated soap, if the skin is greasy.
- Have a balanced diet. Do not take fried foods, chocolates, pastries, spices and aerated drinks.
- Unclog the skin pores by steaming and applying face pack.

4

PIMPLES, ACNE AND SKIN IMPERFECTIONS

PIMPLES AND ACNE

Acne is very common in the teens and twenties. A plague of pimples appears at a time when looking your best may seem so important. Pimples are a serious adolescence problem, which mar many lovely skins in teens and twenties. Pimples and acne appear on the cheeks, forehead and nose usually during adolescence and sometimes during adulthood. Acne is not caused by germs or dirt. At puberty in boys the androgens cause the voice to break, beard to grow, the skin to become greasy and spots to erupt. All women have both female hormones (oestrogen and progesterone) and androgens. Acne is due to an imbalance of these hormones and not to extra male hormones. Greasy skin, excess facial and body hair and the thinning of scalp hair can also be due to this imbalance. Pregnancy improves acne because of the larger amounts of female hormones secreted at this time.

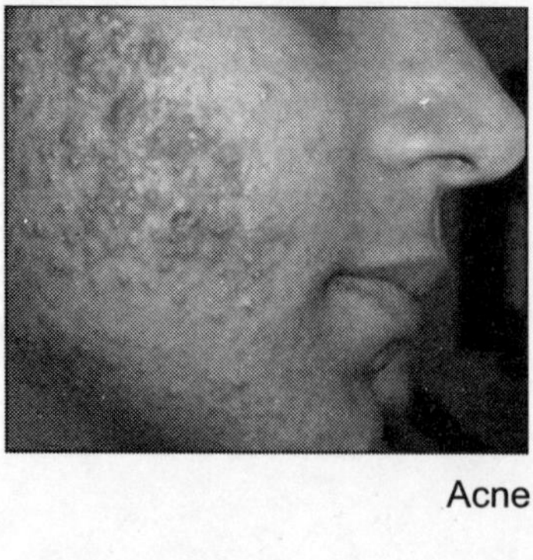
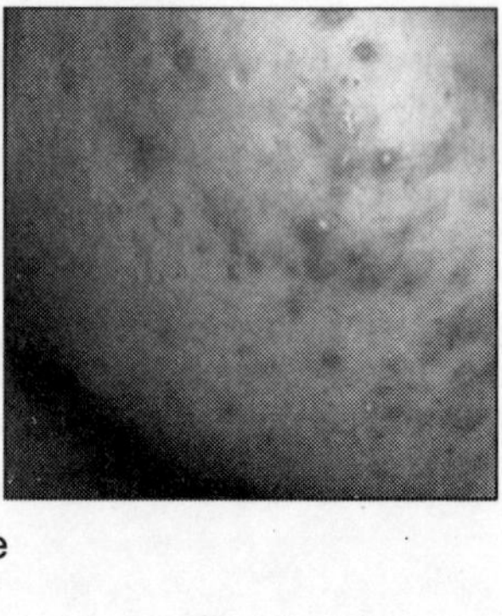

Acne on Face

Why do pimples appear in youth?

The answer to this question is that as soon as one cross childhood and enters the threshold of adolescence, different parts of the body start developing. The oil glands underneath the skin become over-active and ooze grease, which blocks the skin pores, causing pimples to sprout. A special skin care is essential to guard against the pimples. Do not neglect pimples. Be alert as soon as they start appearing. The following remedies are suggested to avoid growth of pimples and acne:

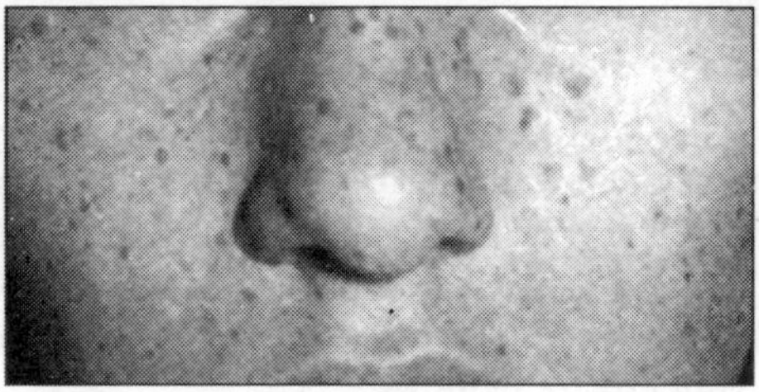

Pimples

1. Acne can be treated very successfully. Bad acne needs a doctor's help early, before you have become depressed and discouraged by no benefit from over-the-counter acne preparations.
2. You cannot wash away acne. Washing will only temporarily remove the grease, which will soon be replaced. Some special washes and cleansers may even make blackheads worse.
3. Peeling of the skin unblocks the pores, which helps blackheads and small spots. Facemasks, light peeling, abrasive scrubs and sponges are helpful to some extent, but the effects are short-lived. Most acne preparations are peeling agent and the most effective preparations contain benzoyl peroxide. Preparations containing other chemical ingredients e.g. resorcinol, sulphur, antiseptics are not good for most of the delicate skins. So consult a skin specialist before you use these ingredients.
4. Antibiotic lotions containing clindamycin or erythromycin are successful in treating acne skin, but consultation of a doctor is must before use.
5. Retinoic acid (rich source of Vitamin A) when using on skin, slowly clears blackheads. But the disadvantages include drying and darkening of black skin. Seek the advice of a doctor.

6. Steroid creams or steroid injections are harmful when put on acne. These help to heal large painful cysts but leave worst effect in the long run and the relief is temporary.
7. Sunlight improves acne. Suntan lotions and oils prevent the benefit of sunshine by blocking pores and should be avoided. However, artificial sun lamps (UVA lamps) are used to treat acne, but they are not very effective.
8. Avoid excessive make up if you suffer from pimples and acne. Thick heavy make-up, use of moisturisers or cleansers make acne worse and must be avoided as far as possible.
9. Doctors usually recommend antibiotics taken in very long course. They suppress the inflammation of the acne spots and cut down skin bacteria. The treatment is lengthy to be continued for 8 to 12 months taking tablets or capsules. Make sure the dose must be too light, however, it may take a long time, but there are no long-term side effects from this.
10. The anti-androgen cyproterone is an effective hormone treatment to relieve acne, which stops the skin and hair being greasy and clears the spots. However, the treatment is not beneficial for male sex as men need their male hormones.
11. Mostly women worry about scarring. The scarring depends on type of skin. The chest and back scars are more often than the face. Avoid picking and squeezing acne lesions, otherwise it leave permanent scars. The types of scars are small ice pick scars (tiny pits), large pits and raised lumpy scars (keloids). Consult a doctor, preferably a skin specialist to treat these scars. Better seek the advice of your doctor. Use Sulphur soap to keep the skin's oil gland clean.
12. Steaming once a week keeps the skin pores open.
13. Remove make-up at night before going to bed. Grease can be removed by use of lemon juice or camphor spirit. Cleansing of stale make-up is very important because stale make-up particles block the skin pores and prevent them from breathing freely.

Herbal Cure to Treat Acne and Pimples

The following remedies should be tried:

1. Yellow Sea Shells (Kauris) should be ground fine, mixed with butter and a little vinegar. It should be applied to the affected skin.

2. Ground together the barks of oris tree (Irsa), neem and turmeric and mix to it water to make a paste and rub on the face.
3. Slake lime in water (in the ratio 1:20). Mix to it a little finely powdered Sulphur. The mixture should be boiled till about half is left. A light coat of the fluid should be applied to the face.
4. Seeds of 'Khurfa' should be ground in milk and applied to the face.
5. The leaves of raspberry, strawberry or blackberry (50 gm.) should be boiled in one litre water for three minutes, then infuse for a further five minutes. This makes a pleasant and soothing wash for skin affected by pimples.
6. Marigold and wheat-germ oil cure scars and blemishes caused by acne. Pound 2 tablespoons of fresh or 1 tablespoon dried marigold petals with 4 tablespoons of warm wheat-germ oil, which is a rich source of vitamin E. Strain into a bottle. Use it to heal those small scars or blemishes caused by acne.
7. Keep the skin clean by thorough washing. Some slightly abrasive soap will help to eliminate blackheads, but it should be used with care, particularly if the skin is inflamed. Smaller blackheads may be carefully removed by the use of Schamberg loop extractor. Warm moist towels applied to the face for 10 to 15 minutes before the treatment will make the removal of blackheads easier. If the pus has formed under the skin, be careful not to open the pimple until it is ready to drain. Squeezing and pinching of the skin may extend the inflammation and delay healing, and may also cause scarring of the face.
8. For mild infections of the face, apply white lotion into the skin. There are many good commercial preparations that may be tried. Here is an simple ointment to treat it by mixing the following:
    - Resorcinol: 1.8 gm.
    - Precipitated Sulphur: 3.0 gm.
    - Hydrophilic ointment: Sufficient to make 60 gm.

    Apply this ointment to the affected areas once or twice daily. Hydrocortisone lotion is also beneficial, especially when combined with neomycin sulphate. Hot compresses applied once or twice daily will help to relieve the inflammation.

9. In severe cases, X-ray therapy may be considered, which should be done by a skin specialist, otherwise it may harm the skin. In the severe cases of abscess formation, penicillin or sulpha drugs may be tried strictly under the guidance of a doctor. This will reduce the infection in the skin. Acne is always worse during the colder months. Exposure to sunlight has proved beneficial but it should not be done for excess time (consult a doctor before treatment).

Acne Rosacea

Acne Rosacea is an abnormal flushing and irritation of the skin on face and nose. It may also affect the cheek, chin and forehead at times. It occurs more often in middle-aged people. But there are times when it is also seen in children and young adults. Certain substances such as coffee, tea, chocolate, nuts and hot spicy foods may be associated with this condition. Alcohol may also bring this on. Medicines containing iodides and bromides may also cause unwanted eruption on the face. Extremes of heat, cold and wind may also aggravate the affected skin. Nervous tension is often a factor. The condition is usually a cosmetic problem. The following treatment is suggested:

1. Try eliminating all suspected foods and medicines. Avoid coffee, tea, chocolate, nuts and spicy foods.
2. The use of alcohol should be discontinued.

Facial Scars

A cosmetic surgeon cannot tell before hand whether the skin of a particular individual will respond well or not to surgery in terms of scarring. Surgeons carrying out life-saving procedures are not concerned about the look of the skin but most of the patients, mostly women do not want to be left with a permanent reminder of the suffering. The use of essential oils before or after surgery treatments may not eliminate the scar completely, but may lessen it. Using essential oils in treatments pre-operatively can lead to less scarring and bruising, quick recovery, less stress and tension and possibly less risk of infection. Essential oil treatments prepare the client both physically and emotionally for the surgery. For the body, choose essential oils that have a relaxing effect. For the face, choose those that have energizing, toning effect.

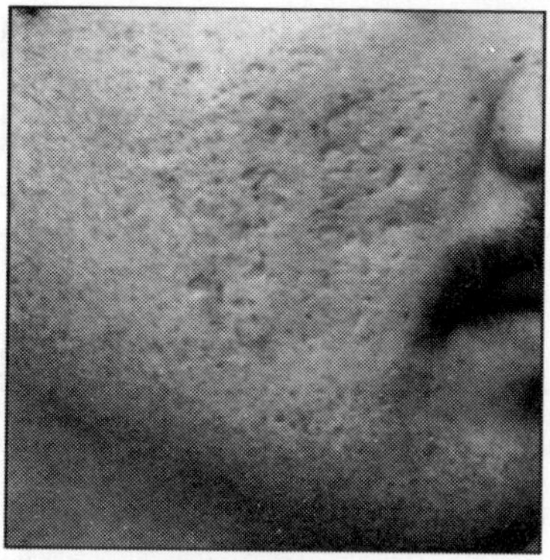

Scars on Face

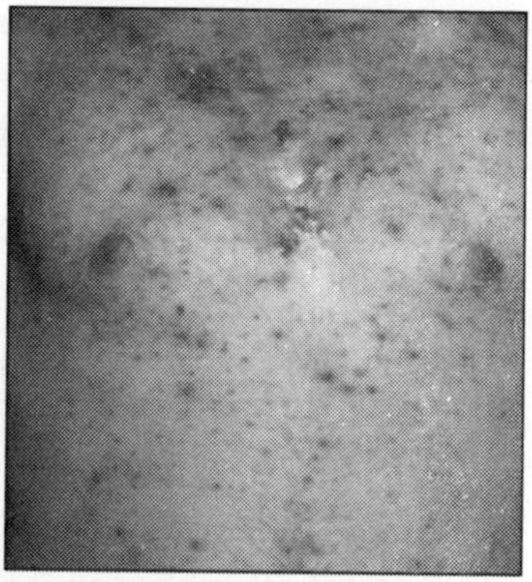

Scars on Chest

Herbal Treatment of New Scars:

New scars response well to essential oil blends which must be applied (not massaged) in the morning and evening for full effect. Choose essential oils that are anti-inflammatory and calming, as these are more effective. Camomile, yarrow, rose and geranium would be good choices. Appropriate carrier or base oils would include camellia oil, macadamia pill, primrose oil, red carrot oil and rosehip seed oil.

Herbal Treatment of Old Scars:

Old scars take much longer time to respond to the treatment. Essential oils that help are frankincense, elemi rose, geranium, fennel, lemon, orange and carrot seed. Very useful carrier or base oils are rosehip seed oil, borage oil, red carrot root oil and macademia oil. Prepare massage oil for the scar area of the skin using the suggested essential oils and vegetable oils. Herbal ingredients such a camphor, sulphur, onion, garlic, curd, yeast, fuller's earth (multani mitti) and vegetable juices are all useful in treating a blemished skin with scars. Here are recipes very useful to clear scars. They have healing, soothing, astringent and tightening effect on the skin.

Herbal Treatments to Cure Scars:

Mix together the ingredients such as ½ teaspoon each oatmeal and camphor, BF crystal and 2 teaspoons orange flower water. Apply the mask on the face. Leave for 15 minutes and wash off with lukewarm water. Two drops of camphor spirit when added to a mixture of 1 tablespoon tomato juice and one teaspoon honey make a strong astringent skin tonic. Leave it on the skin for 15 minutes to relieve scars.

To improve your skin and cure spots, apply home made skin tonic as described below:

Mix the following ingredients and apply mask on the face for 15 to 20 minutes:

Glycerine	1 tablespoon
Borax Powder	½ tablespoon
Distilled water	sufficient quantity to make a paste

Tips to relieve blemishes and Sspots:

1. Rosemary flowers boiled in white wine lighten a sallow skin.
2. Apricot oil rubbed into the most sensitive, soft skin every night before sleep help.
3. An oily skin may benefit from a covering of mashed strawberries.
4. Hard, leathery patches of skin can be softened with pineapple juice or a mash of papaya as both fruits contain enzymes.
5. To clear minor blemishes, apply raspberry mask. Mix 25 gm of mashed raspberries to a paste with 1 tsp each of plain yoghurt and finely ground oatmeal. Leave on the face for ten minutes, then rinse off.
6. Rubbing raw garlic on a spotty, blemished skin has a fine effect to kill spots.
7. Comfrey, honey and garlic pack help to remedy for persistent pustules. Ground a handful of comfrey leaves with enough honey to make a paste.
8. To clear blemishes, melt 25 gm. of beeswax in a bowl on low heat. Add to it 100 gm. of pure honey. Stir until cool, then pot. Keep in a cool place. And apply to the infected skin.

FRECKLES

Small, flat, irregular, brownish spots on the skin generally due to exposure to sun and heat, overactive glands, a poor diet containing too much chocolates and fried foods, emotional disturbances such as quarrels in the family or an unhappy love affair and even lack of sleep and over work. The precipitation of pigments causes freckles. The following remedies may be tried:

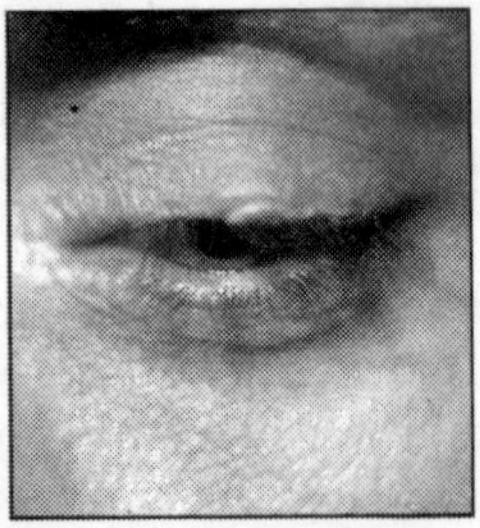

Frackles on the Face

- Mix in a tablespoon of milk cream a few drops of lime juice and apply on freckles at night and wash the face with lukewarm water in the morning.
- Grind turmeric and sesame seeds in equal quantity. Make a paste and apply on the skin.
- Mix yellow mustard in milk and apply to the face at night. Wash the face next morning. Freckles mar the skin beauty of the face.
- Take a watermelon. Make a hole in its rind and introduce some grains of rice in it. The rice should be taken out after a week. Ground into paste and smear over the freckles.
- Grind basal (tulsi) leaves in water and apply the paste to the face.
- Apply rind of the Soap Nut on affected skin. It should be ground in water and the paste applied to the freckles.
- Pound to paste Pumpkin seeds with olive oil. It keeps the skin soft and white and reduces freckles.
- Here is a home recipe to cure freckles:

Collect the following ingredients:

Sour milk	4 tablespoons
Ground oatmeal	4 tablespoons
Freshly grated horseradish	1 teaspoon

Make a paste mixing above ingredients and apply on freckles taking care to avoid near the eyes as fumes can cause stinging. Leave for 30 minutes and wash off.

Precautions

- When the condition is severe, it is better to use a special detergent cleaning solution. This can be used once a day, with medicated soap for the other one or two washings a blemished skin needs each day. Follow by rinsing with clear warm water and dry by rubbing vigorously with a clean towel.
- Avoid dandruff particularly and don't wear hair over face while blemishes persist on the face or this may aggravate spots.
- Avoid fingering the spots, except to remove blackheads and pustules.
- Apply a medicated cream or ointment after cleansing and toning which will blend in with the skin and help disguise spots. Use light liquid make-up.

Cracked Skin, Chapped Lips and Open Pores

The lips get chopped and the skin of hands and other part of body get cracks generally due to cold with the onset of winter or defective functioning of the sebaceous glands. Bad habits, simple neglect and lack of good skin sense make your skin rough and cracked. The basic plan for dealing with chapped skin especially the hands is to avoid water at all costs. Consider water to be just like acid on your skin (especially hands usually exposed to water during household work).

The following remedies may be tried:

1. Rub a little Castor oil or Olive oil on the cracked skin.
2. Apply hot milk cream on cracked skin.
3. Use antibiotic cream and massage the affected skin at night.
4. Instead of using soap, clean your skin or hands with an oil-free skin cleanser to avoid dryness or roughness.
5. Try lemon oil to smooth and soften skin.

The face looks unattractive and the skin gives the appearance of enlarged pores. They are caused by over-active glands during puberty, a poor diet and/or an emotional disturbance.

Remedies include

- Mix 2 tablespoons of honey with ½ tablespoon lime juice and 1 tablespoon rose water. Apply on the face.
- Mix cucumber juice with Fuller's earth (multani mitti) or gram flour. Apply on the face, let it dry for ten minutes, then wash.

Prickly Heat (Miliaria)

Red pustules of size of mustard grains appear on the body, especially on the chest, back and abdomen. It is caused due to profuse sweating during hot or rainy days. A person who has suffered widespread prickly heat by sweating and develops 'heat stroke'.

Try the following remedies:

1. Apply green henna ground in water.
2. Grind leaves of 'neem' in water and apply.
3. Apply Fuller's earth pack, which leaves a cooling effect.
4. If there is intense itching on affected skin and the affected area is scratched, the most effective remedy for treating prickly heat

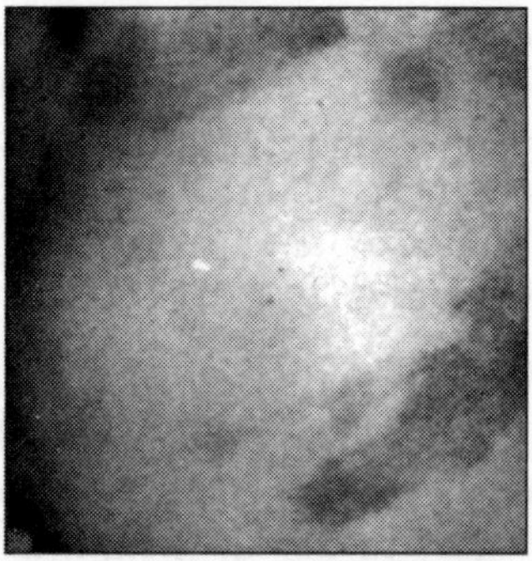

Red pustules on Abdomen

is to take a small piece of sandalwood and rub it on a stone with rose water. Mix to it a pinch of alum (powdered) and apply thrice a week, depending upon condition of skin.

5. Dissolve a tablespoon of soda bicarbonate in half cup of water. Mix to it 1 tablespoon of rose water and apply.

Cold Sores

Also known as Virus-herpes simplex. It occurs usually on lips and other parts of body. Sometimes, it affects the genitalia and the infection is spread by sexual intercouse. This infection can be activated by cold, fever, stressful conditions, emotional disturbance or any serious illness. There are two herpes viruses—herpes simplex virus, which causes cold sores and genital herpes, and another virus which causes chicken pox. The primary attack of herpes simplex is usually severe. The lesions generally consists of multiple, small, vesicles or superficial ulcer on the upper lips on the face (in women), on the male sex organ (glans penis and the shaft of penis) in males. When the attack is mild, the lesions tend to heal in 7 to 14 days. If the infection is severe, antibiotic treatment is usually recommended by the doctor. Consult a doctor. Most people get cold sores (herpes simplex) from someone with a cold sore in childhood. The first attack is the worst, small children may get painful mouth ulcers and swollen glands. Usually, groups of small blisters appear on the lips, form a crust and dry up in a week or so. Cold sores appear in the same place.

Remedies

Cold compress of ice relieves pain. In case of recurrent attacks of herpes, have Acyclovir treatment in consultation with a doctor. The dormant virus cannot be removed from the nerves by any method.

During an attack antiseptic lotions dry up blisters and prevent other germs prolonging the cold sore. Your doctor may prescribe lotion or a cream recommended for anti-virus treatment for very bad cases. If you are prone to repeated cold sores use a sun blocking preparation when sunbathing, climbing mountains or skiing. The following home remedies heal herpes simplex:

Herpes Zoster and Genital Herpes

This disease is caused by varicella-zoster virus when groups of vesicle or bulla occur on a segment of the body including the cranial nerves. The painful lesions start to dry up within a week or so. Proper cleansing of the affected area, local application of calamine lotion, oral administration of analgesic and application of anti-inflammatory agents, which relieve the pain and cure.

This is caused by different strain of same virus, caught by having sex with someone having herpes. It is common in young people. Groups of little blisters appear on the genital area, thighs and buttocks. They are painful, tender and highly infectious. The first infection is worst with swollen glands and a temperature. The blisters crust over and clear in a week or so. The virus becomes dormant in this condition, but may cause repeated attacks.

How to Treat Genital Herpes?

The virus hidden in the nerves cannot be killed. Antiviral creams and lotions may shorten the attack. Warm salt water baths and pain-killers (usually aspirin and paracetamol are recommended by doctor) make you comfortable during an attack. All attacks of genital herpes are infectious to your lover. Avoid having sex during an attack of genital herpes, but once the scabs have disappeared you can have sex again. Condoms lessen the risk of infection.

GENITAL HERPES IN PREGNANCY

Such attack is very serious as an infected mother can pass on the infection to her baby and so she may need to be delivered by a caesarean section. Frequent attacks of genital herpes play havoc with your sex life. Worry and depression, poor general health or lack of sleep and an unhealthy diet may reduce your resistance to infection.

Shingles

After chickenpox, the virus lives in nerves. Later in life, very painful blisters may appear in the skin on one side of the body, which last

7-14 days. Most people have only one attack of shingles. Painkillers help the pain, which is usually worst as the attack is developing, but sometimes comes on for weeks or months after the blisters have gone. Seek your doctor's advice immediately for shingles on the face as it can damage the eyes. The blisters are confined to one side of the face.

Scabies

Scabies is a contagious disease caused by a mite (sarcoptus). This mite lays eggs in the burrows in the skin. The disease spreads through contact with infected individual, clothing, bedding or furniture. The commonly affected parts are finger webs, palm, wrist, front of arm, soles, areas around the nipples and penis. The sole complaint is severe itching (pruritus), which is more at night. Any person who has itching in these areas of the body and is not suffering from allergy or pruritus can be suspected of scabies. The infection due to mite may cause snail papules and there may be a rash. The latter is due to scratching. The incubation period for mite is long, about a month, and it can easily be transferred by normal social contact among a group of people living together. This infectious disease is also transmitted from the pet animals *e.g.,* the dog, cat, horse effecting lower part of the abdomen, ankles, thighs, buttocks, breasts in females, penis and scrotum. Sometimes produce papules, crusts and lymphadenopathy.

Treatment for Scabies

1. All members of the house whether symptomatic or not should be treated. The clothes, linen, towels, etc., should be thoroughly washed and ironed.
2. Local application of 25% benzyl benzoate emulsion (Ascabiol) or 10% gammabenzene hexachloride (Scabiezima, Scarb) as prescribed by the doctor. It is important that all the members of the family are simultaneously treated.
3. There should be separate bath soap and towel of the patient.
4. The clothes should be changed at the end of the treatment.
5. The lotion should not be applied on the face.
6. If the hands are involved, wear cotton gloves.
7. Avoid the use of all harsh soaps and chemicals.
8. Apply silicone protective cream two to three times a day to the irritated area.

9. Emotional upsets should be avoided as far as possible. Make sure that the patient does not have diabetes or some other disease.
10. Apply sulphur ointment to all the body, rubbing it thoroughly after a hot bath. Use 10% sulphur ointment for adults and 5% for children. Apply this on three successive nights. Calamine lotion will help to control the itch. Try not to scratch the skin. For badly inflamed areas, apply neomycin ointment containing cortisone. Treat every member of the family at the same time.

Herbal Cure for Scabies

2 tablespoons juice of green leaves of 'Shahtara' should be taken with a little honey. Alternatively, Ground 'neem' leaves or leaf-shoots with seven grains pf Pepper, strain and drink. There are another recipes as below:

- Boil little quantity of leaves of Oleander (Kaner) in mustard oil till charred. The oil should be used for anointing the parts affected by itch.
- About 250 ml of mustard oil should be heated to a boiling point. Burn into it 21 leaves of Swallow Wort one by one. When the oil has cooled, mix to it finely ground Mansal. Massage the affected parts with this oil.
- Ground in water seeds of Yellow Thisle (Satyanasi). Stain and drink for a week, it will relieve worst type of itch.
- Mix equal quantity of juice of lemon and jasmine oil and rub on itching skin.
- Ground in water Poppy Seeds and mix to it lime juice. The massage of this paste is good for dry itch.

ATOPIC ECZEMA

People who suffer from asthma, hay fever, attacks of conjunctivitis (red, itchy eyes) or atopic eczema are called atopic. This disease usually appears between three to twelve months of age and may persist into the teens. The patches of eczema may be dry, red and scaly or weeping and sometimes split. The children are often disfigured by scratch marks, making the skin thick and ridged. The disease affects the face, especially skin around the mouth and eyes. Following care should be taken to cope with atopic eczema:

1. Usually, a treatment cannot cure this disease and it will go away on its own, eventually. The treatment of this disorder is aimed at making it less troublesome.

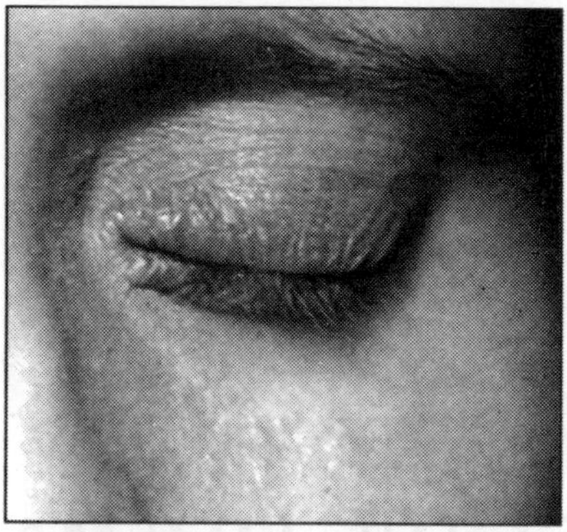
Eczema on Face

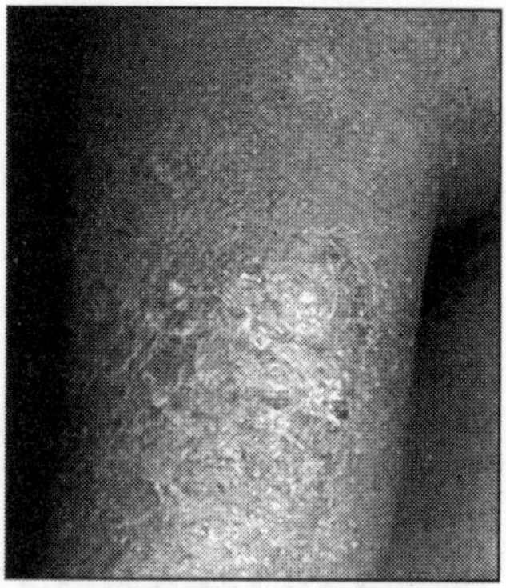
Eczema on Face

2. Breastfeeding only for first six to nine months has been recommended to prevent atopic eczema.
3. A strict diet, free from cow's milk and eggs, improves the condition. The diet can lead to vitamin and calcium deficiency, and must be done under the medical supervision.
4. In case of children, beds and the room of the child must be cleaned daily where children lie or crawl. Dust in bedding, curtains, carpets and soft furnishings contain house dust mite. Allergy to this makes the eczema worst.
5. Wool, nylon and artificial fabrics make the skin itchy.
6. Bubble bath being dry should be avoided. Oil may be added to the bath. Soaps are drying to the skin and should be avoided. A cool bath with a special cleanser to grease the skin is helpful.

5

DERMATITIS: THE ECZEMA

An inflammatory skin disorder in which the cuticle is fissured with a sticky, watery discharge. There is itching and pain over the affected area. This infection is generally caused by the reaction of medicines or cosmetics. In case of cosmetic allergy the face, especially around the mouth and eyes, and the joints are particularly affected. However, there is no permanent change in skin colour or scarring.

COPING WITH ECZEMA IN CHILDREN

Treatment of eczema is aimed at making it less troublesome. Treatments cannot cure it but it will go away on its own, eventually. The following factors help curing allergy due to eczema in babies and children:

- **Diet:** Breastfeeding only for six to nine months has been recommended to prevent eczema. Many mothers have been made to feel guilty bout bottle-feeding their babies, when this is still not proven to be harmful. A few babies and children improve dramatically on a very strict diet free from cow's milk and eggs, when this is still not proven to be harmful. The diet can lead to vitamin and calcium deficiency, and must be done under medical supervision. The main symptoms of allergy include itching of the mouth on eating the food.
- **Dust:** Dust in bedding, curtains and furnishings contain large quantity of house dust mite. Allergy to this makes eczema worse in some children. Beds and room must be vacuumed daily and bedding washed once a week. Carpets must be removed from areas where children lie or crawl.

- **Clothing:** Wool, nylon and artificial fabrics make the skin more itchy and the eczema worse. Cotton clothes and sheets are generally harmless.
- **Bathing:** Soaps are drying to the skin but a cool bath with a special cleanser to grease the skin (such as aqueous cream or emulsifying ointment) is very helpful. Add oil to the bath. Avoid bubble baths, which dries the skin. Chlorinated swimming pools make skin dry, a shower after swimming to wash off the chlorine is essential. However, sea bathing doesn't make eczema worse.
- **Heat:** Heat makes eczema itchy. Hot humid weather often makes eczema worse but sunlight is often beneficial. Cold winter weather, as well as hot, dry atmosphere due to central heating make the skin drier, cracked and itchy.
- **Stress:** Stress and unhappiness leave a harmful effect and make eczema worse.
- **Medicines:** Doctors usually prescribe steroid ointments to reduce inflammation and itch in case of eczema. But only mild steroid ointments such as hydrocortisone can be used for children as steroid may thin the skin. Consult a child specialist before treatment. However, antihistamines taken at night reduce the itch and make child drowsy.
- **Immunization:** If the child suffers from eczema, all the normal childhood immunizations should be given except smallpox; as smallpox vaccination can be fatal in children with eczema.

Eczlema in Adults

Eczema is an intensely itchy rash, which varies from acute redness, swelling and blistering, with weeping crusted areas, to dry scaly patches, thick patches and splits. There is many kinds of eczema as described below:

- **Atopic Eczema:** This type of eczema is rare in adults, but similar to the disease in children, contact allergic eczema is commoner.
- **Hand and Foot Eczema:** This eczema is very disabling as it interferes with work.
- **Housewives Eczema:** Housewives, particularly those with breastfeeding babies and small children suffer dreadfully from very severe chapping of their hands, which get dry, red, cracked and sore. Constant exposure to detergents, washing up liquid, washing powder, bleaches, cleansing fluids, continuous wetting, exposure

to cold weather damage and dry out the skin. Hands, once damaged takes much time to return to normal. Use rubber gloves when having frequent contact.

- **Blistering Eczema of the Hands and Feet:** Unfortunate people have very distressing blistering eczema of the palms and soles in which the attacks start as tiny itchy blisters which dry to form peeling, itchy, cracked skin, which heels in one to two weeks. The disease has frequent attacks every few weeks to continue for months and years. The cause is unknown but stress, heat and sweating all may trigger attacks. A steroid ointment prescribed by your doctor may help to cure, especially after the soaks and in the peeling stage as this reduces the itch.
- **Discoid Eczema:** It produces dry, scaly, itchy patches on the limbs and body. These are occasionally severe and blister or weep. The cause is unknown, but stress makes condition worse. Doctors usually prescribe a steroid ointment.
- **Lichen Simplex:** The patient develops a thick patch of eczema usually at the nape of the neck or leg, resulting in itch and scratches. The skin thickens and itches more. A steroid ointment is recommended.
- **Seborrhoeic Eczema:** A most common form of eczema occurring on the skin and the scalp, which can be severe if not treated. There is occasional patches, redness and itching on the scalp and skin around eyebrows and eyelashes, face, beard area and behind the ears. The other affected parts on the body include centre of the chest, under the breasts, back, body folds on the armpits and groins, pubic area and genitals causing severe redness, scaling, itching, discomfort and embarrassment. Heat and sweating in skin folds make it worse. When the face is affected, one cannot tolerate make-up. Consult a skin specialist for suggesting a suitable ointment/treatment otherwise it will lead to sleepless nights. Hydrocortisone creams may help only mild cases. Avoid all antiseptics, either as creams or baths. Stop bubble baths or bath salts, they will irritate the skin.

Naturopathic Remedies

The following remedies are suggested to cure this affliction:

- Mix Babchi powder with mustard oil and apply on the affected skin.
- Rub the affected part vigorously before bathing.

- An intake of three to four litres of fluid daily flushes the system of the infection.
- Eat maximum fruits and vegetables.
- Oxide of zinc ointment diluted with sweet almond oil should be applied daily. Better consult a doctor.
- Eczema of the face is common among children. If the ears are affected, cover them with a mask and sterilize the surface of ears with a solution of peroxide of hydrogen. If the eyelids are affected, remove and soften the crusts with a blend oil, followed by a light application of Benzoated lard in consultation of doctor. If the nostrils are affected, Boric acid may be applied. When the lips are affected, a tendency to crack may be averted by frequent application of a blend oil, cold cream or equal parts of benzoin, alcohol and glycerine.
- Eczema of the male genitals is most often seen in the chronic form. Careful cleansing, the application of hygroscopic powder and use of suspensory bandage are to be applied. The inflammation of the penis is usually milder than of the scrotum. In acute forms bed rest and application of hot boric acid, as hot as it can be borne, for 60 to 90 seconds, followed by boric ointment.
- Eczema of nipples and breast usually occur in nursing women. The lactating mothers should not employ poisonous treatment.
- Eczema of anus may be treated with carbolic, calamine or hydrocyanic solution. The eczema of nails needs only a protective application.

Eczema—Many sided disease

Though Eczema is a many sided disease, but popular elementary varieties are:

1. The popular erythematous.
2. The vesicular.
3. The pustular.

These lesions constitute the peculiar type, which may remain distinctive or at least predominate throughout the course of the disease. Following are the types of eczema:

- **Eczema Erythematosum:** This variety occurs in the extremes of life, in infancy and also in old age, usually on the face, palm, toes and genitalia. The erythematous spots may remain isolated or rapidly spreading over a large surface. There may be swelling, or even edema, about the eyes and rough scales or fissures or a general weeping of the surface on skin.

- **Eczema Circumscriptum:** When the eruption remains well defined in small patches throughout its course.
- **Eczema Squamosum (Eczema Exfolia Tivum):** When scaling persists to any degree, this condition becomes valid as Eczema squamosum.
- **Eczema Intertrigo:** When swelling and infection occurs on opposing surfaces, as between the genital folds. It is usually associated with a muciform-secretion.
- **Eczema Vesiculosum:** It is the most typical catarrhal inflammation of the skin which may occur on any surface, seen generally upon the face of infants and young children, and upon the fingers, hands, neck and flexor surfaces of the older people. The condition is associated with itching, scratching with scales and crusts.
- **Eczema Papulosum:** Closely aggregated papules may develop into a weeping patch as a result of vesiculation or they may become scaly and may lose their papular character.
- **Papulae Eczema:** It is often refractory to treatment, frequently relapses, and is especially intense itching.
- **Eczema Pustulosum:** When closely aggregated pustules and yellowish or brownish crusts cover the whole or part of the affected area. On the hairy surfaces, such as the bearded portion of the faces of males, the follicles become inflamed and secondary folliculitis complicates the process. Pustular eczema appears on the face and scalp of children, and in adults, it is found on the thighs, lower legs and upon the beards.
- **Eczema Rubrum:** It is secondary form, in which redness, swelling, exudation, infiltration, bleeding and consequent crusting are on the faces of infants, and upon the legs of middle-aged or old adults, who suffer from marked varicosities and often shows the common varicose ulcer.
- **Eczema Madidans:** This aggravates red, raw and weeping eczema in which the moisture constantly come from the surface with burning and itching.

- **Eczema Squamosum:** Scaling and infiltration are the features of this eczema. The scales are greyish-white, thin and flaky. They may involve large areas or small patches.

Medical Treatment of Eczema

Eczema is an inflammatory skin disease in which the cuticle is scaly and fissured with a sticky, watery discharge. There is also severe itching, redness, inflammation and pain over the affected parts. It is more often called 'dermatitis' and is important because majority of cases of skin disorders are eczema. Eczema may be dry with only a patch of thick, itchy skin or weeping, in which case it oozes.

The patients suffering from eczema of hands should wear cotton gloves. Avoid the use of harsh soaps and chemicals. Apply silicon protective cream to the irritated skin. Emotional upsets should be avoided as far as possible. It is important that the patient does not have diabetes or some other disease. Hydrocortisone ointment (0.5%) is often helpful in the treatment of eczema. If there is marked swelling under the skin injections of penicillin may clear up the infection, but seek treatment under the guidance of a doctor, the patient may be sensitive to penicillin.

Herbal Treatment

Bark of Mango and Acacia trees should be boiled in one litre of water and the vapour allowed to play upon the affected part. After this fomentation, the area of skin should be anointed with ghee. Alternatively, the leaves of the Indian Butter tree (Mahua) should be smeared with Sesame oil (warmed) and bandaged over the affected parts. The bandage should be changed after three to four hours.

Homeopathic Cure

The following medicines are recommended:

- **Psorinum:** For old cases when there are ulcers, offensive pus and intense itching (use 200 or 1000 infrequently).
- **Cicuta V:** For treating eczema of hairy parts, specially chin.
- **Croton:** For eczema of face, genitals, scrotum when there is much itch.
- **Kali Mur:** For eczemas in which scaly crusts are formed due to after effects of vaccination in women due to scanty menstruation or amenorrhoea, on the face and head of the children.
- **Sulphur:** For intense burning, itching and offensive body odour.

Birthmarks

These include dark brown patches to fleshy bumps. Sometimes, these are fairly small moles, which disfigure the skin. It is generally called by scratching the pimples, or due to small pox, which leave a permanent scar. The remedial measures include:

1. Dealing minor scars with carbon snow, ray treatment and cortisone injections.
2. Scars can be disguised temporarily by cosmetics.
3. Skin grafting or cosmetic surgery.
4. Peeling treatment, which causes deep cleansing by removing a thin layer of the skin.
5. Strawberry marks can be removed by electric coagulation or by X-ray treatment.

Sunburn

Sunburn is very harmful for you. It ages your skin and may increase risk of skin cancer. Dryness of the skin due to dehydration causes scarring of the skin. It looses complexion and becomes dark, thick, leathery, wrinkled and patchy. This is caused by the adverse effect of sun on the skin. Natural substances such as herbs and flowers not only help reduce symptoms, but may also bring the body back to a state of balance. Observe the following remedies:

1. Drink 8 to 10 glasses of water in a day in summer and 4 to 5 glasses a day in winter.
2. Apply suntan lotion or cream.
3. If skin is dark, apply a mask of a mixture of bleaching powder and hydrogen peroxide.

The dark complexioned people get less sunburn than fair complexioned people. This is because the darker the skin, the more the quantity of melanin in the body. The ill effect of sun-rays are maximum on children between 6 to 8 years of age, on women between 25 to 30 years of age and men between 30 to 35 years of age. Ultra-violet rays destroy the melanin in the body and the skin gets dark. The minute rays cut the skin and crack it. This dries the skin. As a result, the skin swells and rashes appear on it. The fresh melanin comes out and the skin gets blackened. In fact, the sunburn reacts on the body in the same way as does burning by steam or very hot oil. The skin dry, the blood vessels swell and cells are damaged.

Ordinary sunburn can be cured within three to four days, but strong sunburn creates rashes and the skin peels off in layers. Obviously, new cells are born and a new skin does appear again, but it is more dry and thick as compared to the original one. New skin is often brownish in colour. It wrinkles and cracks easily. Such wrinkles are hard to cure.

To cure sunburn, have a cool water bath. But don't use soap; use gel. The degree to which the sun can be tolerated depends upon the type of skin. Direct hot sunrays may be more harmful in the month of June when the sun gets nearest to the earth. Sunrays are dangerously hot between 12 noon and 2 o'clock in the afternoon. Drink as much lemon water during this period of the day as you can for a cooling effect.

Skin damaged by burning or severe inflammation always leaves scars. Surface injuries often heal with temporary discoloration if the burns are not very severe. In case of scars, plastic surgery is done carefully along the expression lines, make the scars invisible. Burn occurs either due to sunrays, sitting too near open fires or using a very hot bottle in winter or fire while cooking is classified as:

1. **First Degree Burn:** These are mild superficial burns, which cause redness of the skin and later peeling. For this no treatment is necessary. Calamine lotion is soothing. The burns usually heal without scarring, with temporary darkening or lightening of the skin.
2. **Second Degree Burn:** These are severe causing blistering, swelling and redness of the skin. There is no permanent scar due to this burn. The blister is made to burst with a sterilised needle and the burn should be kept clean and dry and covered with a dressing.
3. **Third and Fourth Degree Burns:** This type of burns cause serious problems, in which underlying fat, muscle and tendons are burnt down to the bone. The nerves are destroyed and it results in severe scars.

Skin Breaks

Red, itchy and scaling dermatitis causing inflamed hair follicles on the front surface of the thighs and legs. The condition is common at the time of menstrual periods. Treatment to control skin breaks include:

1. The treatment with antibiotics.
2. Restriction of salt intake.
3. Medically supervised therapy to reduce water retention just before the menstrual periods.
4. Hormonal therapy treatment.
5. Avoid wearing tight jeans or wearing trousers with narrow cut. It is seen that large number of skin reactions develop in adolescence among those who wear tight dresses. Wear loose clothes to avoid further skin eruptions produced by pressure or friction, increased heat and humidity caused by tight fit.

Neurodermatitis

It is a chronic type of itching and inflammation of the skin. The itching area may be in some localized spot or it may extend over large areas of the body. The condition may even develop in infants and may disappear after the age of two, only to return in the early teens or later. The condition is more often seen in those who suffer from fever, hives and asthma. The true cause of this disorder is not known, but most of the affected people are allergic to many things, particularly when they are nervous and upset. Many of them are tense and restless which result to dry skin. Many of patients suffering from neurodermatitis are hypersensitive and are often given to itching, especially in the bend of the elbow or behind the knee. The constant scratching leaves deep scratch marks and causes thickening and furrowing of the skin.

Treatment

Rosewater ointment is excellent for this purpose. Another prescription that may be tried is as following:

Aluminium Acetate Solution:	10.0 cc.
Wool Fat:	20.0 gm
Zinc Oxide Paste:	30.0 gm

Apply to the itching area three times a day as needed. For more severe itching, try hydrocortisone ointment, which is very effective during the severe stage. Apply small amount of ointment and rub in thoroughly. Often change of climate is beneficial. Air conditioning is also helpful to cure the disorder. Try to remove all causes of tension and nervous agitation.

Hangnail

Skin infection around the nails is common, especially after improper manicuring or from wearing poorly fitting shoes. The infection may extend under the nail, causing severe pain. Unless the infection is brought under control, the condition may spread to the tendons and other near-by structures.

Treatment

Soak the finger or toe in hot water three or four times a day for at least 10 to 15 minutes. Apply antibiotic ointment on the affected area after consulting your doctor. If pus is present, it must be drained by a doctor.

Beard Infection

Sometimes, the hair follicles of the face become infected, resulting in small tender lesions similar to tiny boils. There may be itching, burning and pain. The following treatment is suggested:

- Wash the face thoroughly with soap and warm water three times a day.
- Remove the hair from the infected follicle and apply antibiotic ointment with the consultation of a doctor.
- Rubbing alcohol applied to the face will help to reduce further spread of this condition.
- X-ray therapy may bring relief.

Athlete's Foot

This is a form of ringworm of the feet. The disease is common in warm climates, and in individuals whose feet are constantly wet because of excessive sweating. When the disease is present over long periods of time, the toenails may become thickened. Treatment includes:

- Bathe the feet thoroughly twice daily, dry them well and rub away the loosened dead skin.
- Apply a suitable dusting powder containing zinc stearate or a powder containing a mixture of equal parts of zinc oxide, zinc stearate and talcum powder.
- Always wear light, airy shoes during warm weather.
- In case of serious infections, use hot foot soaks of potassium permanganate solution. Soak the feet for 20 minutes three times a day.
- Rub feet with cider vinegar.

CORNS AND CALLUSES

Corns are painful thickening of the skin usually found over the joints of the toes and on the soles of the feet. They are tender when touched and often result from wearing badly fitting shoes. Calluses are similar to corns, except that larger areas of the skin are involved. The skin itself is not so tender but is greatly thickened by the extra use on the soles and heels of the feet. Any undue pressure on the feet may produce a corn or callus.

Treatment includes to eliminate excessive pressure over the area by wearing softer, well-fitting shoes. Prevent any undue soreness and thickening of the skin. Thickened skin may also be softened and removed by painting the area each night with the following solutions (with the consultation of a doctor):

1. **Epsom salts and borax:** Fill a bowl with warm water and add to it 2 tablespoons of Epsom salt and 1 tablespoon Borax. Soak the feet until the water is cold. Then dry thoroughly and massage with witch hazel. This will soothe the skin.
2. **Castor oil:** Massage the feet daily with castor oil. A mixture of castor oil and turpentine when massaged harden the feet and hands and make them less susceptible to corns and calluses. If these already exist use a pumice stone after massaging to remove the hard skin.
4. **Cloves:** Five drops of clove oil mix to five tablespoons of sesame oil, which relieves aching feet and soothes sore area.
5. **Soak feet in warm water mixed with bicarbonate of soda:** Then massage feet with sunflower oil mixed with cider vinegar.

Lice Infestation (Pediculosis)

Three main types of lice may affect the human body. One type attacks the scalp and head, another attacks the body and the third attacks the genital areas, and occasionally the eyebrows and eyelashes. The parasites may also be found in the seams of clothing.

- Pediculosis Capitis is caused by the head louse, which infects only scalp hair. In the hair small oval-shaped nits may adhere to the hair shafts in great numbers. These are difficult to remove. In few days they mature, becoming full-grown lice. Itching is usually severe and the skin shows evidence of scratching.
- Pediculosis Corporis (Body Lice) is caused by louse, which live in the seams of the clothes and bites the skin. Body lice are common

in people who are crowded together and living under unhygienic, poor sanitary conditions. They spread rapidly usually during disasters. At such times lice will sometimes transmit serious conditions such as epidemic typhus, trench fever and relapsing fever. In this condition, itching is intense and red bite marks may even be seen in the skin.

- Pediculosis Pubis infects the hairs in the pubic region, axillae, beard, moustche and eyelashes, which many times spread to the trunk. The nits can be seen sticking to the pubic area.

Treatment consists of the following:

1. Application of 1% gamma benzene hexachloride or 0.25% malathion.
2. In case of eyelashes, apply petrolatum to the eyelashes four to five times a day.
3. Thoroughly cleanse the whole body from the scalp to the toes, using plenty of soap and water. Next apply 5% benzyl benzoate emulsion to all itching areas. Rub this well into the scalp at night.
4. Dust the skin with 5 per cent DDT powder especially in the areas where the parasites are found.
5. Thorough laundering of the underclothing and dry-cleaning of clothes will help to get rid of these pasts.

Vaginal odour

A certain degree of odour is normal in the vaginal area. A traditional and effective method of getting rid of odour in the vaginal area or elsewhere in the body, is maintaining cleanliness as a part of the normal shower or bath. Body odour causes by the bacteria acting on perspiration, mucus and sebum (oil) present on the skin. The 'bad' bacteria can invade the genital area, causing one or more symptoms of infectious vaginitis, soreness, irritation, inflammation, vaginal discharge (Leucorrhoea), burning, swelling, reddening of vulva, urinary discomfort and pain during sex. All these symptoms cause vaginal odour. Following care should be taken to relieve vaginal odour:

1. Cleanliness of body and vaginal area.
2. Feminine deodorant sprays can supplement but not replace cleanliness. Consult a doctor in case of a vaginal discharge or odour.

3. Consult your doctor in case of foul-smelling, thin white or blood streaked discharge or white, thick vaginal discharge or grey, fishy-smelling discharge.
4. Garlic is antibacterial and anti-fungal, so it can fight vaginal odour.
5. Using a gelatin capsule of vitamin E as a suppository is very soothing to vaginal tissue, decreasing irritation, redness, swelling and congestion-all these can cause vaginal odour. Insert a capsule once or twice (as recommended by your doctor) daily for a week.

Elephantiasis

It is a chronic hypertrophic disease of the skin and subcutaneous tissue due to the local obstruction of blood and lymph, which results in enormous enlargement of the affected part. The disease is of two types: The endemic form found in the tropical climates and the sporadic occurs in temperate climates. However both types are practically identical in their effect on the parts involved. Usually this disease attacks the legs or feet, the breast, thighs, buttocks, penis, labia, clitoris, upper extremities, individual parts of the face and other regions of the body.

In either of the endemic or sporadic cases, there is infiltration, swelling and redness of the skin. The endemic form often presents antecedent febrile disturbances (fever and sweating), joint pains with nausea, vomiting and chilliness. The genitals, especially the scrotum, show the most pronounced growth, but other parts of the body seldom show such increase. It includes severe itching and varicose ulcers. The disease is more frequent in early adult life. Unhygienic living, poor food and other influences are doubtless contributing factors but the disease is neither contagious nor hereditary. On the other hand sporadic elephantiasis may be recognized by the history of recurrent erysipelatious inflammation and gradual enlargement of the parts.

Myxedema

A constitutional disease characterized by the thickening of the skin and subcutaneous tissue and progressive failure of bodily and mental powers caused by the atrophy or ablation of the thyroid gland. First skin manifestations appear on the face, giving it a swollen, edematous, thickened appearance. The swollen tissue has a yellow, waxy colour and the surface becomes dry and anaemic. The hair falls out, especially if the axillary and pubic regions are involved. The disease usually extends to the neck and extremities and less commonly to other parts of the body. The condition may occur in either sex or at any age, but it is most common in middle-aged women.

Skin Tags

It is very common on the neck and in the armpits and groin. They can be removed by tying a fine thread around the stalks so that they drop off. They can be snipped off with sterile scissors or burnt off, but removing them does not prevent more arriving. Laser therapy is the latest cure to this disorder.

Tattoos

Removing tattoos is difficult and must be done by a doctor. The tattoos can be removed by cutting them out by dermabrasion (replacing the tattoo with discoloured hairless rough skin by laser treatment.

FACIAL WRINKLES

Wrinkles give an old look to a young person and are caused by loosening of skin tissues and muscles, dryness of skin, irritation, annoyance, anger and mental tension. The following measures are suggested to delay ageing:

1. Facial massage is effective to counter wrinkles.
2. Use a cream containing vitamin E.
3. Facial exercise to stimulate the skin.
4. Use a good moisturising cream.
5. Avoid hot sunrays and have a protein rich diet

What causes wrinkles?

As a person ages, skin cells divide more slowly and the inner skin, or dermis starts to thin. Skin loses its elasticity, when pressed it no longer springs back to its initial position but instead sags. The skin becomes dry and scaly. The ability of the skin to repair itself declines. Frown lines (between the eyebrows) and crow's feet that radiate from the eyes appear to develop because of muscle contractions. The skin also age prematurely as a result of prolonged exposure to ultra-violet (UV) radiation, which cause ageing skin resulting wrinkles.

Fine lines are shallow grooves in the epidermis, which can be made to look less obvious by the use of cosmetic products that improve hydration and suppleness. Wrinkles are of two types:

1. **Permanent Wrinkles:** They present a deep wrinkle on sun-exposed skin such as the face and neck and does not appear on stretching.
2. **Non-permanent Wrinkles:** They are fine shallow wrinkles that develop on sun-protected skin such as abdomen and bottom, where the skin becomes thin and wrinkle easily. Fat tissues decrease with age. These wrinkles disappear easily on stretching. Cosmetic products cannot reverse wrinkle development.

The sebaceous glands become less active and the skin becomes dry. The skin loses its elasticity as the elastic fibres harden and the wrinkles appear due to the cross-linking and hardening of collagen fibres. The epidermis grows slowly and the skin appears thinner. Broken capillaries appear, especially on cheeks and around the nose. The facial contours become slack and muscle tone is reduced. Blood circulation also slows down. Collagen production, too, breaks down. Hormone production is reduced. Patches of irregular pigmentation appear on the surface of the skin. Dark circles and puffiness may occur under the eyes.

Hormones Imbalance

There is a relationship between beauty and hormones. Hormones are produced in human body by the organs. Lack of hormones or excess of hormones in the body can prove disastrous. Hormones can be introduced in the system by way of pill or injections to regularize imbalances or make-up deficiencies, and are of various types, but the one which are associated with beauty are androgens, estrogens, thyroids, steroids, insuline and sex hormones. The excessive secretion of androgens cause acne or hair loss and usually is caused by stress and mental tension. Estrogens help to cure acne, pimples, retard wrinkles and make skin clear and shiny. The shortage of thyroids hormones in the system make skin dry and wrinkled. The excessive production of steroids cause skin infections, pigmentation of the skin and acne. The deficiency of insulin hormones harm the complexion and cause skin fungus, bacterial infection and itching, sex hormones are generally of two types. Male sex harmones encourage growth of hair on the body whereas female sex harmones encourage growth of hair on the scalp.

How to Look Younger After 40?

Laughter lines and gray hair give obvious clues to a woman's age. Here are few steps to beat the signs of ageing. The signs of ageing skin include loss of elasticity, increased wrinkles and lack of skin firmness—all these are inevitable. From around the age of 40, our skin cells take longer time to regenerate, due to hormonal changes and decreasing level of vitamin E. When we are younger, skin cells replenish themselves within 21 days. But this rate becomes slower as we grow older.

Drugless modern therapies and deep penetrating aroma oils stimulate the skin and promote its regeneration. Exfoliation encourages circulation, stimulates the skin and removes dead cells. Body brushing, too, stimulates the lymph, helps to detoxify the body and acts as an effective stimulant. Vigorously rubbing or pinching the skin promotes fine lines and encourages wrinkles. Moisturiser should be dabbed lightly and rubbed in gently. Cold showers can tone the skin, and stimulate the nervous system.

In case of signs of ageing, women should avoid sunbathing. Excessive exercise after the age 40 may be harmful. As we get older, the skin can't easily spring back into place, so do gentle stretching and light yoga postures only. The stretch marks on the body pose serious signs of ageing.

Stretch marks are caused by scar tissue just below the skin's surface as a result of stretch and strain on the skin. Retino acid gets rid of stretch marks in early stage. An effective way to fade stretch marks is to use vitamin E, which can regenerate damaged skin tissues. Wheat-germ oil or vitamin E capsules should be cut open and used, which helps to fade the scars. You can have the face of 25 year old, but wrinkles on your hands will give real age you have as hands do not have natural oils and without proper moisturising, the skin begins to lose charm.

Imbalnce of hormones can prove disastrous. Hormones are of various types, but one which are associated with beauty are androgens, estrogens, thyroids, steriods, insulin and sex hormones.

- Excessive secretion of androgen through the sebum of sebaceous glands cause acne and hair loss. It is caused by the stress and mental tension. The imbalance of hormones may be balanced by taking estrogen pills.

- Estrogens cure acne and pimples. Estrogen pills benefit the skin by retarding wrinkles and making it clear and shiny. These hormones are essential after the age of 40, when there is decline in the production of these hormones.
- Avoid taking estrogen pills if you suffer from high blood pressure. Excess of estrogen, sometimes harm the skin causing pigmentation and skin lesions.
- The shortage of thyroid hormones cause skin dry and wrinkled. The steroids also cause skin infections, pigmentation and acne.
- The deficiency of insulin hormones harm the complexion and cause skin fungus.
- Sex hormones are of two types: male and female sex hormones. Male hormones encourage growth of hair on the skin and body, whereas female sex hormones encourage growth of hair on the scalp.

SKIN CANCER (KERATOSIS)

Scaly patches on the skin, on the face such as ear, nose and back of hands. Patches appear on the scalp. The disorder develops in the very elderly, usually on areas exposed to sun. It is caused by too much exposure of fair skin to sun and X-rays or exposure to toxic chemicals. The treatment should be done at a very early stage by radio therapy, surgery and cry-therapy (liquid nitrogen can be used to kill cancer cells by freezing).

SKIN TUMOR

Seborrhoeic warts appear on the skin. This is caused by excessive exposure of skin to sun rays. If not treated timely, leads to skin cancer. It can be removed surgically.

MUDDY SKIN

The skin loses its radiance due to over-tiredness and lack of sleep. Following are the remedial measures:

1. Drink a glass of hot skimmed milk before going to bed at night.
2. Drink four to six glasses of water every day between meals, not with the meals. The water should be cold.
3. Take fresh fruits, green vegetables as much as you can. Have cold drinks and fruit juices without sugar.

SKIN GRAFTING

Skin grafting is simply plastic surgery. When the skin is wrinkled, the extra part of the skin is surgically removed and the skin is stitched. Skin grafting is necessary for optimum healing and to lessen the deformity or disability that occurs when the large area of the skin has been lost by injury or burns, disease like varicose ulcers and surgical excision of some carcinomas. Free skin grafts provide the simplest method of restoring the skin cover. Split thickness grafts are the ones most generally used though they have a tendency to shrink. The skin is usually taken from thighs and the graft may be affixed be sutures.

BEDSORES

A bedsore, also known as decubitus ulcer, occurs when the skin over some bony prominence breaks, because of prolonged pressure over the area. This is most likely to occur when an elderly patient has to spend a long time in bed. These chronic sores are usually found over the lower parts of the back, and over the bony prominence of the legs and ankles. The pressure over the skin cuts off the local blood supply causing necrosis and gangrene. Bedsores are a problem, especially if the patient is unable to control the urine or faeces.

First signs of bedsores are increased redness of the skin, which may later turn darker owing to local cyanosis. Small blisters may also be present in this condition. Eventually the surface of the skin breaks down and an ulcer develops which tunnels through the skin, and into the deeper tissues such as muscles and the bone. Once the skin is broken, infection increases and the ulcer may continue to spread and burrow under the skin in all directions.

Treatment

- Bedsores and decubitus ulcers are easier to prevent than to cure. Take precautions to avoid injury to the skin.
- Turn the patient -from one side to another every hour.
- Use small foam rubber pads to protect these areas. Place fluffed pillows and rolled blankets placed under the knees, so that the pressure will come on the bottom of the heel instead of on the back, where the ulcers are more likely to form.
- Keep patient's bed clean and wrinkle free. Crumbs should not be allowed to remain in patient's bed.

- Keep the skin clean and dry.
- Change bed sheets frequently.
- Good skin care is most important in preventing bedsores.
- Sponge the skin, especially in hot weather, thoroughly drying it after each bath. Then apply rubbing alcohol to keep the skin surface hard. Finally use dusting powder containing talcum or zinc stearate or use silicone spray to protect the skin.
- Stimulate the circulation around the area by gentle massage and infrared radiation. A heating lamp is always useful.
- Apply compound tincture of benzoin to the irritated skin area. Zinc oxide ointment should be applied to the ulcer.

6

CONTAGIOUS DISEASES OF SKIN

LEUCODERMA (WHITE SPOTS)

Painless white spots on patches on the skin of body, which expand, if not treated. A patient is more embarased than a victim of severe pain, as in addition to being a medical as well as beauty problem, it is also a social stigma.

Causes

- Due to loss of pigmentation in the skin.
- Leucoderma is not a contagious disease. An imbalance of melanin in body results in the appearance of white spots.
- Darker skin has more patches because such skins contain more melanin.
- White patches are neither congenital nor hereditary. The children are not affected if the mother is suffering from this disease.

Remedies

- Protect the skin from exposure to heat.
- Have salt-free diet. However, rock salt may be permitted in minute quantity, the absence of salt aids recovery.
- Apply Sandalwood (Chandan) pack on the patches.
- Soak Babchi seeds in ginger juice for 72 hours. Remove their husk, dry and powder, and apply on patches.
- Apply the juice of Goose Foot (bathua) extracted from the leaves, three to four times a day.

- Babchi seeds should be steeped in cow's urine for three days. The seeds should then be rubbed to remove their husk, then dried in shade and powdered. One teaspoon of this powder should be taken daily with fresh milk for 40 days continuously. The ground seeds should be rubbed on the white spots.
- Vegetables like bitter gourd are beneficial for such patients.

LEPROSY

The most serious and disgusting disorder of the skin, which affects not only the skin, but also the mucous membranes and the nerves. It is caused by Mycobacterium leprae. The disease was discovered in 1872. The Leprosy is found mainly in warm climates and is also known as Hansen's disease. Leprosy is of two types:

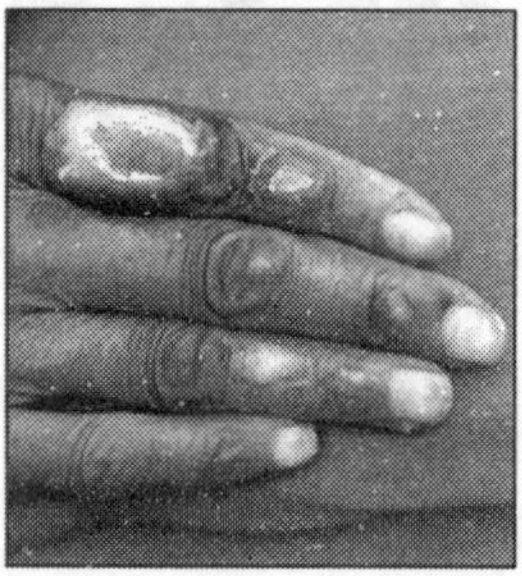
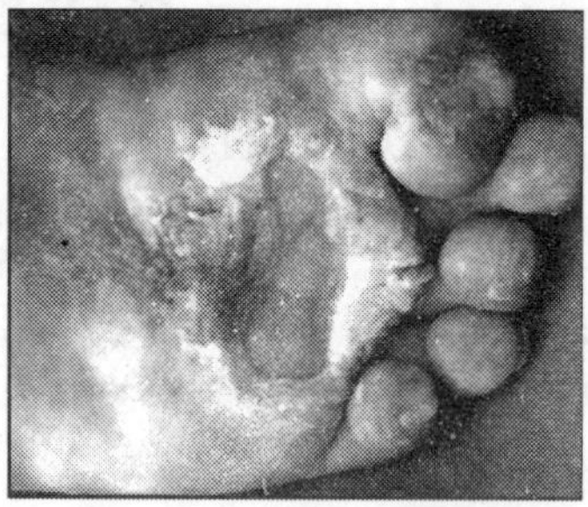

Leprosy

1. **Tuberculoid:** It is not very serious and is self-healing. However, symptoms found in this type of leprosy and the other type Lepromatous are similar. Both the types of leprosy cannot be distinguished easily from each other. The skin starts whitening in the beginning and the massive round lumps are formed on it. Sometimes, this disease affects the eyes also, leading to blindness.
2. **Lepromatous:** In this case the nerves are involved. The manifestation of the disease on the skin runs from the area of whitening to formation of massive nodules visible on the body of the patient. In advances case of leprosy, the fingers start to fell at the joints and the skin over the palms starts rotting. There is pain and in severe cases loss of all sensation in the affected parts. Ulcer may also be found in mouth and the larynx. Ulceration of the extremities can lead to loss of feet and hands.

Since leprosy is infectious disease, the patient suffering from it must be segregated and shifted to a hospital or a leper's home. If that is not possible, better shift the patient to a separate room. Leprosy, in many cases is hereditary and even the seemingly healthy offspring of people suffering from it should be advised not to marry.

Remedy

1. The use of products prepared from 'neem' is a good remedy for this disease. The body of the leprosy patient should be massaged with the 'neem' soap daily for 45 to 60 days. 'neem' oil can be applied on the affected skin. The body of the leprosy patient should be bathed in water in which leaves of 'neem' and 'amaltas' tree have been boiled.
2. The leprosy patient should take a salt-free diet and ensure that he does not get constipated.

PSORIASIS

It is a common, chronic, inflammatory skin disease, the cause of which is unknown. It can appear on any part of the body at any age. It is usually found on the scalp, back of elbows, front of knees, chest, the lower back, the trunk or any part of the body. A lesion consists of scaly plaques, which become silvery when trying to scrape them off the lesions that appear itchy on the skin. Flexural psoriasis lesions have tendency for localisation to the breast-fold region and the groin.

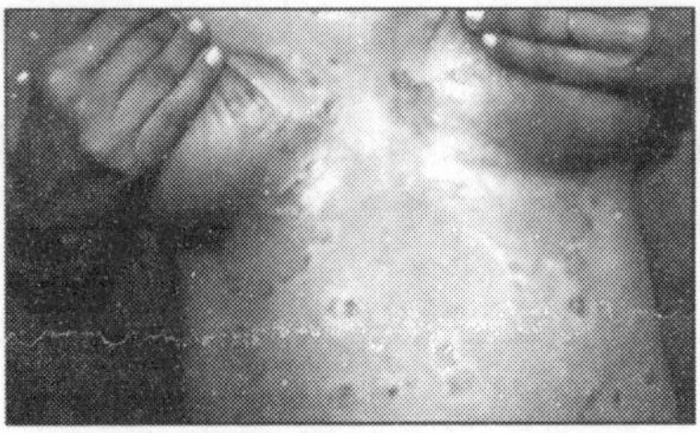

Around the breasts

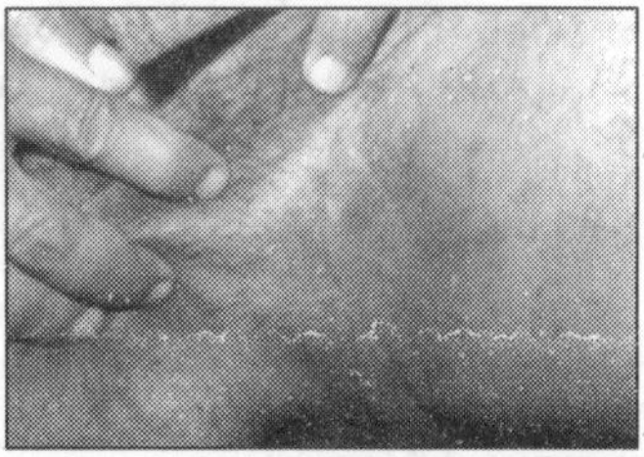

On the Groin

Psoriasis is rarely on the face and can spread by irritation. The main problem is that the skin grows too rapidly in some places on the body, forming a silvery scale over thick patches, which become inflamed and red. The patches of psoriasis give rise to hard lumps and very flaky dandruff on the scalp. The permanent cures are not yet possible. Sunlight helps some psoriasis

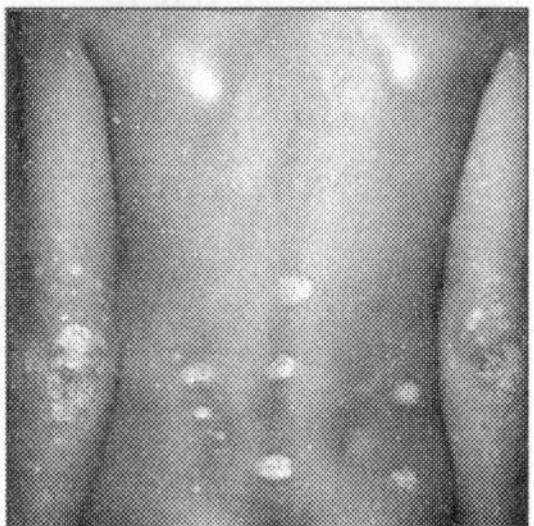

Psoriasis on Back

patients. This chronic condition usually with a little itching also affects the skin behind the ears, front of the knees and behind the elbows does not affect the hair growth, but in few cases the patient may complain of arthritis in the fingers or toes.

Treatment

The following treatment and precautions are needed to cure psoriasis:

1. **Ointments Based on Coal Tar and Dithranol are available:** These ointments, however, take lot of time in curing but are effective in curing psoriasis. The ointments are smelly and stain clothes and the skin, so it is best to apply them at night before sleep.
2. **Exposure of Body to Ultra-violet Rays is Helpful:** For this purpose special lamps are available in the market, which produce rays.
3. **Ultra-violet Radiation from Sunshine:** In which two to three weeks sunbathing is taken, clear the ill-effect of disorder. But this treatment is not permanent.
4. **Regular PUVA Treatment:** However it controls a bad psoriasis, but increase the risk of skin-ageing and skin cancer, especially in fair skin.
5. Many of the anti-cancer drugs slow down skin growth and control Psoriasis, but sometimes leave unpleasant side effect.
6. **Sunlight in Moderate Doses is Beneficial in Most Cases:** The patient should have adequate rest and a well-balanced diet. Every effort should be made to relieve nervous tension. Here is a useful remedy that may be tried:

Collect the Following Ingredients:

Salicylic Acid	0.6 gm
Ammoniated Mercury	0.6 gm
Hydrophlic Ointment	sufficient quantity for 30 gm

Apply this ointment twice daily to the affected areas. Injections of hydrocortisone into the skin, given immediately beneath the lesions, may also help to clear up this troublesome condition. Seek medical advice before having treatment.

NAPPY RASHES

The most common form of nappy rash is ammonia dermatitis. This comes about when a soiled wet nappy is left against the skin for several hours. In this warm wet environment the skin's bacteria break down the urine and it is irritant effect, which can cause the skin to break down, whereupon the bacteria can become even more of an irritant.

Remedies

Remedies include frequent changing and washing of nappies. Emollient cleansing lotions may be more soothing than soap, and zinc oxide or silicon based water repellent ointment will help prevent the skin cracking.

CYSTITIS

Signs and symptoms: These include the following:

1. The frequent urge to rush to the toilet.
2. The burning sensation felt every time you pass urine, the feeling of not quite being able to empty your bladder.
3. The pains and chills during intercourse.

Cystitis is a painful and embarrassing condition. In fact, there are three main phases in a woman's life when she is most likely to succumb as below:

1. At the beginning of her sex life.
2. After childbirth or surgery.
3. With the menopause.

Cystitis is associated with a frequent urge to pass urine, a burning sensation on urination (called micturition in medical terms), a sense of having incompletely emptied the bladder and sometimes backache, feverishness and blood in urine called haematuria).

The word cystitis means bladder (cystis) and inflammation (itis). But more often than just being a bladder inflammation, it is the urethra-the short outlet tube from the bladder, which is most severely affected. In most cases, the entire urethra and the lower part of the bladder are affected. The symptom of frequent urination is usually linked to an irritable or hypersensitive bladder and weakening of the muscles, which control the bladder. The pain on urination is due to a similar irritability in the urethra and inflammation.

In case of trouble, it is very important to visit a doctor to determine whether a particular case of cystitis is linked to abnormally high levels of bacteria in the urine and what sort of bacteria are present. If the bacteria are not present, then find out the cause of this. There is a possibility the urethra suffered physical damage during sexual intercourse, surgery, childbirth, menopause or even a clumsy examination. Or it is an irritant to blame: a soap, deodorant, antiseptic or the effect of a contraceptive cream. Sometimes, an infection of vagina is to blame and sometimes the condition is aggravated by a blocked or tight urethra.

The position and the length of the urethra in women is at the root of this problem. While the urethra in male runs the full length of the penis, has a distinctly separate outlet and is protected by bacteria destroying secretion from the prostate, the female urethra is only one inch long and is very close to and similar to vagina. Both organs have exactly the same mucous lining making them susceptible to the same infections and changes in hormone levels. The outlet of the female urethra is usually situated next to the outlet of the vagina. To the other side of the vagina is the anus, or back passage, which is always a potential source of infection. It is the close proximity of these three outlets that underlies many cases of cystitis.

To add a further complication, some women's bodies do not conform neatly to the prescribed construction of the organ; the outlet of their urethra may in fact be found just inside the vagina, or may during love-making, open temporarily into the vagina when part of this area becomes swollen with sexual excitement. As a result it is likely that organisms from the bowel, which are naturally present around the perineum, could be pushed into the urethra by the thrusting of male organ. The delicate tissue of the urethra can be bruised by lovemaking (the sex act). These tissues can be torn causing inflammation and severe pain.

Remedies

1. Seek medical assistance of a doctor in case of suspected cystitis, who will conduct a detailed examination. A urine sample should be taken for further investigations.
2. X-ray is recommended for women with recurrent infections.
3. Beware of bubble baths, which not only contain chemicals that irritate, but which also lower surface tension and allow soapy water and bacteria to penetrate higher into the vagina than ordinary bath water does.

4. Avoid use of soap, detergents, deodorants, powders, depilatory creams to remove superfluous hair on genital area, nylon undergarments which many times cause allergic reaction.
5. The treatment of drug therapy should be done under the strict supervision of a doctor.
6. Personal hygiene, wearing cotton under-garments, drinking maximum amount of water, washing your perineum from front to back after each time you pass urine are some of the easy ways to cure cystitis.
7. Hormonal therapy, surgery, dilation, urethrotomy, catheterisation are some of the treatments for which consultation of a doctor is very essential.

VITILIGO

Causes and the Symptoms

A skin disorder when the melanocytes in localised areas of the body stop producing melanin. The lesions vary in shape and size, and may appear on any part of the body and mucous membranes spread quickly. The lesions tend to be localised to the skin of arms, knees, elbows, ankles and knuckles. De-pigmentation on forehead is caused by the adhesive of plastic 'bindi', on breast due to the plastic purse usually kept under the brassiere, on the fold of ear by spectacle, frame, on feet by the rubber straps and on the waist due to petticoat string.

URTICARIA (NETTLE RASH)

Causes and Symptoms

Uricaria is also called nettle rash or hives, when areas of skin become itchy and raised into weals, which are red or white. These persist for minutes or hours. In severe attacks the eyelids, mouth and even throat can swell. If the mouth and throat swell, seek help of a doctor immediately. Remember, urticaria is caused not due to an allergy though people assume it is. However, in minority of cases there is a cause for the urticaria as below (the cause is unknown in most cases):

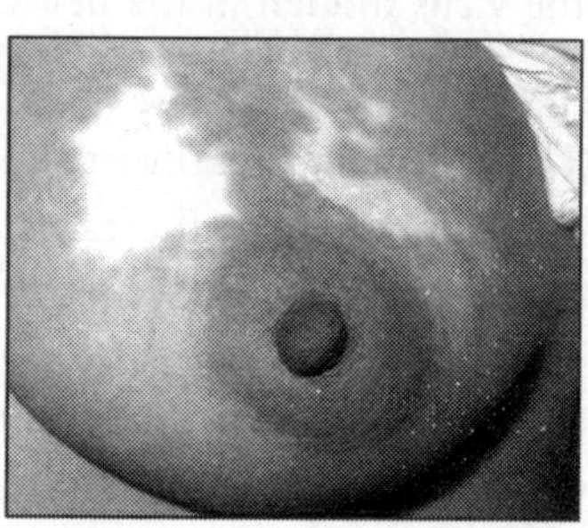

Vitiligo Lesions on Breasts

1. **Food:** may cause urticaria and usually the cause is obvious. Shell-fish, nuts, strawberries or other fruits are the most common. Sometimes, dyes or preservatives in foods can be the cause.
2. Certain drugs such as aspirin, penicillin and antibiotics can also cause urticaria.
3. **Physical Causes:** Heat, cold, sunlight all may cause urticaria.
4. **Stings:** It has been observed that bee or wasp strings can develop urticaria and the mouth and throat swell.
5. Some other causes include change in the temperature, infection due to presence of worms, emotional upset but the major causes are allergy to foods, pollens and drugs.

Treatment

Use anti-allergic drugs till the problem subsides with the consultation of a doctor, who usually recommends antihistamine tablets.

GENITAL HERPES

Causes

Caused by a virus, caught by having sex with someone who has herpes. It is common in young people.

Signs and Symptoms

Groups of little blisters appear on the genital area, thighs and buttocks. They are painful, tender and highly infectious. The infection is the worst with swollen glands and a temperature. The blisters crust over and clear in a week or two. The virus becomes dormant but may cause repeated attacks. When coping with genital herpes, the virus hidden in the nerves cannot be killed completely.

Treatment

The following treatment should be adopted:

1. Apply anti-viral creams and lotions.
2. Have warm salt water baths and pain-killers.
3. All attacks of genital herpes are infectious. Avoid having sex till the scabs have disappeared.
4. Use condoms when having sex, they lessen the risk of infection.
5. Worry and depression, poor genital health, lack of sleep and a unhealthy diet may reduce resistance to infection due to herpes.

6. An attack of genital herpes during pregnancy is very serious as an infected expectant mother can pass on infection to her baby and she may need to be delivered by a Caesarean section.

CANDIDIASIS

Causes

This fungal infection is caused by Candida albicans. It is common in patients who have a fancy for taking drugs like antibiotics or corticosteroids. Patients suffering from diabetes mellitus and hypothyroidism are also prone to this infection. It has also been associated with the use of oral contraceptives. The disorder may involve skin, intestines and vagina. It develops in the gastro-intestinal tract.

Signs and Symptoms

As a result of candidiasis, several disorders are produced as below:

THRUSH

Whitish curd-like deposit on the tongue is common in the infants as well as in the adults with immune deficiency. In adult, a curd-like whitish deposit on vagina is produced on the mucosa with redness in surrounding area (or on the glans in male organ). This condition is known as Vulva Vaginitis. The vaginal infection can be transmitted to the male partner and vice versa.

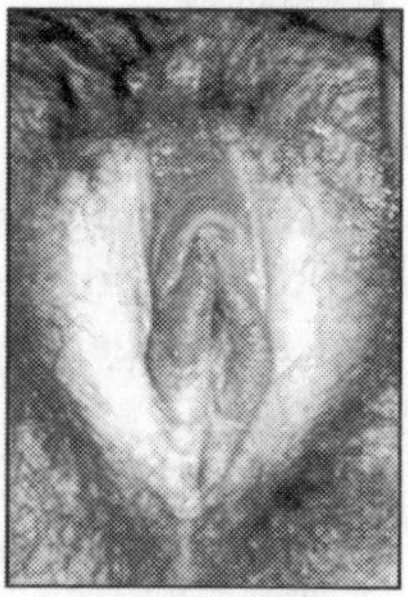

Vulve Vaginitis

Treatment

The treatment of candidiasis consists of finding out the underlying cause.

1. An anti-fungal drug should be given. There are many ointments doctors recommend to treat fungal infection. These are anti-candidial agents and should be used in consultation with your doctor.
2. Avoid wearing nylon panties, tight jeans and moist environment.

WHITLOW

It is also known as Chronic Paronychia, is a term applied to all acute inflammations of the deep-seated tissues in the fingers, whether the structure is affected by the root of the nail, the pulp of the fingertips, the skin of fingers or the bone. A small painful abscess usually forms at the base of the nail or the pulp of the finger. The patient feels intense pain as the bursting of the abscess takes a long time. Whitlow usually affects the housewives. The chronic paronychia is an infection of the nail fold with a yeast-like fungus called Candida. The condition usually starts in the middle finger of right hand as a glazed red swelling of the nail fold and later other fingers may be affected.

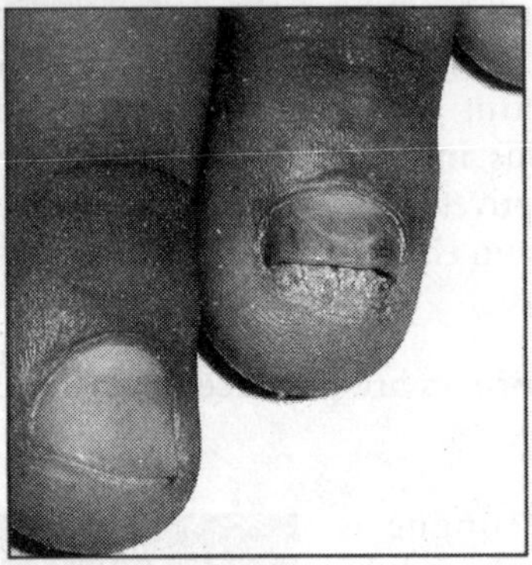

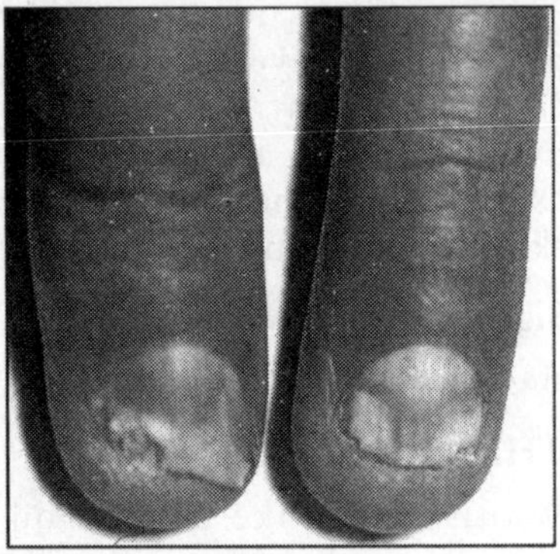

Whitlow

The secondary infection with bacteria causes pain and discharge of pus from the nail fold, many times, the nail is lost in the process and the finger becomes disfigured. Here is a home recipe to cure whitlow:

Mix one part of 'isphagula' in four parts of vinegar, and apply to the infected part. The poultice should be bandaged with a clean cloth and water should be sprinkled over it. Change the bandage after every three hours. The inflammation will subside in three days. Once the pus has been ejected, cooked leaves of 'neem' tree should be wrapped over the site of whitlow.

RED VEINS

The skin becomes red and thin and the blood vessels seem very near the surface. Usually caused due to sensitive skin that has been neglected or ill treated. Try the following home remedies to improve the skin:

- Apply waxy cream. Use moisturizer.
- Avoid going from one extreme temperature to another.
- Avoid rich, spicy foods, very hot drinks and alcohol.

RINGWORM

Causes and symptoms

Round patches are formed on the body especially between the legs, on the face, neck, back and on the buttocks. This malady is caused due to inflammatory infection of the skin produced by certain moulds. It is sometimes due to the effect of extreme temperature. This tiny organism infects the skin and sometimes pustule or sore appear. Round patches are formed on the body especially between the legs and on the scrotum, on the neck, back and buttocks. The edges of pustules itch severely.

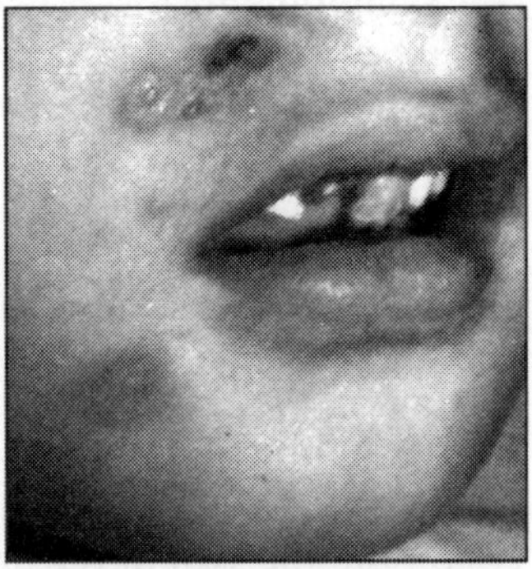

Round Patches due to Rings Worm

Herbal Cure

As a cure apply one of the following remedies:

1. Apply the juice of marigold leaves (genda flower).
2. Make a paste of basil leaves (grinded tulsi leaves) and apply.
3. Scratch the affected skin and apply borax mixed to lime juice.
4. If the ringworm becomes chronic, it should be rubbed with a coarse cloth and the sap of 'akh' plant.
5. Mix 2 tablespoons 'nigandbabri' and seven grains of pepper. Steep in water over-night and drink water in the morning.
6. Ground in water either the juice of marigold leaves or seeds of bastard teak (dhak) and apply on the affected skin.

Homoeopathic Cure

The following treatments are recommended:

- External ointments made from chrysophanic acid used. Mix 4 gm of acid with one tablespoon of olive oil and apply on ringworm.
- Medicines lyce and graphites (for ringworm on lips), hepar (for ring-worm on private parts of the body) and antim crud (for ringworm near the nails or on mustaches) are usually recommended by the homeopathy doctors.

RED NOSE

Causes and Symptoms

The symptoms are severe itching and burning. It is a common trouble with heavy eaters and drinkers caused by sudden change of temperature on delicate skin.

Treatment

The following remedies are suggested:

1. Massage nose up and down with rose water mixed with glycerine.
2. Avoid sudden change of temperature.

RHINOPLASTY

Also known as deformed nose (a hump nose deformity). In this condition, the skin of the upper part of the nose becomes free from the underlying bone and cartilage giving a saddle nose look.

Remedy

Only surgery can cure hump nose deformity. The steps of the operation include removal of hump, nasal in fracture, elevation of the tip of the nose and trimming of the lower part of the nose to suit the rest of the nose.

KERATODERM OF PALMS AND SOLES

Deep painful fissures with bleeding and secondary infection usually occur on palms and the soles.

Treatment

Dressing overnight with 40% urea in glycerine or vaseline. Alternatively mix 10% salicylic acid in vaseline and apply.

EPIDERMOLYSIS BULLOSA

The disorder characterised by a tendency to develop blisters between epidermal layers by degeneration of the prickle or basal cell, ulcers, crusts and scarring on knees and feet with loss of nails sometimes.

Treatment

Protect patient from trauma and infection. Vitamin E is beneficial in this condition.

ICHTHGOSIS VULGARIS

The problem may vary from a mild redness and scaling to a severe condition having diffuse hyperkeratosis. The skin is usually smooth and shiny. It is a common hereditary disorder in which large brownish angulated scales appear on the body especially on legs (not on the face and flexural folds), accompanied by papules over shoulders and buttock. The lesions worsen in winters.

PHARYNODERMA

Deficiency of vitamin A or essential fatty acids lead to Pharynoderma, in which hard keratotic follicular papules appear on the elbows or on the knees or buttocks. Night blindness, spots and dryness of the skin may also be associated.

Treatment

Local application of 10-40% urea cream and 50,000 units of vitamin A twice a day can make lesions disappear in due course.

ANGULAR STOMATITIS

It is caused by deficiency of vitamin B Complex. It manifests as a proliferative growth with a fissure at the angle of the mouth.

ACRO-DERMATITIS ENTEROPJATHICA

Deficiency of Zinc in mother's milk or artificial feed is the main cause of this disease usually in infants or in adults, following gastro—intestinal tract. The trouble leads to vesiculation and ulceration around nose, mouth, anal opening and genitalia.

CHEILITIS

Redness, scaling and swelling appear on both lips.

CHILBLAINS

An exposure to cold, which cause lesions that consist pain, brownish-black discoloration on toes and fingers.

Treatment

Include protection from cold. Use vasodilators during winter. Antibiotics are recommended by the doctor.

PHOTODERMATITIS ERYTHEMA

Scaling and odema on forearm and back of hands are involved due to an excessive exposure to sunlight, following pigmentation, dermatitis, sunburn, redness and inflammation. Use a sunscreen to protect the skin.

IMPETIGO

These are of two types:

1. **Bullous Impetigo:** A large bulla partly filled with pus due to Pyogenic infection (also called Pyodermas). It is more common in children on the face.

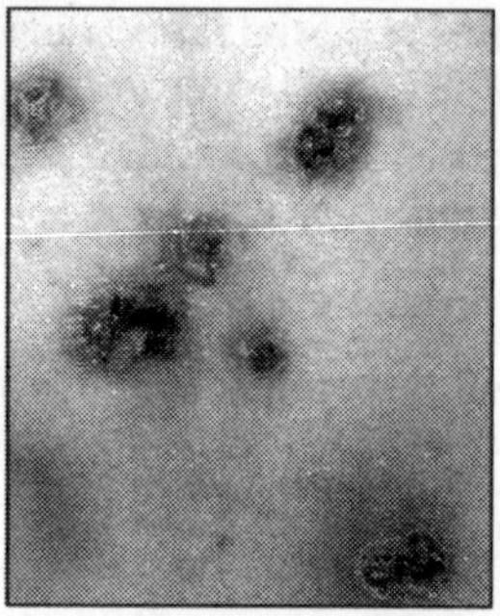

Impetigo

2. **Impetigo Contagiosa:** A superficial pustule and ulcer with yellowish, pussy crust on the face. The disease usually grips the children.

ECTHYMA

Infection having dark brown or black crusts extends deeper into the dermis. The pus may stain with blood.

ERYSIPELAS

The lesions consist of swelling and redness with raised border. The lesions are warm and tender, sometimes associated with fever.

ACUTE PARONGRCHIA

An infection of the nail-fold producing reddish, painful swelling usually in growing nail.

BOILS

Red, small, painful nodules, which start oozing pus and leave tiny scar. Infection of the coarse hair follicle along, with inflammation of the surrounding tissue is called boils. These may produce pus in most of the cases. Boils are more common in children, whereas diabetes patients tend to develop recurrent boils.

The following treatment is suggested to cure boils and pustules:

- Apply paste of 'neem' tree bark.
- Keep bowl clear and avoid eating, fatty or sour products.
- Smear a leaf of 'peepal' tree with ghee and apply as lukewarm bandage on the boil to enable it to burst.
- Systemic antibiotics help cure boils (with the consultation of a doctor).
- Turmeric is cooling herb that can reduce the inflammation of a boil and help prevent recurrences.

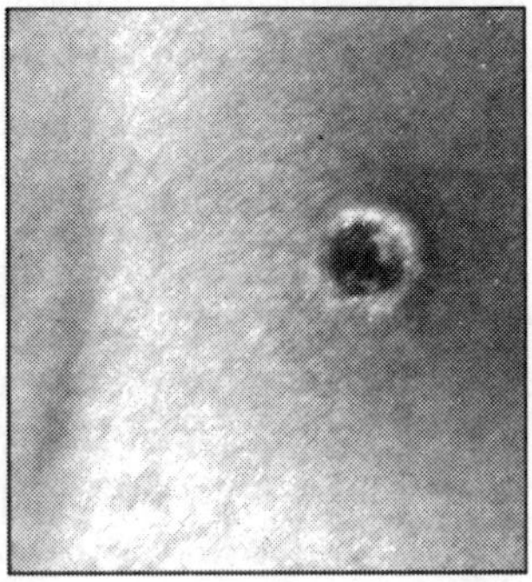

Boil

- For an acute boil-one that pops up suddenly and is not recurrent-immerse a washcloth in hot water (as hot as you can tolerate, but not hot enough to burn), wring it out, and place it on the boil for 15 minutes twice a day.
- Treating the boil with just hot compresses, use alternating heat and cold to draw out the pus. Place hot compress for ten minutes. Then apply another washcloth soaked in cold water for ten minutes. Repeat the cycle three times twice a day to cure boil.
- Here is another recipe to treat boils. Collect the following ingredients:

1 teaspoon	Turmeric powder
1 teaspoon	Epsom salt
One	Baked onion

Combine all in a blender to make a thick paste. Spread it on the boil and cover with cheesecloth to secure poultice with a bandage. Leave the poultice on overnight. Repeat for two days.

- The following kitchen vegetables when applied as compress, help curing boil. They should be changed every few hours:

1. A heated slice of tomato
2. A raw onion slice
3. Mashed garlic
4. A bag of black tea
5. The outer leaves of cabbage

FOLLICITIS

A infection of hair follicles with multiple pussy lesions around hair follicles on legs, thighs and beard region on the face. The condition is common in adult males that occur on any hairy areas on the body.

ECZEMATOID DERMATITIS

A infection of the skin leading to itching and scaly lesions. The presence of bacteria in lesions may be diagnosed from the pus. Sometimes, crusting, scaling and populo-vesicles around the ear on the nape of neck discharge pus. Improved hygiene by bathing with medicated soap and water and a antibiotic treatment is recommended (in consultation with doctor). Avoid use of oil, malnutrition and immune deficiency. Continue treatment till the disease is fully cured to avoid recurrent infection.

PAPULO-NECROTIC TUBERCULID (Tuberculosis of Skin)

Tuberculosis of skin is caused by mycobacterium tuberculosis get implanted through the blood stream or by continuous spread. It manifests in various forms as below:

1. **Lypus Vulgaris:** Group of verrucous plaques (lesions) on buttocks or on the face or any other area of the body. It sometimes leave scar after healing.
2. **Tuberculosis Verrucose Cutis:** Deeply indurated lesions, similar to lypus vulgaris, which affect hands or the foot with scarring.
3. Scrofuloderma/Multiple sinuses start as an infection of underlying tissue (lymph, nodes, bones and joint) with thin yellowish pussy discharge at the opening of the sinus.

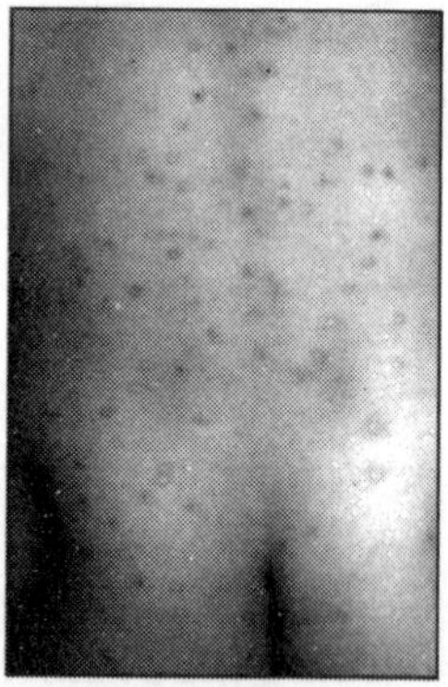

Papules

In case of Papulo-necrotic Tuberculid, the bacteria spread on the body producing multiple nodules and papules on the trunk with scar formation on healing.

UNGUAL DERMATOPHYTOSIS (Nail Plate Destroyed by Fungus)

Usually involved by the deposition of the fungus under the distal-free edge of nail. The disorder has the following characteristics:

1. Nail Plate destroyed by the fungus.
2. White spots appear on nail thick plate.
3. Nails with brownish discoloration.

PITYRIASIS VERSICOLOR

A fungal infection which usually start around the hair follicles on the upper back, shoulders, upper chest and upper arms. It is rare on the neck, face, hands, forearms and the lower limbs of the body. The disease tends to become more extensive in summer.

INTERTRIGINOUS CANDIDIASIS

Redness and lesions grow in the groin, infra-mammary region in adult women, the fingers and at the angles of the mouth in both sexes of any age group. The trouble causes by regular soaking of the hands in water for long period, which damages nail fold and the nail plate. When the inflammation is severe, it may lead to ooze pus.

MOLLUSCUM CANDIDIASIS

Causes by virus and is common in children as well as adults. Skin colour changes with shiny, smooth, infectious lesions (2 to 10 mm. Size). Many times, pinkish papules appear on the body (commonly on the shaft of the penis) occur in clusters. The lesions in the genital area are usually caused by sexual contact.

Treatment

Includes cauterisation of the lesions with phenol or trichloroacetia acid. Consult a doctor for treatment.

Contact Dermatitis

This term is used when the dermatitis is caused by contact with an agent to which one has developed contact hypersensitivity. These sensitive agents include wearing shoes, jewellery, clothes, cosmetics, a plant or contact with a metal.

SEBORRHOEIC DERMATITIS

An inflammation of sebaceous glands causing itchy populous lesion usually occur on the seborrhoeic areas, especially the scalp, the face, retro-auricular areas, upper part of the chest, the back, axillae and the groins.

LICHEN PLANUS

The disease manifests in several forms causing severe itching and pink or whitish papule lesion on the body (back, forearm, legs), on the lower lip, tongue, nail plate, palms and soles and the genitals (on the shaft of penis and on the glans penis).

MELANOCYTIC NAEVUS (PIGMENTARY NAEVI)

These are small black macules or pigmented papules with or without hairs. The affected areas include cheeks, hands, upper chest, back and buttocks. Most naevi can be left untreated. However, a naevus can be excised surgically or with a laser.

BERMATOPHYTOSES (TINRA CAPITIS)

The broken hair in the patch on the scalp occurs either in pre-pubertal children or in adult males. The hair firstly become brittle and tend to break off at the skin surface, followed by the inflammatory skin shows dry scaly patch and itchy lesions leading to localised swelling and yellowish lesions on scalp with a mousy odour is observed.

7

HERBS THAT HEAL

COSMETIC USE OF HERBS

For those in search of beauty and lost youth, herbs have always has held a special fascination, and one that our modern cosmetic industry have exploited. For this reason the cosmetic use of herbs is a subject to those intent on finding beauty. To maintain youth or beauty, people spend a lot, some on surgeons to stitch up double chins or de-bag eyes, others on expensive creams to banish acne and wrinkles. And despite all this, everybody ages and nothing can do stop it. Where certain herbs can help, perhaps, is in improving the faces we were born with and, where possible, delaying the more obvious marks of ageing. In other words, herbs will not create youth and beauty, but will enable us to make the most of what we have of either. An early experimenter in the field of herbal cosmetics was the Greek physician Galen who invented cold cream. He hit upon the idea of melting together while wax and oil of roses in a particular ratio; and then stirring into this mixture a cupful of water laced with spirit vinegar. Since Galen's time the oil of roses has been replaced by almond oil or even liquid paraffin, although the best substitute is sunflower oil particularly rich in vitamin A and vitamin D.

Making your Own cosmetics

Make good use of all kinds of everyday items like fruit, vegetables, nuts, cereals in nurturing their beauty. Even in most beauty conscious there is a definite tendency towards natural therapies. The kitchen larder is a Store House of beauty aids. You just have to follow a few recipes, pick the ingredients, mix them in a required ratio and you will soon have a beauty lotion or cream in hand. These home made herbal preparations help enhance beauty of the skin and complexion and delay ageing without causing harm. Taking care of your skin is a must in order to remain young. During youth the skin is elastic and smooth but as one grows older, the skin loses its elasticity, natural oils and water content. In days gone by, there were hardly any cosmetics available in the market and rural areas, and self-made preparations were used for skin care. Since ancient times vegetable oils, refined animal fats and cream of milk have been used for the care of skin and beauty.

Making your own creams, lotion is easy. By learning to make your own cosmetics, you have at your fingertips not only more luxurious products than you could afford to buy but also those especially suitable for your skin. Most of the recipes mentioned in this book are easy to make. A slight change in proportion changes the character of preparation, be careful when measuring the ingredients.

THE DESCRIPTION OF HERBS

Aloe Extract (Gwarpathe)

A popular botanical recognized for centuries as having beneficial medicinal properties including antibiotic, anti-inflammatory and wound healing.

Aloe Vera

Is used in cosmetic preparations due to its moisturizing, soothing and calming properties. It is excellent for dry and sensitive skins as well as for the treatment of sunburns and other minor burns, insect bites and skin irritations. Aloe extract is obtained from the aloe vera leaves and is also referred to as aloe vera gel. Aloe vera juice is the diluted version of aloe vera gel.

Therapeutic uses of aloe vera

- Aloe vera is an emollient and film forming gum resin with hydrating, softening, healing, anti-microbial and anti-inflammatory properties.
- It has relaxing effect on the skin, making it beneficial for sensitive, sunburned and sun-exposed skins.
- It increases the blood supply to the area of application. Aloe vera is constituted of about 95 per cent water and the remaining

constituents include minerals, polysaccharides, amino acids and carbohydrates.

Alder: This herb plant grows near water, where it can be assured of moist soil. It is commonly found on riversides and marshy ground. Shiny oval leaves of alder enjoy the reputation of curing dropsical conditions caused by disorders of the renal system. The infusion may be used as a lotion for cooling sore, tired feet and prevent fatigue when walking.

Almond: Ground almond are extensively used in face masks. It is good for nourishing and cleansing. The Almond seeds contain 45 to 56 percent oil, which is known as "badam rogan." The oil is very rich and used in various preparations for skin care.

Angelica: A large aromatic plant has drowny, triangular leaves and white or pale-purple flowers. Angelica in both extract and essential oil form, is a herb for the digestion, bringing swift relief from flatulene, colic and heart-burn. An infusion made from the leaves and chopped stem is a tonic, detoxifying and purifying agent. Principal constituents of this herb are volatile oil (about 1%), valeric acid, angelic acid, sugar and a resin called angleoin. Angelica extract is made from the seeds and the roots. It provides an excellent gargle for the treatment of sore tonsils and throats. The plant is used to flavour many alcoholic drinks.

Arnica Extract: A botanical credited with wide variety of properties such as antiseptic, astringent, anti-microbial, anti-inflammatory, anti-coagulant, circulatory, healing and stimulating. Arnica extract is also considered excellent for an acne condition, is effective in gels and creams designed to treat damaged, reddened or tired skin.

Avocado Oil: Oil is obtained from the ripe avocado fruit and seeds, which is rich and nourishing with high vitamin contents. The pulp is used in face masks and the oil in nourishing creams. Avocado oil can function as an emollient and a carrier oil in cosmetic preparations. Its skin-benefiting properties include bactericidal and soothing, particularly to sensitive skin for. In cosmetic formulations, effectively used in cleansing creams, moisturizers, lipsticks, makeup bases, bath oils, sunscreen and suntan preparations. Avocado oil enjoys the highest penetration rate among other oils such as corn, soybean, olive and almond. It consist constituents such as oleic, linoleic and linolenic acid, palmitic and palmitoleic acid, lecithin, phytosterol, cartinoids and a high concentration of vitamins A, D and E.

Balm: A fragrant plant having dark green wrinkled leaves and small creamy flowers. It helps in the treatment of eczema, dry skin and acne formulations and products for blemished or sensitive skins. The herb is credited with calming, soothing, healing, anti-spasmodic, tightening, anti-bactericidal and circulation-stimulating properties. Its use sometimes may cause skin irritation.

Balsam Peru: It is a botanical attributed to strong medicinal actions, recommended for curing scabies and skin diseases. The herb is considered anti-bacterial and sulphur based recommended for use on acne skin and eczema.

Basil (Tulsi): An romantic herb with white flowers and oval-shaped, shiny leaves. Medicinally basil is a potent tonic with stimulant effect. It is particularly good at arresting morning and travel sickness, an effective skin tonic, application in acne preparations and rich in vitamin C. Basil oil is often used as a carrier oil and its properties include stimulating, tonic, purifying and anti-microbial.

Babchi: A well known medicinal herb, used as laxative and anthelmintic. Seeds of babchi cure leucoderma (white patches on the skin).

Babool (Kikar): Used to clean the teeth. The leaves help relieve prolapse of rectum. Useful in cough and asthma. Decoction can help prevent threatened abortion.

Blackberry (Jamun): Berries are not only delicious but good for anaemia conditions as well. The leaves are mildly aperient and accredited with sound tonic virtues. An infusion is applied externally as a lotion to cure psoriasis and scaly conditions of the skin.

Blackberry extract is regarded as excellent for its astringent and tonic properties due to the high tannin content of the root, bark and the leaves. The leaf extract can be used for acne conditions. A standard infusion is made, which can be applied externally as a lotion to cure psoriasis and scaly conditions of the skin.

Betony (Chhitran parni): A purple-flowered plant, is a natural pain killer, especially good for headaches. It purifies the blood and cures pimples, acne and other skin disorders.

Birch (Betula-Bhoj-patra): Birch extract has been described as astringent, antiseptic, softening, curative and circulation-stimulating. They are believed to have curative properties in case of skin diseases. Birch has healing effect on rashes and hair loss. The important

Comfry

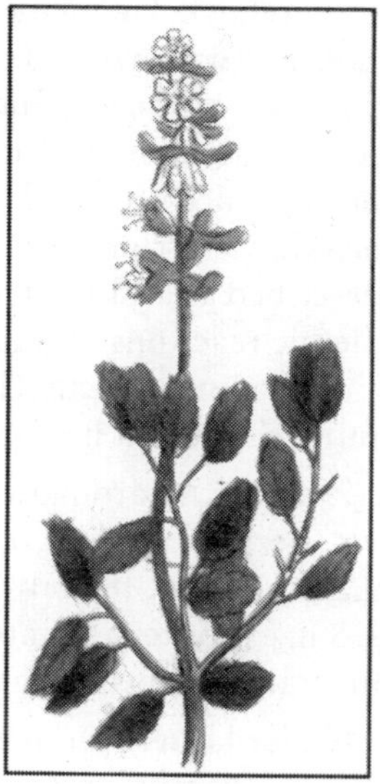

Basil

Common Sorrel

Borage

constituents include glanonoids, hyproside, tannin, saponins and quercetin. Birch extract has anti-irritant and antiseptic properties in acne, eczema and sunburn treatment. The leaves of this plant which have a peculiar, aromatic odour and a bitter taste which secrete a resinous substance with acid properties and contain flavonoids, tannins and essential oils.

Black Pepper Oil: It has cosmetic application, used on skin inflammations and superficial wounds.

Borage (Pattharchur): The plant with blue flower have both leaves and stem covered with white bristles. Borage has beneficial effect on heart, kidneys, adrenal glands and the entire digestive system. The herb cures jaundice and increases the milk flow in nursing mothers. Borage juice obtained from the crushed plant and applied direct to the skin cures ringworm. The tropical application of borage extract is described as anti-inflammatory and beneficial for sensitive skin and allergic reactions. Borage contains potassium and calcium, combined with mineral acid. The oil extracted from seed is an effective anti-irritant and has hydrating properties.

Bergamot (Zabeer): An aromatic herb used to perfume colognes and toilet waters. Bergamot oil is considered an antiseptic and bacterial growth inhabitor, good for oily and acne skin and for seborrhoeic conditions. Sun exposure after applying pure bergamot oil may cause hyper-pigmentation and skin rashes.

Carrot Oil (Gajar-ka-tel): Derived from the carrot root, carrot oil is used since the 16th century for skin diseases due to its cleansing, depurative and draining properties. This carotene-rich emollient has been indicated for curing skin conditions such as dermatitis, skin irritation, rashes and wrinkles. The extract obtained from the carrot leaves has cleansing properties and healing effect due to its strong antiseptic qualities. The juice contains sugar, a little starch, albumen, volatile oil, vegetable jelly or pectin, saline matter, malic acid and carotin.

Calendula (Marigold): Its flowers and leaves are very beneficial for clearing the skin of eczema, spots and grease. Calendula extract is an emollient said to have healing, soothing, antiseptic, anti-itching and anti-inflammatory properties. Effectively used in case of oily and delicate skins as well as for curing acne. The extract is obtained from calendula blossom.

Comfrey: A plant with pinkish blue bell-shaped flowers, and is credited with healing, astringent, and emollient properties. It is used in case of swelling, bruising, cuts, papules and pustules. The extract as traditionally used topically for soothing and anti-itching treatment (a cold compress for eye injuries), as well as for eczema and wounds. The herb contains 0.6 to 0.8 per cent of allantoin and a bit of tannin.

Calandine: The herb plant is found in hedgerows and wastes. Yellowish hairy leaves shaped like oak leaves and small yellowish

Borage (Borago Officianalis)

Angelica
(Angelica archangelica)

flowers. As a wart cure the raw yellow juice should be applied direct to the skin. Some herbalists prescribe an eye lotion made from one part of this infused herb and two parts of water or milk.

Cleavers (lipatni ghas): The plant has tiny white flowers and small round fruits. Cleavers are excellent remedy for diseases of the urinary system. An infusion of this herb, used as a lotion, makes a first-rate tonic for the scalp and the skin. It clears dandruff, cures leprosy and skin cancer. The extract is very useful in treating eczema and spots, and is recommended for normal to dry skins.

Clove (laung): An aromatic spice used in skin tonics and stimulating face masks. It is considered as a powerful antiseptic with a strong germicidal effect. Clove oil may cause strong skin irritation when used in high concentration. The clove oil is obtained from the stems and leaves of the plant.

Camomile (Babuna-ka-paudha): Plant with strong botanical properties and feathery grey green leaves, usually found in waste places. The plant has a distinctive smell similar to over-ripe apples. An infusion of leaves and flowers of this plant (fresh or dried) has wide cosmetic and medicinal uses.

Camomile dissolves tumours, heals ulcers, expels worms, banishes tiredness and treats many female disorders. As a cosmetic the herb can be used as a face-wash to clear complexion. It has been found exceptionally good for treating burns, skin inflammations and

Rosemary

Frech Thyme

dermatitis Camomile is a tonic; digestive and tranquillizing. Camomile oil is considered a anti-allergic, healing, cooling, analgesic and antiseptic agent.

Cinnamon Oil: Said to have a soothing effect on the skin. It is widely recognised for its tonic and antiseptic properties. It is obtained from the plant's leaves.

Codar-wood Oil: Credited with antiseptic, sedative and astringent properties. This clear oil is valuable for use on various skin eruptions such as relieves itching, cures acne, dermatitis, eczema and psoriasis.

Dandelion (kukraundha): The medicinal value of the Dandelion plant with golden-yellow flowers is used to treat all kidney complaints, liver troubles and circulatory disorders. It is widely used for the treatment of arthritis, to disperse acidic deposits from the affected joints, cures pimples and skin spots.

The dandelion extract has tonic properties, refreshes the skin, corrects pH balance, aids in increasing the respiratory capacity of the skin tissues, beneficial for dry skin and also used in acne preparations. The plant root is used for cosmetic preparations rather than the flower, as juice of the root is more powerful part of the plant. The main constituents of dandelion root are taraxac (a crystalline bitter substance), taraxacerine (an acid resin), insulin, gluten gum, potash, citric acid, sterols and vitamin B and C.

Elder (elder vriksh): All parts of this herbal plant are used. Its leaves combined with honey is a standard infusion that clears troubled skin. The infused flowers offer a remedy for catarrh, cough and colds. It soothes burns and scalds. A balm of elder flowers keeps crow's feet at bay. The herb is said to have astringent, antiseptic and emollient properties. It is very useful for problem or inflamed skin and the ointment made from the leaves cure bruises, swelling and wounds.

Elderflower extract is used for eye and skin lotions, particularly beneficial for dry skin. Elderflower water is used to clear the complexion of freckles and sunburn, and keeps the skin in good condition. Elderflower extract is used for eye and skin lotions, particularly beneficial for dry skin. Elderflower water is used to clear the complexion of freckles and sunburn, and keeps the skin in good condition. Elderflower extract is used for eye and skin lotions, particularly beneficial for treating dry skin. Elderflower water is commonly used to clear the complexion of freckles, sunburn and keeps the skin in good condition.

Elm Bark and Extract: Credited with astringent, healing and soothing properties that could benefit surface skin problems. Extract from elm leaves is usually recommended to wash wounds, bruises and sore eyes.

Emblica (Amla): An astringent herb. Rich source of Vitamin C. Useful for hair and skin treatment.

Eucalyptus: An antiseptic used to fragrance cosmetic preparations. Eucalyptus oil has antiseptic, disinfectant and blood circulation activating properties.

Fennel (saunf): It is a herb which has a cleansing effect on the skin, especially as a cleanser and detoxifier for oily skin types. When steaming the face, use it in the water. The principal constituents of fennel oil are anethol, fenchone, plus d-pinene, phellandrine, anisic acid and anisic aldehyde.

Fenugreek Extract: An emollient, anti-inflammatory and healing ingredient used in the treatment of irritated skin.

Garlic (Lehsun): Recognized as an antiseptic and bactericide. The ointment applied externally reduces swelling and useful for treating Acne and Eczema skin problems. The active properties of garlic depend on a pungent, volatile, essential oil obtained by distillation. Rich in sulphur, garlic oil helps in clearing skin problems such as eczema and acne.

Geranlum Oil: Have botanical properties described as refreshing, anti-irritant, mild tonic and astringent. It is good for all skin types, particularly benefit acne skins. This oil is used in perfumery and cosmetics.

Henna (Mehandi): An astringent herb with cooling properties. It is used for hair conditioning. Henna is a colorant that provides a reddish brown shade. It has important constituents which include mucins, phytosterols and napthoquinones. The extract is obtained from the leaves.

Haldi (Turmeric): It helps glow in skin when mixed to a face pack. It prevents inflammation, cures injuries, wounds, used for gonorrhoea (Venereal Disease).

Horse Radish Extract: Traditionally used against sunburns, superficial and other non-extensive burns, give the skin clarity and freshness. Its antiseptic and skin clearing properties are linked to its ascorbic acid content. The extract is made primarily from the plant's roots.

Horsetail Extract (Equisetum-ka-Paudha): General botanical properties include stimulating, astringent, soothing, healing and softening. Horsetail increases skin's defence mechanism, regulates the skin due to rich mineral contents and strengthens connective tissue. It prevents and counteract wrinkles in the eye area. It is beneficial in both anti-aging and relieving acnes.

Houseleek: A herb with healing and astringent properties. It cures warts and ringworm.

Hyssop Oil (zufah yabis): Properties include healing, tonic and stimulating. It is indicated for dermatitis, eczema and wounds. This aromatic plant has long leaves and clusters of light blue flowers. It also regulates blood pressure, clears the chest, calms the nerves, improves digestion and protects the body form infection.

Ivy extract (Labtab): Ivy extract has a slimming and anti-cellulite effect due to its ability to prevent water accumulation in the skin tissue. It is considered anti-bactericidal and soothing, particularly in burn cases. Apparently, ivy also has detergent, anti-parasitic, decongestant and analgesic properties. The leaves are traditionally used to treat various skin eruptions, irritation, dermatitis and skin ulcers.

Jasmine Oil (Chameli-ka-tel): Highly aromatic oil made from the flowers and used as a perfume. Jasmine may cause allergic reaction (swelling). The oil is credited with moisturizing, soothing and healing properties. It is indicated for dry and sensitive skins, and also for skin with dermatitis.

Jatsopha curcas (Ratanjot): Have cleaning, stimulating properties. Very effective to cure scabies, eczema and dermatitis.

Lemon: Rich in vitamin C, it is used in skin tonics and creams. The botanical properties include as acidic, anti-bactericidal and antiseptic. Lemon extract is suggested for treating sunburn, acne problems and oily skin. This extract contains citric acid, vitamin B and C. Lemon oil is one of the most versatile essential oil, is considered a counter-irritant, antiseptic, depurative and lymphatic stimulant. It is widely used in the perfume and soap industry. Lemon grass oil is the volatile oil distilled from the leaves.

Kaner Leander: Plant with white, yellow and red flowers Bark of the root cures many skin diseases and purifies the blood. Oil prepared from this plant is useful in case of scabies and ringworm.

Kalonji: Black seeds resembling onion seeds destroy intestine parasitis, benefit in cases of gall bladder, calculi, gout, rheumatism and sciatica. Ground in vinegar it helps to cure leucoderma (white patches on skin), ringworm, alopecia (patchy baldness) and acne.

Juniper Oil (hapusha): Juniper oil is antiseptic, astringent, cleansing and toning. Also credited with good penetrating capabilities, is considered helpful in treating acne (oily skin), dermatitis and eczema.

Lavender: It has a pleasant fragrance and used for scenting bath water. Used as nerve tonic, curing cough, anti-paralytic and mouthwash. On external application soothes headaches, reduces inflammatory properties include anti-allergic, anti-inflammatory, antiseptic, anti-bacterial anti-spasmodic, balancing, energizing, soothing, healing, tonic and stimulating. Lavender oil works on all types of skins and produces excellent results when used for oily skin as well as in the treatment of acne, burns, dermatitis, eczema and psoriasis.

Lettuce (chukandar): Rich in minerals, iron and vitamins. It is cooling and excellent for sunburn to redness and skin inflammations.

Marigold (Genda): The orange marigold is a prolific garden plant. It opens its petals at nine and closes them at four. A disinfectant herb, marigold is used in effective treatment of ulcers and open sores. The flowers may be eaten raw, taken as a standard infusion when applied as a lotion. The plant cures varicose veins and other circulatory troubles. As a lotion, a marigold infusion (petals only) provides the ideal balance of an over-oily skin and complexions. It has antiseptic healing and soothing effect and heals sunburns and skin rashes.

Marjoram (marwa, sathra): Described as tonic and anti-fungal. Most popular for botanical applications, Marjoram oil is beneficial for antispasmodic, calming and sedative indicating applications for sensitive and irritated skin. Sometimes, it may cause allergic reaction with symptoms being skin redness and itching.

Meadowfoam Oil: Rich emollient. It is widely used in cosmetic formulations because of its dryness and quick penetration into the skin. The extract has strong anti free radical properties as well as analgesic and topical anti-inflammatory activity. The plant grows abundantly at the edges of the river and ditches.

Mimosa: Used in cosmetics for its believed epidermic tissue regenerating, antiseptic, astringent, anti-inflammatory, repairing and protecting properties. Used effectively in post-sun preparations and skin care creams. It may sometimes produce allergic skin reaction.

Mint (pudina): The herb has cooling, tonic, stimulating, antiseptic, digestive and relaxing properties. Mint was traditionally used as an soothing and anti-itching treatment. This aromatic herb is widely used as a fragrance in beauty products and serves as a cleanser for acne and dermatitis treatment. It cures elephantiasis (swelling in tissues and varicose veins).

Myrrh (Benjabol): Said to have disinfectant, antiseptic, anti-inflammatory, anti-itching, tonic, stimulant, sedative and astringent properties. Myrrh extract can be valuable in products designed for acne treatment. Myrrh is a traditionally ancient ingredient for perfumes and incense, was used by ancient Egyptian women in facial masks and other cosmetic preparations.

Myrtle (Vilayati Mehndi): An astringent and antiseptic with strong botanical properties. Suitable for acne and oily skins.

Neroli Oil: A fragrance, used in skin care preparations to stimulate cell regeneration extracted from bitter orange blossom; is one of the most expensive oils; therefore is widely adulterated with the distillation of other citrus blossoms such as sweet orange, lemon and mandarin.

It leave a sedative and soothing effect and most beneficial for sensitive delicate skin types.

Nettle (bichchhubooti): The botanical properties include as anti-inflammatory, astringent, bactericidal, healing, mildly deodorant, antioxidant and stimulating. It is effective for treating eczema and

Majoram
(origanum onites)

Peppemint
(Mentha piperita)

Parslev
(Petroselinum crispum)

sunburn. Nettle is the botanical with the highest vitamin E content. Important constituents include acetylcholine, amino acids, histamine, carotinoids and chlorophyll.

Oak (Majuphall): The botanical properties are described as slightly tonic, strongly astringent, antiseptic, soothing and anti-inflammatory. It reduces inflammation and prevents infection. Oak root is recommended for sensitive skin, protecting it against unwanted reactions such as swelling or redness.

Oat (Jai): Oat extract obtained from the seeds of oats has soothing properties on the skin. It helps to enhance emulsion stability, increase viscosity, leave a smooth after feel and provide a source of whole natural vegetable protein. Oatmeal preparations are beneficial for irritated skins resulting from sunburn, psoriasis, or allergic dermatitis. The oatmeal relieves redness and itching. It acts as a soap-free cleanser and provides a gentle base for facemask, for delicate, sensitive skin. This mask absorbs oil from the skin's surface and reduces the redness of irritated, broken-out skin. Oat flour is an abrasive, absorbent, bulking, and viscosity-increasing substance. It is used in a variety of cosmetic preparations including powders, masks, packs, moisturizers, suntan gels, hand and body creams and soaps.

Olive Oil (Jaitun-ka-tel): A carrier oil with excellent lubrication and low odour. Olive leaf extract has astringent, antiseptic and antioxidant properties. It is used in anti-aging products.

Orange flower oil (Narangi ka tel): Credited with Soothing and calming properties when used in skin care preparations. The oil should not be confused with orange power extract. The flowers from the bitter orange tree yield an essential oil known as Neroli.

Palmarosa Oil: The properties attributed to this oil are soothing, moisturizing, antiseptic and cell regeneration. Its used for acne skin and dermatitis condition. The oil leaves immediate calming and refreshing action on the skin and is widely used in perfumery and cosmetology.

Pimpernel: This little plant with small oval-shaped leaves, long slender stalks, bearing bright scarlet flower was popular since the ancient Greeks to treat eye diseases, jaundice, dropsy and inflammation. The plant has cosmetic value and is applied as a skin lotion to cure skin pigmentation, removing freckles and blemishes, and acts as a hair restorer.

Patchouli Oil: Botanical properties of this herb are described as astringent, tonic, sedative, anti-inflammatory and decongestive. It is useful for acne, aged and chapped skin, and skin redness. The oil has strong, sweet and very persistent fragrance.

Peppermint: Credited with refreshing, cooling, bactericidal and anti-irritant properties. It is used as a fragrance, can produce allergic reactions such as skin rashes and irritation, helps relieve skin irritation and itching and reduces skin redness due to inflammation or acne.

Petit Grain Oil: Widely used in pharmacy and perfumery for its therapeutic and tonic effect. It has fresh fragrance and credited with tonic and antiseptic properties.

Pumpkin: Credited with curative properties. Cosmetic applications include use in anti-acne products and as anti-seborrhoeic.

Quince: Obtained from the dried seeds. Its extract is used in cosmetics for dry skin and eye treatment preparations. The seeds are an emollient, emulsifier and thickening agent.

Rose: Rose extract-rich in vitamin C is credited with astringent, tonic and deodorant properties. It is also used as a fragrance. Rose oil has moisturizing and moisture-retention, slightly tonic and soothing properties. It is helpful in case of skin redness or inflammation, when moisturization and regeneration is needed. Rose oil is beneficial to all skin types, particularly mature, dry or sensitive skins. This oil being most expensive essential oil, is largely adulterated with substances like geranium, lemongrass, palmarosa, and terpene alcohols. About 30 roses are required to make one drop of oil. Rosewater is credited with cooling, soothing, astringent, and cleansing properties. Rosewater is often mixed with glycerine, which provides moisturization and lubrication. Rosewater oil is one of the major perfumery oils useful as a cellular stimulant and tissues regenerator, especially good to sensitive and aged skin, wrinkles, and general skin care.

Rosemary (rusemary): A popular garden plant with spiky dark green leaves and distinctive scent. As a medicine, it is valuable tonic for heart and liver and helps reducing high blood pressure. Rosemary is widely used in the treatment of digestive disorders and menstrual pain among women. Used as a lotion, this herb relieves pain in the head and cough, when a spoonful of the herb mixed with honey and melted butter is taken. Rosemary is a fine tonic for the scalp and skin, adds lustre to the hair and is a useful ingredient in commercial shampoos. It helps to keep the skin free from the wrinkles. Washing with rose water keeps the youth alive. The extract have astringent, toning, stimulating, deodorant, antiseptic, reactivating, softening and invigorating properties which helps curing acne, dermatitis and eczema.

Sage (salvia, sefakuss): An aromatic, sun-loving plant with grey green leaves and mauvish flowers. The herb is used to treat cough, cold, headache, fever, liver troubles, bile and the digestive system. When as gargle or mouth wash the herb helps to cure sore throats and gums. The lotion heals ulcers, sores and other skin eruptions such as acne and oily skin. Sage oil is credited with depurative, astringent, invigorating and healing properties.

Sandalwood Oil: (Chandan ka tel): Credited with astringent, anti-inflammatory, antibacterial, tonic, stimulant, cooling and soothing properties. Beneficial in cases of curing acne and used as astringent for oily skin. The oil may produce rashes on hypersensitive skin, when present in high concentration.

Sesame Oil: (Til-ka-tel): It is commonly used as a carrier oil for cosmetic products. It has emollient properties similar to nut and vegetable oil. Sesame oil derived from the seeds is useful is suntan lotions, and reduces 30 percent of the sun's burning UV rays.

Shahtara (Pitpapda): An herbal plant with fine leaves found in wheat fields, with bitter taste and violet flowers. It has been extensively used for disorders arising out of impurities in the blood, like scabies ringworm besides curing venereal diseases such as Syphilis and gonorrhoea.

Sheesham (Red wood): The oil exuding from this plant is used for many disorders of the skin. It is used as a very efficacious blood purifier curing scabies, ringworm and leucoderma.

Satyanasi (Pela-dhatura): A medicinal plant with yellow flowers and thorny branches. Used as a blood purifier and cures many diseases of the skin. Powder of the seeds use to counteract the itch.

Sorbitol: Obtained from the leaves. Absorbs moisture from the air to prevent skin dryness, leaves the skin feeling smooth and velvety. Used as a replacement for glycerine in emulsions, ointments and various cosmetic creams.

Soapwort extract (saboonbooti): It is credited with cleansing and soothing properties. It helps soothing to the skin and relieves itching and inflammation. Soapwort extract is used for treating acne, psoriasis and eczema. The main constituents of this extract made from the roots, leaves and stem including flavonoids and vitamin C, which leave a magic effect on the skin.

Speedwell: The herbal plant with oval-shaped leaves and pale-blue flowers, also known as veronica is prescribed in medicines for treating catarrh, bronchitis, asthma and digestive trouble. Used as a standard infusion internally as well as externally, it treats most skin eruptions such as sores, ulcers, pimples, eczema and pruritis.

Strawberry: It possesses considerable medical value as well as a remarkable cooling effect on the skin and controls excessive perspiration. Having astringent properties, the herb is useful in dealing with diarrhoea, menstruation disorders, threatened abortion, risk of haemorrhage and the digestive system. Strawberry juice can be used to treat more serious skin ailments. It contains maximum iron contents and cures anaemia. It helps curing serious skin ailments such as eczema, pruritis and sunburned skins.

Thyme (ban ajwain): The herb grows wild on dry banks. It has woody stems, flattish round leaves and heavily scented flowers. Thyme have cleansing properties and its poultice made from leaves combat inflammation and infection. Thyme is digestive used as a liver tonic and cures a wide range of psychological disorders, headaches, hysteria, halitosis and various female ailments. Thyme oil obtained from branches and flowers is considered a powerful product having botanical properties such as antiseptic, tonic, antibacterial, deodorizing, fungicidal and circulation stimulating. The oil is obtained from the herb's branches and flowers.

Tamarind (imli): Credited with astringent, antiseptic and strong immuno-stimulating properties. This botanical is recommended for protecting the skin against environmentally induced damage, stimulating skin repair and for skin with low immuno defenses.

Tea Tree Oil: A natural preservative with antiseptic, germicidal and expectorant properties. The oil cures disorders and infections of all types of skins. It helps fight against seborrhoea, psoriasis, scaling and redness of skin, eczema, itching and dermatitis.

Turmeric: Credited to healing, tonic, mildly stimulating, anti-inflammatory and blood-purifying properties. This herb is useful for a variety of curative purposes including the treatment of acne, eczema, skin infections, ulcers, burns and rashes.

Vervain: The plant having green-grey leaves and small hooded mauve flowers has properties to cure nervous disorders, epilepsy, asthma, the liver, heart and spleen. It relieves mental strain and helps cure infectious diseased, used as gargle or mouthwash for sore throats and gums and as an eye lotion. It is also recommended for curing inflammation and diseases of skin.

Walnut: The extract obtained from leaves and bark of the plant is traditionally used topically soothing and anti-itching, as well as against sunburns and other superficial burns. It can be used in case of acne and other skin diseases because of its fungi static and astringent properties.

Witch-Hazel: Traditionally used in topical treatment of burns, sunburns, skin irritation, insect bites and bruises. It is credited with anti-inflammatory and wound-healing properties, The herb is used for anti-itching, softening and emollient properties.

Yarrow (Sahastrapani, Gandana): Having greyish, feathery, leaves and small daisy-like flowers, yarrow has been used since antiquity for headaches, fevers (influenza) diarrhoea and excessive menstruation. The extract has astringent, antiseptic, anti-inflammatory, healing and calming properties. The important constituents include flavonoid, amino acid, sugar and phytosterol. It is beneficial for oily and acne skins.

SOME DO'S AND DON'TS

The following dos and don'ts should be kept in mind when making a herbal preparation at home:

- Do not expose oils and waxes to direct heat as these can burn and an intense heat can change the properties of the preparation.
- When heating oils and waxes, put them in separate enamel bowls, placed in a large pan filled with hot water (not boiling) and continue stirring with either a wooden spoon or a glass rod or a slow speed electric heater. While stirring, add water to the wax or the oils if it is too thick.

- Add perfume or colouring matter when the preparation is ready and in case of a cream, mix it when it cools and thickens. In case your skin is sensitive or allergy-prone, it is advised to omit perfume.
- Ensure that the contents of the preparation are properly mixed otherwise preparation may turn gritty. Make sure to continue stirring or beating until the cream is cool. If the preparation does not gel, melt it again and repeat the process. You may add a few drops of oleic acid to bind together any cream or lotion.
- The herbal ingredients used in preparing the cosmetics may be easily available with leading general merchandizing shops or an herbal store or dispensing chemists.
- Beeswax, emulsifying wax and cocoa butter can be available with a dispensing chemist. Lanolin is readily available with the chemists. These are usually of two type-anhydrous and hydrous. Anhydrous lanolin is commonly used because it has less water contents. In case, anhydrous lanolin is not readily available, you may procure hydrous lanolin, which has in itself a fairly large water contents. The preparations with anhydrous lanolin will be much more richer and greasier. Oils, herbs, lentils, fuller's earths, camphor, etc. can be purchased from a 'pansari' shop or a good herbalist.
- Home made herbal cosmetic preparations have a short life, which can be lengthened by storing them in a refrigerator. It is suggested to make a small quantity of the recipe and use them lavishly while still fresh. Keep a small jar in the bathroom and the rest in the refrigerator. Nepagin M is an effective preservative. When heating the contents, add a few drops of Nepagin M. Stir constantly until the oily globules disperse. This will enhance the shelf life of preparation.

FRUITS, VEGETABLE AND NATURAL SUBSTANCES USED IN YOUR COSMETIC LABORATORY

Here is a brief description of some of the very useful ingredients required in making Ayurvedic preparations for health and beauty:

Amla (Emblice myrobalan): Cheapest source of vitamin C, which is not destroyed by boiling or other process. A good substance for hair washing and helps in case of falling and premature greying of hair. It rejuvenates the body.

Anar (Pomegranate): A delicious juicy fruit with several medicinal properties. It is cooling and allays uncontrollable thirst in diarrhoea, digestive. Flower of the plant are an ingredient for miscarriage.

The rind of fruit is a astringent and have a tonic effect on the tissues. Bark of root of the plant is used in case of intestinal worms.

Alcohol: It has antiseptic, preserving and grease cutting properties. Used mainly in stimulating astringents and as a solvent for essential oils. Vodka is a common substitute for alcohol.

Arand Kharbuza: Also called as golden tree of life, which acts as a digestive agent because of large amount of pepsin. It is used to reduce inflammation of live and spleen. The sap of tree cures ringworm and intestinal parasites.

Alum (fitkari): A fine white or yellow powder with astringent properties.

Apple: A naturally acid fruit good for the skin. Apple cider restores the acid mantle to the skin. Can be used as skin tonic.

Apricot (Khubani): Rich in vitamin A. Use the pulp in face mask. Apricot oil is very rich in polyunsaturated oil, so it is used in nourishing creams.

Banana: Nourishing and used in masks.

Beeswax: Also known as 'madhu-mom.' It is an easter wax with a high-melting point, ideal for face creams. An emulsifier when mixed with borax. It takes eight parts of honey to produce one part of beeswax. It is one of the oldest raw ingredients used in cosmetic preparations, Beeswax is used as part of the wax composition of solid and paste products such as creams, lipstick and pomades. Beeswax is credited with anti-inflammatory, anti-allergic, anti-oxidant, anti-bacterial, germicidal, skin softening and elasticity enhancing properties. It rarely causes sensitivity, and allergic reaction. Bleached beeswax is white whereas unbleached beeswax is yellow.

Beer: Used to wash the face and as a hair setting lotion. It prevents skin rashes.

Barley: It has nutritional value and is rich in iron and vitamin B. It cools the body, strengthens the nerves, and is excellent tonic food during convalescence.

Basil (Tulsi): Has blood purifying qualities. It is used for ringworm, scabies, leucoderma and leprosy.

Benzoin (Lohban): Essential oil with bactericidal, anti-irritant and anti-itching properties. It is considered a good ingredient for reducing skin redness and is also a preservative of fats. While its primary constituent is benzoic acid, it also contains an oily aromatic liquid.

Borax (Suhaga): It has mild detergent and anti-septic properties. Used as emulsifier in conjunction with beeswax. It cures the patient of ringworm.

Bade (Banyan tree): It is also known as 'bodhi' tree. It has many medicine properties to prepare formulations for spermatorrhae, premature ejaculation etc. Sap of its leaves is specifically beneficial for kibes and corns.

Bakain (Lilac): A tree resembling 'neem'. The leaves have blood purifying properties; recommended for scabies, ringworm, leprosy, leucoderma and to reduce inflammation.

Calamine Lotion: An alkaline lotion used to soothe irritated skin. It contains lime water, glycerine, zinc oxide and calamine.

Camphor: A white crystalline substance used as an antiseptic. It is healing and soothing when used on spot. It is used either camphor cake or camphor spirit. Camphor oil is stimulating.

Castor oil (arandi-ka-tel): A rich oil used in hair products. Leaves of the tree smeared with sesame oil and applied to inflammations tend to relieve them. It has many medicine uses also.

Carrot Juice (gajar-ka-ras): Rich in vitamin A, B and C. Used in nourishing eye creams. Carrot oil has cleansing, depurative and draining properties and cures acne, dermatitis, wrinkles and skin irritation.

Cocoa Butter: Solidified waxy oil from the roasted cocoa beans, used as lubricant in massage creams. It is good for dry skins.

Corn Oil (Gram Seed Oil): A heavy vegetable oil which can be used in body and face creams.

Coconut Oil: Used as a cream base. A raw material in soaps, ointments, massage creams and in sunscreen formulations. Coconut oil is a grouping of primarily short-chain fatty acid bonded with glycerine and expressed from coconut kernels. It may be irritating to the skin and cause skin rashes.

Caraway Oil (Carum Carvi): A carrier oil having ability to remove bruises, and believed to have tissues regenerating properties. It is beneficial for acne (oily) skin.

Citric Oils: Refers to one or a combination of oil from citrus fruits such as orange oil, lemon oil, grapefruit oil and the like.

Corn Oil: Used as carrier oil. This vegetable oil has average emollient properties. It is widely used in cosmetic formulations.

Cottonseed Oil: The oil is used in the manufacture of soaps, creams and baby creams. It is known to cause allergies and be mildly irritating. Expressed from various species of cotton.

Cucumber: It is slightly astringent, cool and refreshing; and used in lotions, cream and masks.

Fuller's Earth (Multani Mitti): An absorbent clay, rich in minerals. Used in facemasks for thickening and cleansing, drawing and stimulating. Also used as dry shampoo. A paste on the skin cures prickly heat.

Cucumber Extract: Credited with moisture-binding, moisture-regulating, soothing, tightening, anti-itching, refreshing, softening, healing and anti-inflammatory properties. It contains amino acids and organic acids that are claimed to strengthen the skin's acid mantle. The extract can be used in aftershave preparations, eye treatment products and treatment for oily skin. It is also effective in emulsions as a tightening agent for stressed skin and in sun-preparations as a refresher.

Eggs: Useful aid to beauty. The yolk is nourishing and the white is drying and tightening. Used in masks and as a hair conditioner. Egg protein creates a film, thereby acting as a moisture rentention agent allowing the skin to build up a supply of water. The moisturizing process tightens and softens the skin only temporarily as the skin cannot utilize the protein contained in a egg. It may cause skin rashes and other disorders in those with an allergy to eggs. Egg lecithin is recommended for sensitive skins. The egg oil extracted form the egg yolk is recommended for sensitive skins. The egg yolk extract is a protein with emulsifying capabilities, contains lecithin sterols and Vitamin A.

Emulsifying Wax: Extremely useful for stabilizing creams. It is an emulsifier and thickening agent used to give body to a formulation. Unlike some waxes including beeswax, this is not a true wax. It is a chemical mixture of emulsifiers and fatty alcohols that permit the formulation of stable creams.

Glycerine: Attracts and holds moisture. Used in face creams and lotions. Glycerine is used in moisturizers due to its water-binding capabilities that absorb water from the air. Glycerine helps the skin retain moisture. Glycerine also improves the spreading qualities of creams and lotions. It is clear syrupy liquid made by chemically combining water and fat that is usually derived from vegetable oil.

Gelatine: A rich source of protein used for hair conditioning or diluted as a setting lotion and nail hardening cream.

Glucose: Has moisture-binding properties and provides the skin with a soothing effect. It is a sugar that is generally obtained by the hydrolysis of starch.

Grapes: Slightly acidic. Good for cleansing and bleaching. It is described as tonic, with anti-inflammatory and decongestant properties. It may act as an antioxidant. Grapes are beneficial in anti-aging, after-sun and other sun care products. Grape seed oil has moisturizing and nourishing properties.

Groundnut Oil: A vegetable oil used in face creams and body lotions. Also known as peanut oil.

Gum Resin: Used as a tightening, fixing and stabilizing agent in the cream. It can be dissolved in water.

Honey: Healing, nourishing and softening. It is used in masks, cream and lotions. A perfect food if taken with milk or lime water. It is helpful in cases of paralysis, cures suppurating, wound and improve eyesight.

Hydrogen Peroxide: A bleaching, oxidizing agent, detergent, antiseptic a skin bleacher in cosmetics. If used undiluted, it can cause burns of the skin and mucous membranes.

Hydrolyzed Milk Protein: Forms a film on the skin's surface that allows the skin to retain moisture.

Kaolin (China Clay): Often used in powders and masks. It is appropriate absorber of the oil and sweet secreted by the skin.

Lanolin: A thick tacky fat, widely used in skin foods for its moisturizing and softening effects. Lanolin is an emollient with moisturizing properties and an emulsifier with high water-absorption capabilities.

Linseed Oil: Botanical properties are listed as emollient, anti-inflammatory, and healing. Derived from the flax plant seed obtained by expression with little or no heat.

Lecithin Powder: A complex, highly nutritious soft yellow powder found in egg yolk and soybeans.

Neem (Margosa Tree): Bitter leaves used as an antiseptic. Neem leaves when ground in paste and applied relieve prickly heat, remove pus from wounds, clean boils on the skin. All parts of the tree are endowed with the quality of purifying blood.

Melon: Used on dry skin for refreshing and cleaning the skin.

Milk: Used for softening, nourishing and cleaning the skin. Milk protein gives a smooth feel to the skin. Milk, primarily is well absorbed by the skin and gives a gloss and fine touch by forming a soft film.

Oatmeal (jai ka atta): A cleansing and soothing agent. Use it for washing with, or in masks. Finally ground oatmeal is found in any grocer's shop.

Onion: An antiseptic. Wash your face with onion juice to prevent blemishes and mix it with honey to make an anti-wrinkle cream. Juice of onion taken in conjunction with honey and eggs is an excellent tonic with aphrodisiac qualities. An excellent preparation against cholera and diarrhoea if steeped in vinegar.

Orange: Contains vitamin C. The juice is used in skin tonics and masks. Dry and grind some orange peel and use it in masks and facial scrubs. Also used in tooth powders.

Olive oil: A poly-unsaturated vegetable oil used in nourishing creams. Olive oil is a carrier oil with excellent lubrication properties. It has pale colour, and low odour. Olive oil is considered an especially good carrier for essential oils.

Papaya: It is also called paw-paw. Have softening and cleansing properties. The enzymes in the fruit have a deep cleansing effect by breaking down the dead cells of the skin. It contains Calcium, Iron, Phosphorus and Magnesium salt.

Peach: Moisturizing, nourishing and delicious smelling. Use the mashed pulp on dry, rough skin in skin tonics and masks.

Petroleum Jelly: A lubricating jelly often used in cleansing creams, and hand and nail cream.

Paraffin: Used in cosmetics as a beeswax substitute. Paraffin is a solid mixture of hydrocarbons obtained from petroleum. Presence of impurities in paraffin may result in irritation, eczema and other skin problems.

Panwar (Mehndi): A herb growing in waste lands. It has seeds like kidney beans. Ground seed applied to skin cures ringworm, leucoderma and blemishes.

Palmitic Acid: Obtained from palm oil, one of the skin's major fatty acids produced by the sebaceous glands. In cosmetic preparations, it is used as a formula texturizer.

Peanut Oil: Utilized as a skin softener, emulsifier and emollient. It is used as a substitute for expensive oils such as almond and olive in cosmetic creams. Peanut oil has a higher vitamin A, vitamin E and nicotinic acid content than other nut oils.

Potatoes: Have cleansing and drawing properties. Clears the skin. Use thin raw potato slices for eye pads to remove puffiness of eyes.

Resin: Used to give gloss, flow, adhesion and water resistance to cosmetics. This is a brittle substance, usually translucent or transparent, that can be either derived naturally or synthetically obtained.

Retinol: Considered a skin revitalizer, retinal is reported to enhance skin radiance and treat conditions associated with aging such as wrinkles and fine lines, acne, and papules.

Safflower Oil: A rich poly-unsaturated oil suitable for all nourishing cosmetics. A carrier oil considered hydrating to the skin, is obtained from the seeds and have astringent, anti-inflammatory and soothing properties especially for sensitive skin and areas with burns.

St. John's Wort Oil (Basant): Considered anti-inflammatory. It is beneficial for sensitive and/or rough, chapped skin as well as skins suffering from acne, irritation and inflammatory circulation.

Sodium Chloride (Salt): Used as a preservative, astringent and antiseptic to treat inflame lesion. Sodium sisqui is a powdery substance, which is a water softener and is used in bath salts. Salt is used with equal parts of bicarbonate of soda as an excellent tooth powder. Also used as an abrasive body rub to tone the skin and improve circulation.

Sodium Bicarbonate (Baking Soda): An inorganic salt used as a buffering agent and a pH adjuster. Used in skin smoothing powders and also serves as a neutralizer.

Sodium Bisulphate: An organic salt used as an buffering agent and a pH adjuster in cosmetic creams.

Sarson (Mustard): A well known oil seed. The seeds of the plant extracting oil used for massage, as cooking medium and also as hair oil.

Stearic Acid: A natural fatty acid. It is crystalline, white, waxy substance, which gives pearliness to creams, hand and body lotions.

Sugar: An abrasive face scrub. Lather the face with soap, then add a handful of sugar and scrub, rinse off and apply lemon juice. This thoroughly cleanses and stimulates the skin.

Sulphur: A yellow powder used in acne preparations. It helps slow down the activity of the oil producing glands. Some people are allergic to it, so before using it on your face, give yourself a skin test behind the ear.

Tea: Contains tannin, which has a soothing and healing effect. It absorbs ultraviolet light and is used in sun creams to help prevent burning. Tea bags are marvellously soothing used as readymade eye pads.

Soybean Oil: Used as a smoothing ingredient. It has high content of phosphatides such as lecithin, sterols and vitamins (A, E, and K). Soybean oil is not irritating.

Spermaceti: A waxy substance used in the manufacture of cosmetics, to thicken the products and give them shine. Spermaceti is non-toxic and non-irritating.

Tamanu oil: Used for the improvement of cell regeneration. It can be found in products used to protect the skin against sun exposure, as well as anti-aging formulations to cure wrinkles.

Tomato: A slightly acidic vegetable containing potassium and vitamin C. Use it on blackheads, open pores and greasy skin.

Turtle Oil: Vitamin enriched oil. Often used in rich nourishing creams. It smells bad.

Vinegar Acidic: Use diluted eight parts water to one part vinegar. Improves and softens the skin.

Vetiver oil (Khus-khus): Produced from the root of a fragrant grass. Considered stimulant and tonic, and used in perfumery as well as in cosmetics.

Vervain Oil: Has been credited with astringent and antispasmodic properties.

Vitamins: Useful for skin and hair. Vitamin A can pass through the skin and is useful for dry skin and acne. Also have soothing properties. Vitamin B promotes health of skin and hair. Vitamin C promotes healing of acne. Vitamin D can be absorbed through skin and has a healing effect on the skin. Vitamin E is said to have healing properties. Vitamin F counteracts dry, chapped skin. Greatly used in face and hand creams, and in hair treatments to counter act brittle hair.

Wheat-germ Oil: Made from twigs of hamamells of alder bush. Widely used in skin tonics for its astringent properties. Traditionally used in topical treatment of burns, sunburns, skin irritation, insect bites and bruises. It is credited with anti-inflammatory and wound healing properties. It is used for its anti-itching, softening and emollient properties.

Yoghurt: A liquor made from milk. It contains enzymes. Used as a base for cleansing and cleaning facemasks.

8

BEAUTY TECHNIQUES

BATHS AND BEAUTY

Hydotherapy is an important factor in the cure of disease, stimulate the vitality of the body and enchance beauty by the use of water and wet packs in various ways at varying temperatures. The application of cold water to the abdomen-the seat of most diseases and disorders leave not only a relaxing effect upon the body system but increase beauty. The application of cold packs to the surface of body draws the blood fom the congested inteior to the skin, relaxes minute blood vessels, opens the skin pores and facilitates the escape of heat from the body. The blood congested in the inflamed skin produces inflammation such as Robor (redness), Tumor (swelling), Calor (heat) and Dolor (pain). Wet packs may be applied to any part of the body. The different types of packs include full Sheet Pack, Spanish Mantle, Body Pack, Abdominal Pack, Chest Pack, Scotch Pack, Throat Pack, T-Pack, Leg Pack, Foot Pack. The purpose of wet pack is to lower high temperature.

Cold and heating compress is an effective means of contolling inflammatoy conditions of the liver, spleen, stomach, kidneys, intestines, lungs, brain, pelvic organs etc. A cold compress soothes dermatitis and inflammations, whereas a heating compress helps accumulation of body heat. Hip Bath is one of the most useful process of hydrotherapy, in which mode of treatement involves the region below the navel, the hips and abdomen. The bath is given in water at alternate temperature. In cold Hip Bath (duration 30 minutes) water temperature should vary between 1 to 18°C. Rub the adbomen briskly from the navel downwards and across the body should remain completely dry during and after the bath. Undertake moderate exercises after the bath to warm the body. It has the following advantages to beautify the body and helps to reduce extra flesh from hips and abdomen besides relieving obesity. A hot Hip Bath is taken for eight to ten minutes at tempeature of water 40 to 50°C. Do not apply friction to the abdomen and drink a glass of cold water before entering the tub. A cold shower bath should be taken immediately after the hot bath. In hot and cold bath (also known as Repulsive Hip Bath), the temperature of water in the hot tub should vary between 40 to 45°C and in cold tub between 10 and 18°C. The patient should alternatively sit in the hot tub for five minutes, and then in the cold tub for three minutes. The treatment should end with sprinkling cold water to the hips.

STEAM BATH (SAUNA BATH)

It is one of the most important water treatments, which induces perspiration. This bath has several queries people want to know as below:

1. Does Sauna Bath helps to slim down?
   - To exercise 15 minutes in Sauna bath is equivalent to running two kilometers. It clears cellulite.
2. Does Sauna Bath helps to beautify skin?
   - Toxins are eliminated through the skin in Sauna Bath, which cure skin problems like acne, dull, lifeless complexion.
3. How long should one stay in the steam?
   - It depends upon the condition and the requirement of an individual.

Steam Bath

4. What dress to wear?
   - Put on the minimum possible clothes on the body. The dress worn at the time of sauna is generall briefs and bras or a swimming costume for women and brief for men. Wear minimum possible clothes on the body. A bare body will reap more fruits that a covered one.
5. In what position and for how much time one should take bath?
   - Sauna bath is a place to relax, to lie prone, speechless.
6. The duration of bath?

- It should be generally 10 to 20 minutes or until profuse perspiration takes place. Start with short sessions and increase the duration when the body will withstand the heat for longer period.

Some Do's and Don'ts when having Sauna Steam Bath

- Do not drink anything for at least one hour after having steam bath.
- Drink one or two glasses of cold water before taking bath.
- Do light Yogic exercises and control your diet when having steam bath.
- Drink one or two glasses of cold water before taking bath.
- Do light Yogic exercises and control you diet when having steam bath, which can do wonders in reducing weight.
- Protect the head with a wet towel when having steam.
- A cold shower taken immediately after the steam bath leaves miraculous effect.
- Have a 30 minutes rest at the end to attain the body's normal temperature.
- Do not wear watch and ornaments when taking steam bath, the steam and heat shall damage them.
- It is preferred to lie on the back and wrap hair in towel when having Sauna bath.

EPSOM SALT BATH

Fill tub with about 13 liters water at 40°C Temperature. Dissolve in it 1 to 1.5 kg. Epsom Salt. Lie down in the tub immersing the trunk, thighs and legs in water fo 15 to 20 minutes. Drink a glass of cold water before taking bath. Epsom salt Bath is very useful for the skin beauty.

Sun Bath: It has the following benefits:

- Clears the skin of pimples and acne.
- Cleanses oily skin, it gives a lovely tan.
- Revives the whole body.

Never expose continuously to the strong rays for more than 30 minutes, which can wither a dry skin, burn a delicate one, distend the veins and cause burns and sun stroke. To enjoy the beneficial effects of the sun is to play, walk or swim in sunligt.

HERBAL BATHS

Tap Water Bath: Is good for skin depending on the skin type. If the skin is extremely dry, washing the body in hard water will be harmful. The salts and calcium in hard water leave the skin further dry. Use a water softener (bath salt or oil to counteract this effect. Excessive rubbing the body will be harmful. Do not apply cold water to breast, only douche the tips of the nipples. Rubbing ice over the tips of the breasts nipples cause a strong static contraction in the mammary muscles of the skin.

VINEGAR BATH

Use for itchy, dry skin.Vinegar soothes and soften the skin.

HONEY BATH

Makes skin smooth and satiny.

STARCHY BATH

Leave your skin beautiful, smooth, tight and soft. Mix one tablespoon each laundry starch and glycerin to bath water.

Mix Bath: Lavender, hyssop, mint, borage, yarrow, rosemary and camomile are useful herbs for the skin when used in bath water.

Lavender, hyssop, mint, borage, yarrow, rosemary and camomile are useful herbs for the skin used in bath water. Baby oil or mineral oil should not be used in bath water as it cannot be absorbed by the skin.

BUBBLE BATH

To prepare Bubble Bath, beat one egg, 1/2 cup shampoo and one teaspoon gelatin. Add the mixture to your bath water when the tap is running.

MILK AND HONEY BATH

Leaves skin feeling smooth, satiny and pampered. Mix ingredients such as two eggs, ¼ cup each almond oil, sunflower oil, olive oil, vodka, milk and 2 teaspoons each honey and washing detergent in bath water.

Precautions while having bath

- Avoid bath within three hours after a meal and one hour before taking meal.
- Avoid Hip Bath and Foot Bath two hours after a meal.
- Do not take bath during periods.
- Pregnant can take only Hip Bath during 1st trimester.

TURKISH BATH

In this bath, the air is heated in a chamber having 43 to 54°C temperature or a hot room having temperature between 65.5 to 76.5°C., followed by a plunge bath. After the bath, the body is given friction to knead the muscles. When the patient begins to perspire, a shampoo bath is given. Rubbing and stroking is continued until the skin is smooth and polished.

Advantages

- Turkish bath helps slimming.
- It cures many chronic diseases.
- Patients lose 800 gm. or even more in a single session of bath of an hour's duration.

Precautions: Avoid bath in case of a:

- Skin disease.
- Diseases of heart, kidneys and diabetes.

THE GRADUATED BATH

It is a form of full bath. The patient is rubbed continuously to produce chilly sensations. The bath is administered every three hours. Rub a cool towel after the bath.

Advantages

- Reduces the fever (body temperature).
- Makes skin healthy and glowing.

Precautions

Those suffering from heart disease should avoid cold bath.

HOT AIR BATH

Consists in exposure of entire undressed body with the exception of the head to a superheated atmosphere having temperature from 48 to 82°C. It may precede a cold douche, a cold wet pack, a cold immersion, a cold sponge or a wet sheet rub, following a hot bath.

Advantages

- The bath increases the tonus of blood vessels and to energize the nerve center of the skin.

Precautions

The hot air bath should be avoided in case of skin disorders, cardiac weakness, in the febrile conditions, in diabetes and in advance cases of nephritis.

COLD FRICTION

A cold bath involves the wet rubbing to the body with cold water. The patient lies on the bed undressed, wrapped in a sheet. The head, face and neck should be wet with cold water. Continue rubbing the body rapidly until it reddens at the trunk, legs, back hips and lastly the feet. Do not rub the soles of feet.

Advantages

Cold friction is employed in case of anemia, chlorosis, tuberculosis, cardiac, dropsy, diabetes, dicrotic pulse, during pregnancy puerperal fever, chronic dysentery, malaria. typhoid, whooping cough, yellow fever, dengue, influenza, lithemia, leprosy, emaciation, scurvy, rickets, anorexia, hypo-pepsia, intestinal catarrh, chronic nephritis, hysteria, neurasthenia, migraine, paralysis and drug habits. A cold friction should be employed two or three times a day.

SUN-CHARGED WATER (WHITE WATER TREATMENT)

The treatment cures several acute as well as chronic diseases such as headache, blood pressure, anemia, gout, paralysis, acidity, abnormal palpitation and convulsions, cough, asthma, T.B., ENT disorders, meningitis, liver troubles, brain troubles, hyper acidity, gastritis, dysentery, constipation, piles, diabetes, irregular menses, leucorrhoea (white discharge from vagina) and uterus cancer.

In this treatment the patient should drink about four glasses of white water (one liter) at a time in the early morning before sun rise. Gradually increase the amount of water. To prepare sun-charged water, stir water in copper container or an earthen pot and drink after 15 minutes. Tap water may also be used after 15 to 20 minutes. Sun-charged water or boiled water has no adverse effect on the health.

COLD WATER BATH

Cold water is good for persons with sluggish or a blemished skin and to stimulate it. Wash yourself with water at different temperatures on different parts of the body: a cold bath to make the bosom firm, and a hot bath to slim the ankles. You need the following items for a luxurious bath:

- Soft bath towel.
- Bath cap.
- Friction mitt.
- Depilatory cream or lotion.
- Bath brush to scrub and stimulate the skin and bring the blood to the surface, remove dead cells, smooth and clean the skin.
- Soap and talcum powder.
- Bath oil.
- Body lotion or massage cream.
- Pumice stone.
- Body cologne or a body spray.

BATH FOR A DRY SKIN

Add to the bath water beaten yolk of an egg and mix to it one teaspoon of lemon juice. This recipe is very useful for dry skin of the body.

SOFT-WATER BATH

Use of rainy water is useful. If you are unable to get rain water, soften bath water by simply adding a little sodium sesqui carbonate, which is very beneficial for the skin.

BATH FOR ITCHY SKIN

A vinegar bath is very useful for a itchy dry skin usually prone to wrinkles. Add a cup of vinegar to the bath water.

BATH FOR A TIRED SKIN

Add two handfuls of Epsom salt to a bucket of bath water to relieve tiredness.

STARCHY BATH TO SMOOTHEN THE SKIN

Mix a few tablespoons of laundry starch and a teaspoon of glycerin to your bath water, which leave your skin beautifully smooth, tight and soft.

HERBAL BATH FOR BEAUTIFUL BODY

Lavender, hyssop, mint, borage, yarrow, rosemary, balm or camomile are useful herbs used in bath water either separately or in a mixture.

SALT BATH

Mix ingredients, such as washing soda, potassium carbonate, one cup aromatic essential oil of lavender or pine and 2 tablespoons iodized salt in a jar and use about a tablespoon in a bucket of bath water.

HERBAL PRODUCTS FOR BEAUTY

Rose

Rich in vitamin C and credited with astringent, tonic and deodorant properties. It is beneficial in case of skin redness or inflammation and especially good to sensitive and aged skin, wrinkles, and general skin care.

Rose

Rosemary (Rusemary)

A tonic for the scalp and skin, which adds lustre to the hair. It has astringent, toning, stimulating, deopdorant, antiseptic, reactivating, softening and invigorating properties, which help curing acne, premature wrinkles, dermatitis and eczema.

Sage (Salvia, Safakuss)

This herb heals ulcers, sores and other skin eruptions such as acne and oily skin. Credited with depurative, astringent, invigorating and healint properties.

Sandalwood Oil (Chandan Ka Tel)

Credited with astringent, anti-inflammatory, antibacterial, tonic, stimulant, cooling and soothing properties. Beneficial in cases of curing acne and used as astringent for oily skin.

Shahtara (Pitpapda)

An herbal plant extensively used for skin disorders arising out of impurities in the blood, such as scabies and ringworm. It helps cure venereal diseases such as Syphilis and gonorrhoea.

Sheesham (Red Wood)

Used for many disorders of the skin and cure scabies, ringworm and leucoderma.

Satyanasi (Pela-Dhatura)

Used as a blood puifier and cures many diseases of the skin.

Sorbitol

Prevent skin dryness, leaves the skin feeling smooth and velvety and is used in various cosmetic creams.

Soapwort Extract (Saboonbooti)

Credited with cleansing and soothing properties. It helps soothing the skin, relieves itching and inflammation, cure acne, psoriasis and eczema.

Speedwell

I help treating many skin eruptions such as sores, ulcers, pimples, eczema and pruritis.

Strawberry

Have cooling and astringent properties. The herb is used to treat more serious skin ailments curing serious skin ailments such as eczema, pruritis and sunburn.

Thyme (ban ajwain)

Botanical properties such as antiseptic, tonic, antibacterial, deodorizing, fungicidal and circulation stimulating. The oil is obtained from the herb's branches and flowers.

Tamarind (imli)

A powerful herb credited with astringent, antiseptic and strong immuno-stimulating properties. Protects the skin against envionmental reactions.

Tea Tree Oil

A natural preservative with antiseptic, germicidal and expectorant properties. Cures disorders and infections of all types of skins. It helps fight against seborrhoea, psoriasis, scaling and redness of skin, eczema, itching and dermatitis.

Turmeric

Credited to healing, tonic, mildly stimulating, anti-inflammatory and blood-purifying properties. This herb is useful for the treatment of acne, eczema, skin infections, burns and rashes.

Vervain

Helps curing infections diseases and inflammation and of the skin.

Walnut

This herbal plant is traditionally used topically soothing and anti-itching against sunburns and other superficial burns. It can be used in case of acne and other skin diseases because of its fungi static and astringent properties.

Witch-Hazel

Traditionally used in topical treatment of burns, sunburns, skin irritation, insect bites and bruises. It is credited with anti-inflammatory, wound-healing, anti-itching, softening and emollient properties.

Yarrow (Sahastripani, Gandana)

The plant has astingent, antiseptic, anti-inflammatory, healing and calming properties. It is beneficial for oily and acne skins.

Eggs

Useful aid to beauty. The yolk is nourishing and the white is drying and tightening. Used in masks and as hair conditioner. Egg lecithin is recommended for sensitive skins. The egg yolk extract is a protein with emulsifying capabilities, contains Vitamin A.

Glycerine

Attracts and holds moisture. Used in face freams and lotions. Glycerine helps the skin retain moisture. Glycerine also improves the spreading qualities of creams and lotions.

Honey

Have healing, nourishing and softening properties. Used in masks, creams and lotions.

Milk

Used for softening, nourshing and cleaning the skin. Milk protein gives a smooth feel to the skin. Contains vitamin C. The juice is used in skin tonics, masks and facial scrubs.

Tea

Contains tannin, which has a soothing and healing effect. It absorbs ultraviolet light and is used in sun creams to help prevent burning.

Tamanu Oil

Used for cell regeneration. It can be found in products used to protect the skin against sun exposure as well as anti-aging formulations to cure wrinkles.

Vinegar

Acidic properties. Improves and softens the skin.

Vetiver Oil (Khus-Khus)

Credited with astringent and antispasmodic properties.

Vitamins

Beneficial for skin and hair. Vitamin is useful for dry skin and acne due to its soothing propeties. Vitamin B promotes health of skin and hair. Vitamin C promotes healing of acne. Vitamin D and Vitamin E has a healing effect on the skin. Vitamin F counteracts dry and chapped skin.

Wheat-germ Oil

Widely used in skin tonics, the treatment of burns, sunburns, skin irritation, insect bites and bruises. Credited with anti-inflammatory, wound healing, anti-itching, softening and emollient properties.

9

HAND AND FOOT CARE

THE COMPOSITION OF NAIL

The nail, a whitish and translucent protein substance is composed of mainly keratin-a protein substance that forms the base of all horny tissue. The nail consists of many parts:

- **Nail Body:** A visible portion of nail attached to the bed.
- **Nail Root:** At the base of the nail, embedded underneath the skin and attached to a growing tissue, known as the matrix.
- **The Free Edge:** The end portion of the nail plate over the tip of finger and toe.
- **Nail Bed:** Which has many blood vessels that provide the nourishment necessary for the growth of nail.
- **The Matrix:** The part of the nail-bed that extend beneath the nail root and contains nerves, lymph and blood vessels to nourish the nail. The matrix produce cells, which harden the nail.
- **The Lunula:** It is also located at the base of the nail.

The structure of the nail: It include

- **The Cuticle:** Overlapping skin around the nail.
- **The Eponychium:** Extension of the cuticle at the base of nail.
- **The Hyponychium:** Portion of the epider-mis under the free edge of the nail.
- **The Perionychium:** Portion of surrounding the entire nail border.
- **The Nail Walls:** Folds of the skin overlapping the sides of the nail.

- **The nail grooves:** Slits, or tracks at the either sides of the nail upon which the nail moves.
- **The mantle:** Deep fold of the skin in which nail root is embedded.

THE GROWTH OF THE NAIL

The growth of nails is influenced by:

- Nutrition.
- General health.
- Disease.

The average growth of normal nail is about 1/8" per month, which grows faster in summer than in winter. Children nails grow more rapidly as compared to adult nails. The nail of middle finger grows faster than the thumbnail, which has slowest growth. The toenails grow more slowly than finger nails, Toenails are thicker and harder.

Nail irregularities	Symptoms and causes
Corrugation	Uneven growth due to injury or wavy ridge illness.
Furrows	Run either lengthwise or across the nail due to illness or an injury to nail cells, pregnancy or stress.
Leuconychia	White spots caused by injury to the base of the nail.
Onychauxis	Overgrowth of nail caused by a local infection.
Onychatrophia	Nail loses lustre, becomes small and sheds due to injury or disease.
Pterygium	Cuticle adheres to the base of the nail caused by circulatory problems.
Onychophagy	As a result of nervous habit that prompts to chew the nail or harden the cuticle.
Onychorrbpxis	Split or brittle nails caused by injury, vitamin deficiency, illness and exposure to strong soaps.
Hangnail	Nail splits due to dryness of cuticle, cutting off too much cuticle.
Eggshell nails	Have thin white plate usually caused by a chronic illness or defective circulation.
Blue nails	Poor blood circulation or heart disorder.
Bruised nail	Darker, purplish spots due to injury and bleeding in the nail bed.
Treating cuts	Caused by accident during a manicure. Apply anti-septic immediately. Do not buff or apply nail polish on it.

DISEASES OF NAILS

Any nail that shows signs of infection or inflammation causing redness, pain, swelling or pus is a diseased nail. Oxyctosis is the medical term applied to nail disease. People who use hands in water frequently or in an alkaline solution are usually prone to nail disease.

Ringworm of the nails is a highly contagious disease, caused by fungus on the nail bed. The disease invades the free edge and spreads towards the root. There are several nail diseases that you may encounter. Any nail disease that shows sign of infection or inflamma-tion such as redness, swelling or pus must not be treated in a beauty salon. A medical treatment is required for all nail diseases. More than 80% nail infections are seen developed more readily in people, who regularly us their hands in alkaline solution. Natural oil of the skin is lost by frequent exposure to soaps, solvents and other substances. Here are some of the common terms applied to nail diseases.

- **Oxyctosis:** A technical term applied to nail disease.
- **Oxychomycosis (Ringworm of the nail):** An infectious disease caused by a fungus. A common form is while patches that can be scrapped at the surface. The disease invades the free edge and spreads towards the root. The infected portion is thick and discoloured in the third form to deep layer of the nails are invaded causing the super facial layer to appear irregularly thin. These infected layers peel of and expose the diseased parts at the nail bed.
- **Ringworm of the hands:** Highly contagious disease caused by a fungus. The principle symptoms are red lesions are occurring in patches or rings over the hands itching may be tight or severe. Athlete foot may also exist, and in acute conditions, deep, itchy, colourless blisters appear. They spread over the sole and between the toes. When the blisters rupture the skin becomes red and oozes. The lesions dry as hey heal. Prevention of infections and beneficial treatments are accomplished by keeping the skin cool, dry and clean.
- **Koilonychia (Spoon shaped nail):** Causes due to iron deficiency in the body.
- **Parenychia (or felon):** An infectious and inflammatory condition of the tissue surrounding the nail, characterized by gradual thickening and brownish discoloration of the nail plate.

- **Oxychia:** Inflammation of the nail metric accompanied by pus formation.
- **Ingrain Nails:** The nail grows in the flesh on sides, and usually cause infection due to wearing ill-fitting shoes.
- **Oxychoptosis:** Periodic shedding of one or more nails.
- **Oxycholysis:** It is loosening of the nails without shedding. It is frequently associated with an internal disorder.
- **Oxychophosis:** It refers to growth of horny epithelium in the nail bed.
- **Remember:** A nail technician should never draw blood by the careless use of instruments and abrasive buffers. It is better to rely on softening creams and gels to remove dead skin.

TEN IMPORTANT NAIL TIPS

- If you have very soft nails, file them while the polish is still on.
- Apply hand cream every time you wash your hands.
- Wear rubber gloves when doing the washing-up.
- If you have very weak nails, try painting base coat and nail polish under the tips.
- Dry wet nail polish with a cold jet of air from the hair dryer.
- Leave a tiny polish-free gap at the base of the nail where the cuticle meets the nail (the place where new nail cells are growing).
- If you are planning to do some gardening or messy work, drag your nails over a soap bar. The undersides of your nails will fill up with soap and dirt won't be able to get in.
- Clean stains from your fingertips by using a tooth brush and tooth paste on the affected areas.
- Hide cracked or chipped nails under stick-on false ones. This is a temporary solution.
- Use a cotton bud (swab) with a pointed end to clean under your nails.

MANICURING AND PEDICURE

The word manicure is derived from the Latin manus (hand) and cura (care), and means the artful treatment and care of the hands and nails. The word pedicure has its root in the Latin 'Ped' for foot and means the care of the feet and toenails. The purpose of manicures and pedicures is to improve the appearance of the hands, the feet, and their nails.

EVERY WOMAN MUST KNOW

Every woman should have the basic knowledge of:

- The structure of the nail, the composition of the cosmetics used in manicure.
- The ability to give a manicure and pedicure efficiently and effectively.
- The ability to care for the manicuring problems or concerns.
- Thorough knowledge to be able to distinguish between disorders that may be treated by self, in the salon and or by a doctor.
- Thorough awareness of the procedures involved in sanitation and disinfections.

Implements and Tools

The following are the implements you will need for a complete manicure and pedicure services:

1. **Cuticle Nipper:** Small cutting tool used to nip or cut excess cuticle at the base of the nail reusable.
2. **Cuticle Pusher:** Implement used to loosen and push back the cuticle around the fingernails or toenails. It is shaped to conform to the shape of the nails reusable.
3. **Emery Board:** Used for shaping the nails with the coarse side, and smoothing them with the finger side. Hold the emery board at a 45-degree angle and using light pressure. File on the top or underside of the nail.
4. **Nail Brush:** Small brush used to clean under and around the nails, warm water and soap.
5. **Nail Buffer:** Instrument made of leather used with a polishing powder to polish the nails to a high lustre.
6. **Nail Clippers:** Implement used to shorten nails. If the nails are long, Clipping will reduce filing tines.
7. **Nail Filer:** Metal instrument with a specially prepared surface. It is used to file and shape the nails. Use 7" or 8" file and strict sanitation guidelines must be followed before using metal files.
8. **Orangewood Stick:** Stick made from the wood of the orange tree, used to loosen the cuticle around the base of the nail or to clean under the free edge. It should be discarded after use.
9. **Tweezers:** Implement used to lift small bits of cuticle from the nail.

NAIL COSMETICS

The following are some of the most important nail cosmetics. One must develop a strong working knowledge of the cosmetics:

1. **Antiseptic:** Used to prevent infection when there are minor injuries to tissues surrounding the nails.
2. **Base Coat:** Colourless liquid applied to the natural nail before the application of coloured polish. Allow the nail polish to adhere readily to the nail surface. It forms a hard gloss, which prevents the colour in the nail polish from staining the nail plate.
3. **Cuticle Cream:** Special creams that usually have a base of lanolin, petroleum or beeswax. It is designed to prevent or correct brittle nails and dry cuticles.
4. **Cuticle Oil:** Special oil used to soften and lubricate the cuticle around the fingernails and toenails.
5. **Cuticle remover or Solvent:** Solution of alkali, glycerine and water used to soften and remove dead cuticle from around the nail.
6. **Dry nail polish:** Powder or paste used with chamois buffer to add shine to the nail.
7. **Hand cream and hand lotion:** It is recommended for dry, chapped or irritated skin. Hand creams are made up of emollients and add a finishing touch to a manicure. Hand lotions are similar in composition to hand cream but have a thinner consistency due to higher oil content. Hand cream or lotion can be used as oil in a hot oil manicure.
8. **Liquid nail polish or Lacquer:** Keeps nail polish thin enough to flow freely. If the polish is thick, add a little polish solvent and shake well.
9. **Nail bleach:** Used to remove stains and whiten the nails.
10. **Nail conditioner:** Contains moisturizing ingredients to combat dryness and brittleness. Used independently of a manicure, usually overnight, on clear and dry nails.
11. **Nail hardener:** Product designed to prevent nails from splitting or peeling. It must be applied before the base coat to nails that must be thoroughly clean, free of oils or creams and dry. There are three types of hardeners:
    - Protein
    - Formaldehyde
    - Nylon fibre

12. **Nail polish remover:** An organic solvent used to dissolve and remove nail polish. To offset the drying action of the solvent, oil is frequently present in nail polish remover. Use non acetone nail polish remover for women who have artificial nail, because acetone weakens or dissolve tips, wraps glues and sculptures nail compound.
13. **Polish thinner:** Product uses to thin out nail polish where it has thickened, contains acetone or some other solvent.
14. **Top coat or sealer:** Colourless nail enamel applied over polish to protect it, prevent chipping and impact a high gloss.

Materials used during a Manicure or Pedicure:

These include:

- Absorbent cotton, cotton balls for application of cosmetics to nails.
- Cleanser for finger baths preferably in liquid form.
- Cleansing tissue.
- Plastic cups for use in oil manicure heater.
- Plastic spatula for removing creams from jar.
- Powdered alum or alum solution. Aluminium salt used as a styptic (used to stop bleeding).
- Terry cloth. Use fresh towel for each one.
- Chamois for replacing soiled chamois on buffer.

PROCEDURE FOR MANICURE TREATMENT

- **Prepare Manicure Table:** Use soft disinfectant and clean the table. Place a bowl of soft soapy water. Wash your hands with disinfectant. Analyse the skin of hands.
- Take off old polish with an oily remover with the cotton from base of the nail to the tip. Do not smear the old polish into the cuticle or surrounding tissue.
- **Shape Nails with a Nail Filer:** File the nails of left hand from the little finger towards the thumb. Use the filer or emery board to shape the nail. File each nail from corner to the centre, going from right to left and then from left to right. Avoid going too deep into the corners of the nails
- **Soften Cuticles:** After completing the left hand, file the nails of right hand. Then dip fingers of left hand in soapy water for softening the cuticles. Finish filing nails of right hand.

- **Dry Fingertips:** Hold towel with both hands. Carefully dry the left hand Gently loosen and push back the cuticle and skin adjoining on each nail.
- **Apply cuticle remover:** Take a thin layer of cotton on the blunt edge of an orange wood stick considering it as an applicator. Apply cuticle solvent around cuticles of left hand.
- **Loosen cuticle:** Take the spoon end of cuticle pusher and gently loosen the cuticle, keeping cuticle moist and in flat position. To remove dead cuticle stuck to the nail without harming the nail plate.
- Avoid too much pressure while using both cuticle pusher and orange wood stick, to enable save the live tissue from damage.
- Clean under the free edge with cotton tipped orange wood stick dipped in soapy water and clean under free edge from the centre towards each side with gentle pressure.
- Trim cuticle using cuticle nippers or cutter or scissors to remove dead cuticle, hangnails or uneven cuticles.
- Bleach under free edges with cotton tipped orangewood stick. Apply hydrogen peroxide or other bleaching preparation under free edge of each nail of left hand.
- Apply ordinary or cuticle cream or oil around the sides and base of the nail and massage with thumb in the rotating movement.
- Now soften cuticle of right hand. Immerse right hand into finger bowl for giving soap bath. Continue to treat left hand. Remove right hand from the soap bath and treat cuticles as explained above for left hand.
- Dry hands and nails.
- **Bevel nails:** Re-examine the nails for defects. Use fine side of emery board like a nail file to give the nails a smooth bevelled edge.
- Apply liquid polish lightly and quickly, using sweeping strokes from the base to the free edge of the nails. Always keep the polish thick enough to flow freely. If the polish is excessive thick, add a little of polish solvent and then shake it well.
- Remove excess polish. Dip a cotton-tipped orange wood stick into the nail polish remover and apply carefully around the cuticle and nail edges to remove excess polish.
- Apply hand lotion with light manipulations over the hands from wrists to fingertips after the nail polish coat is completely dry.

- A hand massage should be included with each manicure to keep hand flexible and well-groomed and the skin smooth.

DELUXE MANICURE

A deluxe manicure consists of the following steps:

Bleaching

Bleach for 20 minutes. A bleach pack is prepared by mixing the following ingredients:

2 to 3 teaspoons	Kaolin Powder
2 teaspoons	Hydrogen Peroxide (H202)
1 teaspoon	Ammonia

- Perform a normal manicure after massage.
- Conduct vibratory massage for 2-3 minutes.
- Apply Hand Pack by mixing the following ingredients:

3 teaspoons	Almond oil
3 teaspoons	Olive oil
3 teaspoons	Til oil
One	Egg yolk
2 teaspoons	Honey
Kaolin powder	asper requirement

Make paste and apply on hands. When dry, wash it off. Lastly rinse in vinegar water to remove smell of egg.

SUPER DELUXE MANICURE

It is also called Oil Manicure. Bleaching is not done in Super deluxe manicure. The following steps are performed in this manicure treatment:

1. Take 1/2 cup Almond oil.
2. Dip finger in lukewarm oil for 10 to 15 minutes.
3. Give steaming hot towel or cover hands on electrical mitts.
4. Apply hand pack for 10-15 minutes. A thermo herb can be given for wrinkled and aged skin of hands and fingers.
5. Remove pack with lukewarm water.
6. Apply moisturizer.
7. Apply nail varnish or nail paint, if required.

FRENCH MANICURE

There's one look that never goes out of fashion, and that is the French Manicure. It leaves your nails looking clean, fresh and healthy—and matches any style of make-up you wear. There are three steps for doing French Manicure:

1. The basis of the French Manicure is two coats of pale pink polish. Do it in three strokes—one down the middle and one on each side. Apply two coats, giving each one plenty of time to dry. To turn a French manicure into an American manicure, switch the pink polish for a beige one.
2. Now it is the time to paint the tips of your nails with a white polish. If you find it difficult to then free hand, try using the stick-on nail guards that come with many French manicure sets. Rest your hands on a firm surface to keep them steady.
3. Once the white tips of your nails are dry, paint on a clear topcoat of polish and create a chip-resistant finish.

COLOUR CODING OF NAIL POLISH

- **If you have long elegant fingers:** You can carry off any shade of polish, including the dramatic deep red reds, russets and burgundies.
- **If you have short nails:** These nails look best with pale or beige-toned polish.
- **If you have broad nails:** Pale colour will suit. However, you can make them appear slightly narrow by leaving a little space on the sides of each nail unpainted.
- **In case of a tanned skin:** Coral polish and pearlized formulations work wonderfully.

SOFT, SMOOTH HANDS

The age of a person can be guessed from the skin of his or her hands, so the care of hands is as important as for the face and the hair. Here are few steps to keep your hand healthy, soft and smooth:

- Apply a good hand lotion whenever going out.
- Use a good hand cream every time you wash your hands.
- Keep your nail file with a nail-cutter and a pair of nail scissors to prevent infection.
- Change your nail-varnish once a week. Let your nails breathe for the night and apply fresh nail-varnish next day.

- Have a professional manicure once in a month in a beauty parlour.
- Apply milk cream to your hands at night. Add a few drops of lemon juice and glycerine to it and rub to your hands.
- Massage hands and fingers with almond oil at night before going to bed on alternate days.
- Mix glycerine, rose water or cucumber juice in equal quantity and rub on hands with a cotton wool swab to clean the skin and improve its complexion.
- Wash hands with water mixed to vinegar or lemon juice to ward off the ill effects of hot water, soda, soap and detergents.
- Use hand lotion in winter to relieve dryness of the skin. If the skin is too dry, add carbolic acid to vaseline and rub in your hands.
- If skin of your hands is rough, take a spoonful of sugar or honey mixed to lemon juice on your hands. Rub palms till sugar dissolves, then wash off with cold water.
- If the skin of your hands is coarse and rough, rub pulp of boiled, peeled potatoes on the hands and fingers.
- Hairy hands look ugly. Unwanted hair can be removed by waxing, or hidden by bleaching once a fortnight or a month.
- Use a rich cream after steaming the hands, if the skin is wrinkled.
- Use skin-food cream and wear gloves over night, if the skin of your hands is cracked.
- Use bleaching cream and wear cotton gloves during night on tanned hands.

TREATMENT FOR HANDS, FEET AND NAILS

The hands and feet benefit from essential oil treatment, as much as any other part of the body does. Besides beautifying and providing protection, they help in healing wounds, burns and viral or fungal infection. Certain vegetable oils are often most important ingredients in the treatment of hands and fingers for softening cuticles, correct splitting or flaking nails, strengthening them and encouraging new growth. Essential oils and vegetable oils provide the tools for effective hand treatments. They are used in hand massage, intensive hand therapy, as well as in treatments for specific conditions such as eczema, psoriasis, warts, infections, wounds and burns. However, by using appropriate essential oils and vegetable oils, the therapist or nail technician has the tools to perform the following tasks:

- Soften the skin
- Tone the skin
- Help reduce the visible signs of ageing
- Heal broken skin
- Reduce any fuel congestion in the hands and fingers
- Soothe aching muscles

HERBAL PREPARATIONS FOR HAND AND FEET

Add 10 drops of essential oil (choosing from essential oil profile depending on the function you wish to perform) in the following ingredients, which can be blended to make a basic hand cream:

Cocoa Butter	15 gm.
Bees wax	15 gm.
Almond oil	40 ml.
Evening primrose oil	5 drops
Carrot oil	5 drops

Melt the cocoa butter and the beeswax. Add to it almond oil, evening primrose and carrot oils. Mix together well. The basic hand cream can be made thinner by adding more almond oil, or thicker by including less almond oil at the outset. Add essential oil when the blend is complete, and mix in well. The follow-ing essential oils can be added to basic hand cream, or to vegetable oils, or to products especially designed for the addition of essential oils. The choice of essential oils depend on the specific function you require of the hand massage, and is not limited to those below:

- Geranium
- Rose
- Peppermint
- Lemon
- Palmarosa
- Lavender

Foot Freshener Astringent

Mix the following ingredients into a large bottle and shake well:

Rose water	¼ cup
Witch-hazel	¼ cup
Distilled water	¼ cup
Spirit of camphor B.P.	1 tablespoon
Alum	a pinch

Dab on with a wad of cotton wool to cool hot, tired feet. Cucumber juice also cools aching feet, especially in summer.

Thyme and Rosemary Foot Lotion

Add a few drops of the essential oil of either herb to a cup -ful of olive oil and rub into the affected area.

Rosemary Jelly

Collect the following ingredients:

Rosemary water	8 tablespoons
Glycerine	1 tablespoon
Arrowroot	2 tablespoons
Arrowroot	2 tablespoons

Heat rosemary, water and glycerine in two separate bowls over water bath. Stir the arrowroot into glycerine to make a smooth paste, then add to it rosemary water. Continue to heat over simmering water, stirring all the time, until the mixture becomes like jelly.

Balm for Corns

Collect the following ingredients:

Coconut oil or lard	50 gm.
Camphor oil	30 ml.
Turpentine oil	15 ml.

Melt oil or fats in a bowl over boiling water. Beat the remaining ingredients until the mixture cools. Rub corns with this balm daily in the morning and at night.

Lanolin Cuticle Cream

Lanolin is an excellent cuticle cream. Mix to a paste two tablespoons lanolin with two teaspoons of kaolin or powdered lecithin.

Petroleum Jelly Cuticle Cream

Mix two tablespoons of pure petroleum jelly with ½ teaspoon glycerine and a drop of red food colouring. Beat them together to make a paste.

Hand Paste

To make a protective hand paste, mix together into a paste yolk of one egg, two teaspoons kaolin and one teaspoon almond oil. This paste can also be used on knees, elbows and feet.

Oatmeal Hand Mask

Mix to a paste the following ingredients:

1.5 tablespoon	Oatmeal
1 tablespoon	Warm Water
1 teaspoon	Olive oil
1 teaspoon	Lemon juice
1 teaspoon	Glycerine

Apply to your hands this mask for 10 to 15 minutes, and it leaves them beautifully soft.

Hand Massage Strokes

These are divided into five parts as below:

- **Fingers:** Massage the nail plate, cuticle and knuckle clockwise, then anti-clockwise. Now twist the fingers twice and pull. Finally, rub between finger and pinch. The last step is, physiotherapy of finger clockwise and anti-clockwise.
- **From knuckle to the wrist:** Start with vibration 3 times. Now iron out with both hands holding tightly. Iron out again.
- **Palm:** Vibrate 3 times from palm to fingertips. Now inter-lock the fingers and rub the palm, then hold the finger between thumbs and shake the hands. Now inter-lock the fingers again and rotate the wrist clockwise, anti-clockwise, up and down.
- **From wrist to elbows:** Vibrations 3 times, then cupping the elbows massage on inner elbow.
- **From elbows to the wrist of the fingers:** Massage with pinching, hacking and vibration movements going upward. Continue with roll patting movement coming downward. Have physiotherapy of elbows and release tension from the middle finger.

Applying Hand Pack

Collect the following ingredients:

3 teaspoons	Almond oil
3 teaspoons	Olive oil
3 teaspoons	Till oil
2 teaspoons	Honey
One	Egg yolk
Sufficient Quantity	Kaolin powder or gram flour.

Make a Paste

Apply on hands. When dry, wash it off. In the last rinse in vinegar water to relieve smell of egg.

Remedies for Smelly Feet

- Use an infusion of whit willow bark mixed with a pinch of borax and use as a footbath.
- Mix 1/2 teaspoon powdered alum with 300 ml of warm water and use as a footbath. This reduces sweating and acts as a deodo-rant.
- Massage feet with a mixture of 6 tablespoons of witch-hazel and one teaspoon each glycerine and tincture of arnica. Avoid using in case of broken skin.

Herbal Preparations for Kibes and Corns (feet and hands)

Persons not wearing socks generally suffer from cracking of feet (known as Kibes). Most of the times, lack of moisture and oil can bring about such a condition. In most cases, it is not a painful condition, but in some cases where the inner muscle is involved, it is very painful. The herbal preparations described below are helpful in treating this condition.

Beeswax Ointment

Boil together the following ingredients:

Bees-wax (madhu-mom)	1 teaspoon
Sesame oil	4 tablespoons
Finely ground resin	1 tablespoon

Wax and oil should be boiled and finely ground resin be nixed to it. The mixture should be further cooked for a few minutes till it gains the consistency of an ointment, which fills the cracks.

Astringent Foot Freshener

Collect the following ingredients:

Rose water	¼ cup
Witch-hazel	¼cup
Distilled water	¼ cup
Spirit of Camphor B.P.	1 tablespoon
Alum	a pinch

Mix all the ingredients into a large bottle and shake well. Dab on with a wad of cotton wool to cool hot, tired feet.

Almond Hand Cream

Almond Hand Cream is very luxurious cream and should be used after washing your hands. Apply to your hands for 10 to 15 minutes, and it leaves them beautifully soft. Mix to a paste the following ingredients:

Lanolin	2 tablespoons
Cocoa butter	1.5 teaspoons
Beeswax	1 tablespoon
Light liquid paraffin	5 teaspoons
Almond oil	1 teaspoon

Melt together the above ingredients over a water bath and slowly add to it borax dissolved in water. Mix ¼ teaspoon borax in two tablespoons water and stir thoroughly so that it is dissolved completely.

Vinegar Hand Lotion

Vinegar when mixed to oil and rubbed together on the hands produces a magical effect.

Nail Stains Remover

Mix the following ingredients together:

Glycerine	1 tablespoon
Hydrogen peroxide	4 tablespoons
Rose water	5 tablespoons

Apply the above recipe to bleach the skin of your fingers. This recipe is very useful for ladies who smoke, and their fingers get stained due to nicotine.

Nail Bleaching Lotion

If your nails become discoloured, apply lemon bleach in a bottle and use:

Orange flower water	3 tablespoons
Lemon juice	1 teaspoon

Nail Varnish Remover

Add a teaspoon of glycerine to 50 ml bottle of acetone and apply to your nails. Glycerine prevents acetone from drying. Acetone can be procured from a chemist shop.

Nail Hardening Lotion

Paint the nails with hardening or strengthening solution on tips at night for a month and then weekly. Massage a nail lotion into cuticles once or twice a week. Another way is to soak brittle nails to warm oil several times a week. You can use olive oil, almond oil or even castor oil. The same oil can be poured back into the bottle.

For nail strengthening, there are few recipes.

- Take daily a dose of 1 tablespoon of unflavoured gelatine.
- Two to three kelp tablets can be taken daily to strengthen the nails.
- Blue iris flowers steeped in water overnight and brushed regularly on the nails will strengthen the nails.
- To prevent brittleness, make an infusion of elm leaves. Steep clean nails in this preparation daily.

HAND MASSAGE AND EXERCISES

Hand massage and exercise both help the circulation and relieve tension and stiffness. Always massage towards the wrist using the thumb and index finger. Make small rotary movements on each joint with little finger. The following exercises should be practised daily:

- Stretch your fingers out as tautly as possible, relax and then throw them out again. Repeat this several times.
- Shake your hands until they are completely relaxed and limp.
- Circle your hands from the wrist, making the circle as deep as possible. Repeat this several times.

CARING THE FEET

Beauty starts with the feet. The most beautiful face will show the strain of tired, aching feet. They will also cause a loss of balance in your walk and promote tension and irritability. Never wear high heels, pointed shoes etc. as these prove harmful with difficult feet. The following simple exercises will help a great deal when the feet have been constricted in shoes all day:

- Sit with legs crossed. Rotate the feet six times towards each other and six times away from each other.
- Sit with legs stretched, straight out in front. Bend the toes up as far as possible and then down as far as possible.
- Put a pencil on the floor and try to pick it up with your toes; this will strengthen the feet.
- Sit on a chair with feet on the floor and spread out the toes as far as you can. This will tone up the feet muscles.

WARTS ON HANDS AND FEET

Warts on the fingers and hands are very common and are often difficult to cure. Warts are caused due to a virus, anti-viral essential oils are used in their treatment. Warts are small epidemic growth, which vary in size and shape and are commonly of three types: Plane warts, common warts and planter warts. Plane warts are the simplest of all warts, and usually small, smooth and skin-coloured or brownish lesions, which rise on the surface of the skin. The common place of occurrence for such warts is usually the face and outer surface of the hands. The most commonly affected are children and young adults. A step more than plane warts are common warts. These are largest and firmer elevations with a rough surface and usually occur on the hands, forearms, knees and upper side of the feet. Planter warts are slightly different and appear on the weight-bearing areas. They do not protrude much above the surface and normally contain blood vessels.

Herbal Remedies to Cure Warts

- **Banana Skin:** Strap a small piece of banana skin, soft side down, over the wart and leave overnight. Repeat this for seven days. A piece of pineapple wrapped over the wart works equally well.
- **Garlic Rubbing:** Rub your wart with garlic.
- **Onion liquid:** Cut an onion in half. Scoop out the centre of one half and fill the cavity with coarse sea salt. Allow this to dissolve and use the resulting liquid on the wart for at least 30 days.
- **Lemon and Vinegar use:** The pure juice of a lemon or vinegar in which the rinds of two lemons have been macerated is a simple remedy.
- **Celandine, dandelion, figwort, houseleek or fig stalk:** The juice of any of these herbs, applied through a small piece of cardboard with a suitable-sized hole cut in it will remove a wart if used for three to four days.

Herbal Cure For Nails

It is usually seen, aroma therapists have no trouble with their own nails, which grow strong and long because of constant contact with the essential oils. Fixed vegetable oils also play an important role in nail care. The vegetable oils, such as jojoba, rosehip seed, borage, apricot and kernel are very useful for nail bed treatment. Whereas, vegetable oils such as avocado, wheat germ, red carrot root are beneficial for softening the cuticle.

The nails often become discoloured and appear unhealthy because they have been continuously covered with varnish for long periods of time, or following acrylic nail remover. When the nails become soft and unhealthy they are at risk of infections, including fungal infection. Suggested essential oils in this regard include tea tree, lavender, lemon, thyme linalol and lemon grass.

Chemical Reaction

Be careful with the health problems or an adverse skin or nail reaction or allergies caused by the chemicals found in nail related products as described below:

Chemical	Potentialm Problem Attributed
MMA	Headache, dizziness, toxicity, dry hands, itching, rashes and allergies. Acetone Skin irritation, rashes, dry patches on the hands or the body.
Benzoyl peroxide	Harsh on sensitive and delicate skin, inflammation.
Formaldehyde	Headache, dizziness, faintness, and nausea.
Hydroquinone	Rashes, redness and dry skin,
Oleic acid	Skin rashes and itching.

Foot Treatment with Essential Oils

When essential oils are used for foot treatments, they help to stimulate the circulation and refresh, or relax the whole body. Treatment can begin with a Foot Bath, using a cleansing product that contains essential oils with anti-bacterial and anti-fungal action. Simply add essential oils with those properties to the water. Foot infections are picked up by walking barefoot in public places, swimming pools, gyms and even beauty parlours. Anti-bacterial or anti-fungal essential oils can be used in foot treatments, whether you have a problem or not. Following a bath, dry the feet and spray with a refreshing hydrolat.

FOOT MASSAGE

Essential oils can be diluted in fixed vegetable oils, or added to the cream or lotions designed for use with essential oils such as tea tree, thyme linalol, nutmeg, grapefruit, rosemary, spear-mint and frankincense. Fixed vegetable oils, with or without essential oils, can be used to soften cuticles, or after the removal of hard skin. In case of nail bed infection, apply neat tea tree. However, verrucas and athelete's foot disorders are not within the scope of beauty therapy, but these essential oils can be very effective in these areas.

The feet are extremely well supplied with nerve endings. Reflexology utilises this fact to stimulate precise areas of the foot that correspond to organs and certain areas of the muscular and skeletal system. Gentle foot massage (reflexology) provides fantastic result. Use essential oils that have an effect on the whole body, by being either relaxing or stimulating.

Procedure for the Pedicure

Care of feet, legs and toenails is said as Pedicure treatment. Foot cares not only improves personal appearance but adds to the comfort as the whole weight of the body rest on feet alone. Abnormal foot conditions include corns, callous and ingrown nails. People with athlete foot (watery blisters) and thick white skin between the toes or other foot infection should not be given a pedicure.

Equipment and Material required for a Pedicure: The equipment required for a pedicure are the same as for manicuring. The following additional items are needed:

1. Low stool for cosmetologist.
2. A tilted (sliding) seat or stool to rest foot.
3. Two basins of warm water enough for footbath (electrically operated foot-bath tub with water heater are available in market).
4. Waterproof apron or Turkish towel placed over the lap to protect dress of the pedicurist.
5. Two towels for drying feet.
6. Special toenail nippers.
7. Antiseptic solution.
8. Cotton or foot powder.
9. A foot mat.

Preparing for a Pedicure

- Seat the customer on the chair and let her remove the shoes and socks.
- Wash hand with antiseptic lotion.
- Let the customer keep her feet on the footrest.
- Fill both basins with warm water sufficient to cover the ankles. Add antiseptic to one basin and place both feet in it for 3-5 minutes.
- Remove feet from the basin, dry.
- Add soap and antiseptic to other basin. Make lather.

Procedure

The following steps are undertaken:

- Remove oil nail polish from the nails of both feet.
- File nails with emery board. Shape the nails straight across.
- Do not cut or file the corners of nails. Smoothen rough edges with fine side of emery board.
- Place left foot in warm soapy water.
- Shape nails of right foot.
- Remove left foot from basin and dry.
- Apply cuticle solution with cotton tipped orange wood stick and under the free edge of each toenail.
- Place right foot in bath.
- Loosed cuticle gently on left foot. Keep it moist and loosen with the cotton tipped orange wood stick.
- Rinse the left foot and dry massage each toe with cuticle cream or oil.
- Repeat the whole process on other feet.

How to Massage Feet?

- Apply coconut oil or cream over the feet for massage.
- Commence the massage with fingers with firm rotating movements.
- Slide thumbs firmly and repeat same movement, from instep down to the centre of the toes and back.
- Start at the heel and work down to the centre of the toes.
- Slide back forcefully to heel and repeat massage movement on both feet alternatively.

- Hold small toe in one hand and big toe in the other hand and give three rotating movements. Repeat the same on the other toes.
- Slide right hands to the ankles and palm of your left to the ball of the foot. Apply six firm rotating movements. Repeat the same on other foot.
- Remove coconut oil from both feet with warm moist towel.
- Apply astringent with cotton wool. Complete with dusting powder.

How to Keep feet Odour-free, Silky and Sexy?

To keep feet odour-free, take the following steps:

1. Dry feet and your toes after bathing because bacteria thrive in moist conditions.
2. Spray feet with a mixture of water and rose water after working.
3. Soak your feet in a tub containing tepid water to which a little lavender oil has been added.
4. Change your socks in case you sweat a lot, after changing shoes.
5. Wear open-toed sandals and shoes as your feet and nails need breathing space.
6. Dry out your shoes overnight if they are sweat-wet.
7. Gently scrub hard soles with a mixture of lemon juice and sugar to prevent calluses.
8. Use a mix of wheat bran and milk to cleanse off the grime and to smoothen and to smoothen rough skin.
9. Mash five strawberries and mix to it 2 tablespoons of olive oil and 1 tsp salt. Massage into your feet for 5 to 10 minutes. Rinse with warm water and pat dry. This will result soft, smooth and sweet-smelling feet.
10. Mix a tablespoon of oatmeal in a cup of water. Dip a fine pumice stone or a sponge in it and rub it over the base and sides of your feet. It will smoothen dull skin and slough off the dead skin.
11. Massage and exercise feet by placing a ball or feet roller under the feet and gently roll it along the foot's entire length.
12. Mix half-teaspoon turmeric powder to half of a freshly grated coconut and gently massage it on your feet. Leave on for five minutes and rinse with warm water. Now make a paste of 250 gm grated carrots and 2 tablespoons of gelatine and pamper your feet with it. It helps condition the skin with essential nutrients after the exfoliating process.

13. Dip your tired feet in a bowl of milk to which heavy cream has been added. It gives lot of pleasantness to your feet.
14. Rough, cracked heels can be cured with a good soak in warm water to which a few drops of tea tree oil and 1 tsp of glycerine is added. When the water cool down, remove your feet, pat dry and rub camphor on the heels. This relaxes tensed muscles of your feet.
15. Mix some precious pearl powder with cream and slather feet with it. This will nourish the feet.
16. Massage your feet with sandalwood essential oil (diluted in water). This will ease the foot pain (if exist) and enhance sexual awareness in you.
17. Soak your feet in warm olive oil or sunflower oil for 10 to 15 minutes.
18. Use a mix of wheat bran and milk to cleanse off the grime and to smoothen rough skin.

Mudras—To heal without medication

1. **Gyan Mudra:** Touch tip of thumb with the tip of the index finger and the remaining fingers straight. You may perform this mudra with both hands, anywhere any time for duration as long as possible. Benefits: Cures mental disorders, diseases like madness, Hysteria, depression, laziness, angry behaviour, mental concentration and cures sleeplessness.
2. **Prithvi Mudra:** Touch ring finger and thumb, and press them to each other. Perform practice for as long as you desire. Benefits: Helps to gain weight. Increases the lustre of skin and removes all kinds of physical weakness.
3. **Varun Mudra:** Put together tips of thumb and little finger. Benefits: Restore moisture in the body and remove impurities of the blood and disorders like gastroenteritis and pain due to cramps.
4. **Vayu Mudra:** Keep index finger on the base of thumb and press. Practice this mudra for 45 minutes daily.

   Benefits: Cures rheumatism, arthritis, gout, Parkinsone's disease(trembling of hands), palsy of face, stiff neck or cervical spondylosis.
5. **Shunya Mudra:** Keep the middle finger at the top of Venus and press with thumb. Practice this mudra for 40-45 minutes daily.

6. **Benefits:** Cures deafness, diseases of ears. In case the deafness is since birth, the treatment will not be effective.
7. **Surya-Mudra:** Bend ring finger and press with the tip of thumb as shown in the illustration. Practice daily twice in the morning and evening for 5 to 15 minutes.

   Benefits: Include to reduce extra weight and mental tension.
8. **Jalodarnashak Mudra:** Bend little finger touching the base of the thumb pressing hard.

   Benefits: Cure diseases caused by excess water.

10

FACE MASSAGE

HOW TO MASSAGE THE FACE?

Remove a little cleansing cream from the jar and blend it with the fingers to soften it. Using both hands apply cream over the face. Start at the chin and with a sweeping movement slide to end of jaw, from base of nose to temple, along the side of nose, between the brows, and across forehead to temples. Take additional cream, blend it, smooth down the neck, chest and back. Start massaging at the center of fore-head, move lightly around eyes, then towards temples and back to the center of the forehead. Slide down nose to upper lip, smooth to temples and forehead, then move lightly down to chin and finally slide up towards jaw line, temples and forehead. Remove cream with cleansing tissues or warm moist towel. Emollient (tissue) cream selected according to skin type should be applied in the same manner as indicated above. Use lanolin or hormone cream for a dry skin and cold cream for an oily skin.

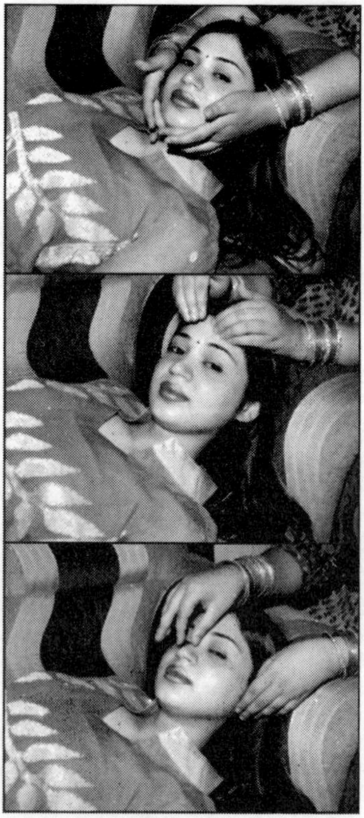

Face Massage

Selection of Cream

For neck, face, shoulder and chest, apply emollient cream. Apply eye cream (readily available in market) under the eyes gently with fingertips. Use muscle oil around the neck. For massaging face apply a massage cream giving manipulations using slightly cupped hands and fingers. Start massage under the lower lip with two fingers. Repeat process several times. Pinch gently along the jaw line, working outward ears.

Massage—The Magic of Hands

Massage is one of the easiest ways for attaining and maintaining health, youth, vigor and beauty. Aches, pains, insomnia, tension and stress can be alleviated with the simple instrument-Hands. A touch of massage has great value in maintaining beauty and body. According to expert's advice, when couples touch each other and embrace, can prevent physical and mental illness. It improves circulation, relaxes muscles, aid digestion by stimulating the lymphatic system. It eliminates waste products, provides energy, refreshes and revitalize the body.

WHAT IS 'MASAH'?

The word massage has been derived from the Arabic word 'Masah'—which means the magic of hands. Early morning massage just after waking up has a miraculous effect on the various organs. To get beneficial results, it is important that massage is given in a comfortable environment. For that choose a warm, peaceful place with dim lights. Always lie on a firm, padded surface to relax the back and the stomach. Place a cushion under the knees to reduce the arch of the lower hack. Also place a small cushion or folded towel under the head to raise it. An hard bed is ideal if you want to give a soothing massage, which can leave you relaxed and sleepy. Keep your hack straight throughout the massage and use the weight of your body to give rhythm and depth to the massage. Keep in mind the following precautions when giving a massage:

- Never stay in one position when massaging.
- Wear loose-fitting washable clothes and flat shoes, or be bare-footed.
- Remove ornament before massage, it can cause scratches.
- Support a sway back with a cushion under the waist and put a cushion under one shoulder for a relaxing massage.

EXERCISING THE HANDS

Exercising the hands increase their sensitivity and flexibility. The following exercises keep the hands supple:

1. Hold a rubber ball in one hand and squeeze. Relax the finger repeatedly. Then follow this procedure on the other hand.
2. Rotate and stretch each finger and thumb in each direction one by one. Then pull it gently with the other hand.
3. Press and hold the fingers against each other. The palms, however, should not touch.

MASSAGING TIPS AND TECHNIQUES

1. A rhythmic massage sends waves of relaxation throughout the body.
2. If you feel pain or an uncomfortable situation during massage, inform the masseur.
3. Mould your hands to the contours of the body.
4. Vary your pressure from very light to very strong. The massage should be lighter over bony areas and firmer over the muscles.
5. Do not apply heavy pressure when massaging.
6. Concentrate on the massage. Avoid talking when massaging.
7. Feel totally relaxed for a good massage.
8. Do not worry if your initial movements seem clumsy. Practice will make you perfect.

Avoid Massage, if you suffer from:

- An infection or a contagious skin disease.
- High temperature.
- Skin infection, bruises or an acute inflammation.
- An inflammatory condition such as thrombosis or phlebitis.
- Inflammatory cases of cases of joints.
- Infectious diseases like diphtheria and gonorrhea, which causes formation of pus; a massage may spread the pus to entire system.

Precautions When Massaging the Face?

1. For an effective massage, clean the facial skin.
2. Start massage from the neck upward and end at the forehead or temples because all veins and tissues get blood circulation.
3. Do not press the delicate skin around the eyes.
4. Massage for a minimum of 15-20 minutes as cream takes that

much time to get absorbed. Wipe off extra cream with a cotton swab.

5. Wash hands with soap before starting massage.
6. Remove all traces of stale make-up or fresh make-up before massage, otherwise the skin pores will get blocked.
7. Remove oiliness with cleansing milk or pH acid, if the skin is too oily.
8. Use moisturizer before massage, if the skin is over dry.
9. Use astringent lotion before massage, if the skin is damp.
10. If the skin is fleshy use a massage cream.
11. The best time to massage a face is at night before going to bed.

Important Facial Massage Movements

Movement	*Place on the face*
Linear movement	Applied with fingers on forehead and temples.
Circular movement	Start at eyebrow towards the hairline.
Criss-cross movement	Start at the forehead and back.
Stroking movement	Over brows, forehead and temples with pressure by the fingers.
Brow and eye movement	Around the eyes.
Down to the mouth	On the side of nose towards down.
Lip and Chin movement	Upper lip towards lower lip and chin.
Optional movement	Around the mouth from upper to lower lip.
Lifting movement	From mouth to ear and nose to ear.
Rotational movement	From chin to ear lobes on cheeks.
Tapping movement	From chin to earlobe on both sides of face.
Stroking movement	On the neck in front side, downward and on sides.
Circular movement	At the back of ears towards shoulders and across the chest.
Slow and fast massage	Done slowly and lightly with soft fleshy fingers. Done by the front halves of both the palms. This movement helps in removing wrinkles.
Pressure Massage	Applied with fleshy fingertips. Removes pouches under the eyes.
Stroking Movement	On cheeks. Recommended in case of broad nose.
Pinching Movement	Skin to be massaged is held between the thumbs and fingers. It cures wrinkles and double chin.
Kneading Movement	Done as if kneading the flour. Start from chin to the cheeks upwards.

TEN STEPS FOR TEN-MINUTES REFRESHING MASSAGE

1. Rest your forearms on the shoulders to reduce tension.
2. Stroke firmly up the back on either side of the spine.
3. Knead the muscles across the top of the shoulders with both hands, squeezing and releasing the flesh.
4. Calm the shoulder muscles pressing gently to drain out tension.
5. Place your thumbs on either side of the spine holding the pressure for few seconds, followed by stroking the upper and lower back and shoulder blades.
6. Massage the back of the neck at the base of the scull with the right hand applying circular pressure and supporting the head with the left hand.
7. Use both hands to massage head, including the area around the ears, temples and forehead.
8. Rub hair briskly back and forth with fingertips to relieve tension.
9. Stimulate shoulders and upper back with the sides of the hands. Keep hands relaxed.
10. Soothe the whole back with rhythmic massage movements, followed by the feather stroke.

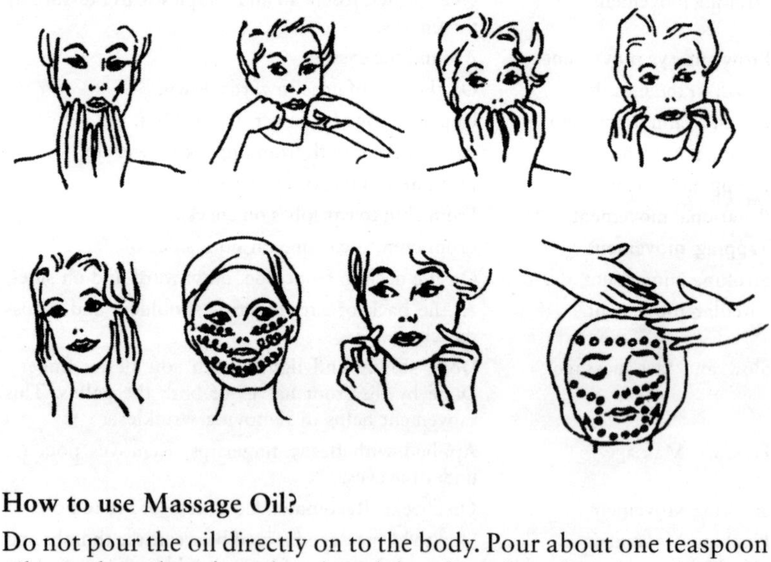

How to use Massage Oil?

Do not pour the oil directly on to the body. Pour about one teaspoon oil into the palm of one hand. Rub hands and stroke oil on the body.

Massage with essential oils is very useful for the skin, vigor and vitality. Some people with excessive oily skin use talcum powder for a dry massage. Use a light vegetable oil scented with few drops of essential oil.

FEW MASSAGE TECHNIQUES

Reflexology and Relaxation Massage

It is a 75-minute treatment in which finger pressure is applied to the reflex zones of the feet to stimulate the internal organs and systems of the body, helping to activate the body's natural healing ability and to restore balance. A relaxing massage promotes the further release of the tension in the nervous and muscular systems.

Reflexology in the neck and head is a 30-minute treatment focusing the head and the neck. It helps to produce a decongestive effect, stimulate blood circulation, reduce inflammation, lower blood pressure, alleviates migraine and headache pain. It is highly relaxing and strongly recommended for eliminating stress.

Relaxing massage is a special 50-minute treatment for relieving accumulated stress, reducing muscle fatigue and improving blood circulation.

Therapeutic Massage

It is an ideal massage for the treatment of sensitive areas affected by muscular tension, stress and fatigue.

Sports massage is another 50-minute treatment for before or after sports activities. It helps to maximize performance potential, reduces muscle fatigue and eliminates toxins produced in the muscles during physical exercise.

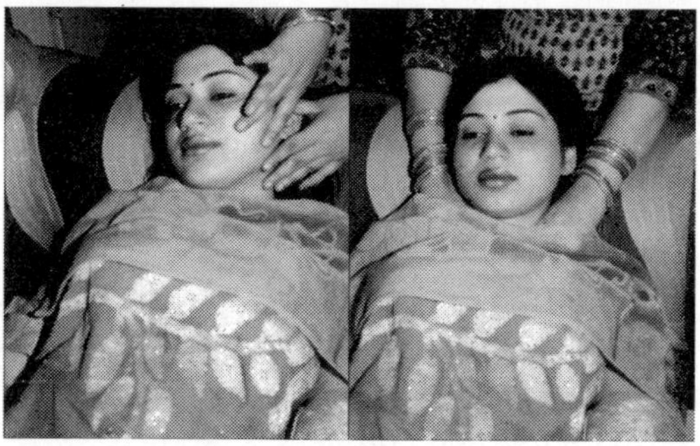

Face Massage

Anti-cellulite Massage

A reductive massage that works in zones with the highest concentrations of cellulite. Special movements are used to generate heat to help dissolve body fat. Ideally, it should be followed with a Sauna session and completed with a Shower bath.

Lymphatic Drainage

A massage therapy technique, which helps to detoxify the skin and promotes its renewal. The massage movement helps to drain toxins and prevents premature ageing.

Shiatsu Massage

In Japanese 'Shi' means finger, and 'Atsu' means the pressure. This massage movement in which the fingers, palms and sometimes elbow are used to exercise pressure on specific points of the body to stimulate energy channels and the internal organs. This massage technique reduces stress, alleviates aches, pains, fatigue and symptoms of a variety of diseases.

Ultrasonic Massage Therapy

This therapy provides glow, improves blood circulation, activates sebaceous glands, improves dry skin and is especially effective for dull and sallow skin. It works through an electric device. It is a highly effective massage treatment in deep penetration of skin much beneficial to do in winter.

Suction Massage Therapy

This massage therapy can suck out the infection, unfriendly bacteria, dirt, dust, germs from the upper layer of the epidermis and from deeper stratum in order to treat the secretion from the root. This electric therapy is totally safe, which is performed by the compressor. The benefits of this therapy include tightening of the skin, leaves skin germs free, helps in controlling sebum, improves blood circulation and removes infection.

Thai Massage

Thai Massage is a therapy recognized as an effective mean of reducing stress, pain, muscular and general relaxation, recovery from injury, circulation of blood and lymph and restoration of metabolic balance.

Traditional Thai massage is a combination of acupressure, breathing technique, gentle stretches and beautiful postures. Thai massage stimulates the free flow of energy along the lines and the balance is restored to the whole person physically, emotionally, mentally and spiritually. Thai massage should be performed on the floor with matteress on it, which takes every joint through its range of movement and stretch of every muscle, leaving the body relaxed and revitalized.

Thai massage was started in Thailand around the same time as Buddhism, about the 3rd century B.C. Its benefits include:

1. Deep relaxation pressure on feet and legs are sedating.
2. Releases point of tension in the body, which blocks the natural flow of energy, including hormone stasis balance and harmony.
3. Releases strength and increase energy.
4. Increases flexibility and range of motion.
5. Helps in alignment and postural integrity of the body.
6. Improves blood circulation.
7. Strengthens the internal organs.
8. Promotes inner peace and quite mind.
9. Most suitable for postnatal mothers.
10. Improves neurological functions.

THE REJUNVENATION THERAPIES

Siddha Vaidya and Ayurveda are the useful therapies in which special herbal oils and herbs are used that trigger changes in mind and organs of the body to bring balance and harmony to the overall system. The herbs called adaptogens react in the body that is appropriate to achieve a state of homerostasis or balance. They affect the autonomic nervous system, the endocrine system and the blood pressure. Adaptogens are credited with these properties. Help the body adapt to stress, achieve body balance, increase protein biosynthesis, elevate body enzymes synthesis, promote general endocrine synthesis, improve mental power, increase physical ability, fight free radicals, improve eyesight, beneficial to cardio-vascular and respiratory system and improve specific resistance to various stressors like heat, cold, wind.

The following naturopathic therapies are beneficial:

1. **Shirodhara:** Thin thread of warmed oil is poured over the fornd scalp. Shirodhara calms the mind, pacifies vatha, cleanses, stress calms and balances the nervous system, relieves/stress and improves mental power. Shirodhara improves the body's heat

and is used before the rejuvenation (Kriya Karma) therapies, Shirodhara should be repeated three to four times a week for optimal benefit.

2. **Nasaya:** A procedure aimed at reducing waste products from the head, throat and nose in human body. Nasaya is the introduction of medicated substances into the nose, stimulate secretion, remove impurities of the head and neck. The primary effect of the treatment is to improve the connection between different organs of perception. Nasaya is used in headaches, sinusitis, nervousness, migraines, vascular headache, stiff neck, running eyes, ear infections, hearing loss, tinnitus, loss of smell and much more. This treatment can be used several times a week in conjuction with other therapies like reflexology and head massage.
3. **Rasayanas:** This means rejuvenate system and tissue—is a beneficial treatment for the face and the scalp to encompass a head to toe beauty along with other treatments such as:
    - Massage (abhyanga)
    - Steam (svedana)
    - Pastes and masques (snehana)
    - Use of herbs
    - Foot reflexology
    - Face and scalp treatments
    - Aromatherapy
    - Colour Therapy (chromotherapy)
    - Panchkarma (cleansing and strengthening)
    - Kriya Karma (rejuvenation)
    - Crystals and gems therapy)
    - Purva Karma (for maintaining health to help Panchkarma or Kriya Karma)

    The above therapies and body treatments leave your skin looking and feeling fresh and healthy.
4. **Siddha Massage:** It promotes relaxation, calming of vitha, kapha and pitha. It balances and increases the circulation of body's largest eliminative organ—the skin. It also aids and facilita-tes the removal of waste products into the central circulation from where it is removed. It increases lymph flow, strengthens the immune system and relieves muscle tension. The mobility of the ligaments, tendons and joints is increased, thereby adding to the

flexibility of the body organs besides helping to clam, relax, tone and balance nervous system. It can be used to treat sleeplessness, Siddha massage regulates the other systems and organs such as the digestive and eliminative system known to increase the production of collagen and elastin fibres and aids in the removal and preventing wrinkling and suppleness of the skin besides to relieve muscle spasm and pain of chronic and acute origin.

5. **Abhganga:** The therapy is recommended for muscle soreness, joint pain and stiffness, nervousness, tension, stress, lack of energy, restlessness, immune dysfunction, fatigue and tiredness, paralysis or presis of traumatic origin injury, poor digestion, poor elimination, sleeplessness and ungrounded feelings.
6. **Panchkarma:** Panchkarma means, 5 action—'an ancient scientific system for detoxification.' It rejuvenates the whole system, bringing youthfulness and strength on the body and calms openness to the mind. Traditionally, it is undertaken as preventive therapy at the change of seasons, the aim to cleanse the body not only of waste materials in the body, but also excessive in subtle energies or tissues, thereby promoting positive health and longevity through the changing climatic conditions.
7. **Ozone Therapy:** It includes producing alkaline rays used for both scalp and facial skin treatments such as itchy scalp, dandruff, acne, pimples and busting pussy infection. This therapy is performed by using anti-allergic, antiseptic and sterilized powder.
8. **Micro Therapy:** It is a power massaging therapy to treat, ageing, skins showing signs of laughing lines, frown lines, crowfeet. This therapy helps to improve blood circulation, stimulate nerves and muscles, regenerate cells and tissues, face lifting and promotes the elastic fibers of the skin.
9. **H.F. Therapy:** The primary action of this treatment is thermal heat produced due to rapid vibrations but without muscular contractions. This therapy helps solving eye disorders and contributes for life-long physiotherapy techniques to give instant and excellent results. The beneficial results of HF therapy include relieving dark circles under the eyes, puffiness under the eyes and regenerates crow feet and shrunken eyes.
10. **Derma Brasion:** Various skin problems are solved by this therapy, in which layers of skin damaged due to acne, scars, blemishes, pigmentation marks, uneventone are removed.

11. **Shirobasti:** Pour oil on the head for about 60 minutes stored in a leather cap and sit on a comfortable chair, cozy in blankets and pillows. The oil is cooked with herbs, is poured into the cap to cover hair and scalp. Start with 30 minutes and gradually increase to 60 minutes. The treatment is followed with gentle head, neck and shoulder massage.

    Shirobasti is traditionally used to treat several conditions which include insomnia, chronic headaches, anxiety, hair-loss, premature hair graying, skin complexion, etc.

12. **Akashi Tarpan:** Akashi stands for eye, Tarpan stands for nourishment. It is a beneficial therapy to provide nourishment to eyes. It helps to relieve tension in the eye sockets, regain to loss of vision, pain in eyes, fatigue, glaucoma, night blindness, cornal inflammation and conjunctivitis. This therapy also helps to make eye lustrous, remove wrinkles and dark circles under eyes.

    In this therapy, eyes are washed with medicated ghee or oil in the morning or afternoon. A circular wall is build around the eyes, in which medicated ghee or oil is poured up to the eyelashes. The ghee or oil is allowed to remain in the eyes for 15-30 minutes depending upon the conditions. If Akashi Tarpan is over done, it can cause itching and other kapha disorders. Avoid the therapy on cloudy, very hot or very cold days.

LYMPHATIC MASSAGE

The heart is on the left hand of human body, whereas the lymphatic duct is on the right hand side. This helps in purifying the blood from the heart. There are 18 lymphatic nodes in human body. Lymphatic massage has several advantages as below:

1. By opening the lymphatic nodes, the waste products are released from the body.
2. It helps in fighting infections and removes wastage from tissues.
3. It improves blood circulation.
4. It removes waste products like oil, grease and bacteria from the body.
5. It relaxes nodes.
6. All the fluids get removed from the veins through urine.
7. This massage is excellent for curing acne.

Following precautions are essential during lymphatic massage:

1. Lie down straight before starting the lymphatic massage.
2. Avoid lymphatic massage if the age is below 16 years.
3. Wrongly done lymphatic massage is harmful for the body and may result in vomiting and headache.
4. Lymphatic massage can be done on every type of skin.
5. Removal of make-up before massage.
6. Cleaning up the skin thoroughly.
7. The massage movements should be carried by Touch Therapy, Effleurage movement and with the help of electrical gadgets.

MOTOR NERVE POINT

Motor nerve points help to obtain the maximum benefits from the massage, as these nerve points affect the underlying muscles. The location of the motor points varies among individuals due to differences in body structure. Motor points are used for Lifting the face. In this treatment face lifting and toning machines are used. The machine has two rods, through which electric current is produced. The rods are used on motor points, which help in tightening and lifting the skin and bring back to its actual position. The flow of electric current is adjusted according to the skin type.

Corrective Line Treatment

Corrective Line Treatment or massage is basically meant for mature and oily skins. With the growth of age, fine lines usually develop on the skin resulting in loosening of the skin. This type of massage is done in people above 30 years of age. Corrective line massage can be done by two processes:

- **Mild Process:** Massage is given with the help of thumb and fingers.
- **Strong Process:** In this process a lifting gadget is used.

11

BODY MASSAGE

The word body massage come from an Arabic word 'Massa', which means to touch or stroke. Massage is a scientific method of giving manipulations to the body by rubbing, pinching, kneading, tapping or stroking with the hands, fingers, or an instrument. In ancient times, women had their body massage with vegetable or animal oil to keep their skin soft. Among the many benefits of body massage, few are as follows:

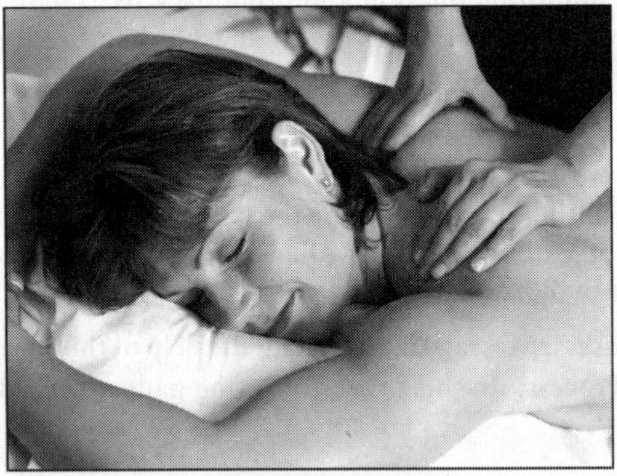

Massage

1. It stimulates and smoothen the nerves.
2. It relieves body tension.
3. It increases circulation of blood.
4. It causes muscles contraction when the movement is firm and rapid.

5. It stimulates the action of skin glands.
6. It helps to relieve pain in the muscles.
7. It softens the skin when massaged with cream.
8. It calms and relaxes a person and relieves emotional tension.

Precautions

1. Do not massage over an area where redness, swelling, pus is present.
2. Do not break contact with the skin until the massage is finished.
3. Always massage towards origin of the muscles.
4. Keep your fingernail short enough, to avoid scratching the skin.
5. The massage movement should be carried out rhythmically from the insertion to the origin of muscles.
6. Massaging in a wrong direction causes muscles and the skin to sag.

THE THEORY OF BODY MASSAGE

Massage is a method of manipulating the soft tissue of the body. It is one of the oldest and most useful methods of physical treatment employed for the reason of health and beauty accomplished by means of hands with the aid of mechanical or electrical appliances. Massage should always be applied by cream, ointment or oil to permit better hand movement and prevents drag or damage to tissue.

Some don'ts and do's

Massage should not be used when the following conditions exists:

- Heart disease.
- High blood pressure.
- Inflamed or swollen joints.
- Glandular swelling.
- Abrasions of the skin.
- A skin disease.
- Broken capillaries.

Massage should be applied with

- A firm, sure touch.
- Must develop strong flexible hands.
- Self control.
- Quiet temperament.

- Use of psychology.
- Leveled nails to prevent scratching of the skin.
- Firm, warm and dry palms (hands).
- Direction of the movement from the insertion of a muscle towards its origin.

Five Classical Massage Movements

Effleurage (Stroking movement):

A stroking, light, continuous movement applied using the palms and fingers in a slow and rhythmic manner over the skin. No pressure is employed. Over large surfaces the palm is used, while over small surfaces the cushions of the fingertips are employed in flowing and rhythmically. Effleurage is frequently applied to the forehead, on face, neck, chest, shoulders, back, arms and hands. A facial massage usually begins and ends with this rhythmic movement, which quicken the circulation of blood near the surface of the skin. The fingers should be slightly curved, with just the cushions of fingertips touching the skin. Do not use the ends of the fingertips as fingertips cannot control the degree of the pressure and free edge of the fingernails is likely to scratch the skin. The whole hand is held loosely, the wrist and fingers are kept flexible and fingers slightly curved to conform to the shape of the area being massaged.*

Petrissage (Kneading Movement):

This movement involves soft tissue away from the underlying structures using palm of hands, pads of fingers/thumbs with light but firm pressure, usually limited to back, shoulder and arm massage. Various movements involve light and heavy kneading, rolling and squeezing movement,

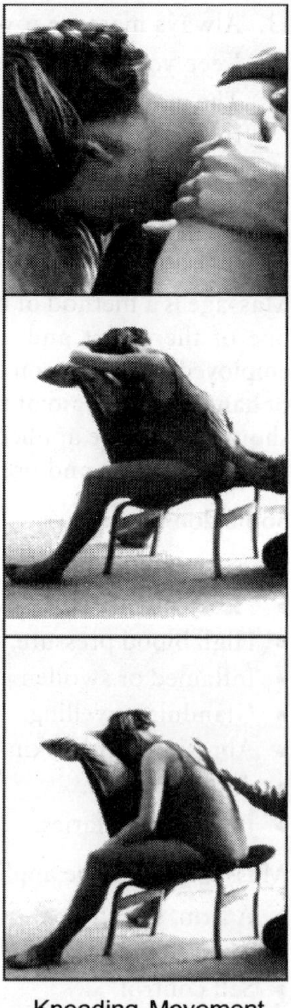

Kneading Movement

which deeply stimulates the muscles, nerves and skin glands, and promotes circulation of blood. The movement must be rhythm and never jerky. Petrissage has the following effects:

- Softens and relaxes hard contracted muscles.
- Eliminates fatigue.
- Stimulates sensory nerves.
- Increases blood circulation and lymph circulation.
- Helps to tone and strengthen muscles.

Tapotement (or Percussion)

Tapping, slapping and hacking are various movements, which are most stimulating when applied with sides of hand usually with partly flexed fingers or fingertips. In facial massage, light digital tapping are brought down against the skin with flexible fingers in rapid succession. In slapping movements, flexible wrists permit the palms to come in contact with the skin in light, firm and rapid movements. Hacking movements employ the wrists and outer edges of the hands in fast, light, firm, flexible motions against the skin.

Tapotement have the following effects:

- Increases blood circulation.
- Strengthens and tone the muscle.
- Stimulates sensory nerves.
- Increases lymph circulation.
- Redistribute fatty tissues.

Friction (Deep Rubbing Movement)

Light circular movement produced by the pads or fingertips or thumbs of the hands are used on the scalp, arms, face and neck. This movement requires pressure on the skin while it is being moved over the underlying structures. Friction has a marked influence on the circulation and glandular activity of the skin. The movement has the following effects:

- Breaks down nodules and fibrous adhesion.
- Increases the blood and lymph circulation.

Chucking, rolling and wringing are variations of friction, which are employed principally to massage arms and legs.

Chucking movement: is accomplished by grasping the flesh firmly in one hand and moving up and down along the bone, while the other hand keeps the arms or legs in a steady position.

The Rolling Movement: requires the tissue be compressed firmly against the bone and twisted around the arm or leg.

Wringing Movement: is a vigorous movement in which the hands are placed a little distance apart on both sides of the arms or leg. While the hands are worked downwards, the flesh is twisted against the bone in opposite direction.

Vibration (Shaking) Movement: A fine trembling movement, using pad of fingers and thumb of hand. This movement is always given along a nerve path with rapid muscular contractions. The balls of the fingertips are pressed firmly on the point of application. It is highly stimulating movement. Massaging in wrong direction cause muscles and skins to sag. Vibration movement has the following effects:

- Stimulates the nerves.
- Loosen scar tissues and stretch adhesion.
- Relieves pain.

Shiatsu Therapy

This therapy, also known as acupressure. It is used to treat disorders by pressing various pressure points on the skin of the body, which has nearly 600 Shiatsu Points on the human body, and among them few are very important to cure disorders. Pressure on such points produces energy that flows in the body. It takes about 45 to 60 minutes to treat the whole body.

How to give Shiatsu treatment?

Shiatsu treatment is given on the floor. Lie face down. Keep both hands moving rhythmically along the meridians from one point to the other pressing on each point from three to five seconds. It takes 45 to 60 minutes to treat the whole body, which improves the circulation and induce relaxation. The following steps are carried out to practice shiatsu:

- Press down either side of the spine.
- Press down the buttocks and the back of the legs.
- Press down on the points on the arms, hands and on the front of legs.
- Press gently on abdomen working clockwise in circles.
- Press from center of the chest outwards bet-ween the ribs.

Precautions while Applying Pressure

1. Let the pressure come from shoulders.
2. Keep arms straight when applying pressure.
3. Press with the balls of thumb.
4. Increase pressure steadily and evenly lean-ing body weight on hands.
5. Keep knees apart when applying pressure.
6. Swing hips forward to apply gradual pressure.
7. Rest fingers lightly when applying pressure on back.
8. Apply pressure lightly, steadily and evenly on abdomen.

Pressure Points on the Face

- Center of hairline to crown of head.
- On the center of eyebrow.
- On the upper edge of cheekbone (below eye).
- Groove between nose and upper lip.
- Between the eyebrows.
- Inside corner of the eyes.
- Below the end of eyebrows.
- Groove at the side of nose.

Preparations to carry out massage:

- The lighting should be dimmed.
- Many people do not like to hear music while having massage. Some enjoy in total peace and quiet. Few may like to talk during the massage. The best is to choose gentle, unobstructive music (including instrumental music) that can suit most tastes.
- Have two large towels suitable to cover the whole body to prevent oil evaporating after the massage has been completed.
- To help support the breast, a small rolled towel or other support can be placed under the sternum. A soft pillow may be used by the women having heavy breasts.
- Remove all clothes before massage for better treatment.
- Have the client sit on the couch with their back towards you, and:

Carry the following Examination

1. Examine the vertebrae for any misalignments, redness or lumpiness.

2. Note the posture. Lean forwards with the head hung down. Are the shoulders rounded?
3. Smooth one hand over the whole of the back to feel how tense or stressed the muscles are. This will help in your choice of essential oils and help determine the body work technique that is required.

Carry out a brief skin analysis to help choice of essential oils and body work techniques and see that:

1. Pale skin indicates poor blood circulation or a medical condition such as anaemia or low blood pressure.
2. Discoloured areas of body may indicate toxicity or previous bruising.
3. Yellowish skin may indicate kidney problems or liver conditions.
4. Bluish tinge may indicate poor blood circulation.
5. Cold hands and feet may indicate poor blood circulation.
6. Varicose veins may indicate colon problems, back problems, lack of exercise, stagnant energy and fluid flow.
7. Spongy tissue may indicate water retention or poor nutrition.
8. Tension in the muscles may be caused by injury, stress or holding the body in a fixed position.
9. Knotted fibrous tissue may indicate scar tissue or congestion.
10. Hard and congested areas on body may indicate crystallisation.
11. Thickened toe nails may indicate fungal rheumatic condition.

AROMA MASSAGE

In 1928, Rene-Maurice Gattefosse used the term aromatherapy. He became aware of the power of lavender in treating his own severe burns. He also discovered that synthetic oils were not as effective as the pure essential oils found in nature. Essential oils have a therapeutic effect on the body as they are: Analgesic, Antibiotic, Anti-fungal, Anti-inflammatory, Antioxidant, Antiseptic, Anti-spasmodic, Anti-viral, Carminative, Depurative, Digestive, Diuretic, Expectorant, Hepatic, Laxative, Hypertensive and hypotensive, Sedative, Stimulant,Toning and many more.

Effects on Mind

Essential oils restore balance to the emotions and mind, which are capable to:

- Soothe nervous tension and settle a worried mind.
- Calm anxiety and apprehension.
- Improves concentration and memory.
- Boost morale and pacifies anger and frustration.
- Uplift depression and negativity.
- Enhance love and relationship.
- Strengthen the spirit to help indecision.

Benefits of Aroma Massage:

They help to:

- Induce deep relaxation, relieving both physical and mental fatigue.
- Improve circulation to the muscles, thereby inducing inflammation and pain.
- Release neck and shoulder tension and backache.
- Relieve neuralgic arthritis and rheumatic conditions.
- Help sprains, fractures, breaks and discolorations and heal easily.
- Promote correct posture and help improve mobility.
- Improve the function of every internal organ.
- Improve digestion, assimilation, elimination and relieve constipation.
- Increase the ability of the kidneys to function efficiently.
- Flush the lymphatic system by the mechanical elimination of toxins and waste matter.
- Reduce high blood pressure.
- Help disperse headaches or migraines.
- Stimulate mind and body without any side effect.
- Stimulate the immune system.
- Help relieve suppressed feelings.
- Trigger the release of mood altering chemicals such as encephalin and endorphin.
- Encourage deep breathing.

MASSAGE FOR EXPECTANT MOTHERS

Careful, smooth and gentle massage movements benefit a woman during pregnancy, but do not forget to consult a doctor. Massage during this period helps alleviate many complications such as tension, backache, insomnia and faulty deposits on the body. A pregnant woman should avoid, deep pressures and percussion movements.

A careful massage during three trimesters of pregnancy and even before conception helps to increase the fertility of a woman. You can use all stroking techniques suggested for abdomen, back shoulders and legs and feet massage but the massage strokes should be gentle and very light. Use cushion under the shoulders, lower back and knees to reduce curves and discomfort while massaging. Massage done by a trained masseuse makes childbirth easier. Lower back and the shoulders are the areas for relieving tension with massage. For a back massage, a woman expecting baby should lie on her side when having massage or sit on a chair facing towards the back of chair.

Various massage movements for a pregnant

1. Gentle stroking with one hand, then both hands, one following the other clockwise on the abdomen.
2. Stroking softly on the side of the waist upwards with one hand after the other till both hands reach the navel.
3. Then gently glide the hands toward the abdomen and move down the sides to complete the stroke.
4. Cup your hands over the navel for a few seconds until you feel the heat, then lift your hands slowly.
5. Avoid talking during massage.
6. Leg massage is especially beneficial as it soothes, relaxes and relieves swelling and pain in the legs.
7. Varicose veins and cramps are some of the problems faced by expectant mothers. The best remedy is to always sleep with the legs slightly raised above the level of the head. The sleeping posture relieves swelling in the legs by draining the manual lymphatic system. The manual lymphatic system is a purifying and drainage system of the body. The system drains waste products from the body and helps to cure many skin disorders like acne, eczema and dermatitis.
8. If a doctor advises restriction on abdominal massage to expectant mothers, they can go for the arm massage, which has a soothing effect on the body. An arm massage can be given to a pregnant woman gently and rhythmically. Backache and morning sickness are the most common complaints during pregnancy, which can be relieved to a great extent with back massage.

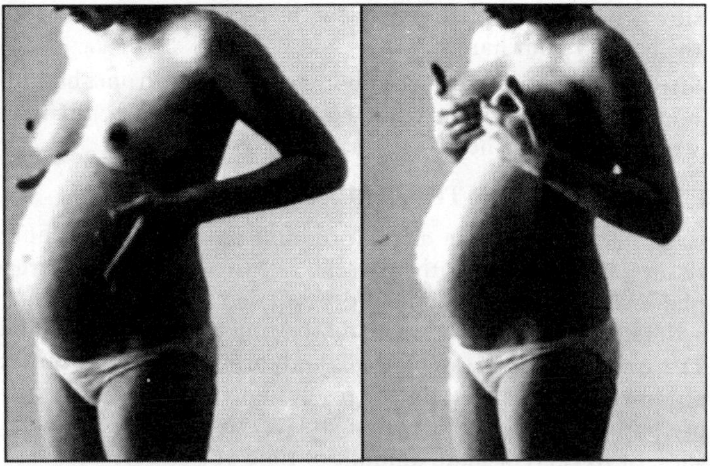

Expectant Mother Massage

9. Avoid deep pressure to the lower back during the first trimester of pregnancy. Stroking movements gently calm the muscles and several complaints by expectant mothers, which can be alleviated with plenty of smooth and flowing stroking movements on the mid back just above the waist at the base of spine and between the shoulder blades. Press firmly applying circular pressure with your thumbs on the hips and buttocks. This will relieve lower back pain.
10. Foot massage and pressing few Shiatsu Points, can relieve pain during labor (childbirth) and help speedy delivery. Stroke the sole of feet firmly with the heel of your hand, applying deep pressure with the thumbs in the center of the sole to the heel of the feet, which helps easy delivery of child and reduce labor pains.

MASSAGE AFTERCHILD BIRTH

Deep massage to abdomen for 40 days after delivery energises the mother, cures body aches and brings the uterus back to its original position. To give an abdominal massage to a woman after childbirth, the following abdominal massage movements should be applied:

1. Stroke the abdomen in all directions.
2. Knead firmly on hips, then gently across the abdomen.
3. Stroke gently clockwise in large circles on the abdomen. Stroke

slowly up the abdomen, starting at the public bone pressing with the heels of your hands.

4. Stroke slowly on the lower abdomen, starting from the pubic bone to the navel. Cup your hands over the navel, lift hands when you feel the heat.

ESSENTIAL OIL BODY TREATMENTS

Massage helps to increase circulation and oxygenation, stimulate the tissues, relax and tone the muscle, release tension and increase lymphatic flow. It helps with the process of digestion, stimulating the body to release and remove waste matter and toxins from the body. There are many types of essential oils and forms of massage, the type of movement used depend on the result aimed for. You may visit a beauty parlor to have a full body massage, to relax, to ease aching muscles, or to carve a small amount of time out of busy life.

The body massage treatment using essential oils can be for:

1. Slimming
2. Toning
3. Energizing
4. Relaxing
5. Healing

The role of massage can be seen in several distinct ways:

1. **To reduce Tension:** A full body or back massage, neck massage, foot massage and shoulder massage.
2. **Weight Reduction:** A massage, which emphasis on a specific area.
3. **Lymphatic Drainage Massage:** Aims to reduce oedema conditions and build-up of fluids.
4. **Massage Incorporating Acupressure/Reflex Points:** Can treat specific conditions or help maintain good health.
5. **Sports-massage Techniques:** These are used to tone, or release tension from muscles and in many cases to treat or prevent injuries. Therapists use a wide range of oil-based products, which enable the hands to glide over the body effortlessly. These include oils, lotions, creams and powders. Many commercially produced products claim that they contain essential oils, whereas in reality they do not contain pure essential oils in sufficient quantity at all.

However, using a therapeutic essential oil product intended for professional massage is a different experience, and many beauty therapists and users are surprised at the pleasure they derive from using such products. The percent of essential oils within a massage oil has been controversial area of discussion within aromatherapy for many years. In fact, scientifically nobody can give a definite answer as to what an appropriate dose should be, and there are no rules, only guidelines about this and dermatological sensitivity tests are carried out using various percentages of essential oil diluted in various mediums. The scientific testing of essential oils is most often carried out for cosmetic and perfume industry, who have to consider that their product is likely to be applied on a customer's skin every day in different climates and different skins, including most sensitive. Remember, in beauty therapy treatments, it is always best to use less essential oil rather than more. Real essential oils, used in correct dosages, provide therapeutic activity and have a very real effect on the client's well being. The following percentages of essential oil has been suggested to use for body treatment purposes in case of a sensitive skin, or is on medium, or is considerably biologically aged:

- 1–5 to 2 % for general relaxation.
- 2 to 2.5 %for general body massage.
- 3 % when treating a specific condition; or aches and pains; or during slimming, cellulite or toning treatments. The following reflex points can be included during the massage treatment using essential oils, as well as using finger pressure, finger pressure is applied by placing the middle finger over the index finger. Use the lower finger to massage the points with small, stationary, circular movements. The word stationary indicates that the fingertip doesn't move over the skin, but stays at one reflex point, moving in imperceptibly small circles. The pressure should be applied for not more than three seconds each time. A natural rhythm will emerge and it is possible to incorporate pressure of the reflex points within the flow of massage. Effleurage can be applied between each pressure point.

Body Treatments

- **Back:** Place one hand flat on the back and other on the sacrum area. Then remove the towel, apply oil and commence the massage. Incorporate the reflex points outlined in sketches. Finish by holding once again over the back and the sacral area.
- **Legs and Feet:** Remove the towel covering the legs, and use the hand holding positions—first on the soles of the feet, then behind

the knees, then on the thighs. Pour a little oil into your hand and rub both hands together in a friction move-ment. Smooth over enough oil, and commence your leg massage. When you have finished, use reflex points on both feet, then cover the legs with the towel.

- **Abdomen:** Hold one hand over the lower abdomen, and the other hand over the chest area covering the thymus gland. Now start massage by working on the abdominal area, incorporating front of the body reflex points that you feel to be appropriate. Cover abdomen and breasts with a towel, starting on the left side of the chest, and using a light effleurage movement with one hand following on from the other in a continuous flowing movement, drain along the clavicle, into the armpit. Now repeat the movement on the right side. And finish with general effleurage movements used in massage, not forgetting to incorporate the shoulder area.
- **Arms:** Press the reflex point at the center of the hand for three seconds. To finish, use holding pressure on the inner arms in three sections e.g. lower arm, inner upper arm and inner arm. Repeat the draining movement before moving to other arm.
- **Neck:** Use gentle sweeping movements up the neck, to the base of the occipital. Then use small circular movements with three fingers, traveling in upper direction, either side of the cervical vertebrae. Starting again on the left side of chest repeat the light continuous effleurage movement one hand following on from the other. Then repeat on the right side.

Precautions When Using Essential Oils

Essential oil massage provides immediate results. The molecules enter the body through inhalation and absorption through the dermis. They also enter the blood stream. They penetrate the skin and tissues quickly. The oil molecules are inhaled constantly because of the proximity of the nose. The following basic rules are essential when using an essential oil:

1. The oil should be diluted before application on the face and the neck.
2. The application of oil to the face should not exceed more than 30 minutes at each massage session. The session should be spaced at 7 to 14 days' interval for a series of six to ten treatments.
3. If the skin is sensitive, carry out a patch test before performing the treatment. Use essential oil between 1/2 to 1%.

4. Skin with acne needs to be treated very gently. The percentage of essential oil used will depend on the type and severity of the acne being treated, varying between 2 to 3 %.
5. Those suffering from allergic reactions to foods or cosmetics should use 1/4 to 1 % essential oil.
6. Avoid using essential oils in case of side effects and allergic reaction resulting in a burnt, scabbing appearance.
7. Do not use essential oils, if undergoing radiation or chemotherapy treatment.
8. Pregnant and lactating women should avoid use of the following essential oils:

- Aniseed (saunf)
- Basil (tulsi)
- Bey (kaiphal-ka-paudha)
- Birch (bhojapatra)
- Black pepper (kali mirch)
- Clove (laung)
- Fennel (saunf)
- Hyssop (zufah yabis)
- Juniper (hapusha)
- Marjoram (marwa, sathra)
- Parsley seed (ajmod, prajmoda)
- Rosemary (rusemeri)
- Sage (salvia, sefakuss)
- Thyme (ban ajwain)
- Valerian (jalakan, mushakbala)
- Wintergreen (gandhpura)
- Yarrow (gandana, sahastrapani)

Essential Oils of Herbal Plants used on the Skin

The following herbal plants are recommended for different types of skin:

1. **Normal Skin:** Use Arnica, Lavender, Melissa, Neroli, Rose petals, Rosemary and Sage.
2. **Oily Skin:** Use Calendula, Marigold, Jasmine, Lavender, Melissa, Peppermint, Rosemary, Sage, Thyme and Yarrow.

3. **Dry Skin:** Use Borage, Calendula, Camomile Roman, Elder flower, Jasmine, Lime, Marshmallow, Rose petals and Sage.

Cellulite Treatment with Essential Oils

Normal body fat is smooth, following the outline and curves of the body. Cellulite in the adipose of tissue is often found in areas that have poor circulation and elimination, such as the hips, thighs, buttocks, abdomen and the inner part of the upper arms. Cellulite is caused by accumulation of waste and toxic matter becoming trapped in the tissue, leading to lack of cell nourishment with swelling and thickening of tissue which often feel like scar tissue. A sluggish lymphatic system can lead to lumps and nodules of hard fat. Even women involved in hard labor, long distance runners and athletes can have areas of cellulite in their body. It becomes more obvious with age, when connective tissues and elastin become weakened. Cellulite is often seen in people whose weight fluctuates frequently. Cellulite is very stubborn problem once it has taken hold, and a complete reversal of the body functioning needs to take place.

Essential Oils are Useful in Treating Cellulite by the Following Methods

1. Body brushing and massage, which increase circulation and lymph flow, improves the tone and texture of the skin.
2. Regular exercise is very essential.
3. Correct nutrition is of the utmost importance.
4. The patient should be advised to go on a de-toxification diet. Cut out wheat, dairy products, red meats, alcohol, coffee, tea and fried foods.
5. Drink plenty of water and consider taking a vitamin and mineral supplement.

ESSENTIAL OIL MASSAGE

Apply essential oil diluted in vegetable carrier oil over the back, avoiding cellulite area. Then apply the same massage oil, but at a 20% higher dilution, over the stubborn cellulite areas. Suitable essential oils to use in the massage oils are lemongrass, thyme linalol, rosemary, cypress, grapefruit, black pepper, juniper, fennel and eucalyptus.

Essential Oil Massage during Pregnancy

Essential oil massage can be very beneficial during pregnancy. Regular massage can even prepare the body for an easier delivery. The women having regular massage with essential oils during pregnancy experience fewer tense muscles and become used to allowing the body to relax. Suitable essential oils during pregnancy period include the following:

1. Palmarosa
2. Tangerine
3. Geranium
4. Camomile roman
5. Rose
6. Jasmine

Use of Essential Oil during Childbirth

During labor, essential oils can be diffused in the labor or delivery room. There are few essential oils that cannot be used during pregnancy as hormonal and physiological changes take place during this period.

SECTION 2: HEALTH

12

KNOW YOUR BODY

Many of the questions we ask ourselves about our own body. I have come across several men and women, some of them even going to be married or to conceive or near to the delivery of child. Many of such expectant mothers know least about the organs of their own body. Most of the teenagers feel hesitant to question about male or female genitals to their elders though their knowledge is essential for everyone. It also allays fears and misconceptions.

Adolescent Period of Development

The teenage period between the ages of twelve and twenty is considered to be the adolescent period of the life. This is the period when sex functions mature, roughly between 12 and 15 years of age in girls and 13 and 16 years in boys. In fact this is the most important period of life, because it is the time when there is the most rapid growth and most sudden changes in physical, psychological and physiological development in the body. Girls tend to mature one to two years earlier than boys. Heredity factors play an important role on the development of body. Usually at the onset of menstruation, a girl will be the same age her mother was when she began to menstruate. It is seen, the girls tend to mature and to menstruate at an early in summer climate. When menstruation starts, it is irregular for the first few months. The amount of flow varies widely. The periods become regular after two to three years. It may occur every two to three weeks or may occur only once in every two to three months and there is no need for any treatment. If a young girl is irregular in her periods after two years of start, she must consult a doctor for thorough examination.

A rectal examination will give the necessary information as to the state of the uterus and ovaries. It is not necessary to do a vaginal examination on such girls. Breasts usually begin to develop about one year before the onset of menstruation. It is common in a fair number of children when one breast or one nipple develop before the other. The unequal development of breasts mean that one breast always remains larger than the other. The other breast will eventually catch up in its development and both breasts will be approximately of the same size in due course. During the developing stage of breasts, there is sometimes pain and tenderness. At about ten to twelve years of age girls must be explained about the menstruation so that they are prepared for its onset. Parents should impart sex education to their growing children. The parents should instruct their children about adolescence, puberty and sexual changes. If the mother is not able to do it, then someone who is educated in the field, such as school teacher or a medical advisor should inform the child. It is the best that a female child gets the information from mother or elder sister from an older person rather than from her friends, who may be misinformed.

Following are the major evidence of puberty in male boys:

- Increase in the size of the external genitals.
- The appearance of pubic and underarm hair.
- The appearance of hair on the face and upper lip.
- Voice change, with deepening in tone.
- The development of muscles and masculine figure.

The major evidences of puberty in young females are the following:

- Breast development.
- The appearance of pubic and underarm hair.
- The assumption of the female types of figure.
- The onset of menstruation.

Developmental Changes in Children and Teenagers

The organs such as the pituitary gland, the ovaries and testicles are responsible for the developmental changes of a child, because they begin to secrete larger quantities of the sex hormones and thus bring the changes seen in adolescence. Sometimes, breast enlargement is seen in a boy during puberty. There may be a nodule formed beneath the nipple at some time or other in boys between the age of eleven and fifteen years. This enlargement of the breast usually disappears spontaneously and requires no treatment. Both boys and girls tend to develop pimples and blackheads during adolescent period. This condition is called acne.

Special diet, special methods of keeping the facial skin clean and Correct medications prove helpful. This skin disorder among adolescents and teenagers has been described in detail in another chapter. The parents should handle the psychological problems of adolescent carefully by providing assurance and encouragement, warmth, love and proper guidance to their children, who often are seen restlessness, disobedient, disrespectful and awkward during adolescence due to lack of important psychological changes that take place during this period.

Most of the children has increased sexual urge during adolescence, which is a normal phenomenon and neednot be discouraged. It is normal for boys and girls to want to get to know one another and get along each other. Sexual curiosity is a part of that desire to learn more about the opposite sex. During this period sexual curiosity should be controlled gently and children should be directed so that their curiosity doesn't result in harmful pursuits. Now the question arises about the sex education among children. A child should be educated gradually from his or her earliest years when they start taking interest in sex. By the time adolescence is reached, children should know about sex so that they are better to manage their sexual urges. Ignorance about sexual matters often results in unwanted pregnancies or venereal infections among youngsters. It is natural for boys and girls to masturbate during adolescent period and the parents should not make them feel guilty about this practice. In most of the cases, in both boys and girls, late or delayed adolescence requires no treatment. In most of the cases hormonal treatment is administered, which may leave a harmful effect due to a tendency towards slowing up of glandular function when the hormone treatment discontinues.

When to Menstruate?

Wait for the treatment in case of delayed menstruation until a girl is sixteen or seventeen years of age before consulting a gynecologist. A treatment is necessary if a girl doesn't menstruate up to the age of eighteen. There are unusual cases of girls who begin to menstruate at the age of seven, eight or nine years. Also there are boys who may develop voice changes, genital enlargement and a beard at a similar age. Such cases generally signify that there is an abnormality in the development of one of the glands. These children should have a thorough investigation by a doctor. Sometimes, certain cases of tumor of the pineal gland in the brain may lead to such precocious development.

Menstrual habit refers to the duration of menstruation, and indirectly to the amount of loss. The average duration of menstrual cycle is five days, but it varies greatly in different persons. The extremes are cases where the menstruation lasts for an hour or so, and there are cases where it goes on for more than 8 to 9 days. It tends to be greater in hot climates, less in cold and, greater in urban dwellers and those living in luxuries and eating stimulating food. Sexual stimulation and habits of thought tend to increase it.

There are four forms of menstruation as below:

- **Amenorrhoea:** The absence of menstruation during the active sexual period of life from puberty to the menopause. Amenorrhoea is one of the early symptoms of pregnancy and it persists in 60% of the women during first few months of lactation.
- **Metorrhagia:** It means bleeding from the uterus in the intervals between menstrual periods.
- **Menrorrhoea:** It means excessive hemorrhage at the menstrual periods.
- **Dysemenorrhoea:** A painful menstruation.

Physical Growth of Both Sexes During Adolescence and Puberty

Adolescence is the stage of life between childhood and adulthood usually beginning somewhere between the age 11 and 15 years. During adolescence you experience many physical, mental, emotional and social changes. These changes prepare you to be an adult. Physical changes are a sign that a male or a female is going through the development stage called puberty.

Puberty is the time when you develop physical characteristics of adults of your own gender. During puberty, males' and females' bodies begin to change. These changes are a normal part of becoming a healthy adult. The chart below describes how male and female bodies change during puberty.

Males	Females
Male hormones production increases.	Female hormonal production increases.
Sudden, rapid growth occurs.	Sudden, rapid growth occurs.
All permanent teeth come into place.	All permanent teeth grow.
Acne may appear.	Acne may appear.
Underarm hair appears.	Underarm hair appears.
Pubic hair appears.	Pubic hair appears.
Perspiration increases.	Perspiration increases.
External genital grow.	External genital grow.
Shoulders broaden.	Breasts develop.
Muscles develop.	Hips become wider.
Sperm production starts.	Body fat increases.
Facial hair appears.	Ovulation occurs.
Larynx gets larger and voice deepens.	Menstruation starts.

Role of Hormones and Glands in Human Body

Hormones are one of the things that make your body change. Hormones are chemical substances produced in certain glands that help to regulate the way your body functions, and are produced by the organs of the endocrine system. The endocrine system is the system of glands throughout the body that regulate body functions. Each gland of the endocrine system makes one or more specific hormones. The pancreas makes the hormones insulin and glucagons. When the pancreas releases insulin into the blood, it lowers the level of sugar in the blood. When pancreas releases glucagons, it raises the blood sugar level. If the blood sugar is too low, you feel weakness and lightheaded. If it is too high, you can feel nauseated.

Role of the Endocrine System and Related Diseases

This system controls many of the changes in the body as below:

- **Parathyroid glands:** Located within the thyroid glands. They regulate the levels of calcium and phosphorus into the blood.
- **Adrenal glands:** Located on the top of kidneys that produce hormones and help regulate the balance of salt and water in the body. They also aid digestion and control body's response to emergencies and excitements.
- **Ovaries in female:** Female reproductive glands. Hormones produced in the ovaries control sexual development and the maturing of eggs.

- **Testes in male:** Male reproductive glands. Hormones produced in testes control sexual development and the production of sperm.
- **Pituitary gland:** Located at the base of the brain and produces several hormones that control the glands and organs, such as thyroid glands, adrenal glands and kidneys. Pituitary gland hormones regulate the body's growth and development.
- **Thyroid gland:** Located alongside the trachea or windpipe. They regulate body growth and the rate of metabolism.
- **Pancreas:** Located behind the stomach and controls the level of sugar in the blood, and provide the small intestine with digestive chemicals called enzymes.

The following are prominent diseases of the endocrine system

- **Diabetes:** Germ fighting cells in the body attack the cells of the pancreas that produce insulin, thus there is too much sugar in the blood. If not treated the patient can fall into a coma. Regularly inject insulin to keep blood sugar at the right level. People with this disorder are usually overweight and may feel tired a lot. They may also have infections and wounds that do not heal. Such patients should control their diets and engage in a regular physical activity. They also need medication and consult a doctor. Diabetes patients may suffer from poor circulation, nerve damage, heart disease, kidney failure or blindness.
- **Thyroid diseases:** Diseases of the thyroid glands affect metabolism and a person can develop a condition called hypothyroidism, and usually feel tired and cold, have dry skin and gain extra weight. It delays growth in teens. Consult a doctor in this condition.

What is leucorrhoea?

A white or yellowish vaginal discharge (not blood) from the uterus. This discharge may arise from 'trichomonas vaginalis' – an infection due to a small parasite that normally inhabits the bowel. Other causes of leucorrhoea are pelvic congestion, endocrine disturbances, lacerations, injuries and atrophy of the vaginal tissues following the menopause. It is seen, the presence of infection in any of the tissues usually causes whitish discharge, also called leucorrhoea. There are several causes of vaginal discharge in females. In young girls the discharge may be due to any of the following reasons:

- An irritation of the labia or external genital organs due to soiled undergarments, dirt, intestinal worms and masturbation.

- When the irritated tissue may become infected with 'staphylococcus' germs present in the skin.
- When the girl reaches puberty due to over-activity in her sex glands and organs causing excessive white discharge.
- There is slight discharge at the time of ovulation, which doesn't indicate the presence of any disease.
- A profuse, yellowish discharge associated with burning, intense itching on urination due to a serious infection or a venereal disease.
- A thin watery discharge due to the presence of cancer in the uterus or cervix.
- A creamy, slightly blood stained discharge due to trichomonas (a kind of infection) or some other infection.

Why Menopause in 20s?

Menopause or 'change of life' is a condition usually occurs between the age 40 to 50. The menopause, sometimes, occurs in females in their twenties. The female reproductive time of life begins at adolescence in the early teens and continues until the beginning of the menopause. The early symptoms of menopause are the following:

- Increased nervous tension.
- Menstrual disturbances.
- Hot flashes.
- Chilly feelings.
- Excitability.
- Easy fatigue.
- Depression.
- Crying spells.
- Sleeplessness.
- Palpitations.
- Dizziness.
- Headaches.
- Numbness, tingling and other annoying symptoms.

Body Organs

- **The womb**: A compartment of female body in which the baby forms and grows till birth. It is also termed as uterus. A pear shaped muscular organ situated deep in the lower abdomen usually of size 3"×2"× 1" when in non-pregnant state. It stretches gradually in size to store a fully formed baby. The lower part of the uterus is narrow and is called cervix with an opening in its tip.

- **The cervix:** It protrudes into a long stretchable passage, which opens outside. The fluid containing sperms flows through this during sexual intercourse. The passage is called vagina.
- **The Vagina:** About 4" in length vagina runs interiorly and caudally from the cervix between the bladder and rectum. It is directed from perennial opening upwards and backwards. Its upward end is closed.

Vagina

- **Uterus:** The upper broad end of uterus opens on either side into two long tubes called the fallopian tubes, each ending in a funnel-shaped opening guarded by five finger-like projections. The funnel-shaped opening lies close to the ovary on either side, which is a spherical, walnut sized organ responsible for producing female hormones and eggs called ova. Ovulation occurs somewhere in the middle of a menstrual cycle e.g. middle of an interval between two consecutive periods (roughly 14 days before any period). During a woman's reproductive life, only 400 ova are shed. When ovulation occurs, the ovum is picked up and travels down the fallopian tube towards the uterine cavity.
- **The Penis:** The male genital organ, which serves a dual function of erection and as a route of excretion of urine and semen. It is composed of three cylindrical structures of cavernous. The blood supply to the penis is primarily via the right and left internal arteries, which enter the base of the penis. Psychological factors account for most cases or cause of impotence. However, latest studies reveal that majority of cases of impotence have organic reasons. Vasculogenic impotence is one of the most frequent causes for erectile failure generally due to poor arterial inflow into the penis or excessive venous leakage of the blood from the penis or both. The frequency of the various causes of impotency is an below:

1. Vasculogenic	37.5%
2. Diabetes mellitus	20%
3. Psychogenic	11.7%
4. Neurogenic	6.7%
5. Malignancy	5.8%
6. Testosterone and Trauma	3.3% each
7. Other causes	11.7%

The Liver

The largest organ in the human body weighing approximately 1500 gm. in a adult, which lies in the right upper quadrant of the abdomen. The liver is divided in three lobes - the right, the left and the center lobe. It has many important functions to perform said to be a great chemical laboratory of the body. The liver is affected by a number of serious disorders e.g. virus infections, parasites, disturbance of the circulation, stone formation in the bile duct due to poisonous substances and various kinds of food we eat after having been digested and absorbed from the gastro-intestinal tract. Various abnormalities of liver are liver cyst, jaundice, hepatitis, infections, fatty liver, cirrhosis of the liver and liver cancer.

Gallbladder

A small pear-shaped, muscular organ closely attached to the under surface of the liver varying in size and the shape from person to person. The disorders of gallbladder include acute or chronic cholecystitis and jaundice. Sometimes, cancer occurs in the gall bladder.

Pancreas

Pancreas is an important gland situated below the liver, which produces strong digestive juices necessary for assimilation of food. Pancreatitis is mild or very severe inflammation of the organ. Avoid taking alcohol in such condition; this may only aggravate the condition. Avoid stress as far as possible.

Urinary Tract

The human body is a living engine, which burns fuel (the food) and requires a constant supply of oxygen, water and various chemical substances to provide energy to the organs of body, repairing damaged tissues and keeping check on kidneys. Normally, the body filters about 300 liters of fluid each day leaving approximately one liter of urine to be excreted from the body. The urine flows down the tiny tubules towards the center of kidneys and finally it is collected in the renal pelvis, from where it is eliminated from the body through the ureters and bladder. The common diseases of kidney are kidney infection, kidney stones, poly-cystic disease, bright's disease (nephritis), cancer of the urinary track, hydro-nephrosis, prostate gland, tuberculosis of the kidney, urethritis (inflammation) and uremia (toxic condition associated with kidney failure).

Uterus

The size of pear-shaped uterus ranges from 2 to 3.3 cm in length and 0.5 to 1 cm in diameter. As puberty approaches, the uterus gradually increases in size. The maximum dimensions of the uterus are approximately 8 cm. in length by 5 cm. in width by 4cm. diameter during pregnancy. Congenital uterine abnormalities occur in about 0.5% of females and are associated with an increased incidence of abortion and other obstetric complications.

Ovary

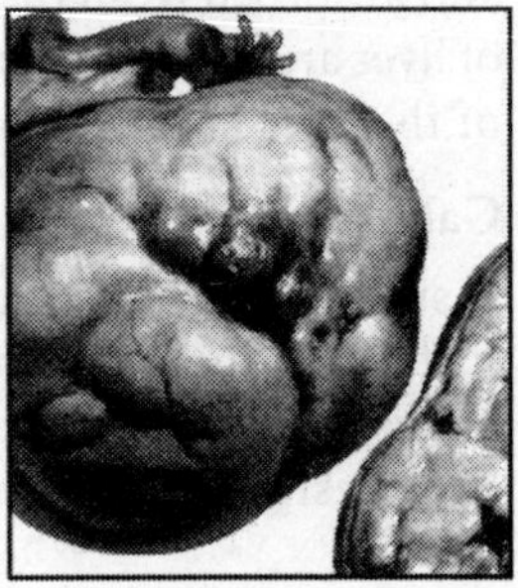

Ovary

Ovaries have 1.5 inch length, 0.75 inch breadth and thickness resembles the egg of a pigeon in appearance, and is almond-shaped connected with the base of the uterus by means of the ligament tightly attached to fallopian tubes. The most common ovary disorders are amenorrhoea, hirsutism (unwanted hair on body), obesity and infertility. Poly-cystic ovarian disease include functional cysts, follicular cyst, the corpus luted cyst, theca-luteal cyst, ovarian remnant syndrome (causing pelvic inflammatory disease or tumor), parovarian cysts, post-menopausal adnexal cysts, endometriosis (presence of tissue outside the uterus), torsion of the ovary associated with cysts or tumors, ovary cancer, epithelial tumors and neo-plastic lesions. All need immediate medical treatment.

The Adrenal Glands

There are two adrenal glands, one on each side of the body, located just above the kidneys. These glands are triangular in shape measuring approximately two by one inches in diameter. They are composed of two separate parts: a cortex and a medulla, which constitute separate organs. The adrenal medulla secretes the chemical and hormonal substances that are secreted into the bloodstream. The functions of cortex of the adrenal glands are the following:

- The utilization, storage and maintenance of body sugars, proteins and fats.
- The balance of water and minerals in the body.
- The secretion of certain male and female sex hormones.
- The manufacture of chemicals concerned with the body's response to stress, strain and injury.

The following are diseases related to adrenal glands:

- **Pheochromocytoma:** A tumor sometimes occurs within the medulla of the adrenal gland. The tumor causes elevated blood pressure, attacks of anxiety, palpitation, overactive metabolism and increased blood sugar. This tumor can be removed surgically through an incision made in the abdomen.
- **Addison's disease:** A condition in which there is a chronic deficiency of the adrenal cortex. As a result of this disease there is a gradual increase of fatigability, weakness, weight loss, loss of appetite, nausea, vomiting and emotional instability. There is also a peculiar discoloration and pigmentation of the skin and mucous membranes. This disease can be treated by the use of cortisone-like hormones, which correct adrenal deficiency.
- **Cushing's disease:** It has the following characteristics:
  1. Redistribution of fat to the upper torso, neck and shoulders.
  2. A fattened and rounded 'moon' shaped face.
  3. Purplish streaks in the skin of the abdomen, thighs and arms.
  4. Development of male body characteristics in female and vice versa.
  5. Elevated blood pressure.
  6. Elevated blood sugar content.

  Cushing's disease can be treated by X-ray treatment of the pituitary gland in the skull, which lessens adrenal secretion or the part of adrenal gland having tumor can be removed surgically. If not treated, the patient will succumb to it after a period of several years.
- **Conn's syndrome:** It is allegedly caused by tiny tumors of the adrenal glands, which cause a variety of symptoms as following:
  1. High blood pressure.
  2. Generalized weakness.
  3. Periodic paralysis.
  4. Excessive thirst.
  5. Excessive urination.
  6. Frequent headaches.

Male Reproductive System

The main job of this system is to produce sperm and semen.

Sperm: are male reproductive cells. Each sperm can join with a female reproductive cell and make another human. Testes are the pair of glands that produce sperm. Testes are located in the scrotum. Sperm leaves the testes and travel to the urethra.

Semen: is a mixture of sperm and fluids that protect sperm and carry them through the tubes of the male reproductive system. The semen is released from the urethra through the penis. The body's release of semen is called ejaculation. There are three to four million sperm cells in each ejaculation.

Parts of Male Ejaculation System

- **Penis:** Made of a spongy tissue with many blood vessels.
- **Urethra:** Small tube that runs through the penis, from the bladder. Urine and semen, at different times, leave the body through the urethra.
- **Scrotum:** A pouch that contains the testes.
- **Testes:** The glands that produce sperm and testosterone – the hormone that regulates male sexual development.
- **Prostate gland:** Produces fluids that protect sperm and move through the reproduction system.
- **Epididymis:** The collection of tubes is located next to testes to store sperms.

Problems of Male Reproductive System

- **Inguinal hernia:** Caused due to weak muscles. Can be treated through surgery.
- **Testicular cancer:** Uncontrolled growth of abnormal cells causing lump or swelling of the testicles during 15 to 35 years of age.
- **Prostate enlargement:** Blocks the flow of urine due to pressure on the urethra.
- **Prostate cancer:** Common in elder persons when tissues of the prostate gland become cancerous.
- **Sterility:** Males who produce no sperm.

Functioning of the Organs of Female Reproductive System

- **Ovaries:** Hold the female eggs. Make estrogen and progesterone hormones. Control female sexual development and other reproductive organs.

- **Uterus:** In which a developing child is nourished.
- **Fallopian tubes:** Through which the eggs travel from the ovaries to uterus. Eggs are usually fertilized in these tubes.
- **Cervix:** Narrow part of the bottom of uterus. The opening of the cervix enlarges to allow a baby to leave the uterus during birth.
- **Vagina:** The passage way that leads from the cervix to the outside of the body through vagina. Sperm enter the female reproductive system through the vagina. The baby is delivered through vagina.
- **Labia:** The fold of the skin that cover the opening of the vagina.
- **Ovulation:** The process by which the ovaries release mature eggs. Usually, one each menstrual cycle from ovary is released.
- **Menstruation:** The flow of blood, tissues and fluid that results from the break down of the lining of the uterus that oozes from the vagina.
- **Fertilization:** The joining of a male sperm cell and a female egg cell to form a fertilized egg, which travels to the uterus.
- **Yeast infection:** An infection of vagina caused by changes in the amounts of bacteria and fungi that normally live in the vagina. As a result, the female experiences itching and irritation in the vulva folds as well as a white vaginal discharge with a yeasty odor. The patient has pain during urination and sexual intercourse. See a doctor, if self-treatment doesn't work. Have a Pap smear, visual examination and other simple tests to sort disease out. The following treatments are suggested:
    1. To reduce leakage from your vagina, use suppositories and creams at bedtime. Wear a sanitary pad or panty liner during treatment to protect your clothing.
    2. Try a vinegar douche. Flush your vagina with a dilute solution of vinegar and water occasionally. Douching kills off bacteria in the vagina.
    3. Apply or eat yogurt. If you are applying yogurt, be sure to use plain, unsweetened yogurt to your vaginal opening.
    4. Use dry and cotton underwear and wear loose clothes so that air can circulate in them.
- **Vaginitis:** An infection of the vagina (due to a yeast infection, trichomonas vaginalis or sexual transmitted trichomonad parasite)

causing itching, discharge and sometimes pain. See your doctor if you notice pain or itching in your vagina and in the area of your vulva – the lips outside the vagina, reddening of your vulva, pain while urinating or sexual intercourse, a greenish-yellow frothy and foul smelling discharge, a foul-smelling thin whitish or blood-streaked discharge, heavy whitish thick and odorless vaginal discharge and white or gray and fishy smelling discharge. The following remedies are helpful:

Vaginitis

1. Take antibiotics to suppress infection quickly.
2. In case of swelling and itching, cool compresses are often beneficial. Coolness causes blood vessels to constrict, which makes you less red and swollen.
3. A plain tea bag soaked in water, cooled in the refrigerator and applied externally can relieve itching.
4. Take a warm bath, which soothes irritated genital tissues.
5. Avoid use of soap. Soap destroys skin's natural oils.
6. Scrub your bathing tub thoroughly. Bathing tubs are regular germ storage sites. Clean and disinfect bathing tub quite often to keep bacteria and mold under control.
7. Good toilet hygiene is a good habit. Wipe from front to back after a visit to the toilet to avoid transferring germs from the rectal area to forward your genital area.

Uterine Prolapse

The following symptoms may signal uterine prolapse and the patient should see a doctor immediately:

- Pain or feeling of a heaviness in the lower abdomen.
- Lower back pain.
- Pelvic pressure when you are standing.
- When you see the uterus protruding through the vaginal opening.

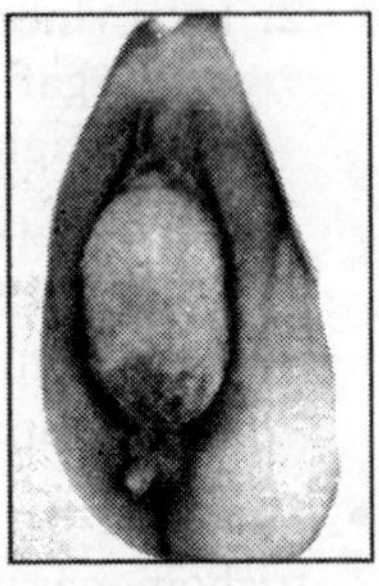
Uterine prolapse

The following treatments/precautions are necessary to strengthen pelvic muscles:

1. Practice exercises to strengthen cervical muscles.
2. Avoid heavy lifting.
3. Do not smoke. Coughing from smoke increases intra-abdominal pressure and tends to have an increased incidence of uterine prolapse.

Rectal Itching

Rectal itching may be associated with diabetes or incontinence. They often spread pinworm, an infection that causes the skin around the anus to become irritated. Other possible causes include allergic reactions to scented soaps, drinking coffee, tea or alcoholic beverages or eating citrus fruits and chocolates, which are common bowel irritants. To avoid chronic rectal itching following home remedies are suggested:

- For quick relief apply a little bit of petroleum jelly to the site of itch, generally in the morning.
- Wipe until it is clean. Make sure that you leave no trace of stool on the toilet paper. Usually hard stool can be hard to clean. If you have wiped a few times, and your anal area still isn't clean, wet toilet paper may work better. Then pat dry with a fresh section of toilet paper.
- Make sure that your bottom is dry. A wet bottom irritates the skin around your anus. Keep it dry. Pat with a disposable cotton ball and sprinkle powder.
- Deodorized or perfumed soap can irritate your rectum. To keep your rectum itch-free, choose unscented soaps.

Toxic Shock Syndrome (TSS)

A rare bacterial infection caused by using a single tampon for more than 24 hours. It should be treated promptly. A female should change her tampon every four to six ours.

Cancer

Cancer can occur in breast, ovaries, uterus and cervix in women. It is caused by uncontrolled cell growth in the tissues of these organs. Early detection is the best way to prevent serious complications of cancer. Cancer can be treated through surgery, radiation or chemotherapy. Cancer is not contagious. But a recent study indicates that certain cancers are associated with virus invasion and therefore

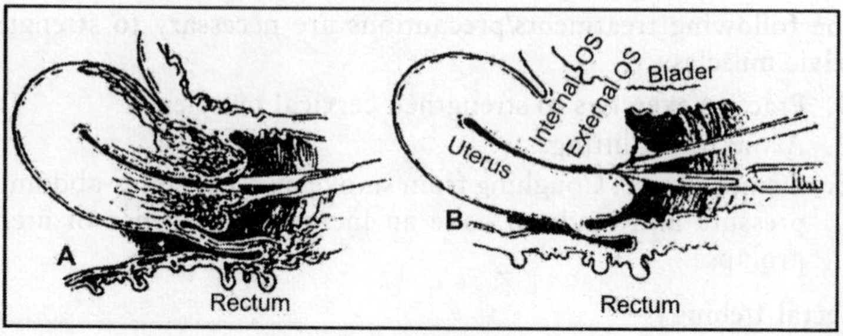

Uterrus cancer

might conceivably be transmissible. The tendency for cancer to occur is approximately the same in both men and women. However, certain types of cancer show up more often in one sex. For instance, lung cancer is more prevalent among men; breast cancer among women.

Estimated Cancer Incidence by Site and Sex

Site of cancer	In men	In women
Skin	3%	3%
Oral	4%	2%
Lung	20%	11%
Breast	-	28%
Pancreas	3%	3%
Colon & rectum	14%	16%
Prostate	20%	-
Urinary	10%	4%
Leukemia & Lymphomas	8%	7%
Uterus	-	10%
Ovary	-	4%
All other	18%	12%

Estimated Cancer Deaths by Site and Sex

Site of cancer	In men	In women
Skin	2%	1%
Oral	2%	1%
Lung	35%	20%
Breast	-	18%
Pancreas	5%	5%
Colon & rectum	14%	14%
Ovary	-	5%
Prostate	11%	-
Urinary	5%	3%
Leukemia & Lymphomas	9%	3%
All others	20%	20%

How Does Cancer Spread?

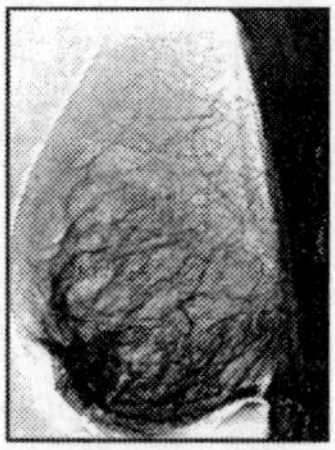
Breast cancer

There are three main routes:

- By direct growth and extension to surrounding structures.
- By spread through the lymph channels to distant organs.
- By spread through the bloodstream to distant organs.

Sterility

When a person is unable to produce children. Can be caused by the following factors:

- Untreated sexually transmitted disease.
- Hormonal imbalances caused by stress, diet and over-exertion. Aging.

The following precautions are undertaken:

- Undertake self-examination every month.
- Shower or bathe daily.
- Keep track on menstrual cycle. See a doctor in case of missed menstruation for several months, pain during menstrual flow and heavy menses.

Premenstrual Syndrome (PMS)

Common symptoms include headaches, breast tenderness, fatigue, dizziness, nervousness, irritability, outbreak of acnes, abdominal cramps, breast swelling or tenderness, decrease or increase in sex drive, food cravings, diarrhea or constipation. Consult a doctor for treatment. The following treatments are beneficial:

- Control over the diet. Sufficient rest and exercise can help to cure disorder.
- Cut out alcohol in the week before your period. Skip salt, sugar and caffeine found in coffee, tea, sodas, and chocolates one week before periods.
- Eat small meals, often six times a day to maintain a steady level of blood sugar.
- Add grains, fruits and vegetables to your daily diet.

  Reduce stress. Practice yoga and meditation daily.

- Take warm baths. Get a massage.
- Take 50 to 100 milligrams of vitamin B-6 and 250 mg of magnesium daily.
- Get enough calcium, zinc, copper and vitamin A and E. Amino acids and enzymes also help.
- Dandelion leaves (an herb) ease bloating and breast swelling. Steep 1 tablespoon dried or 2 tablespoons fresh leaves in a cup of boiling water and drink four times a day.

Care Taken During Pregnancy

- Eat healthy foods during pregnancy.
- Have regular monthly check ups.
- Beware of infections.
- Avoid use of tobacco or drinking alcohol.
- Avoid taking drugs without consulting your doctor.

Adulthood

At about age 19, the stage called young adult begins. At this time, physical growth slows significantly, but young adults continue to grow mentally, emotionally and socially.

Sexually Transmitted Diseases (STD)

Disease	Symptoms (treatment)
AIDS:	Sore throat, fever, swollen glands in the neck or underarms and groin, fatigue, chills and night sweats, cold sores, oral fungal or yeast infection, sudden weight loss, chronic diarrhea, dry cough, breathing problems, sores, vision loss, confusion and memory loss. (Get an HIV test, early treatment to slow the onset of AIDS)
Chlamydia:	This bacterial disease result in pelvic inflammatory in women, watery mucus from penis in men or vagina in women, burning with urination, mild lower abdominal pain 1-3 weeks after infection. Sometimes, there may be no symptoms. (See a doctor who may recommend antibiotics)
Genital herpes:	Viral infection spreads through sex, cold sores and transferred from mother to baby during childbirth. Symptoms include itching or burning pain in genital area, red bumps or blisters on genitals. (Consult your doctor. Avoid sex until heals)
Genital warts:	Causes due to infection by human papillomavirus (HPV). Symptoms include small, round, red, flat, itchy bumps on genitals, around anus or inside the vagina and in the mouth (Consult a doctor immediately)

Gonorrhea:	Bacterial infection. If left untreated may spread to joints, tendons or heart. Symptoms include pelvic inflammation, thick yellow discharge from vagina or penis, burning and itching while urinating, abdominal pain and bleeding between periods. (See your doctor, who usually recommends antibiotics)
Syphilis:	Bacterial infection. Can damage brain, nervous system and heart. Common symptoms are painless sores in genitals and rectal area, or mouth, enlarged lymph nodes near sores, mild fever, rashes, hair- loss in patches (alopecia) and sore throat. (Consult a doctor immediately, usually recommend antibiotics)
Trichomoniasis:	An infection caused by parasite. There is heavy greenish-yellow vaginal discharge, pain during intercourse, vaginal odor and pain while urinating. Usually, men have no symptoms. Generally, baby born to infected mother will be premature or underweight. (Doctors usually recommend antibiotic treatment. Avoid sex until treatment is finished)

13

GUIDE TO HEALTH, TESTS AND SCREENINGS

A General Guide to Health Tests

	Purpose	Age	How often to be tested
Blood pressure:	To detect hypertension-a major risk factor for cardiovascular disease	21+	Annually. More frequently if over 140/90
Breast self-examination:	To detect changes in breast tissue or its appearance	20+	Monthly, 7-10 days after onset of period
Cholesterol test:	To check cholesterol content of blood is too high-a major factor in heart disease	45+	Every 5 years or as advised by the doctor
Colorectal exam:	To detect signs of colorectal cancer, which can be cured if detected early	50+	Fecal Occult Blood annually. Flexible Sigmoidoscopy with digital rectal examination (DRE) every 5 years. May have Colono-scopy and DRE every 10 years.
Mammogram:	To detect changes in breast tissue that are too small to be felt.	40+	Annually
Pap Smear:	To detect cervical abnormalities, including cancer	21+	Annually or if referred by the doctor
Pelvic exam:	To detect uterine abnormalities, including cancer	30+	Annually
Breast exam:	To detect changes in breasts that remain unnoticed	20-40	Every three years

Treatment of Common Women Health Problems

Health Problem	Usual Symptoms	Treatment
Dysmenorrhea:	Painful cramping during periods, usually caused by high levels of prostaglandins. Symptoms are headache, nausea and diarrhea.	Exercise and high-fiber diets. Have medicines to reduce prostaglandins or to reduce pain.
Endometriosis:	Caused by bits of the uterine tissue growing outside the uterus. This condition can cause severe, steady pains few days prior to periods, which goes away after menses.	Hormones therapy helps some patients, whereas it need to have the excess tissue surgically removed.
Osteoporosis:	Loss of bone mass occurs in both sexes, but is more severe in post-menopausal women due to hormone changes. Loss of body height, back pain and hunch back are common symptoms.	Regular weight-bearing exercise and a calcium rich diet help. Hormone therapy can stop loss of bone mass.
Pelvic inflammatory disease (PID):	PID is an extremely serious infection of the uterus, fallopian tubes and ovaries. Symptoms include severe lower abdominal pain, unusual bleeding, vaginal discharge, fever and chills.	Oral//intravenous antibiotics and a bed rest is the only best treatment for PID. Better consult a doctor.
Pre-menstrual syndrome (PMS):	Women experience PMS one or two weeks prior to their periods. The condition have depression, confusion, sleeplessness and weight craving.	Low-fat low-sugar diets, vitamin supplementation, adequate rest and regular exercise relieve PMS.
Sexually transmitted Diseases (STD):	STD include syphilis, gonorrhea, chlamydia, herpes and AIDS. It usually occur due to sexual contact. Symptoms include discharge, pain, sores etc.	Treatment depends upon the STD, but often antibiotics are recommended. However, there is no cure for AIDS. Practice safe sex.
Vaginitis:	Caused by bacterial or yeast infections of the vaginal tissue. Symptoms include yellowish, white or curdled looking discharge, burning, itching, soreness and a painful intercourse.	Oral medication (antibiotics) or a vaginal suppositories or creams are usually suggested by the doctor. An early treatment is advised.
Stress:	It is a physical and psychological reaction to change. Persons under stress may have changed sleeping or eating patterns, feel fatigued, irritable and generally anxious.	A stress management class can help you learn coping and relaxation techniques. Yoga and meditation helps to alleviate stress.

(The author thanks to the experts of renowned Fortis Heart Hospital, Mohali for advising above health guidance tips for this encyclopedia).

Today the world is on its wheel. Scientific and technological research has become the watch-ward of progress. New discoveries and inventions have brought radical changes in human life. In the field of medicine and surgery miracle drugs and treatments have been introduced to alleviate the suffering of human being. On the other hand incidence of diseases has shown an upward trend in decline of human health due to general negligence and fast changing culture in our society. According to a medical survey more than 50 percent females and 20 per cent males today are suffering from the genital disorders for one reason or the other.

Negligence is the root of general decline of human health. Women in particular, it is observed, have the origin of their diseases, in some disorders in their genital organs. But these women blame their fate, keep suffering under the veil of superstitions. Ignorance and superstitions cause too many casualties and mishaps. A timely treatment, however, may control such mishaps to large extent.

It is quite true that the instinct of motherhood is too strong in a woman yet she is shy and disturbed usually at the time of her first cohabitating with male partner. Lack of proper knowledge on the subject and general ignorance lead many newly married couples to commit such mistakes, which keep them repenting for the rest of their life. Subjects like pregnancy, expectant mother's care, maternity, stages of labor, various sexual diseases, breast-feeding, postnatal care and taking care the baby are the subjects have been widely described in coming chapters of this book.

Periodic Health Examination

Generally people want to know how often should periodic health examinations be performed? In people under 45 years of age a periodic health examination be performed once a year – after that a check up twice a year is advisable. In case you feel perfectly fit, it is most important to have yourself examined, as many conditions of serious nature can exist for a long time without producing symptoms. Diseases can sometimes be spotted in its very early stages, when it is easier to cure. One should go to the family physician for periodic health examination, who may refer to specialists if he thinks additional tests or examinations are required. Total body scanner (also known as CAT scan) test is valuable, but the test is very expensive, is possible for those who are suspected of having a serious disease such as cancer.

Adolescence and Puberty?

The teenage period between the ages of 12 and 25 is considered the adolescent period. It is the time when there is the most rapid growth and the most sudden changes in physical, psychological and physiological development.

The period when sex functions mature, roughly between 12 and 15 years of age in girls, and 13 to 16 years of age in boys is considered the puberty.

Irregular Menstruation in Young Girls

Girls tend to mature one or two years earlier than boys. Usually, at the onset of menstruation, a girl will be the same age as her mother was when she began to menstruate. In warmer climates the girls tend to mature and to menstruate at an earlier age. When menstruation starts, usually it is irregular for initial few months. It may occur every two to three weeks or may occur only one in two to three months. Also the amount of the flow varies widely. Anywhere a period from one to three years is required for regular menstruation cycle and it requires no treatment. If a young girl is irregular in her periods for a year or two, it is wise to have her examined. A rectal examination will give the necessary information as to the state of the uterus and ovaries. It is not necessary to do the vaginal examination on these young girls.

Development of Breasts in Young Girls

Breasts usually begin to develop about one year before the onset of menstruation. It is common for one breast or one nipple to develop before the other in most of the young girls. It is perfectly normal. Both the breasts will eventually catch up in its development and will be approximately the same size. There is sometimes pain and tenderness in the developing breasts; this requires no treatment unless it is very severe. At about 10 to 12 years of age all girls should be told about menstruation so that they are prepared for its onset. The child's mother should instruct girls about the adolescence, puberty and sexual changes. It is best that she should get the information factually from an older person rather than from her friends, who may be misinformed.

Organs Responsible for the Onset of Adolescence?

The pituitary gland, the ovaries and the testicles begin to secrete larger quantities of the sex hormones and thus bring on the changes seen in adolescents. Both boys and girls tend to develop pimples and blackheads during this period. This condition is called acne. Special diet, special methods of keeping the face clean and medications prove helpful.

Increased Sexual Urges of Children During Adolescence?

A child should be educated about sex gradually from his or her earliest years when he or she first evinces interest in sex. By the time adolescence is reached , children should know a great deal about sex so that they are better able to manage their sexual urges. Ignorance about sexual matters, often result in unwanted pregnancies or venereal infections among young ones. Generally, there are so many myths about boys and girls to masturbate during adolescent period. It is important not to make them feel guilty about this practice. In majority of cases, in both boys and girls, late or delayed adolescence requires no treatment. Eventually, all children reach physical maturity without the need for medical treatment. A hormonal treatment if there is faulty menstruation, would be safe to wait until she is 16 or 17 years of age. Better consult a gynecologist.

14

DISORDERS OF SKIN DURING AND AFTER PREGNANCY

Skin Allergies

Any substance, may be the pollen from a tree, the dander from a cat, or a dog, the dust, ill effect of cosmetic, perfumes, strong fumes, foods, drugs, dyes, chemicals, bites or stings of insects – are enemies of your skin due to allergic reaction. The substances that cause allergy are known as allergens. Apart from reacting skin, allergies can manifest themselves in vomiting, diarrhea, abdominal cramps, headaches, severe rashes and other symptoms. Common allergic diseases include hay fever, bronchial asthma, eczema, hives, perennial allergic rhinitis or vasomotor rhinitis. Allergies are not contagious, and are not transmitted from person to person by contact. To perform allergy tests, serum obtained from the blood of the allergic patient is injected into several sites in the skin of a non-allergic individual. The allergic tests are then done on these sites.

Pigmentation of Skin

Discoloration of skin is often mistaken for scarring. Initially, all scars are red, pink or purple. This color fades over the next year. The blood vessels in a scarred area may be very noticeable. All color changes can be camouflaged with make-up or special covering cream and many scars become temporarily lumpy during healing and later flatten. The skin may darken because of pigments deposited in the skin, which are iron and melanin.

Color cells (melanocytes) produce a brown pigment called melanin. All races have the same number of color cells in the skin but they produce different amounts of pigment and the color increased by sunshine. The color of the skin also depends on the blood supply to the skin. An extensive network of blood vessels runs underneath the epidermis and they react to heat and cold. The skin too reacts to heat and cold in many ways. The body needs a constant internal temperature to function properly. The skin regulates the body temperature by reducing loss of heat when the atmospheric temperature is less, or the body is too hot. In hot weather, warm clothes cause the body temperature to rise, redden the skin due to enlarging of the blood vessels, swelling of the skin and sweating.

Many skin diseases especially eczema provoke the color cells of the skin to over produce pigments which drop down into the dermis of the skin and leave brown marks when the skin trouble disappears. This is called post-inflammatory hyper-pigmentation. Fortunately, the body can slowly remove this pigment and most darkening fades over one to two years. The darkening is worst in dark skin and may occur even after acne. The early treatment will help prevent the color change.

Effect of hormones: Increased hormone levels in the body during pregnancy stimulate the color cells of the face and the brown patches appearing specially around the eyes, on cheeks and on the upper lip. The contraceptive pill can cause similar brown patches. Hormones occurring naturally cause this problem mostly in women who are not on the pill or are pregnant. The brown patches last for many months and then slowly fade away. It is most important to avoid sunshine, which will darken the existing patches. One should use sun-blocking cream with the consultation of a skin specialist over the brown patches together with a sunshade or sunhat.

Allergies due to perfumes: Allergies to a perfume may also produce dark patches on the face and the neck. These perfumes are present in after-shave lotions, cosmetics and creams, in addition to perfume sprays. It is important to wash off all perfumes before sunbathing. Very dark patches may develop in the groins and armpits in later life. They can also be signs of illness so get them checked by a doctor.

Various Conditions of the Skin

Urticaria, psoriasis, scabies, warts, candidiasis and moniliasis are various conditions of the skin – every pregnant must be familiar with these conditions. Throughout life the skin changes according to our age, mood, hormones and exposure to foods and chemicals.

Therefore, at certain times we are prone to develop certain skin problems. There are many ages of the skin:

- **Infancy**: In babies and infants skin bacteria can break down urine to produce ammonia, which is very irritating to the skin and may cause a nappy rash. This forms sores and ulcers on the skin. It is very important to wash the skin at each nappy change to remove bacteria. Many babies are prone to getting a rash, which often looks like a bad nappy rash but also affects the creases of the bottom and is very red and crusted all over the bottom. This is a form of eczema, known as seborrhoeic eczema of infancy. It needs protective creams for baby's bottoms –zinc and castor oil etc. Avoid use of detergents and soaps. There are detergent-free emulsifying ointment or aqueous cream available from the chemists for washing infants. Many times the rash become infected with thrush and small pustules are visible. Babies who are kept too warm and become damp from sweating and urine often develops crops of red spots, which may blister usually in the folds. Milk spots may be alarming in lactating mothers especially with the first babies and the infants. They are tiny spots, which appear on cheeks, normally between the ages of 2 to 6 weeks and soon disappear. Infancy is also the age when atopic eczema starts.
- **Adolescence**: The major affliction of adolescence is the tendency to develop acne, which affects every teenager when the puberty starts. It is important to take acne seriously and to treat it quickly to prevent scarring. Another problem may be the enlargement of birthmarks or an increased awareness of birthmarks at the time of developing relationship with opposite sex. Male pattern baldness may also develop in late teenage years. Rapid growth of height may give rise to stretch marks on the trunk, abdomen and limbs - which may further get worsened by additional physical stress (weight- bearing).
- **Ageing**: As we age the skin becomes thinner both in the outer layer and in the supporting tissue resulting in wrinkled skin, which becomes less elastic. This is increased by exposure to sun so is often noticeable initially on the neck and face (with yellowish lumps with a scraggy appearance). The blood vessels lose some support and bruising occurs. Over bathing, especially with foam bath may give a very dry and itchy skin. Older skin tends to develop lumps and bumps – warts, skin tags, freckles, white patches and skin cancers. Hair thinning may occur all over the scalp.

Effect of Ultraviolet Radiation (UVR) on Skin

We can neither see nor feel ultraviolet radiation from the sun – it is neither heat nor light. UVR increases in summer and is maximum between 11 am and 3 pm. UVR stimulates the color cells (melanocytes) of the skin to produce a brown pigment (melanin), which absorbs UVR and protects the skin from the damage by a suntan and by skin thickening. Basically, the skin is classified in five types as below:

- Which never tan but always burn.
- Which always burn but sometimes tan.
- Which sometimes burn but always tan.
- Which never burn but always tan.
- Which cause pigmented skin.

Harmful Effects of UVR

Sunbathing is pleasurable and makes us feel more attractive. Suntanned to the requirement is beautiful. A beneficial effect is that our skin can synthesise Vitamin D, preventing rickets. The following effects of UVR are harmful for the skin:

- **Skin Cancer:** The skin cells are continuously damaged by UVR and eventually develop into skin cancers.
- **Skin Freckles:** Harmless lumps and bumps appear on sun-exposed skin. These include freckles, pale white patches and rough scaly keratoses.
- **Ageing:** UVR damages the elastic and supporting tissue of the skin, which loses its elasticity and tends to wrinkle.
- **Allergies to UVR:** Skin allergies to UVR tend to appear on the sun-exposed areas. The commonest allergy to UVR is called polymorphic light eruption and affect women more than men. Usually mild rashes appear during summer season, which are called as 'heat bumps' or prickly heat. It consists of juicy red spots on the face, arms and hands.

How to Protect Your Skin?

- If you are fair skinned, you should protect your skin with clothing and sun blocking creams as much as possible and avoid direct sunshine.
- Avoid going out in warm weather between 11 am to 3 pm as far as possible.

- Wear a hat with a brim and long-sleeved clothing.
- Some suntan lotions contain plant products (such as bergamot), which increases the risk of tanning resulting skin cancer and skin ageing. Better consult a skin specialist before purchasing such lotions.
- Fake suntans manufactured by chemicals usually stain the skin surface. These chemicals do not provide protection against burning, so a sun-blocking cream should be used.
- Prolonged UVR can be harmful to the skin but limited exposure with avoidance of sunburn will produce no harm unless you have an allergy to sunshine.

Burns

The most common burns woman generally has come from either working in kitchen while cooking or for using curling rods in dressing room. Even a small burn can cause pain, redness, throbbing, swelling and even blistering. Unless properly cared for burn can leave a brownish scar. To help diminish unattractive brownish scar or a spot left behind. The following tips are suggested:

- Bleach away the scar by applying a mild skin bleaching cream readily available in the market. Cream containing hydro-quinone help lighten the scarred or spotty area. Do not apply cream after the burn has healed.
- Faster scar fading results are possible by applying glycolic acid product (alpha-hydrox), which helps peel away the top layer of the skin.
- Cool the affected burn skin when a burn is minor, which helps keep pain and skin damage to a minimum. Apply cool water immediately to stop burning and skin damage to a minimum. Don't use ice because it is too cold.
- Cool the affected area with a compress applying a washcloth or towel soaked in cool (not icy) water.
- Be gentle with the blisters. The fluid in the blister is the white blood cells that the body sends to help protect against infection and help the healing process.
- Clean the burn gently twice a day with mild soap and cool water or with hydrogen peroxide, which kills the germs.
- Take aspirin or ibuprofen (after consulting a doctor) as an anti-inflammatory medication within the first hour or so after the burn. It prevents the burn from getting worse.

- Apply anti-bacterial ointments to prevent infection. Change the ointment if it causes a red, itchy allergic reaction due to some ingredients in it.
- Bandage the burn with gauze dressing in case of large burns. For small burns an adhesive strip will serve the purpose. Keep bandage loose and move the joint or burned area as much as possible, which boosts fast circulation to the area and clears out fluid build up.
- After the wound has healed over, moisturize the skin as healing burn can have lots of itching and cracking and interferes with the skin's ability to moisturize itself. Moisturizers can help restore elasticity to the skin and reduce dryness and flakiness. Use fragrance-free lotion.
- Drink plenty of water as water keeps skin hydrated and helps burnheal quickly.
- Eat plenty of protein foods such as skim milk, lean meats, nuts, beans, eggs, peanut butter and fat-free cheese.
- Vitamin C helps re-build collagen in tissue and speeds healing. Vitamin C is found in fruits and vegetables such as orange, grapefruit, broccoli and tomatoes.
- Apply Vitamin E or aloevera oil to burn.
- Use Vitamin A and D ointment for healing minor burns.
- Apply butter on a burn for temporarily soothing. If the butter contains salt that may cause additional tissue damage.
- Use of sliced raw potatoes on a burn work quick healing. This is a remedy that provides cooling first and then a protective layer of starch on the skin.
- You must see a doctor immediately in case:

  1. The burn is larger than the palm of your hand, deep or severe.
  2. The burn is characterized by deep ulcers and open sores.
  3. The burn is small but deep.
  4. The burn is extremely tender, painful, swollen and blistered.
  5. The burn occurs on the face, hands, feet or genitals.
  6. The burn has pus, yellowish drainage or yellowish crust.
  7. The area around the burn looks red or feels hot.
  8. There is a sign of fever.
  9. The burn causes unbearable pain.
  10. The burn has been caused due to electric or chemicals.

Razor Burn

Razor burn is actually a skin irritation. When you shave, you peel off part of your epidermis – the top layer of skin, which becomes red and swollen. Blood flow increases to the area to heal the wound and blood vessels dilate and become red. Razor burn is hard to get rid of as every time you shave, you re-irritate the skin. Here are few tips to reduce embarrassing redness due to razor burn:

- Apply a dab of 1% hydrocortisone cream to the area after you shave But avoid using it daily otherwise your skin could become habituated to it and become redder and more irritated.
- Lubricate your skin after shaving. Use moisturizing lotion, which helps to reduce dryness and itchiness. after you shave.
- Shave after you bath or take a shower as the skin won't be dry and your hair will soften.
- Always shave the hair in the direction that it grows in a downward motion that will not irritate the hair follicles.
- Use acne preparations containing 2.5 to 5% benzoyl peroxide, which helps to minimize razor bumps.
- Switch to electric razors, it gives a smooth and more even shave than a regular razor.

Unwanted Hair on Bikini Line

Even if a woman have slim and trim attractive figure and self-confidence to wear a swimsuit, still she have one serious problem: pubic hair that peeks out from behind from an abbreviated front panel. Use of a depilatory cream is not recommended as the skin along the lower abdominal area adjoining the upper thigh is too sensitive and some depilatory creams can cause irritant reactions. Permanent method to remove unwanted hair by electrolysis is harmful and sometime leaves scars on sensitive skins. Doctors usually suggest shaving the best way to get rid of unwanted hair along the bikini line with an outbreak of little bumps and red rashes – signs of bikini line infection. The skin in this area harbors a lot of bacteria that your razor can pick up and drag into hair follicles – the pores from which the hair shaft grows. The infected follicles erupt into little bumps, a condition called folliculitis. Here are few tips to remove pubic hair safely:

- Scrub your bikini-line area with antibacterial soap before you shave.

- Pat area dry before shaving.
- Apply an astringent after you wash.

Marks or Scars on the Skin

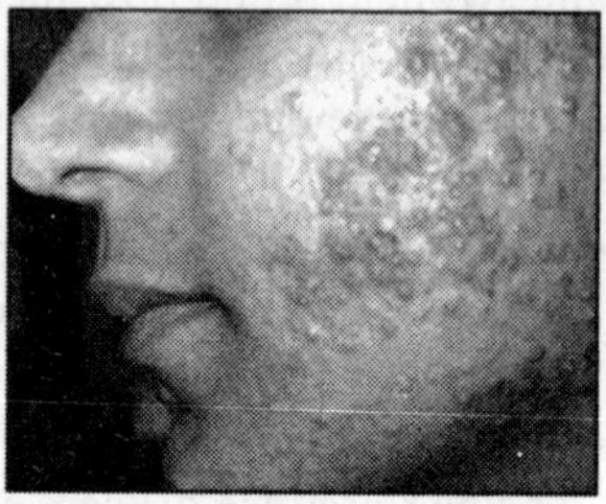
Acne scars

A scar is raised or indented section of fibrous tissue formed by the body's healing process in response to an injury that penetrates the skin. If the injury penetrates only the top layer of the skin (the epidermis) the healing process may leave only a light, temporary marks. But if the injury penetrates the body's deeper layer of skin (the dermis), then the body may form a scar. Besides cuts, scrapes and burns, picking a pimple or scratching a chicken pox sore can also leave a scar. The following measures are adopted to prevent scar:

- If the scar is lighter or redder than the rest of the skin of your body, application of a good foundation cream can eliminate it.
- Apply a topical antibiotic once a wound is clean and bleeding has stopped. Smear on an antibacterial ointment after consulting a doctor.
- Take Vitamin C, which can speed healing of a wound that may cause a scar.

Effect of Heat and Burns on Skin

Heat causes the body temperature to rise. The following symptoms are seen:

- Reddening of the skin due to enlarging of blood vessels. The skin appears red and flushed, and feels warm to the touch.
- Swelling of the skin (also called oedema) causing leakage of watery fluid.
- Sweating is the most important and essential way of losing body heat. People who do not sweat collapse from heat stroke in warm conditions.

Prickly heat (miliaria): When the body is hot, sweating occurs. In hot humid conditions, the sweat doesn't evaporate and swells the skin, causing blockage of the entrance to the sweat pores. This causes small itching blisters filled with sweat, which then burst and dry up.

A person who has suffered widespread prickly heat cannot lose heat by sweating and develop heat stroke or heat collapse.

Burns: Heating the skin causes a burn There are four types of burns:

- **First Degree burns:** Mild burns causing redness of the skin and later peeling do not require any treatment. Calamine lotion is soothing. They heal without scarring. However, there may be temporary darkening or lightening of the skin. In case of pain, plunge the burnt area in cool water to lessen pain and irritation.
- **Second Degree burns:** These are more severe with blistering, swelling and redness of the skin. In case the blister is filled with fluid, get it burst by a doctor. The burn should be kept clean, dry and covered with a sterile dressing. There may be a slight change in color but no permanent scarring.
- **Third and Fourth Degree burns:** These are very serious problem in which the whole skin and underlying fat, muscle and tendons are burnt down to the bone. The burn is usually black and charred as the nerves are destroyed. Seek medical attention to avoid infection. There is often severe scarring when the burn heals.

Skin Blemishes

Blemishes are clogged pores consisting of dead skin cells, oil secreted by tiny sebaceous glands in the skin that produces bacteria. There are three types of blemishes lasting for three to four weeks: blackhead or whiteheads, papules and cysts. Blackheads and whiteheads develop close to the surface of the skin. With a blackhead, the oil and accumulated debris forces the pore open the oil oxidized to black. A whitehead is similar to blackhead, but is closed in which the oil and debris remain beneath the skin surface. A papule is a red bump that occurs because of an inflammation under the skin at a hair follicle. Cysts occur deeper within the pores in the form of swollen red or white papules. There are several remedies to get rid of blemishes:

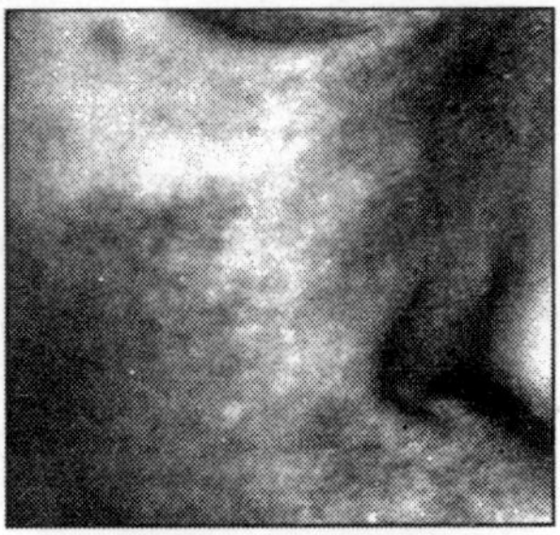

Skin blemishes

- A good treatment for emerging pimple is to apply ice. Wrap an ice cube in a washcloth and hold it to the pimple for five minutes. Cooling it will decrease inflammation.

- Products with benzoyl peroxide can help get rid of blemishes and prevent new ones from forming.
- Blemish cover cream is designed to use with regular cover creams. Let it set for a couple of minutes, then apply foundation cream for deep coverage.

Blisters

Blisters are caused by friction and foot is the most frequent site usually because of shoes that do not fit properly. The activities like running, dancing and sports can also cause blisters. Even a tiny blister needs to be treated by a doctor. See a doctor in the following cases:

- If the blister or blisters are painful and doesn't heal.
- A blister suddenly shows signs of infection, pain, swelling, redness, weeping or a yellow crust.
- Blister is accompanied by fever.
- You develop a wide-scale eruption or blisters.
- Blisters continue to form over time without an obvious cause or a friction.
- You develop single or repeated episodes of a cluster of tiny blisters.
- You develop blisters during pregnancy.

The following simple remedial measures are suggested to treat blisters:

- Gently clean the blister with soap and water to eliminate bacteria that could cause infection.
- If a blister is open, apply a anti-microbial ointment to kill bacteria and prevent infection.
- After applying an ointment, cover the blister with a bandage to keep it clean.
- Protect the blister with petroleum jelly or Vaseline to prevent friction further and to keep skin moist.

Sunburn

Redness, pain, swelling, discomfort and even the blisters are the signs of sunburn. Sunscreen protects against wrinkles and skin cancer. People with fair skin suffer from sunburn quickly. The following measures are helpful in case of sunburn:

- Have a cool bath if your body has been affected by sunburn.
- Step into an oatmeal bath. To relieve itchiness of dried, sunburned skin, add powdered oatmeal in bath water.

- Soothe on cortisone ointment. This anti-inflammatory ointment helps keep down inflammation and swelling.

Boils

A boil occurs when bacteria invades a hair follicle in the skin, travel down the follicle and form a collection of pus at the base and the result is a swollen, hard red bump on the skin, mostly appearing on the buttocks, inner thighs and under your arms - the areas with lot of moisture. You should immediately contact a doctor in case:

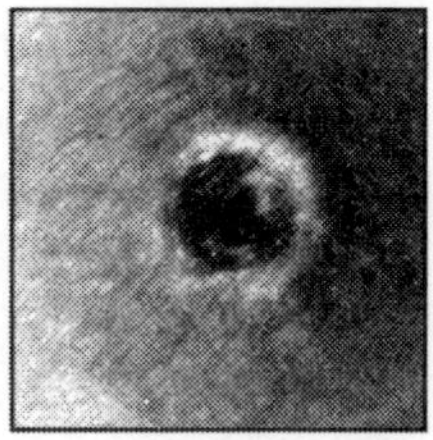

Boil

- The area around the boil becomes too red.
- The boil is deep and contains lot of pus. The doctors usually drain out pus with a steroid to decrease swelling and inflammation.
- You develop multiple boils.
- You develop a boil on the upper lip, nose cheeks, scalp or forehead as an infection in these areas can gain easy access to the brain.
- You develop a boil on the breast, which could pass highly infectious bacteria to your infant.
- You get boils frequently.

Try the following remedial steps:

- Apply warm compresses. Warm, moist heat increases blood flow to the area, which may bring the boil to a head and speed healing. If the boil is large, the acne preparation benzoy peroxide may help dry it out.
- Try a saline solution. Apply salt water to draw out pus and fluid and dry it out. Mix a spoon of salt to a cup of hot water. Dip a washcloth in it and wring it out on the boil. When it cools re-dip it and reapply.
- Wash away the germs with a liquid antibacterial soap and water when the boil has started to drain.
- Apply antibacterial ointment.

Cold Sores

Cold sores crop up around the edges of the lips, on the skin between the mouth and nose, sometimes inside the mouth and on genitals caused by the herpes simplex virus, which is transmitted by direct contact by kissing or sexual intercourse and can linger for years in nerve cells in the body. Many doctors opine that outbreaks follow stress, illness, too much sun exposure, onset of menstruation, allergic reaction due to foods, even dental procedures. Cold sores sometimes break down to form a scabby sore that lasts for a week or so. The following remedial measures heal cold sores:

- Use a sunscreen regularly. Sunlight triggers one of every four cases of cold sores.
- Yogurt has a reputation to relive formation of cold sores.
- Rub fresh aloe-vera juice on the spot as soon as tingling starts. It prevents cold sores.
- Petroleum jelly helps keep the cold sore from cracking and bleeding, which may cause infection.
- Kissing an ice cube can chill out a cold sore and prevent the sore from erupting. Ice helps prevent spreading the infection to the adjoining area and ease the pain, swelling and inflammation.
- Vitamin C stops cold sores.

Urticaria Allergic

Urticaria during pregnancy is an eruption of wheals – itching, pale or pink, edematous, raised lesions resembling those caused by the sting of a nettle – which last for a short time of a few hours only, but re-appear at the same or different sites. Swelling may be produced on the face (on lips and eyelids and groin) because of looseness of subcutaneous tissue where large amount of fluid can accumulate.

Allergic urticaria is the commonest allergic condition of the skin. Substances, which cause allergic urticaria enter the body by inhalation or injection. Drugs like antibiotics, penicillin, sulphonamides, aspirin, tetracyclines and even B-complex vitamin are among the commonest causes of urticaria. Many foods like shellfish, pork, eggs, mushrooms, milk, wheat, rice and pulses, nuts, strawberry or other fruits etc. can also cause urticaria. The widespread allergic urticaria can be due to pollens, dust, effect of dyes, horse dander, anti-toxin injections, intestine infection and stings of mosquitoes. At times a focus of infection in the throat, sinuses, ears, teeth or kidney may also cause urticaria. Physical factor like cold, heat, exertion, ultra violet radiation and pressure can produce urticaria in sensitive individual. Psychological stress resulting from sex and domestic problems has been known to cause urticaria in some women. Treatment of urticaria is carried out by administering antihistraminic (strictly as per doctor's prescription). While having these drugs one requires mental alertness as they cause varying degree of drowsiness.

Psoriasis

Psoriasis is a chronic disease of the skin in which there are patches of redness, itchy, raised cracking accompanied by loose silvery white scales. The cause is not yet known. But there are several indications that show that psoriasis is hereditary. The condition can start at any age. The number and extent of lesions differ from patient to patient from time to time. There may be few lesions or the whole body. Common sites of involvement are scalp, elbows, knees and buttocks. It tends to come and go with repeated attacks after an interval of few weeks or so. Psoriasis flares up in winter and improves in the summer. Some women notice that it's worse just before their menstrual periods. Scalp lesions are well defined and are covered with heavy mass of scales. In more than 50% patients suffering from psoriasis there is abnormality of nails like pitting, ridging, thickening and discoloration.

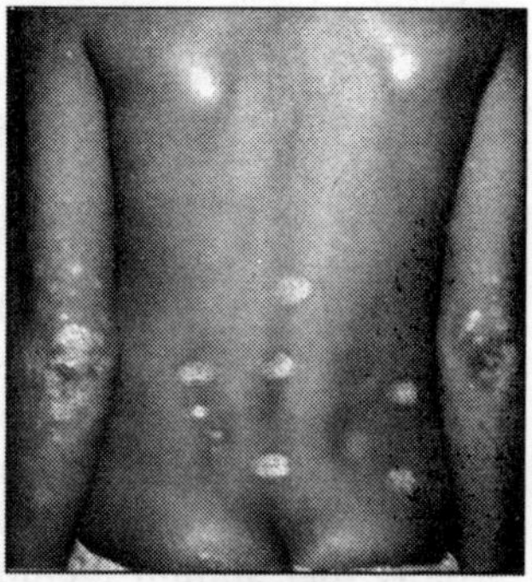

Psoriasis

Psoriasis runs in families. Patches of psoriasis develop over areas where the skin is frequently knocked with painful fissures and troublesome itching. It tends to get better in summer and worse in winter. Most of the treatments are ointments based on coal tar with the recommendation of your doctor. Ultraviolet radiation (2 to 3 weeks sunbathing) from sunshine may clear psoriasis. Tars of different types have been the most used agent in the treatment of psoriasis. 5% of crude coal tar in soft paraffin is most effective though messy. Coal tar solution of 10 to 20% is probably equally effective and more acceptable. The following natural treatments help control psoriasis:

- **Water:** Drink 6 to 8 glasses of water for internal cleansing of your body of toxins.
- **Stewed fruits:** Eat two stewed figs, apples, raisins, apricots, pears, peaches or prunes daily. Their laxative effect will help clean your bowels.

- **Exercise:** It is a vital part of regimen for clearing psoriasis, which stimulates the internal structures of the body, increases circulation, activates the glands, oxygenate the blood, opens the pores and filter the blood through liver and kidneys. An aerobic session for 30 minutes a day (walking, swimming, bicycling or playing tennis) is sufficient.
- **Moisturizing skin with oils:** Rub castor oil on thick skin lesions and a mixture of olive oil and peanut oil (in equal ratio) on thinner lesions.
- **Hydrotherapy:** Cleanse body with lukewarm water to which you have added one cup of apple cider vinegar and one cup rolled oats and powdered cornstarch. This will soothe the nerves and cure psoriasis.
- **Food:** Avoid saturated fats. Saturated and hydrogenated fats cause inflammation and must be avoided. Use olive oil for cooking. You daily diet should include 70-75% fruits and vegetables, whose high fiber content helps to cleanse the colon and the large intestine of toxins. The remaining 25% should be grains, poultry, fish, low fat, low-sodium dairy products.
- **Yellow saffron:** Prepare tea by mixing ¼ teaspoon of saffron in a cup of boiling water. Let it stand for 15 minutes and drink once a day until your psoriasis clears.
- Target your skin with tar. Preparations such as creams and lotions containing ingredients made from coal tar are readily available at chemist shops.
- Add bath oil to your bath water, which tends to coat the skin and block out water.
- Moisturize after bathing, which keeps your skin hydrated so that it's less likely to crack.
- Coat your skin with cortisone cream, which can help cure itching and swelling.
- Use shampoo readily available at chemist shops, containing either coal tars or salicylic acid.
- Spend a few minutes in the sun as exposure to ultraviolet rays improves the condition.
- Go on changing the brand of shampoo frequently.

Planter Warts – Painful Blemishes

If it feels like you have a pebble in your shoe when you step down and put weight on the feet, you may be suffering from Planter Warts.

The other common symptoms include an hard and flat growth on the sole of your foot, which hurt when you try to move it from side to side and there are tiny, pinpoint dots of blood in it. A planter wart is similar to any other wart, except that it is found on the sole. The red dots are at the ends of capillaries that are trapped in the wart. The wart is a non-cancerous growth caused by the virus, which is contagious and can be spread from person to person. The wart virus thrives in moist places and usually picked up by walking barefoot at swimming pools, health clubs and public showers. You are more susceptible if your feet sweat more than average. Planter warts can be small or large enough to cover the entire heel or ball of your feet. The larger warts are more painful. Planter warts can be treated by the following methods:

- Take a footbath. Dunk your feet in a basin of water mixed with a special drying preparation – a solution of aluminum salts that dries out and toughens the skin. Mix it into the water and soak feet in it for about 15 minutes.
- Keep you feet dry. Use towel to dry off your feet after showering, then apply foot powders containing talc to dry your skin.
- Products containing salicylic acid dries out warts.
- Cushion the blow. Callus pads can help take the pressure off a painful wart.
- Avoid touching or fiddling with your planter wart to avoid spreading warts to fingers. Make sure to wash hands immediately after applying wart treatment to avoid spread of wart virus.

Nail Fungus

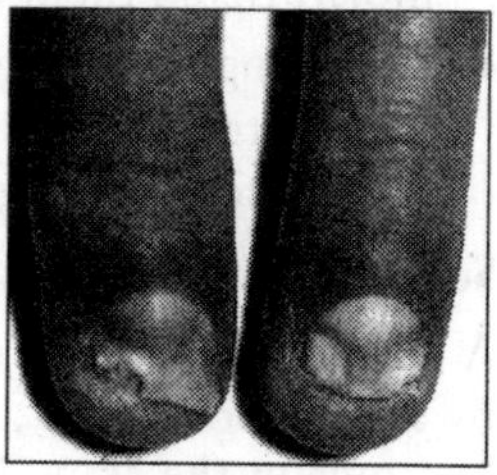
Nail fungus

Fungus of the nails can be stubborn with nails thicken and turn white or yellow, appear scaly and crumbly, begin to split and sometimes nails may even shed. Artificial nails are glued on, but these are not recommended as moisture can get accumulated under the tip creating fungus to grow and spread infection, pain in nail folds, swelling and throbbing. Yeast infection of the nails can pose a problem for the women who have their hands in water quite often. The signs of a nail bacterial or fungal infection include painful swelling around the nail folds causing separation. There is often yellow, white, green or brown discoloration. Consult a dermatologist for an accurate diagnosis and proper treatment. The following care should be taken:

- Avoid wearing artificial nails to relieve nail fungus.
- Keep hands and nails dry.
- Wear cotton-lined latex gloves.
- Apply moisturizers to avoid dryness, cracked cuticles and infection to nails and skin.

Brittle Nails

Nails gets weak and brittle, then split or cracked. Exposure to household work, chemicals and detergents tend to dry out the nails. The nail dryness is mostly due to aging when our nails become more brittle and thinner and split easily as we grow older. Here are few tips to strengthen brittle nails:

- Moisturize and lubricate with petroleum jelly or a thick, water-washable cream, which acts as an emollient. Apply cream at night, then wear cotton gloves overnight.
- Soak nails in olive oil for 15 to 30 minutes.
- Soak hands in diluted bath oil for five minutes once a day. Bath oil capsules are available at chemist shops. Apply a moisturizer or a cream with alpha hydroxy in it, which helps hydrate the skin of your hands and nails.
- Beware of nail polish remover that contains acetone and is drying. Frequent manicures, too, dry the nails. Always moisturize your hands and nails after a manicure.
- Take your nail polish off the night before a manicure and then moisturizing them with cream or ointment.
- Trimming your nails closely minimizes the problem of brittle nails. File or trim them after bathing, which minimize the chance of damage or splitting.

Scabies

A contagious disease of the skin caused by a mite 'Sorcoptes', which lays eggs in burrows in the skin. The disease spread through contact with infected individual, clothing and bedding. The commonly affected parts of the body include fingers, webs, palm, wrist, front of arm, armpits, buttocks, abdomen, inner side of thighs,

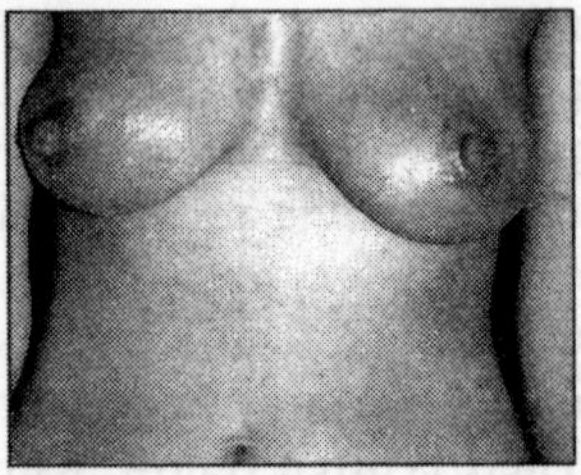

Scabies

around breast nipples, female genitals and male organs. There is often severe itching and irritation especially during night at affected part. Sometimes, a thin fluid oozes out of the scratched surface and later forms into scabs. Very often external genitalia in males are also affected. Scratching might result in lesions getting secondarily infected with bacteria producing pus and containing lesions of impetigo, boils, abscesses etc.

Treatment

- To treat this disorder boil leaves of oleander (karbir) till charred. in 250 ml mustard oil. The oil should be used in massaging the affected parts.
- The juice of lemon and jasmine should be mixed and rubbed on the itching surface.
- Another remedy is to ground poppy seeds in water. Add to it lemon juice. Massage the paste on itchy skin.
- Gamma benzene hexachloride used in 1% lotion or cream cures scabies. Better consult doctor in this regard.
- Scabies is treated with the local application of 25% benzyl benzoate emulsion (Ascabiol) or 10% gammabenzene hexachloride. It is important all members of the family are simultaneously treated. Before applying the medicine the patient must have a thorough scrubbing, and a bath with soap and water. The lotion is applied all over the body except on the face. The clothes must be changed at the end of treatment and laundered.
- Scabies should be treated in consultation with a skin specialist.

Crow's feet

Cow's feet are usually the earliest wrinkles to appear on a woman's face usually due to exposure to the sun – called as photo-aging as a result of loss of elasticity, resulting in temporary wrinkles pattern formed at the corners of the eyes, which eventually become permanent. Woman smokers may develop crow's feet earlier than women who do not smoke. The following measures are taken to prevent crow's feet:

- You can minimize crow's feet by moisturizing the area with an eye cream that contains glycolic acid. – a moisturizing agent in the cream to prevent wrinkling and dryness.
- Use sunscreen around the eyes. Sun rays destroy skin's elastin and collagen fibers.
- Avoid smoking.

Thrush Infection

Thrush (candida) is a common infection, which causes sores at the angles of the mouth, especially in false teeth wearers where it lurks above the dental plate. Babies may get white patches of thrush on the tongue and sides of the mouth. Thrush infection of vagina with itching is common in females. Vaginal thrush also called vulva vaginitis is common in women with severe itching and discharge accompanied by redness in genital area or on the glans in male organ. The vaginal infection can be transmitted to the male partner and vice versa. Contraceptive pills can create conditions, which encourage thrush. If you are suffering from vaginal thrush, avoid wearing nylon panties, tight jeans and moist environments. Seek the help of doctor to cure thrush infection.

Vitiligo

A pigment disorder of the skin, when the melanocytes in the localized area of the body stops producing melanin. The lesions vary in shape and size on the skin of the body and spread quickly.

Herpes (cold sores) in Childhood

There are two herpes viruses – herpes simplex virus, which cause cold sores and genital herpes and another virus, which causes chicken pox. Cold Sores are tiny white blisters have popped up in the corners of mouth and around the lips. Most people get cold sores in childhood from someone with a cold sore. The first attack is usually worst and the children may get painful mouth ulcers and swollen glands, when group of small blisters appear on the lips, forms a crust and dries up after seven to ten days. The virus sometimes becomes dormant in the nerve and can be re-activated by illness and high fevers, especially colds and sore throats. Some people get cold sores. Once in a while, and some get them almost non-stop.

In an infant or young child, a case of herpes can be dangerous because of dehydration and the spread of the infection to the hands and eyes. If your child has oral herpes, take him to the doctor. In adults, conventional medicine offers no cure, but the prescription medication acyclovir taken with the consultation of doctor help keep cold sores under control. Those suffering from chronic cold sores can take medication regularly for preventing occasional outbreaks.

To cope with cold sores, the dormant virus cannot be removed from the nerves by any method. During an outbreak anti-septic lotions help to dry up the blisters and prevent other bacteria prolonging the cold sore. Doctors usually prescribe use of anti-virus treatment applying creams and lotions. If you are prone to repeated cold sores and suffer badly, consult your doctor. Always use a sun blocking preparation when sunbathing, climbing mountains or skiing. There are several natural remedies for preventing cold sores, shortening outbreaks and providing pain relief as described below:

- **Increased intake of Lysine:** Protect yourself against cold sores by increasing your intake of lysine in consultation with a naturopathic physician. Foods containing ample lysine include cheese, avocado, eggs and chocolate.
- **Foods must have:** If you are prone to oral herpes, include foods with arginine, which include nuts (almonds, cashews, peanuts and walnuts), seeds (sunflower and sesame), pork, milk and cheese. Yogurt also help counter herpes virus and heals during an outbreak of chronic cold sores.
- **Application of ice:** It provides cure at the first sign of a sore and stop the blisters from forming. Wrap an ice cube in a napkin or washcloth and apply on the affected skin for 15 to 30 minutes.
- **Herbal cure:** The herb Astragalus boosts your immune system and kills viruses causing cold sores. The capsules or tincture form herb is generally available with naturopathy physicians.
- **Curing with minerals:** Calcium and Magnesium help to keep body's pH alkaline – necessary in preventing or rapid healing cold sores (Recommended daily dose 1,000 mg each for calcium and magnesium). The nutrient Zinc, too, builds the immune system, resists cold sores and strengthens the epithelial tissue on the lips and inside of the mouth (Recommended daily dose 15 mg).
- **Vitamin E for fast healing:** It helps speedier healing in case of chronic problems. This nutrient builds up immunity and integrity of the epithelium. (Recommended daily dose 400 international units). Beta-Carotene strengthens the mucous membranes of the mouth and speeds the healing of cold sores (Recommended daily dose 80-100 mg). Vitamin C speeds healing in case of chronic cold sores (Recommended daily dose 2,000 mg).
- **Lemon balm:** The herb lemon balm ointment readily available with health food stores is very soothing to cold sores.

Genital Herpes among Pregnant

Genital herpes is a sexually transmitted virus that usually can erupt 7 to 10 days outbreak of itchy, burning blisters and sores in genital area repeatedly. If you are having an outbreak of genital herpes with small, irritating, fluid-filled blisters and red, burning, itchy sores on your genitals, buttocks, thighs and groin, see a doctor immediately for an accurate diagnosis and treatment. Remember, a herpes infection in a pregnant woman can threaten the unborn baby in womb and must be treated by a gynecologist. An attack in pregnancy is very serious as an infected mother can pass on the infection to her baby, so she may need to be delivered by a caesarean section.

Genital herpes is caused by a different strain of the same virus, caught by having sex with someone who has herpes. The blisters appearing on genital area, thighs and buttocks are very painful, tender and highly infectious. The first infection is usually the worst with swollen glands and temperature. The virus becomes dormant but may cause repeated attacks. These viruses hidden in the nerves cannot be killed easily. There are several antiviral creams and lotions to shorten an attack. Warm salty water bath and painkillers make you comfortable during an attack. Remember, such attacks of genital herpes are highly infectious to your lover or beloved. Avoid sexual intercourse during an attack, but once the scabs have disappeared, you can have sex again. However, condoms lessen risk of infection. Remember, frequent attacks play havoc with your sex life. Worry and depression, poor general health conditions, lack of sleep and an unhealthy diet increase the risk to infection. The following treatments help stop an outbreak:

- **Lysine works well:** Amino acid rich lysine is a natural healer to fight off the virus (Recommended daily dose 200 to 500 mg capsule four times for two weeks as prescribed by the doctor).
- **Food to be avoided:** Foods, such as whole-wheat products, brown rice, oatmeal, chocolate, carob, corn, dairy products, raisins, nuts and seeds must be avoided.
- **Olive leaf extract:** It gets rid of the lesions and helps prevent them from coming back (Recommended daily dose 500 mg tablet three times for three weeks).
- **Vitamins and minerals:** A herpes break is a sign of stress your body have. The following vitamins and minerals help to reduce stress, shorten the herpes attack and reduce its severity (consult a doctor for correct quantity to be taken).

1. Vitamin A (Recommended dose 20,000 international units (IU) twice a day for 4 days).
2. B-Complex vitamins (Recommended dose 50 mg twice a day for 30 days).
3. Vitamin C (Recommended daily dose 500-1,000 mg thrice a day for 4 days).
4. Vitamin E (400 IU twice a day for 1 to 2 week).
5. Zinc (10 mg twice a day for one week).
6. Calcium/Magnesium (500 mg and 250 mg twice a day for 30 days).
7. Selenium (200 micrograms daily for 2 weeks).

- **Intake of water:** Drink a lot of water, which helps flush toxins out of your body and awaken immune system.

Shingles (herpes zoster)

After chicken pox, the virus lives in the nerves. Later in life, very painful blisters may appear on the skin on one side of the body, usually lasting between 7 to 14 days. Mostly people have only one attack of shingles caused by a rash infection by virus. There are many reasons that the virus can reactivate years – even decades – later and cause shingles.

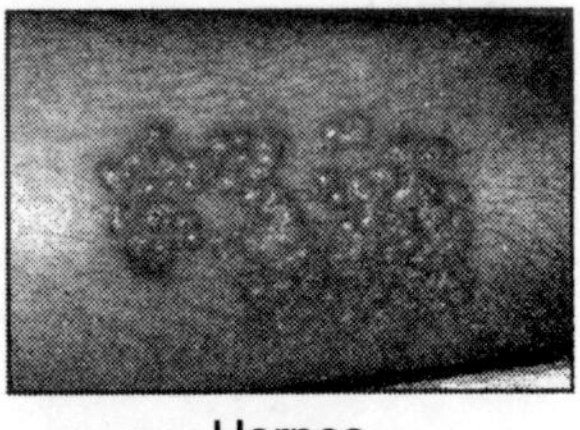

Herpes

Shingle is a painful, itchy but relatively harmless infection that can be treated with either medications or home remedies. In some people particularly those over 70, the pain of shingles never leaves a condition called postherpetic neuralgia. If you have shingles blisters anywhere on or near your head or you are immuno-compromised (means that you are suffering from AIDS, cancer or any other immune-weakening disease) consult a doctor immediately. Contact a doctor if you have difficulty in eating or drinking during an attack or if you are having trouble with hearing and balance. These symptoms may mean that you have internal blisters, which can be very serious. It can damage eyes. The following home-remedies help to treat shingles. It is important to seek advice of a doctor:

- **French clay and tea tree oil:** Mix 2 drops of tea tree oil to a teaspoon of French clay to make a paste. Apply a thin covering of the paste directly to the blisters. Leave the poultice on for two to three hours. Clean the area with a warm cloth. When applying the poultice, avoid touching the blisters directly with your hands or any other part of your skin.

- **Activated charcoal removes virus:** Add enough water to small quantity of activated charcoal and equal quantity of cornstarch or ground flaxseed to make a paste. Let stand for 20 minutes. Apply paste to the blisters with a piece of muslin.
  Leave the paste on for 12 hours. Wash it off. Reapply till blisters are completely dry and heal.
- **Hydrogen peroxide:** A gel of hydrogen peroxide contains high levels of oxygen, which is believed to kill viruses. Apply gel to the blisters every 2 to 3 hours until they have dried and healed.
- **Capsaicin ointment:** It is an outstanding treatment for postherpetic neuralgia – a condition that occurs mainly in people over age 70.
- **Multivitamin/mineral supplement:** Vitamins and minerals contribute to the strength of the immune system when taking high-potency multivitamin/mineral supplement to prevent shingles.
- **Vitamin C:** It is the most important for healthy immune functioning to prevent shingles (Recommended dose 50 mg twice a day).
- **Alpha-lipoic Acid:** It has powerful antioxidant properties and helps prevent shingles outbreak (Recommended dose 50 mg twice a day).
- **Lysine amino acid:** It helps decrease the recurrence of shingles.

Skin Cancer

The skin tumor is caused by excessive exposure of sunrays and in case it is not treated in time it leads to skin cancer. Avoid excess exposure to X-rays. Keratosis is another form of skin cancer in old age when numerous scaly patches appear on the scalp and other areas such as face, ear and back of the hands. Fleshy, rapidly growing lumps or bumps in the skin may spread to the other parts of the body and should be dealt with immediately. Skin cancer rarely spreads to the rest of the body but needs to be removed by an experienced surgeon by radiotherapy or surgery and cryotherapy (a process in which liquid nitrogen can be used to kill cancer cells by freezing). Try to get skin cancer diagnosed earliest by an experienced doctor. It is easier to treat it at a early stage.

There are several types of skin lightening creams or bleaching creams available in the market. They all contain a chemical called hydroquinone, which interferes with the production of melanin. These creams cannot lighten the post-inflammatory pigmentation, which is the common cause of brown patches. They can lighten the normal skin, birth- marks and freckles. It is generally very irritating to the skin and produce inflammation with more darkening of the skin or blotchy discoloration. In case of itching and redness stop using bleaching creams immediately. Use of hydroquinone creams especially in high concentration preparations sometimes damages the underlying tissues leaving black lumps and cysts. Better use cream unless advised by a dermatologist, because it can cause permanent color loss. It is advised to have treatment in consultation with the doctor.

Round Patches in Rainy Season

Generally during rainy season round patches are formed on the body, especially on the face, neck, back, buttock, inside of thighs, groin and genital area – which itch badly. It is an inflammatory infection of the skin produced by certain moulds in which round patches are formed on the body on different parts. They produce pustules. The edges of small pustules itch badly and it becomes difficult to resist. It is better to consult a skin specialist. Here are few home remedies for the cure:

- Apply juice of marigold-petals (genda flowers).
- The leaves of basil (tulsi) have a curative effect on the condition.
- Apply borax mixed to lime juice.
- Rub with a coarse cloth and the sap of swallow-wort (Akh) applied to it. This process is painful but is a sure remedy.

Infection is also caused by a group of fungi called dermatophytes. They affect the horny layer of the skin, nails and the hair. The lesions are red and scaly. They are circular patches, and may ooze pus too. There can be one or more lesions. Itching may be from moderate to intense. If the trouble exists on genitalia, use clean under-garments. This is a highly infectious disease of the skin, so a contact of this portion should be avoided. Friction warmth and moisture promote fungus.

Warts on Face and Body

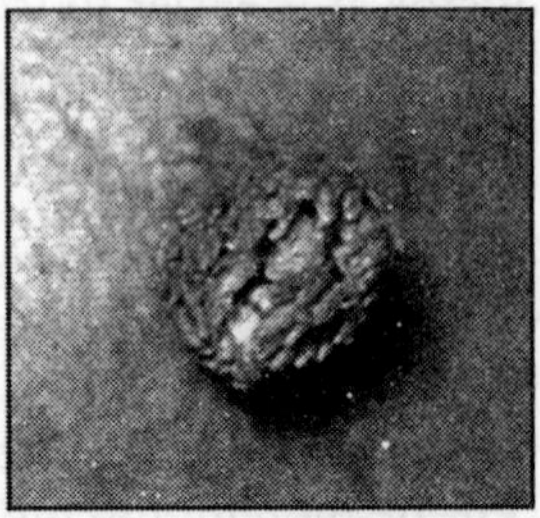

Warts

Warts are viruses that can take up anywhere on the surface of the body having unpleasant characteristics – itching, burning and oozing. The best way to get rid of warts is to have it frozen off by a doctor. Warts should be diagnosed accurately and treated appropriately. Once the warts are diagnosed, they should be removed/ treated early. Do not wait until they spread and enlarge and become more difficult to eliminate. Warts can be easily removed by cryosurgery or freezing with liquid nitrogen or electrocautery – a procedure that burns the wart off with an electrified surgical tool.

Children usually catch the wart virus at school from someone else's wart. After three to four months the warts appear. No treatment can kill the wart virus. The wart disappears itself. The treatments include scraping, burning or freezing. These physically destroy the wart but it often comes back and unpleasant scars can result. Treat your wart with natural methods as below:

- **Homeopathy cure:** Two homeopathy remedies to get rid of warts are 'thuja occidentalis' and 'antimonium crudum' (in 30X potency) readily available in market. They make the wart soft, fleshy and oozes or bleed easily.
- **Garlic – an antiviral:** Garlic oil is traditional remedy for warts. Swab the oil on the wart or on the bandage applied to the wart overnight, and strain out the garlic the next day. Take garlic capsules or tablets.
- **Multivitamin/mineral supplement:** Patients with warts should take daily multivitamin/mineral supplement. This will help to strengthen the immune system so that it can easily destroy the virus.
- **Olive leaf fights infections:** An herbal extract from olive tree contains powerful anti-infectious compound, which may help to get rid of a wart.
- **Stay dry:** Warts thrive on moisture, so keep the skin dry for early cure.
- **Applying lemon:** Soak lemon slices in apple cider with a little salt. Let stand for two weeks and rub the lemon slice on the wart.
- **Rubbing:** Rub wart with a piece of chalk or a raw potato.

- **Applying banana:** Tape the inner side of banana skin to the wart.
- **Vitamin E:** Apply vitamin E oil, clove oil, aloevera juice, milkweed juice, juice of unripe figs directly on the wart.

Genital Warts

They are transmitted by contact in the sexually active individuals. Other diseases may be caught at the same time. They may be related to the development of cervical cancer. So if you have warts, get them treated properly and have regular cervical smears. Mind-body techniques such as self-hypnosis can be very effective for healing warts. You might sit comfortably in a chair (or on the toilet seat). Relax your body with a few deep breaths, and form a mental picture of a patch of snow over your wart, which creates a pleasant, refreshing, tingling in the area, then melts the wart as it melts away. Do this visualization technique every day for 5 minutes or more. Salicylic acid plasters, salicylic acid collodion, salactol (combination of salicylic acid and lactic acid) are common wart preparations available for the treatment.

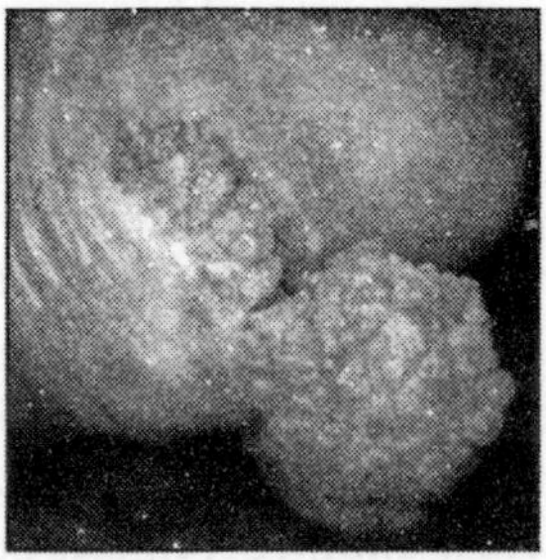

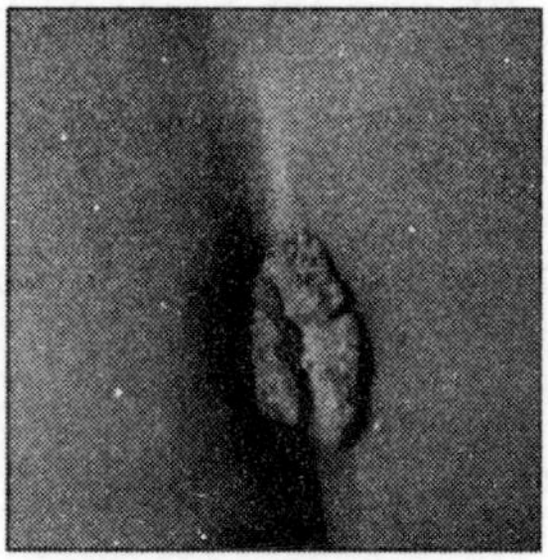

Warts on genital organs

Boil and Pustule

Boil is a bacterial infection of a sweat gland or hair follicle, typically on the face or in the armpit or groin caused by a pore or follicle being blocked by dead skin cells and other debris. Sometimes, infection of hair roots with bacteria (usually staphylococci) cause boils. Repeated attacks are common in teenagers and young adults. A red, painful lump develops a head of pus surrounded by redness, swelling and pain, which burst and leaves a scar. Recurrent boils are caused by the following reasons:

- Gastrointestinal bacteria entering the bloodstream and promoting a skin infection.
- Eating too much sugar (either refined sugar or sugar from fruit).

You should never lance or press a boil to open it, this can spread the infection causing permanent scarring. There are effective ways to heal small boils of less than ½ inch across. If you have a boil that doesn't heal within few days, consult a doctor for suitable treatment. Courses of antibiotics, draining or a steroid injection may clear single attacks of boils. People who have repeated attacks may need intensive skin dis-infection. To clear the germ from the nose, the armpits and groin, you need a nasal antiseptic cream and antiseptic bath solution (prescribed by your doctor). Do not apply hard antiseptic lotions available in the market. If you notice red lines radiating from the boil or you have fever or swelling or if the boil is extremely tender or exists under a thick layer of skin, consult your doctor immediately. The following natural techniques can help heal boils:

- **Hot compresses:** Using hot compresses on a boil will bring blood to the area and may diminish bacteria. In case of acute, non-recurrent boil use a hot washcloth. Immerse washcloth in hot water (as hot as you can tolerate), wring it out and place on the boil for 15-20 minutes twice a day. Using hot and cold compresses alternately draw out the pus.
- **Antibacterial herbs:** Echinacea and goldenseal help kill the bacteria in the boil. Take one tablespoon each tincture of both herbs three times a day until the boil clears. It is very bitter in taste.
- Turmeric extract is very beneficial for treating boils. (Recommended dose 450 mg three times a day). Use it to make a skin paste that bring boil to head. Here is another recipe as below:

  In a blender, mix 1 teaspoon each turmeric powder, Epsom salt and a baked onion and water to make a thick paste. Apply paste spreading over cheesecloth before sleep at night with a bandage. Leave the poultice over night and remove next morning. Repeat for two nights.
- **Don't spread it around:** When the boil is draining, keep the skin around it clean. Take showers instead of baths to reduce chance of spreading infection.
- Tie poultice of the following vegetables over the boil:

  1. A heated slice of tomato.
  2. A raw onion slice.
  3. Mashed garlic.

4. The outer leaves of cabbage.
5. A bag of black tea.

Red Pustules: This is a common condition during the hot and rainy season, known as prickly heat. The reason is that there is profuse sweating and the body is not exposed to the air. Red pustules of the size of mustard grains appear on the body especially on the chest, back and abdomen. There is an intense itching and if the area of affected skin is scratched it gives temporary relief, but there are chances of getting septic too. Persons subjected to prickly heat should avoid heavy garments and try to expose the affected area to the air. Take cool water bath twice daily and follow few other easy remedies as below:

- Dissolve Fuller's earth (multani mitti) in water to make a thin paste. It should be smeared over the affected parts. When the paste has dried, wash it with cold water.
- Apply green henna ground in water on the affected skin.
- Grind leaves of 'neem' tree in water to make a paste and apply on the affected skin.
- Rub a small piece of sandalwood on stone mixing to it rose water to make a paste. Mix to it a pinch of powdered alum and apply to the affected skin twice or three times a week.

Chapped Lips, Cracked Skin

During winter season lips get dry and chapped and the skin of the body and face gets cracked. Lip barrier creams are available in the market and should be applied on chapped lips before going out in winter or in the sun. The exposure to sunshine also causes the lips to become swollen, sore or irritated. Hands, too, get cracked during winter and hot season. If you have splits and cracks on your hands, you have got hand eczema and it's a sign you should see a dermatologist. Chapped skin of hands is usually prone to little blisters along the sides of the fingers. It is caused to those whose occupation (doctors, nurses, chefs and housewives etc.) requires them to immerse their hands for prolonged period. There are several easy home remedies for cracked skin.

- The skin should be properly scrubbed, dried and ghee or mustard oil smeared over them.
- The best application is the cream that forms over the boiled milk when it has cooled down.

- The affected skin should be massaged with lubricating oil or cream during the night while going to sleep.
- Even chapped lips can be smeared with this cream at night. On waking up, you will find the lips tender and soft.
- To remove the top layer of dead skin cells, put your hands in oatmeal. Blend oatmeal until you have a very fine powder. Immerse the hands in powder in a large bowl. Rub hands in the powder and gently remove dead skin. Rinse with cold water, pat dry and lavish on hand cream.
- When you are suffering from chapped skin of hands and fingers, the juice of raw meat and vegetables like potato, onion, tomato and carrot being toxic to the skin will further irritate the skin.
- Use cotton gloves to protect hands.
- Put on good layer of moisturizer when going out.
- Hydrocortisone creams and ointments are of great value in treating chapped skin.
- Instead of applying balm (which contains antiseptic ingredients like phenol and camphor), use cocoa butter (which is nontoxic and rich in emollients an moisturizer) on chapped lips. Cocoa butter will help re-hydrate your lips.
- Drink sufficient water if your lips are chronically dry. To hydrate your lips and the skin, you need to sip hot water or decaffeinated tea, which gently dilates your circulatory system so that the moisture can reach the tissues. Take one or two sips every 10 minutes throughout the day.
- Sun damages the lips causing dryness and scaling. Use a sunscreen as sun fries lips. Use a product with built-in sunscreen. A creamy lipstick would help soothe chapped lips.
- Nutritional deficiencies, such as those of B-complex vitamin and iron can play an important part in scaling of the lips. A multivitamin supplement is necessary.

Ulcers produced from ruptured blisters should be dressed with antibiotic creams. Chilblains and cracked skin occur due to reaction of cold weather. Chilblains develop with the onset of winter. Young people, especially girls are more often affected. That happens, particularly during winter because of defective functioning of the sebaceous glands. Chilblains consist of bluish red discoloration, swelling and sometimes blistering of toes and fingers. Nose, ears and cheeks are rarely involved. The affected person experiences severe itching or burning. The condition heals with the arrival of summer. To avoid recurrences in winter, as a therapeutic and prophylactic measure the patient should keep himself warm with the use of properly fitting gloves and socks. Peripheral vasodilators like nicotinic acid can produce relief to symptoms. You may seek advice of a doctor also.

Red Veins

Red veins indicate a sensitive skin that has been neglected or ill - treated. The skin is very thin, the blood vessels are very near to the surface and are affected by poor circulation or by extremes of temperature. Washing the face with very hot water or splashing it with icy cold water usually cause this condition and sometimes makes it much worse. If you suffer from broken veins, following precautions should be taken care of:

- Protect the skin from weather conditions by using a moisturizer.
- Apply lotions and waxy creams to be used in high altitudes, which give added protection. You may consult a skin specialist or a beauty consultant.
- Avoid going from one extreme of temperature to another. Always wait for few minutes in a place with intermediate temperature.
- Petroleum jelly can be used safely on the face to help soften and smooth the skin in the way any other emollient is used. The oily film will prevent evaporation of the moisture and protect the skin from irritation. Petroleum jelly also feels too greasy and will not go on or come off the skin as readily as regular cosmetic cream.
- Avoid rich spicy foods, hot drinks and alcohols when suffer from this condition.
- Moisturize the skin as much as possible.
- Electrical treatment process helps drain the blocked blood vessels and seals them. Seek the help of an experienced beauty therapist for treatment.

Birth-marks and Scars

Scars and birthmarks worry many people – especially women and it is worth consulting a doctor before disguising the marks cosmetically. You can make them fade considerably, especially when they are not too large. Apart from medical treatment, almost any birthmark, naevus or scar can be disguised nowadays with the wide range of cosmetic covering creams available in market.

Scars and birthmarks are difficult to remove completely. However, surgery can often reduce them to such an extent that they become almost unnoticeable. Minor scars can be dealt with electrolysis, carbon snow, ray treatment and cortisone injections etc. Birthmarks are fairly small moles. However, some birthmarks are very large, brownish colored and more disfiguring. They are often hairy. They can only be removed surgically. Birthmarks are of many types as described below:

Moles (pigmented naevi)

These are extremely common and harmless lumps in the skin. They are not visible at birth but appear during childhood and early adult life, varying in size and color from dark brown patches to fleshy bumps. In the early stages moles may be inflamed and red, but they eventually settle and become less obvious. If new moles develop after the age of 40, they should be check by a doctor. Moles become darker and more noticeable during pregnancy, and with the use of contraceptive pills. It is advisable to get the mole removed surgically if:

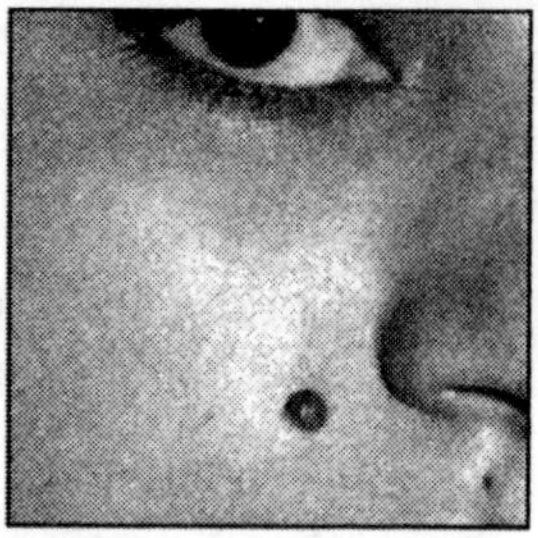

Mole

- There is increase in blackness of the scar.
- The color is uneven.
- There is constant increase in the size of mole.
- Changes in the edge of the mole an uneven or red edge.
- There are tiny black dots around the mole.
- There is bleeding or ulcer on the surface of the mole.
- There are itchy moles.

Stains, Marks and Patches

- **Port wine stains:** These are flat, red marks usually found on the face and scalp. They cannot be removed by surgery. These should be treated by laser treatment and infra- red treatment. They can be camouflaged.
- **Strawberry marks:** They are developed soon after the baby is born and grow rapidly from a bluish small mark to bluish-red fleshy

lump of blood vessels. They can bleed also. The mark increases in size very fast but eventually it shrinks. By the age of ten only a white scar remains. Avoid surgical treatment for it will cause a worse scar in the end.

- **Stork's bill mark:** Some babies have red birthmark on the nape of the neck, which is usually covered by hair.
- **Dark patches:** Very large areas of brown hairy thickening may develop on the arms and the trunk in the teens. It is not possible to remove them as large scars are left and these reappear after a short time.
- **Mangolian spots:** These occur in babies. They may have bluish birthmarks over the lower back. These are harmless and usually fade after 18 to 24 months.
- **Skin tags:** These are small tags of skin very common on the neck, in the armpits and groins. They can be removed by tying fine thread around the stalk. They can be snipped off with scissors or burnt.
- **Seborrhoeic warts:** By the age 60, sometimes lots of greasy warts appear on the face, neck and trunk. Very often, people worry about them as being skin cancers. They may become itchy and sore. These can be removed by scraping or freezing.

15

COMMON DISORDERS BEFORE/ AFTER YOU CONCEIVE

Varicose Veins

Enlarged superficial veins usually into and around the legs due to increased pressure on the veins, which cause to lose the elasticity and become elongated. Varicose veins look like a bluish snake-like appearance.

As the blood returns to the heart it passes through special thin-walled channels called veins. These vessels are easily distended and swell as the blood builds up behind it. Blood flowing from the head and upper chest flows downward towards the heart. On the other hand, blood coming from the lower extremities must flow upward. To make it possible nature has provided valves in the veins so that blood can flow only towards the heart, never in other direction. Constipation, smoking and hot baths are all contributory factors to varicose veins.

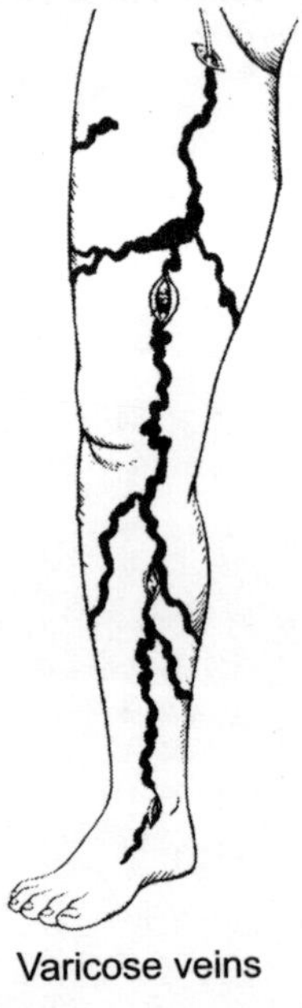

Varicose veins

The valves in the varicose veins in the legs especially around the ankles and thighs are incompetent to prevent a backflow of blood resulting in stagnation followed by swelling, pain, inflammation or phlebitis. When the person suffering from varicose veins has been standing for a long time usually lead to reduced blood supply to the muscles. Varicose veins seem to run in families. This ailment is more frequent in pregnancy and obesity due to increased pressure in the pelvis or abdomen region, which slow the flow of blood to the heart from the lower extremities. The following measures are suggested to treat varicose veins:

- Check weight as every extra amount added to the weight increases the pressure on venous circulation.
- Blood sugar should remain within prescribed limits.
- Avoid prolonged standing.
- Wear comfortable padded low-heel shoes.
- Wear varicose vein stockings available at a chemist or surgical store.
- A hot and cold footbath before bed time improves circulation, prevents varicosities and helps to heal.
- Walking or jogging in water (in a swimming pool) is very helpful to relieve varicose veins.
- Vitamin C strengthens vein walls (Recommended dose 2,000 to 3000 mg daily).
- Rosemary tea with honey and elderflower tea are old-fashioned remedies to aid the circulation.
- Raise the legs several times a day and sleep with the foot of the bed raised six to eight inches higher than the head side.
- Massage the legs gently but do not scratch varicose veins because the varicose ulcers may result in from a sore place and can be very unpleasant. Excellent massage oils for varicose veins are olive oil, sweet almond oil, essential oils of cypress, calendula, rosemary and lavender.

The signs of trouble include swelling along the course of the veins, followed by muscle cramps and a tired feeling of legs behind the knees. Sometimes, the skin over the lower part of the leg may break down forming a large, ugly painful ulcer, especially when thrombophlebitis develops in legs. Surgery is the best treatment, especially when the large veins of the legs and thighs are involved. However, regular practice of yoga relieves varicose veins and cramps.

Vaginal Infections

Very common in females of every age when a yellowish discharge from vagina accompanied by itching can be due to fungal or bacterial infection. Candid V6/V3 is used for treating fungal infection. For bacterial infection certain other medicines as recommended by a doctor are useful. Get a high vaginal swab for culture sensitivity done. There is great need of cleanliness of genital area during pregnancy. The following are some of the common warning signs during pregnancy:

Warning Signs	Possible Problems
Vaginal bleeding	• Miscarriage • Placenta previa • Premature labor
Abdominal pain	• Ectopic pregnancy • Premature labor contractions
Leakage of fluid from vagina	• Rupture of membranes
Puffiness or swelling of face, hands and feet	• Preeclampsia (toxemia)
Severe/ persistent headache	• Preeclampsia (toxemia)
Pain/ burning while urinating	• Urinary tract infection • Sexually transmitted disease
Irritating vaginal discharge, genital soreness or itching	• Urinary tract infection • Sexually transmitted disease
Nausea or vomiting	• Hyperemesis gravidarum • Infection

Loose Vaginal Muscles

Loose vaginal muscle has ruined many happy marriages. Remember, One cannot prove that women with loose vaginal muscles are not virgin, nor these muscles will be an hindrance in satisfying the male partner. Practice of yoga exercises help relieve.

Vajroli Mudra is a yogic postures, which helps to tighten and strengthen loose vaginal muscles, relieve the disorders of pelvic region and strengthen all sex organs among both sexes. This exercise strengthens the anterior and posterior parts of the pubic muscles. A pregnant woman should do about 5 to 6 rounds of this posture daily strictly in consultation with a doctor. To practice Vajroli Mudra, sit in Padma Asana (Lotus Pose) or any comfortable meditative asana. Place hands on knees, close eyes, feel relax

Vajroli Mudra

and breathe through nose. After a deep inhalation, hold breath and try to draw the sexual organs upward by pulling and tensing the lower abdomen contracting the pelvic muscles as if one has an urge to pass urine but wishes to hold one for some time. Now exhale, relax and repeat the posture. This posture also helps those suffering from premature ejaculation and delay climaxing (orgasm) when involved in intercourse.

No Periods Due to Closed Hymen

Sexually well-developed teenage females sometimes do not have menses despite good health, although they feel periodic pains for few days every month besides having pain in the lower belly during these days. In few cases an ultrasound report shows a completely closed hymen. Surgical operation helps to start normal periods. Consult a doctor.

Marriage in Blood Relation

Marriage between blood relations is genetically unhealthy as both father and mother may carry the same type of unhealthy genes, which could intensify the unhealthy manifestation in the offspring. Here is an example of a couple both were closely related having blood relation. Their first baby was mentally retarded. They had an abnormal second baby. The third, a premature died at birth. The fourth also premature was, too, far from normal.

Duration of Having Sex

It depends upon the couples to involve into a pattern to suit their moods and needs. The frequency of the relationship varies from couple to couple. Some need sex everyday, others once or twice a month even in their early stage of marriage. With increasing age there is decline in sex in most of the couples. During pregnancy, frequent sex is not advisable and a couple must seek advice of a gynecologist. In case of problem pregnancy, better avoid sex as far as possible. In case of blood spots do not indulge in sex, this may lead to a abortion.

Honeymoon Urethritis

Over- enthusiastic love making, excessive handling of clitoris during foreplay and frequent intercourse lead to severe inflammation of the urethral opening resulting in honeymoon urethritis. If the vagina has become infected or the infection is severe, pus cells pass into the bladder. Consult a doctor immediately for the treatment.

Sucking of Breasts

Sucking of breast by the husband is not harmful. If your husband wishes to suck the breasts, he should not be discouraged. This is natural and healthy exercise for the nipples and the breasts.

Natural Contraceptive Methods

Various contraceptive methods for the family planning are of three types as described below:

- **Coitus interrupts:** This is a unreliable and unhealthy method of contraception usually practiced by traditional couples in which the sex act is interrupted at the time of male ejaculation and the male organ is quickly withdrawn out of the vagina before the semen discharged out. However, long-term practice of coitus interrupts can cause pelvic congestion with the formation of ovarian cysts in the female.
- **Rhythm method:** This method follows the natural ovulation pattern in women, which happens once a month on the 14th day of the cycle (immediately before and after this day are the most fertile days for ovulation). However, the days following the menses and preceding the next period are the least fertile. The ovum is capable of getting fertilized for two or three days after its liberation as the discharged sperms remain vital for three or four days in the upper regions of the female genital tract. If the intercourse is avoided during ovulation and three to four days before and after, the chances of conception are minimal. The husband's cooperation is very necessary to avoid having sex for over a week in the mid cycle or use a condom during this period.
- **Lactating the baby**: In many women, during total lactation, ovulation stops and menses do not take place. During this period a woman cannot conceive or has very low fertility. This method, too, is not hundred percent reliable as there are instances, despite lactation, the woman conceives even before menstruation restart. In some cases, menstruation and ovulation commence within three months. The early restart of sex brings on quicker menstruation and ovulation due to hormonal effect on the system with breast milk decreasing.
- **Vasectomy and tubectomy**: Sterilizing the male or the female is the best way for permanent stop to birth of a child. In males the operation is called Vasectomy in which the ducts (vas) carrying

the sperms from the testes to the urethra in the penis is cut on both sides and tied beneath the skin of the scrotum. This operation is usually100% successful. Vasectomy has no fears about loss of libido, difficulty to perform the sex act and general debilitating effects. Vasectomy if performed un-hygienically can produce infection in the internal genital organs. In few cases the operation causes minor nerve pain during erection. In female the operation is known as tubectomy in which the fallopian tubes on either side are cut and ligatured. The operation is performed easily, even a week after the delivery of child when the uterus is still high up in position and tubes are easy to ligature. The operation is performed by laparoscopy technique by a pencil like instrument fitted with microscope (micro surgery) with hardly an inch long cut into the abdomen.

Displacement of Uterus

The uterus or the womb is slung in the pelvic cavity and has sufficient movement in all directions. However, its natural position is upwards and forwards between the bladder and rectum. Displacement of uterus occurs because of several reasons and is usually accompanied by inflammation. The downward displacement of uterus is known as pro-lapse. In this condition the uterus slips downwards in the space between bladder and rectum. This condition is more common in overweight or too weak women.

The disorder is frequent in women having repeated deliveries. The uterus gets distend during pregnancy when the fetus grows. The muscles supporting the uterus become to week to bear the burden of the growing child in it. After the delivery of child the uterus and surrounding muscles lacks the former shape and the size. The symptom, which indicate displacement of the uterus include backache or headache and heaviness in the bowels. Nerve centers are badly affected due to the displacement of uterus. The patient feels irritable and depressed. Doctors generally advise surgical interference for the treatment.

All external or internal muscles of the body if become loose, their tone and strength start malfunctioning resulting in such ailment. Inactive muscles may also acquire extra coats of fat and become unserviceable. Lack of proper exercise, acquisition of a coat of fat, deposition of morbid matter in the body and an inadequate diet lacking in essential vitamins and mineral substances can lead to weakness of the muscles of the body. A healthy woman doesn't experience any difficulty in childbirth and there are no complications even afterwards. Remember, antenatal care and proper diet can ward off the danger of displacement of uterus. If the patient is weak and old, it could take long to put her back in shape. The following natural steps are recommended:

- Have good diet containing enough fruits, milk and green vegetables.
- Rest in the bed and relaxation drain out tension from the body.
- Have a regular exercise plan designed to tone up the muscles supporting the uterus. Also seek advise of a naturopath doctor.
- Rub the parts immersed in water vigorously while having Hip Bath.
- Keep a hard pillow under the buttocks instead of under the head. This will help the uterus to return to its initial position.
- Lie on the floor with your knees touching your breast, which help the uterus to resume its normal position.
- Lie down after a meal with a pillow under your back.

Premature Ejaculation in Males

It is a malfunctioning due to psychological reasons generally found in males who are sexually more aroused than the females, who need a bit of foreplay to be ready for the intercourse. Too much anticipation of the sex act, too much of excitement can lead to premature ejaculation giving a feeling of failure or lack of fulfillment, which should follow the act of sexual intercourse. The following are natural ways to treat premature ejaculation:

- Apply Mud Pack on pubes before sleep at night.
- **Kegal Exercise:** Squeeze the muscles in the anal area as if you are trying to stop the flow of urine. This exercise strengthens the pubic muscle, the urethra (urinary tube) and the rectum. A regular practice will help you to control over ejaculation.
- **Self-stimulation:** If you want to learn to slow your minutes' ejaculation reflex for four to six times during each session, masturbate three to four times a week, just bringing yourself close to orgasm but without ejaculating.
- **Scrotal Pull Technique:** During self-stimulation try practicing to pull down on your scrotal sac before you reach the point of no

return. During sex, you can do it yourself or seek the help of your partner.

- Press the area on your perineum, the space between the anus and the back of the scrotum, which stimulates the prostate – the gland that supplies the fluid for semen during ejaculation. Pressing on this spot when you are highly aroused helps block the ejaculatory reflex and can be quite pleasurable and delays ejaculation. Press on it firmly and rhythmically at any point on the area during sex after you have achieved a maximum erection.
- Mix in equal quantity seeds of 'Lajwanti' and sugar and take with the milk in the morning.
- Avoid constipation and digestion disorders.

Male Impotence

Impotence (sexual weakness) is the inability to perform sex - it may be partial or complete, temporary or permanent. Impotence can be in two categories: as a result of organic reasons or psychological reasons as described below:

Organic impotence: is caused by the following reasons:

- Lesions of the external genitalia such as a tight foreskin.
- Disturbances of endocrine glands, such as diminished activity of the gonads, thyroid glands or pituitary glands.
- Diseases of the central nervous system.
- Severe disturbance of health.
- Diabetes plays an adverse effect in this case.

In case of treatment of impotency due to organic factors, deal with the disease, which has caused it.

Psychological impotence: is caused by the following factors:

- Ignorance about sex.
- Fear.
- Weak-ness or abnormality of sexual desire.

The psychological treatment of impotence is to find the true reason and realize what has caused it. Treatment for impotency includes the following:

- The best remedy for impotence is a healthy diet and exercise.
- A wet pack (dipped in cold water) on the spine can help body to

energize and strengthen the nervous system. Lie naked on the bed so that the wet bandage remains in constant touch with the spine.

- Drink plenty of water in a day to draw away all the morbid matter that has been poisoning the body system.

Frigidity in Females

Frigidity is a condition in women, where she is unable to give herself sexually to male partner and enjoy sex usually due to the following reasons:

- Psychological fear.
- Wrong notions about sex.
- Physical incapacity.
- Hormonal and genital defects.
- Cultural taboos and social position.
- Intellectual upbringing and emotional status playing a significant role in female sexual behavior.
- Sexual indifferences (which is the major reason) or disliking for sex.
- Physicals causes such as inflamed vagina, a very rigid hymen, urinary problems or uterine infections.
- Displaced ovaries.

Nocturnal Emission

Involuntary discharge of semen (the fluid produced by testicles in male) during sleep or nocturnal emission is one of the common disorders among youths or even in middle-age persons. Night emission among youngsters is generally due to excitement because of reading vulgar literature or seeing a motion picture having exciting scenes. The following treatment are recommended to get rid of this psychological disorder:

- Avoid thoughts of sex.
- Eat rich food.
- Have dinner three hours before sleep.
- Have evening walk followed by a bath.
- Go to the bed early, not later than 9 p.m.
- Application of a Mud Pack on pubes during sleep at night.
- Hot and cold hip bath.

Excessive Sex

There are women who are extremely passionate and feel uncontrolled desire of sex. They are constantly attracted towards opposite sex. This is often due to the following reasons:

- Deep sense of insecurity produced by neglect in childhood and adolescence.
- Genetically, some females are hyper-fertile and highly sexual.

Excessively sexual women need psychotherapy. Hormone therapy neutralizes the effect of estrogen by administering progesterone hormones help to large extent.

Painful Intercourse

The disorder is also known as Dyspareunia, which may arise from muscular spasm of the vagina. Sometimes, there is a superficial ulceration following some injury and tissues are painful to the touch. Bladder infection is common in such cases, which may lead to further complications. Some of the causes of a painful intercourse are following:

- Tightness in the female genital area after a surgery. In such case usually tissues may have been drawn too tightly together.
- Pelvic inflammation may cause pain during intercourse.
- Nervous tension usually due to unconsciously afraid of pregnancy.
- Problems like body odors, halitosis etc.
- Lack of understanding on the part of male partner.
- May cause her pain during marital relations.

When Urine Escapes

This disorder of leakage of urine while laughing or carrying an heavy luggage is generally due to weakness of urethral opening or weak vaginal muscles, and sometimes as a result of repeated childbirths and prolonged labor. The overstretched urethral opening loses its elasticity. Sometimes, the urine escapes out with increased abdominal pressure due to short length of urethra in females.

Night Discharge

Involuntary discharge during sleep or at night while dreaming is common among youths. Reading cheap and vulgar literature or seeing sexually exploiting movies and TV serials may lead to frequent night discharge during sleep. There is misconception in our country that semen is produced from blood. Semen in males is, in fact, the fluid produced by testicles and its production during intercourse or involuntary discharge during sleep is not much of a concern as the quacks have us believe. Those concerned by frequent night discharge should take a clean, healthy living. Sexual thoughts and rich foods should be completely avoided. Rich foods only disturb the digestive system. Dinner should be taken three hours before sleep. To cure night ejaculation, get up early in the morning. Sunbath has a curative effect. Go to bed early preferably with a mud- pack on the pubic area. This regimen is equally beneficial for hysteria patients, to treat menstrual irregularities and in case of frigidity in women.

Premarital Sex

Premarital sex is uncommon in Indian males as well as females due to early marriages. Sex life starts with marriage in most of the cases. Women feel the risk of pregnancy and avoid premarital sex. When a female goes through an abortion, it has physical risks to health and can produce hemorrhage, rupture of uterus, pelvic infection and other serious complications to catch pelvic infection, vaginitis, urinary infection and risk of sexually transmitted diseases.

Sex After Menopause

Menopause is not the end of sex life and a woman can continue normal sex for years after she has stopped her periods. Many women enjoy satisfying sexual partnership even in old age. There are numerous couples in 60s who are involved in active sex life. Sometimes, menopausal women face problems having sex due to severe dryness of genital organs with pain during intercourse. Lubricating creams or estrogen ointments help to prevent the rapid atrophy of the vaginal mucosa.

16

PREGNANCY AND ABORTION

Signs and Symptoms of Pregnancy

- Stoppage of menstruation (monthly bleeding known as periods).
- Laziness, heavy feeling, irritability and presence of physical disturbances.
- Morning sickness and vomiting from second month onwards, which usually stops in the fourth month, or in some cases continues throughout pregnancy period.
- Heaviness in breasts.
- Breast nipples get prominent and areola starts turning darker from pinkish.
- Tightening of abdomen after about four months.
- Urge to frequently urination due to pressure of the pregnant uterus on the urinary bladder.
- Genitals feel warmer due to more blood and congestion.
- Vagina remains excessive moist.
- The fetal movement starts usually in the fifth month onward.
- Vagina is usually hot and moist.
- Uterus rises above the pelvis when the pregnancy is advanced.
- The movement of the fetus increases, feeling the limbs, head and neck of the fetus.
- Nausea and vomiting (start two weeks after the conception).
- Exhaustion and tiredness.
- Change of taste.
- Strong liking and disliking for certain foods.

Abortion

Loss or failure of early pregnancy in several forms: complete, incomplete, inevitable, missed, septic and threatened is known as Abortion.

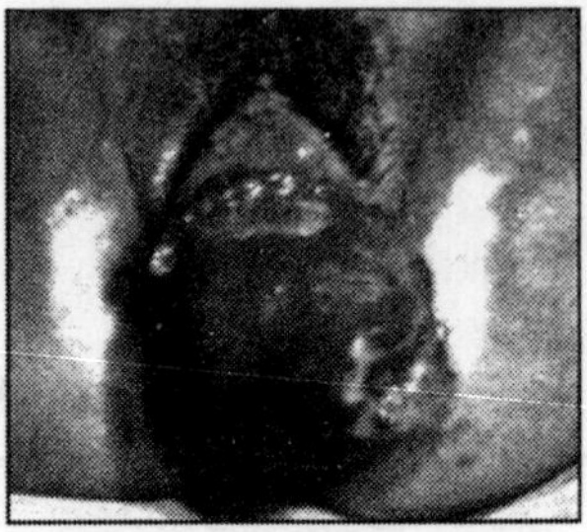

Abortion

Complete abortion: The termination of a pregnancy before the age of viability almost in 50% cases. It occurs at less than 20 weeks from the first day of the last normal menstrual period or involving a fetus of weight less than 500 gm.

Incomplete abortion: The spontaneous passage of some of the products of conception associated with uniform pregnancy loss.

Inevitable abortion: A pregnancy in which rupture of the membranes and/or cervical dilation take place during the first half of the pregnancy period.

Missed abortion: The retention of a failed intrauterine pregnancy, which can be detected by an ultrasound.

Septic abortion: A variant of an incomplete abortion due to infection.

Threatened abortion: A pregnancy in which vaginal bleeding or uterine cramping occurs. 50-60% such pregnancies come in the category of complete abortion.

Causes of Abortion

There are several causes for an abortion. Some of the prominent causes are the following:

- Endocrine abnormalities (in 25-50% cases).
- Genetic factors (in 10-70% cases).
- Trisomy (in 40-50% cases).
- Monosomy (in 15-25% cases).
- Reproductive tract abnormalities (in 6-12% cases).
- Tripoidy and tetraploidy (in 5-15% cases).
- Abnormality of placenta.
- Effect of venereal diseases.

- Chronic cardiovascular disease and chronic renal disease.
- Diabetes mellitus.
- Environmental factors such as alcohol, anesthetic gases, effect of drugs, radiation, smoking and toxins.
- Other factors such as advanced maternal age, delayed fertilization, short interval between pregnancies.

Signs and Symptoms

These include the following:

- Vaginal bleeding (bright red to dark colored).
- Abdominal cramping (rhythmic accompanied by pelvic or low back pressure).
- Cervical dilation with tissue visible at the cervical openings.
- Severe vaginal hemorrhage.
- Cervical polyps and cervicitis.
- Urinary tract infection and lower abdominal discomfort.
- Loss of early symptoms such as fullness of breasts or morning sickness.
- Disseminated intra-vascular coagulopathy can occur when an intrauterine fetal demise in the second trimester has been retained beyond six weeks after the death of the fetus.

Specific Measures

- Rh-negative mothers should be treated with Rh immune globulin after completion of the abortion, because ovulation may occur as early as two weeks after an abortion.
- After an abortion, control the bleeding, prevent infection and relieve pain.
- Ensure that all the products of the conception have been expelled from the uterus. If retained tissues are present and cannot be rules out, curettage must be performed immediately.
- Septic abortion requires urgent and aggressive management. Antibiotics, fluid therapy and prompt evacuation of the uterus are indicated.
- If significant pain or bleeding persists, especially bleeding leading to hemo-dynamic alterations, evacuation of the uterus should be conducted.

Maternal Disorders and their Effect on the Fetus

Disorder	Adverse effect
Toxemia of pregnancy:	Intra-uterine growth retardation, respiratory depression of the fetus due to use of sedatives and need for curtailment of pregnancy.
Antepartum hemorrhage:	Fetal and birth asphyxia, premature labor and anemia.
Polyhydramnios:	Anencephaly, high intestinal obstruction and ectopic pregnancy.
Oligohydramnios:	Bilateral renal agenesis or hypoplasia obstructive, obstructive uropathy, deformed limbs or face.
Rupture of membranes:	High risk of pneumonia in the baby.
Malnutrition:	Intrauterine growth retardation, anemia (iron deficiency).
Thyrotoxicosis:	Neonatal thyrotoxicosis and goiter.
Maternal diabetes:	Premature delivery often by cesarean section, intrauterine death, early asymptomatic or symptomatic hypoglycemia.
Maternal infection:	Abortion, intrauterine death, fetal growth retardation, multi-system involvement such as hepatitis, anemia, congenital malformation with viral infections during the first trimester of pregnancy.

17

TYPES OF PREGNANCY

Radiological diagnosis of pregnancy: This is widely used method for the diagnosis of pregnancy. The main reasons for the employment of radiography are the following:

1. The diagnosis of pregnancy.
2. The demonstration of the fetus in relation to presentation and position, maturity, structural abnormalities and multiple pregnancy intra-uterine death.
3. The demonstration of the uterus with reference to hydramnios and placental situation.
4. Localization of fetal abdomen for the purpose of intra-uterine transfusion.
5. Demonstration of material pelvis and lumber spine.

Radiological method of diagnosis should not be employed before the 28th week and are rarely necessary thereafter to find out the structural abnormalities and in twin pregnancy when one head is nearer the X-ray tube than other. To find out multiple pregnancy, the demonstration of the uterus and placental situation, hydramnios and placenta praevia, tube shift method is employed in the following ways:

- Find out first view of the pelvic inlet demonstrated in contour in the anterior posterior projection. The X-ray tube is centred above the patient's pelvis, so that the central ray of the X-ray beam passes through about three inches behind the anterior border of symphysis pubis.

- The radiograph is taken with the patient lying on the left side in between the left loin to keep the lumber spine straight. The thighs are flexed 5 degree towards the abdomen and knees are flexed 90 degree.
- The radiograph to show the transverse diameter of the outlet and the sub-pubic angle is obtained by placing the patient in sitting position. The X-ray beam is directed vertically downwards so that it passes through the mid point of the line joining the two tuberosities.

Types of Deliveries

Fertilization is the union of a mature ovum with a sperm. If sexual intercourse takes place within 12 to 24 hours of ovulation, then one of the thousands of sperms deposited in vagina unites with the ovum to fertilize it after traveling uterine cavity and reaching fallopian tube. Once the pregnancy has not established, the production of the hormones- estrogen and progesterone continue but there is no shedding. The menstruation stops and a woman is said to have conceived. The fertilized ovum gradually grows into the fetus and it takes about 266 days for a fertilized egg to grow into a baby. There are various types of deliveries.

Normal Vaginal Delivery

It is aided with a small cut of the vaginal outlet sometimes, the process in known as **Episiotomy,** which is done to help quicker delivery and undue downward pressure on uterus and adjoining parts like bladder and rectum. A normal delivery is generally done with a small cut at the vaginal outlet.

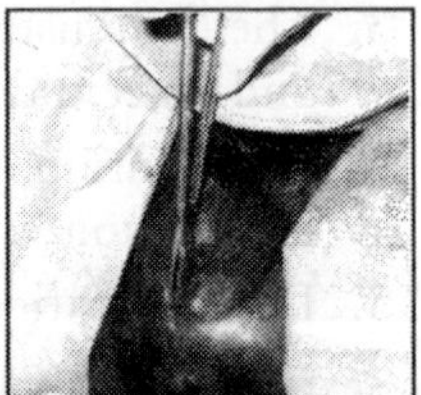

Episiotomy

Suction Delivery

It is a process in which suction is applied to the low descending head of the baby to hasten deliver. It is also called *vacuum method of delivery* and helps the mother to deliver quickly. Anesthesia is not required in most of the cases.

Forceps Delivery

In which baby's head is helped out with the use of forceps e.g. a large pair of tongs, which grasp the baby's head for applying a downward pull. Mild anesthesia is given to the mother to avoid excessive pain. The following are essential conditions for the application of Forceps:

Forceps delivery

1. The cervix must be fully dilated.
2. The head should be in the cavity of pelvis.
3. The head should be in a suitable position. A forceps delivery must not be attempted until the operator is quite certain of the presentation and position of the head.
4. The membranes must be ruptured.
5. The bladder and rectum should be emptied.

Risk of Forceps

- Injuries to the soft passages may be caused by carelessness in application of the blades or by too rapid extraction.
- Hemorrhage may be caused by too rapid extraction.
- Injuries to the child (e.g. fractures of the skull, intra-cranial hemorrhage, injury to eyes, facial paralysis, sphyxia for compression of head).

Multiple Pregnancy

Do you have any history of multiple births in the family? If yes, then you must watch out and tell your doctor to diagnose seriously. It can be diagnosed by the size of womb or pelvic examination or USC scanning of abdomen. In case of signs of multiple pregnancy, visit your doctor more frequently and have complete rest between 30th to 37th week, to avoid premature delivery. Multiple pregnancy means an extra trouble and sometimes there is a possibility of a caesarean section. Plural births require highly skilled pediatric care. The fetal mortality is much higher: pre-maturity, pro-lapse of the cord and asphyxia of the second twin takes a high toll. Congenital abnormalities in uniovular twins are common. Locked Twins is a rare complication, where the first child presents by the breech and the second by the head.

Delivery of the Head

This is the critical phase, because delay may cause havoc. The reasons for the delay are the following:

- The head passes into the pelvic cavity, which is no longer subject to the expulsive power of the uterus.
- The passage of head is resisted by the vulva ring at the outlet. To avoid such risk, episiotomy should always be made in a primigravida when the buttocks are distending the perineum. However, when the child is small and the maternal passages roomy, spontaneous delivery may occur without giving a cut at the outlet of vagina.

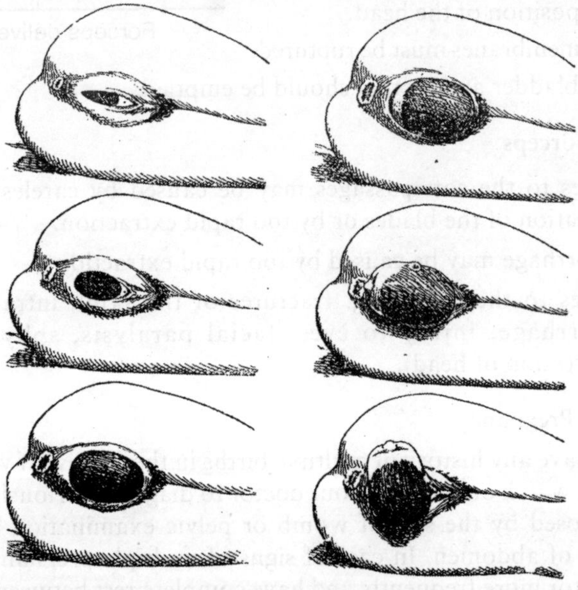

Delivery of the Head

The usual method of delivery is to hold the child's body slightly downwards, straddled over the left hand and forearm, and exert gentle pubic (nor fundal) pressure on the head as the head enters the pelvic cavity. Gentle traction will deliver the face and head.

Ectopic or Tubal Delivery

It is a rare complication in which the fertilized ovum or embryo becomes blocked in its passage through the fallopian tube. There the

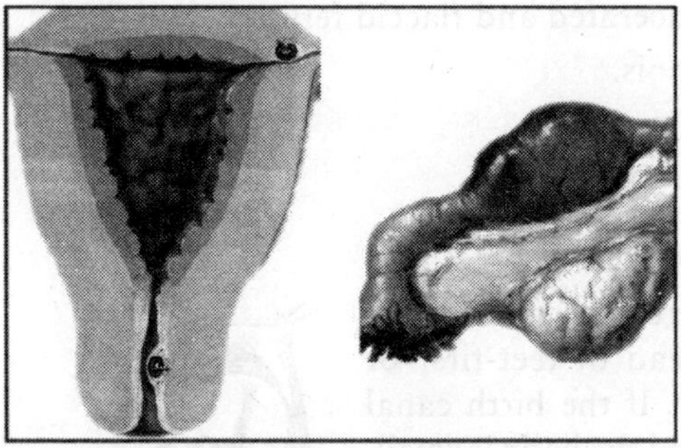

Ectopic or Tubal

embryo continues to grow as it normally would within the uterus. However, the space between the tube is too small to allow expansion, that may rupture, causing a serious hemorrhage and also intense pain in the pelvis. This may also result acute appendicitis. Consult a doctor for necessary surgery as soon as a tubal pregnancy is suspected before the occurrence of hemorrhage. Ectopic pregnancy remains one of the leading cause of maternal death, the pain, abnormal vaginal bleeding and a palpable adnexal mass is present in most of the patients with ectopic pregnancy.

Induced Delivery

In this connection, labor is brought on or induced artificially by rupturing the membranes and letting out a little amniotic fluid, which stimulates labor pains. When the pains are too feeble or the delivery is overdue, labor is induced by administrating medicines, which contract the uterus.

Premature Delivery

The termination of pregnancy after the fetus has become viable such as capable of living independently, is called premature birth. And if the fetus is born dead, it is stillbirth. Causes, which produce abortion can endanger the growth of the fetus resulting in still birth or a premature delivery. Premature delivery is usually the problem with the placenta to the faulty blood supply to the fetus, defective hormone production and effect of injurious toxins and chemicals through the blood to the fetus. The causes of premature delivery are the following:

1. Obliquity of the uterus.
2. Uterus subseptus.
3. Premature fetus.

4. Dead, macerated and flaccid fetus.
5. Hydramnois.
6. Placenta praevia.
7. Pelvic tumor.

Breech Delivery

Most babies are born in head-first position instead of feet-first or shoulder first. If the birth canal is adequate and the baby is small, there may not be any serious difficulty because of breech position. If the baby is bulky and the birth outlet small, this could be dangerous to both mother and the baby. Avoid traveling or bulky jerks during the last few days.

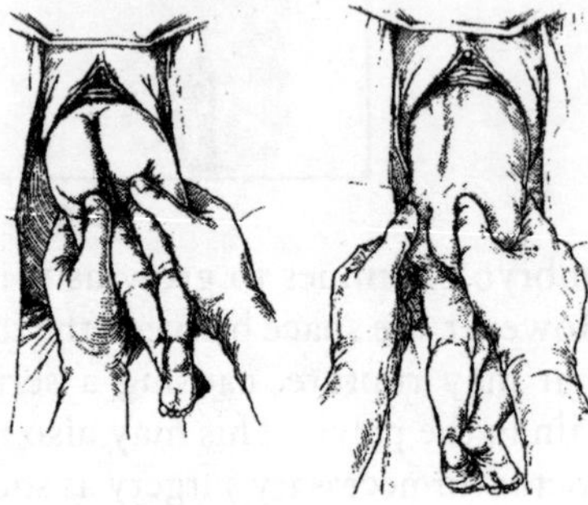

Breech delivery

Internal Version

1. In case of membrane intact or not ruptured recently, avoid internal version.
2. The abdominal and uterine walls must be relaxed.
3. An anesthesia should always be given.
4. The cervix must be dilated sufficiently to admit the entire hand in uterus.
5. The position of the fetus must have been exactly mapped out by the palpation before the hand is introduced in the uterus.
6. The vulva and the vagina must be thoroughly cleansed.
7. Sterile rubber gloves should be worn.

Pass the hand into the uterus in cone-shape and seize a foot. The patient should be placed on her side or her back. If the knee is felt, the foot or knee should be brought down through the cervix. The head must be pushed up into the fundus of uterus by external hand.

Vaginal Hysterotomy

In this process artificial dilation of the cervix is conducted by the fingers or by hydrostatic bags in the first stage in an operation, which has been nowadays almost replaced by cesarean section - better and a safer operation.

Under general anesthesia the cervix is exposed by adequate vaginal retraction. With the scissors the cervix is cut at points in clockwise direction. The cut extends to the junction of the cervix and the vaginal wall. Following delivery by the forceps the cut is carefully sutured. The final results of the healing are usually unsatisfactory and lead to reverse hemorrhage sometimes. Incision of the cervix is now very uncommon operation. Attempt to dilate the cervix by the fingers is always almost followed by cervical lacerations and the operation of the incision of the cervix is always preferred.

How to do Vaginal Hysterotomy?

This operation has been almost entirely supplemented by abdominal hysterotomy. The steps of the operation are described below:

1. Cervix drawn forcibly down longitudinal and transverse incisions in anterior vaginal wall.
2. Dissection of bladder from uterus and vaginal wall.
3. Splitting cervix anteriorly. Bladder and vaginal wall drawn up by anterior retractor.
4. Cervix split anteriorly. The membranes bulging down.
5. Posterior incision sutured. Suturing anterior incision.

Displacement of Uterus

It may be diagnosed by:

- Increase in backward displacement.
- Pain on micturition occurs, passing into retention if incarceration occurs.
- Undue enlargement of abdomen.

Generally, the enlargement of uterus and abdomen occurs due to pregnancy plus large tumor, hydramnnios, multiple pregnancy or even a mere mistake as to the date of conception. The bladder must be carefully emptied by catheter before examination.

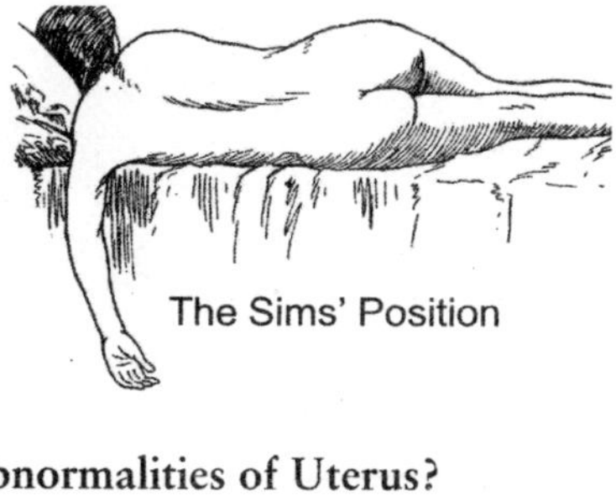

The Sims' Position

How to Treat Displacement and Abnormalities of Uterus?

1. If by12th week the uterus is still retroverted, then a large ring pessary is inserted into the vagina.

2. The patient is instructed to adopt the semi-prone position and remain in bed for a couple of days in the **Sim's Position.** It is found, after 24 to 48 hours the fundus can be felt in the abdomen. The pessary should be left in vagina until after the 16th week of pregnancy (under doctor's supervision).
3. If the uterus remains retroverted after 48 hours, then manual reposition of the uterus may be undertaken. Simple manual reposition is done by inserting two fingers in the posterior fornix and pushing the fundus upwards and forwards. The cervix is then caught backwards by one finger and the other hand on the abdomen to catch the fundus. After the uterus has been replaced a large ring pessary should be inserted and not removed until after the 16th week of pregnancy.
4. In case of patient with a history of preveous abortions, a laparotomy should be done immediately.

Abnormalities of Uterus

The malformations of the uterus are usually the result of incomplete fusion of two mullerian ducts or of incomplete absorption of the septum between then. The complications recorded include a high incidence of abortion, premature labor, inertia during labor, retained placenta, of transverse lies and breech presentations.

18

PHYSICAL EXAMINATION DURING PREGNANCY

The doctor often asks certain questions regarding the previous pregnancy such as difficulty in previous delivery, abortions or miscarriages (if any) in past, the birth of premature or macerated fetuses or death of children occurring in early infancy. The blood of both parents should be examined. Patient should be questioned about her present health, existence of cardiac or pulmonary disease or toxaemia, for example breathlessness, palpitation, cough, excessive vomiting, persistent headaches, swelling of the hands or face, diminished amount of urine, dimness of vision, condition of the bowels, the presence of vaginal discharges and their nature, swelling of the feet or legs, presence of hemorrhoids or varicose veins etc. should be enquired into.

After preliminary questioning is finished, the patient is asked to undress and lie upon an examination couch. Firstly, a general survey of circulatory, respiratory and digestive system is made. See that the doctor inspects the breast noting their development, the condition of nipples, areola (the darkish part around nipples) and the presence and the amount of secretion from them (if any). The mouth should always be examined for septic teeth, gums and tonsils. The blood pressure should be checked by the instrument- sphygmomanometer. It is important to find out blood group of the expectant mother for the investigation of hemoglobin and Rh group. The patient's height is recorded and it may be worthwhile to mention that women of short stature (five feet or below) are more likely to have small pelvis than taller women. The patient's weight is noted and a check on weight gain is made during the pregnancy.

Abdominal Examination

In early pregnancy, note the size of uterus and exclude any morbid abdominal conditions. Prior to the 26th week of pregnancy abdominal diagnosis of presentation and position is often inaccurate. The level of the fundus, the presence of uterine soufflé, hearing the heartbeat should be examined. At the 38th week, a final review is carried out and relationship of the fetal head to the maternal pelvis determined. A study is made to determine the size of the head related to the pelvis brim. It is important that in a primigravida, the head should normally become engaged in the pelvis during the last two or three weeks. It may be still movable during the last fortnight of pregnancy due to pelvic contraction, an abnormally large head, a posterior position of the occiput, placenta praevia, a pelvic tumor or simply due to faecal accumulation in the pelvic colon and rectum. A thorough examination of abdominal region should be carried out by the doctor to find out the head is able to enter the pelvis.

Pelvic Examination

The objects are twofold-to investigate the condition of the pelvic organs and to estimate the size and shape of the pelvic canal. It is necessary to measure the pelvis by your doctor by means of a bimanual examination. The diagnosis of pregnancy is confirmed and the presence or absence of pelvic swellings such as uterine fibroids or ovarian cysts can be determined. If the fundus of the uterus can be palpated abdominally there is no need to carry out the pelvic examination at the first visit and can be postponed until need arises. There are three methods of pelvic examination as below:

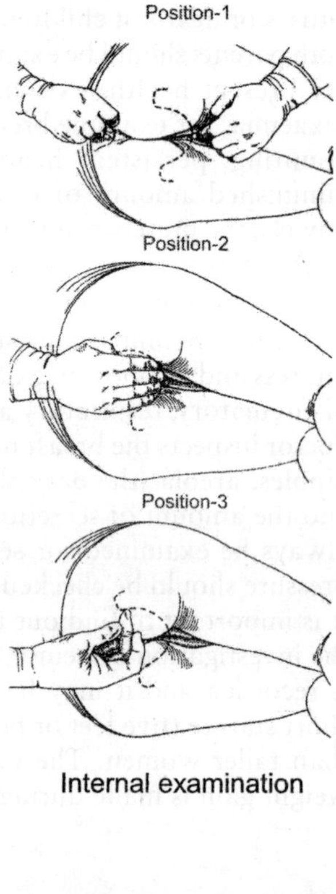

Internal examination

1. **External examination:** The measurements are made with a pair of calipers to find out any deformity to be recognized at once.
2. **Internal examination**: Internal diameter is measured with calipers.

The two, anterior-superior spines are located, where the points of caliper are placed on their outer· lips and the measurement read off. Normally it is 9-1/2 to 10 inches (24 –25 cm.). The Intercristal diameter is also measured at the points passed slowly round the iliac cresta until the points of greatest separation are found when the measurement is read Normally, it is 10-1/2 to 11 inches (26-27 cm.).

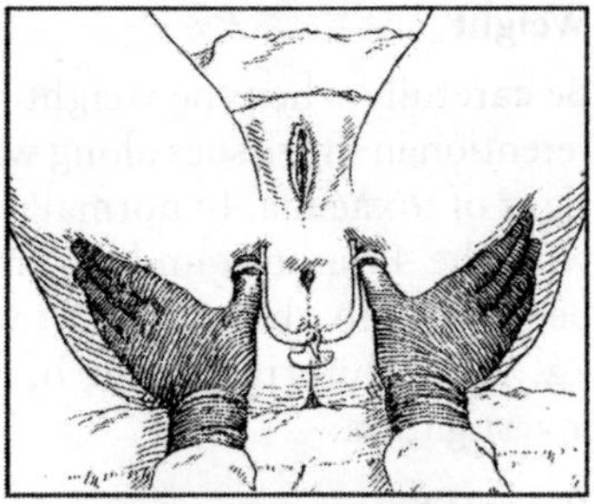

External examination

3. **By X-rays:** The size of the pelvis and the fetal head can be assessed by X-ray. This process is known as Radiographic Pelvimetry.

Blood Pressure

The blood pressure of the patient should be ascertained at each antenatal visit. During pregnancy the blood pressure should not rise above 140/90. If after a suitable period of rest, the pressure remains above this figure, then hypertension is said to exist. During the middle trimester of pregnancy the blood pressure is often low and the reading of 110/70 may be recorded. This physiological drop is of great interest and is called the 'mid pregnancy drop' in blood pressure.

Urine and Hemoglobin

Usually, the patient is asked to pass urine before she undresses for the physical examination. Examination of urine is most important throughout pregnancy. The possible presence of albumin is most important point to attend to, besides checking the presence of sugar, pus and other abnormalities. Urine should be examined once a month in the first six months, thereafter more frequently as pregnancy advances. If the albumin is present in the urines along with a vaginal discharge, a mid-stream specimen of urine should be obtained and a doctor should be consulted. The hemoglobin should be checked throughout pregnancy. It should be estimated as routine in all pregnant women at the 30th week. If you are suffering from anemia, there is plenty of time to correct this. All Rh Negative patients have their blood examined for the presence of antibodies at regular intervals.

Weight

Be carefully when the weight increases during pregnancy, since fluid retention in the tissues along with the increase in weight, is the earliest signs of toxaemia. In normal pregnancy, the increase in weight begins with the 4th month and continues at an average rate of about 2 kg per month to about the 39th week, the total weight being about 12 kg. Any abnormal gain in weight should determine a careful investigation.

Vaginal Secretion

The vaginal secretion in a healthy pregnancy differs only in its increased quantity from that of a healthy non-pregnant woman. It is whitish in color, containing epithelial cells, leucocytes and mucus. It also contains numerous large 'vaginal bacilli'. It has been observed that the acidity of the vaginal secretion is inimical to the life of other organism than the 'vaginal bacillus', followed by the appearance of organism in the vagina. Thus during the puerperium the lochia (discharge from the uterus after labor) is alkaline, which contain many organisms, mostly saprophytic are found.

Method of Cleaning Genitals

The birth canal can be divided into three parts:

1. The vulva, including the entrance to vagina. This area swarms with organism of various sorts. It may therefore be designated the Septic Tract.
2. The vagina, containing the vaginal bacilli with their acid secretion, a few fungi, and some leucocytes. This is Antiseptic Tract.
3. The cavity of the uterus, separated by the plug of mucus from the vagina, is entirely devoid of any form of organism. It is therefore the Aseptic Tract.

Cleansing of Vulva

Wherever possible the patient should have a complete bath at the very commencement of labor, and the nurse should see that the rectum and bladder are emptied. It is usually suggested that the patient should be given an enema in every case, irrespective of whether the bowels have acted naturally or not, unless the patient is in strong labor when the nurse arrives. The nurse should then pay special attention to the genitals. The hair should be shaved. Before a vaginal examination is made, the vulva is swabbed with a antiseptic solution. The labia minora must be separated and wiped with pledgets of wool soaked in an antiseptic solution. The pledget must always be drawn from being backwards to prevent carrying forward any septic matter from near the anus. No pledget must be used for more than one wipe.

Puerperal Infection

The term puerperal infection can be used to describe any infection during or after labor, it generally applies to infection of the uterus and surrounding tissues after delivery. This can vary from mild to life threatening in severity. Some of the most severe infections may appear within hours of the delivery and are often opportunistic and non-associated with reliable risk factors. Vigilance and aggressive diagnosis, and treatment are required. The puerperal infection causes due to colonization and infection of the tissues of uterus, peritoneum or surrounding organs. Abscesses usually contain both aerobic and anaerobic bacteria. Nearly 50% of the ascending uterine infections involve chlamydia trachomatis. The risk factors of this infection includes a Cesarean delivery, invasive procedure during labor, prolonged rupture of the membranes, prolonged labor, multiple examinations, retained placental fragments, urinary catheter, intravenous line(s), low socioeconomic status and chronic diseases including diabetes. Better seek the advice of your doctor for treatment.

The signs and symptoms of the infection are fever and tachycardia often developing rapidly after delivery, uterine tenderness, signs of septic or cardiovascular shock, hypertension, anxiety, disorientation, prostration, impaired renal function, hemolysis or hemoconcentration. The infection can be diagnosed by the following:

1. Urinary tract infection including Pyelonephritis, in which large number of white blood cells and cultures are positive.
2. Wound infection.
3. Infection in intravenous line or site and contaminated fluids.
4. Disturbed abscess.
5. Septic thrombophlebitis.
6. Necrotizing fasciitis.
7. Transfusion reaction.
8. Amniotic fluid or pulmonary embolism.
9. Cardiogenic shock.

10. Toxic shock syndrome.
11. Mastitis.
12. Afelectasis.

Possible associated conditions include septic shock, adult respiratory distress syndrome, acute renal failure and disseminated intra-vascular coagulation.

Vaginal Examination

The use of abdominal palpation instead of this method of examination in normal cases has already been recommended. Where a vaginal examination is necessary it must be done with care. The patient should be on her back rather than on her side, so as to diminish the risk of the hand coming into contact with the anus. Cleanse hands and vulva before conducting the examination. The labia minora is separated apart by the left hand fingers. The fingers of right hand are introduced in the vagina without coming into contact with vulva at all, or at least only the inner surfaces of the labia minora, which have also been cleansed. In case the patient is passing through the stage of labor, it is well to introduce the fingers into the vagina during a pain and prolong the examination until it passes off. One can learn the state of matters both during and between pains. Ascertain the following points during vaginal examination:

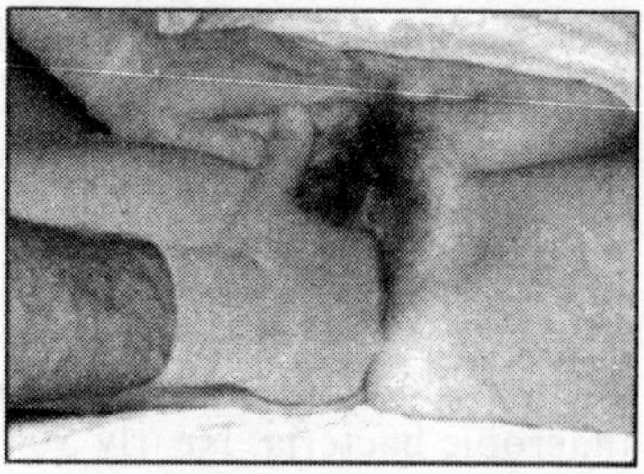

Vaginal examination

1. State of labor; how far advanced it is?
2. Presentation and position?
3. Are the membranes ruptured? (if not, be careful not to rupture the same).
4. State of vagina and perineum to check rigidity, moistness or dryness.
5. Is pelvis normal?
6. Is cord prolapsed?

19

40 WEEKS OF PREGNANCY

How Pregnancy Develops?

The upper broad end of the uterus opens on either side into two long tubes called the fallopian tubes, each ending in a funnel shaped opening guarded by five finger-like projections called fibria, which lies close to the ovary - a spherical walnut sized organ producing female hormones and eggs called ova. Ovulation occurs usually in the middle of a menstrual cycle (between two consecutive periods). At birth, each ovary has thousands of follicles and each follicle is capable of giving one mature egg. During a woman's reproductive life about 400 ova are shed. When ovulation occurs, the ovum is picked up and travels down the fallopian tube towards the uterine cavity.

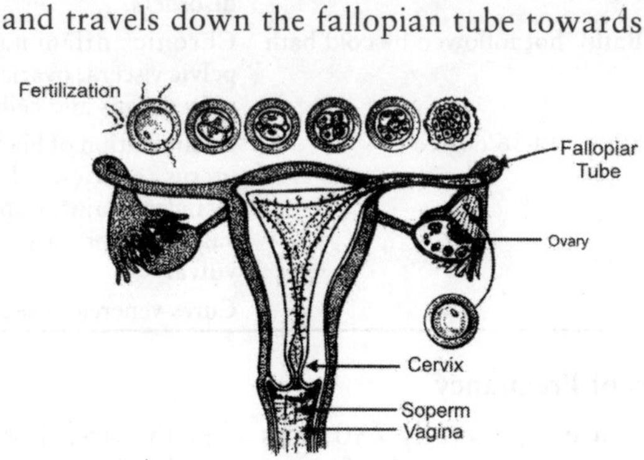

Fertilization

Menstruation is a process of 28-day cycle in which follicle matures and ovaries produce oestrogenic hormones. When an ovum matures, it is shed and start traveling. The follicle, which contains this ovum produces the hormone progesterone. In case there is no pregnancy, the level of the hormones falls and is shed off along with the blood. This is called menstruation.

Fertilization is the union of a mature ovum with sperm. If sexual intercourse takes place within 12 to 24 hours of ovulation, then one of the thousands of sperms deposited in vagina unites with the ovum to fertilize it after traveling down uterine cavity and reaching the fallopian tube. Once the pregnancy has got established, the production of hormones: estrogen and progesterone continues but there is no shedding. The menstruation stops and a woman is said to have conceived.

Enhancing Sex Power Through Therapeutic Baths

Type of bath	Water temperature	Genital advantages
Cold Hip Bath	10-18 degree C	Cures irregular menstruation, uterine infection, pelvic inflammation, prostate glands, seminal weakness in men, impotency, sterility, ovary and uterine displacement.
Hot Hip Bath	40-50 degree C	Cures pelvic inflammation, chronic urine infection, irregularities of menstruation, impotency in men, disorders of ovaries and uterus.
Epsom Salt Bath	1.5 kg salt in water	Cures genital diseases and kidney disorders.
Alternate Hip Bath	hot followed by cold bath	Chronic inflammation in the pelvic viscera, ovaries, genito-urinary organs and cellulite.
Neutral Hip Bath	30-36 degree C	Inflammation of bladder, urethra, uterus, ovaries, fallopian tubes, testicles, painful spasms of the vagina and pruritis of the anus and vulva.
Mud Bath		Cures venereal diseases.

Three Stages of Pregnancy

The delivery date is generally 280 days after the first day of the last period. The 40- week period of pregnancy is classified into three trimesters as below:

- The first trimester: Period starting from 1st to 12th week.
- The second trimester starts from 13th week to 28th week.
- The third trimester starting from 29th to 40th week.

The child in womb becomes theoretically capable of living a separate individual existence about the 28th week of pregnancy. It is important to know the age of a fetus or embryo both for clinical and medico reasons.

- **At the end of 4th week:** The embryo is much curved, head and tail being close together. It measures from 2.5 to 4 mm. from crown to rump. The brain and cord are enclosed, eye and ear vesicles are visible. The heart is prominent and is beginning to divide in four chambers.
- **At the end of 8th week:** The embryo is about an inch (25 mm.) long in crown rump measurement. The head has a human shape, whereas the tail has nearly disappeared. The hands and feet begin to appear. Eyes, nose and ears are recognizable. The external genitals are visible, but sex is not distinguishable. The embryo now becomes the fetus.
- **At the end of 12th week:** The fetus is about 3-1/2 to 4 inches long weighing about 50 gm. The intestines are enclosed in the abdomen and umbilical cord is beginning to show spiral turns. Sex can be determined by the presence or absence of the uterus. Most of the bones are beginning to show centers of ossification.
- **At the end of 16th week:** The fetus is about six inches (15 cm.) long and weighs about 190 gm. Sex is clearly defined at this stage. The fine downy hair starts appearing on the skin.
- **At the end of 20th week:** The fetus is about 7 to 8 inches (18-20 cm.) long and weigh about 450 gm. The head is still relatively large. The cord is about 12 inches long.
- **At the end of 24th week:** The fetus is about 9 inches (23 cm.) long and weighs about 930 gm. Fat begins to deposit under the skin. Hair appears on the head.
- **At the end of 28th week:** The fetus is about eleven inches (28 cm.) long weighing about 1300 gm. The eyelids are now open and the papillary membrane starts disappearing. The body is now covered with fine hair (lanugo). A child born at this time very seldom survives.
- **At the end of 32nd week:** The fetus is nearly 12 inches long weighing about 2075 gm. The hair on the scalp is thicker.
- **At the end of 36th week:** The length of fetus is nearly 14 inches weighing about 2500 gm. The subcutaneous fat has increased, and the face is less wrinkled and the body more round. A child born at this time has a very fair chance of survival.

- **At the 40th week:** The total length reaches 20 inches weighing about 3200 gm. The fingers have complete nail, the skin is pink and smooth. The diameter of the head becomes normal. In the male the testicles are in the scrotum.

Prenatal Examinations

The following tests and examinations are performed at the first or second prenatal visit to doctor, which helps assure the birth of healthy baby:

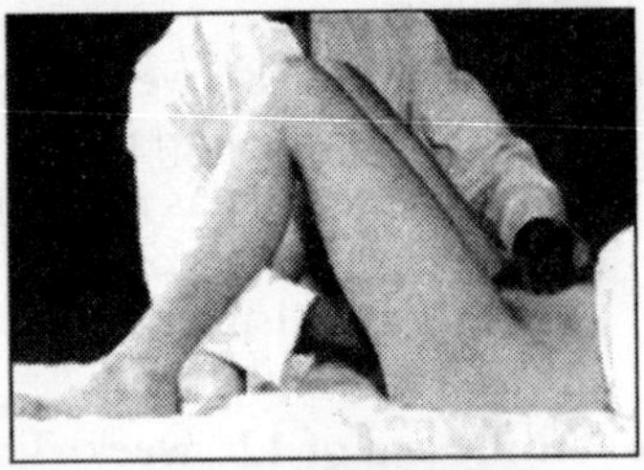

Vaginal examination

- A complete medical history and physical examination.
- A pelvic (vaginal) examination to confirm pregnancy, estimate the size and shape of your pelvis, to do a Pap smear to detect cervical cancer and to test for gonorrhea.
- Blood test to determine your blood type, Rh factor, test for anemia, infection, syphilis and German measles immunity.
- Urine test to check protein, sugar and any infection.
- At each prenatal monthly visit to your doctor check up for weight, blood pressure, urine and abdominal examination to measure the growth of uterus, fetus and estimate the size and position of fetus should be carried out.

Warning Signs During Pregnancy

Warning signs	Possible problems
Vaginal bleeding	Miscarriage, placenta previa, abruptio placentae and premature labor.
Abdominal pain	Ectopic pregnancy, abruptio placenta and premature labor contractions.
Leakage of fluid from vagina	Rupture of membranes.
Sudden puffiness or swelling on body	Preeclampsia (toxemia).
Severe, persistent headache	Preeclampsia (toxemia).
Disturbance of vision, spots or flashes	Preeclampsia (toxemia).
Dizziness	Preeclampsia or supine hypo-tension.
Pain or burning on urination	Urinary tract infection and sexually transmitted disease (STD).
Vaginal discharge, sores or itching	Vaginal infection and STD.
Fever (oral temperature)	Infection.
Persistent nausea	Hyperemesis gravidarum and infection.
Reduction in fetal activity	Fetal distress.

First trimester of Pregnancy

The important sign and symptoms include:

- Missed period, but sometimes the pregnant woman keeps having their periods two to three months after they conceive.
- Nausea and vomiting, many times, such women do not have nausea and vomiting.
- Exhaustion, tiredness and excessive giddiness all the time.
- Morning sickness.
- Change of taste.
- Strong liking and disliking for certain foods.
- Frequent urge to urinate.
- Engorged and tender breasts.
- Increase of discharge from nipples.

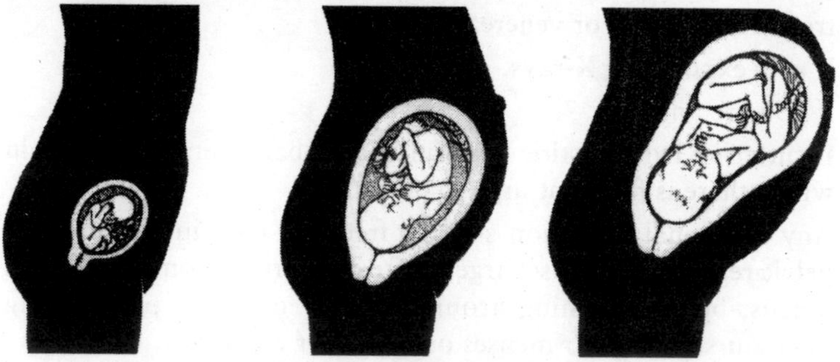

Three Stages of Pregnancy

After conceiving, the fertilized egg travels down the fallopian tube to get embedded in the lining of the womb in the 3rd week. By the 6th week, the embryo is 1.25 cm long but doesn't look like a baby. It has large head with pits for eyes and a tail. By the 12th week the baby measures about 9 cm weighing approximately 9 gm. It appears like a human embryo with all internal organs. The fetus takes nutrition from the mother and discharges its waste material into her blood through placenta. Always take medicines as prescribed by a doctor. Placenta, full of blood vessels, is formed partly by the fetal and partly by the uterine tissues. Placenta produces hormones necessary for the pregnancy. After baby's birth the placenta gets separated from the uterine wall and is expelled from the uterus.

On finding the symptoms of pregnancy, the pregnant woman should consult a doctor and tell him/her the following:

- The date of the first day of last menstruation period.
- The duration and heaviness in menstrual flow having in past.
- Any complication faced in previous pregnancies.
- The number of children and their usual weight at the time of birth in previous cases of pregnancy.
- The duration of lactation (breast feeding) in past cases.
- The number of years of marriage and the number of children.
- Any miscarriage or termination of pregnancy in past.
- If undergoing any treatment at the present or in past. In case of a past surgery, inform the doctor.
- Past history of health with detail of prolonged suffering such as diabetes, high blood pressure, epilepsy or heart disease.
- If yourself or your husband or any close blood relation is suffering from a hereditary or venereal disease.
- If ever exposed to X-rays.
- If you are anemic.
- If suffering from cystitis (painful and embarrassing condition in which there is frequent urge to urinate).
- Any abnormal condition such as frequent pain in abdomen or pelvic region, blood discharge, white discharge accompanied with mucus, boils or itching around urinary opening, pain during intercourse, irregular menses or any other condition.

A pregnant woman must undergo the following monthly tests/ examination by the doctor:

- Weight gain.
- Recording blood pressure.
- Oral hygiene checked.
- Signs of anemia, swelling of legs, feet and hands.
- Inspection of heart and lungs.
- Examination of breasts to check for any lumps and abnormality of nipples.
- Vaginal examination. During the first 12 weeks the uterus cannot be felt by placing hand on abdomen. To confirm pregnancy, an internal pelvic examination has to be performed between 6th and 10th week of pregnancy.

To find correct picture and determine the size of the uterus gently insert two gloved fingers into the vagina and push firmly on abdomen to assess the uterus thoroughly. The patient is made to lie flat on the examination table bending legs in such a way so as to keep the feet on the table and pelvic muscles relaxed.

A pregnant woman should avoid the following during first trimester:

- Wearing tight clothes.
- Drinking excessive tea and coffee.
- Jerky or long traveling.
- Over-exertion.
- X-rays.
- Strong medicines without doctor's prescription.
- Smoking or drinking.
- Standing for a long time or getting up suddenly from sitting position.
- Contact with animals, especially cats and birds, which may lead to abortion, premature delivery or birth of a sickly baby.
- Not consulting the doctor on finding symptoms such as bleeding or excessive discharge through vagina, abdominal pain, painful burning urination, persistent vomiting, frequent fever and feeling of dizziness. If you feel dizzy sit down with your head between your toes.

A pregnant should take the following precautions during first trimester:

- A monthly check up and consultation with the doctor.
- Have frequent small meals – about 6 to 7 times a day.
- Get 8 to 10 hours sleep during night and minimum two hours rest during the day.
- Restrict fluid intake in the evening to avoid frequent urination during night.
- Hormonal changes lead to a feeling of lethargy and exhaustion during the first trimester of pregnancy, so a complete rest is essential in this period.
- Consult a doctor in case of burning sensation while passing urine.
- Eat hygienically cooked food.

- Relax for few minutes with your feet up during lunch hours.
- Take anti-vomiting drug in consultation with the doctor in case of severe nausea and vomiting.

How to Do a Vaginal Examination?

Where a vaginal examination is necessary it must be done with care. The patient should lie on her back rather than on her side, so as to diminish the risk of the hand coming into contact with the anus. Cleanse hands and vulva before conducting the examination. The labia minora is separated apart by the left hand fingers. The fingers of right hand are introduced in the vagina without coming into contact with vulva at all, or at least only the inner surfaces of the labia minora, which also need cleansing.

Second Trimester of Pregnancy

Signs and symptoms during 2nd trimester include the following:

- No nausea and vomiting.
- Desire to urinate frequently subsides.
- Movement of growing baby in the womb is noticed by the 18th week in case of first delivery, otherwise by the 16th week of pregnancy.
- Enlargement of breasts visible.
- Gradual increase of bulge in abdomen.
- Skin around the nipples becomes dark.
- Clear watery secretion from nipples becomes thick and yellowish when squeezing by the 16th week.
- Small, pinkish and white streaks become visible on the lower abdomen.
- The skin of the upper thighs gets stretched by the 20th week.
- Appetite lost during 1st trimester of pregnancy returns. There is 20-25% increase in appetite of a pregnant woman during the last trimester of pregnancy.

Some essential checks during 2nd trimester of pregnancy are the following:

- Have a regular check over the blood pressure as during pregnancy it is slightly lower than pre-pregnancy stage. Consult a doctor in case blood pressure start rising as it is harmful for the mother as well as the baby.

- A check over the growth of baby in womb is essential during this period. After 12th week the womb lying deep in the pelvis starts rising out of bony pelvis, which can be felt by placing a hand on the lower abdomen. A doctor may easily assess the size of womb and the baby besides having a check if it is a multiple pregnancy.
- Check weight after the first trimester of pregnancy. The total weight gain during three trimesters of pregnancy should not be more than 10 to 12 kg. After the first trimester, there should be an increase in weight ranging from 0.7 to 1.4 kg. On completion of 20 weeks, the total increase in weight should be up to 4 kg. In case of lesser weight than the normal required gain, it indicates poor growth of the baby and there is need for the improvement in mother's diet. If the weight is more than the normal gain coupled with increase in blood pressure, consult a doctor immediately. Avoid excessive intake of wrong kind of food.
- Ensure regular urine test for proteins as you may be suffering from pre-eclamptic toxaemia (PET), which is common disorder in expectant mothers having high blood pressure.
- Around the 7th week of pregnancy visit your doctor for an ultrasound. You can hear baby's heartbeats around the 14th week of pregnancy. The doctor must observe the rate and rhythm of the baby's heartbeats.
- Urine test is a must to find out the traces of sugar every month, indicating diabetes and functioning of kidneys.
- Swelling of hands, ankles and legs should be examined by your doctor every time you go for check up once a month. Have a hemoglobin test to detect early signs of anemia, if any and should be treated accordingly.
- Even in case of a normal pregnancy, between 16th to 20th week of pregnancy, a routine ultrasound scan is advised to find out the growth of the child and position of placenta. In case the position of placenta is near or on the cervical opening there are chances of severe bleeding and immediate attention of a doctor is required.
- Carry out alpha feto protein test during 15th to 18th week of pregnancy. Alpha feto protein is a substance produced by the baby, which passes into the mother's blood stream. There are chances of congenital defect or there may be two babies in the womb, in case of abnormally high levels of this protein.

- Amniocentosis test is carried out between the 14th to 18th week of pregnancy to detect any abnormality in the baby. It is carried out only when the age of the expectant mother is more than 35 years and has delivered a malformed baby previously.
- During 2nd trimester of pregnancy, tetanus toxoid injections are administered twice at an interval of one month on the advice of your doctor.

Avoid the following during 2nd trimester of pregnancy:

- Do not take greasy and spicy foods, otherwise there are chances of excessive weight gain.
- Drink 7 to 8 glasses of water a day.
- Avoid constipation.
- Avoid excessive intake of sugar and salt.
- Avoid canned and processed foods. Take extra fruits and pulses.
- Avoid eating at unhygienic places.
- Sexual intercourse is not permissible in the 2nd trimester of pregnancy in case of previous miscarriage or in case of vaginal bleeding. However, normal sex is permissible within the physical constraints imposed by the growing womb. A pregnant woman can, however, fulfill her husband's needs with love and tenderness, omitting intercourse.
- Avoid strenuous exercises in this trimester. Start with light exercises for 5 minutes and gradually increase the duration to 20 minutes.
- Take complete bed rest if bleeding occurs.
- Do not exert to the point where you get tired. A walk in the open in the early morning is the best exercise during this trimester.Besides the physical toning up, it has a calming and relaxing effect.
- Do not wear high-heeled shoes. Wear flat shoes as far as possible.
- Do not bend your waist while picking up any object from the ground. Keep your back straight and bend at your knees and hips.

3rd Trimester of Pregnancy

The period from 29th to 40th week of pregnancy is the last stage and need a lot of care. As the arrival of new baby draws nearer, expecting mothers are filled with excitement to see the new arrival as well as the fear of the delivery of child. The expectant mother should visit a doctor once a week in case of any complication or once in a fortnight in case of normal condition. During the final month, between 37th to 40th week, the following medical check up and precautions are essential:

- There must be three or more movements of the baby in one hour during the last weeks of pregnancy. In case the movements are less, consult your doctor.
- Get checked blood pressure and urine.
- Check any swelling on the face and feet and inform your doctor.
- Consult your doctor for finding the position of the baby in the womb, size and growth, heartbeats of the baby etc. by an abdominal examination. These information help during the process of delivery.
- In case you find any abnormality in breast nipples, consult your doctor. A nipple exercise will be beneficial to treat disorder.
- Avoid sex during this period as it becomes cumbersome and physically difficult because of bulging abdomen. Sex should strictly be avoided if there is a history of bleeding during pregnancy or there is risk of premature birth of baby or such a thing has happened in the past. However, there is no harm if the intercourse is done carefully after consulting your doctor, lying in such a position that there is no pressure on the abdomen, preferably in a position having back to your partner.
- Take 8 to 10 hours of sleep during the night and minimum of 3 to 4 hours rest during the day.
- Continue light exercises during this trimester, which are important for good health. Make sure the exercises are done to the extent where you do not get tired. Avoid lying flat on back during late pregnancy. Consult your doctor before starting exercise.
- You may feel breathlessness and discomfort during the last two months of pregnancy usually due to the growing womb, which pushes the other abdominal organs upward. In such condition, rest as much as possible. Use an extra pillow to prop yourself up while lying down.
- In case you feel faint and dizzy during the last four weeks of pregnancy generally due to low blood pressure, take complete rest. Avoid standing for a long period.
- There is often feeling of frequent urination during night in the last 8 to 10 weeks of pregnancy generally due to womb pressing down on the bladder. Do not worry if there is no burning sensation while passing urine.

- In some cases there is burning sensation in the upper abdomen during the last phase of pregnancy because the enlarged womb presses against the stomach, thus pushing food contents up into the food pipe resulting in pain and burning sensation in the upper abdomen and below the ribs. To prevent this, avoid taking spicy and fried foods. Take smaller quantity of food at short intervals instead of taking heavy meals at long intervals.
- Leakage of urine on light jerk is another common problem during the last trimester of pregnancy due to weak pelvic floor below the womb. Avoid lifting heavy weights and constipation. Empty your bladder frequently. A light pelvic exercise will help a lot. To exercise pelvic, lie on the floor with back and knees bent so that your feet lie flat touching the floor. Now tighten the muscles by pressing hips and thighs drawing your vagina in as much as possible.
- Reddish, moist rashes may develop in the skin folds usually under the breasts and in the groin region during the last stage of pregnancy (mostly in summer). The expectant mother should keep such area dry and clean and avoid use of nylon underwear. Always use cotton undergarments.
- Painful contraction of muscles, usually in the calves, is another problem during the last trimester of pregnancy generally due to deficiency of calcium. Take calcium tablets with the consultation of doctor. Massage the affected area and in case the calves are affected, walk for sometime to regulate blood circulation.
- Heavy swelling of the feet, fingers and other parts on the body usually occur in late pregnancy and is called pre-eclamptic toxemia (PET) – which is a combination of swelling on ankles, fingers and vulva (also known as oedema of vulva) followed by puffiness of the face with increased blood pressure and presence of protein in urine. The risk of PET is more common among obese women and females getting married in teenage. Women with family history of high blood pressure are prone to this risk and consult a doctor immediately. A delayed treatment may cause a risk of fits and birth of a retarded child.
- Expectant mother in the habit of smoking and drinking cause severe damage to the baby in the womb. Intra-uterine growth retardation is a condition where the growth of baby in womb is severely impaired due to anemia and malnourishment. To ensure a healthy baby, it is important to completely part with smoking

and taking alcohol. Smoking is the root cause of certain diseases like high blood pressure, chronic kidney diseases, heart ailments and several infections harmful for mother as well as for the child's health and growth. Excessive smoking affects production of breast milk and alcohol taken by the mother passed into the baby cause severe side effects.

- The gums start bleeding and become inflamed during the last trimester of pregnancy. Brush your teeth thoroughly after taking meal and massage gums gently.
- There is a complaint of leakage of urine while walking briskly, laughing or sneezing by the expecting mothers during the last trimester of pregnancy due to loss of strength of muscles of the pelvic floor, which support the intestines, urinary bladder and womb. Here is an exercise to treat this disorder. Lie on the floor with back and knees bent keeping feet flat on the ground. Tighten the muscles, squeezing as if trying to stop the urine. Draw your vagina in, pause for a while and then relax. Repeat for 10 to 15 times.
- Expectant mothers develop the problem of piles in the last trimester of pregnancy due to constant pressure of the baby on blood vessels around anal region. This also results in soreness, itching pain and bleeding while passing stool. Avoid constipation and standing for a long time. Consult a doctor to prescribe an ointment to reduce pain and itching.
- The expectant mothers feel uneasy and cannot sleep properly in the night usually during the 3rd trimester of pregnancy. Reading or a warm bath before going to sleep helps a lot. Lie on your side with a pillow under the head.
- Constipation is another problem common during the 3rd trimester because the bowel movement slows down under the influence of progesterone hormone. As such the stools become hard and infrequent. Take plenty of fluids besides regular exercise. Avoid laxatives. Consult a doctor.
- Problem of excess sweating arise during the last trimester of pregnancy generally attributed to hormonal changes. Wear loose clothes, especially during night and take plenty of water.
- Many times, there is thick curd-like discharge with severe itching in the vaginal region. A slight increase in the clear or whitish

vaginal secretion is normal. The hormonal changes during last trimester of pregnancy make one more prone to vaginal thrush with a thick discharge and itching, which make urination painful. Avoid use of soap and nylon undergarments and keep the area around the vagina dry.

- The risk of complications during delivery is more pronounced in women suffering from anemia. The red blood cells contain a substance called hemoglobin, which carries oxygen. The normal level of hemoglobin is 11 to 14 gm. In case its level falls to below 10 gm, one is considered anemic. An anemic expectant mother may have a smaller than the normal child or a premature baby. The risk of pregnancies also increases during delivery in anemic women.
- Multistage pregnancy can easily be diagnosed by the size of womb or USG scanning. In case of a multiple pregnancy consult your doctor more frequently and take complete rest between 30th to 37th weeks to avoid premature delivery. There may be a possibility of a caesarian section in case of a multiple pregnancy. In case of caesarian section the delivery of baby is made through an incision in the uterus rather than the baby's exit through cervix and vagina, where incision is done in the low lying transverse region in the lower abdomen where becomes hidden under pubic hair.

Pregnancy Calendar at a Glance (First Trimester)

Fetal growth: After conception, up to four weeks the fetal length is about 1/4th inch. The eyes, ears, mouth, brain, spine, spinal cord and umbilical cord start forming. The heart starts beating by the 25th day. It is called **ovum** until two weeks. By the end of 8th week, the length of fetal grows up to 1-1/8 inches with the formation of arms, legs, bones, internal organs, the brain and tooth buds. It is called **embryo.** By the end of 12 weeks the fetal growth ranges to 3 inches long when the movement of arms and legs starts. The fingers and toes are formed. Sex is distinguishable and can urinate. It is called a **fetus.**

Placental and uterine changes: Uterine lining becomes thick with increased blood supply. Uterus starts enlarging, cervix becomes softer, implantation of ovum is usually in upper back portion of uterus and there is formation of placenta and umbilical cord. By the end of 8 weeks, the uterus is of size of a tennis ball. By the end of 12 weeks the size of uterus is like a grapefruit, the fundus is just above pubic bone, amniotic fluids fills uterine cavity and is continually replaced. At this time there is complete exchange of nutrients and waste products through placenta. The placenta is the major source of estrogen and progesterone.

Common physical and emotional changes: The following changes are observed in expectant mother by the end of 12 weeks:

- No menstruation.
- Has fullness or ache in pelvis.
- May be nauseated and may vomit frequently.
- Feels tired.
- Has increased vaginal secretion.
- May feel faint.
- Urinate more frequently.
- Breasts are fuller, nipple may tingle and areola is darker.
- May lose or gain up to 2 to 2.5 kg.
- Moods widely vary.
- There is always focus on body changes.
- Sexual relationship in both partners may change.

(Second Trimester)

Fetal growth: Till 16th week the fetal is 6 inches long with strong heart beats, active muscles, thin and transparent skin, downy hair covering the body, formation of fingernails and toenails. By the end of 20th week the fetal length reaches 10 to 12 inches and there is presence of hair, eyelashes and eyebrows. By the end of 24 week the fetal length reaches 11 to 14 inches, the skin gets wrinkled and the meconium starts collecting in bowel.

Placental and uterine changes: Till the end of 16th week the uterus is placed 3 inches above the pubic bone and the placenta performs nutritional, respiratory, excretory and most endocrine functions. The amniotic fluid increases in amount. By the end of 20th week, the uterus is placed at level of navel and the size of placenta covers half of the inner surface of uterus. By the end of 24 weeks the uterus reaches above the level of navel.

Common physical and emotional changes: These are the following:

- Fetal movement is noticeable.

- There is no nausea during this stage.
- Mask of pregnancy (chloasma) may appear.
- Usually become constipated.
- Have food cravings.
- Sometimes develop vaginitis.
- There is usual problem of nasal congestion.
- Have leg cramps frequently.
- Change in voice.
- Painful groin from round ligament contractions.
- Weight gain.
- Pregnancy becomes more enjoyable.
- Sexual desires may change.

(Third Trimester)

Fetal growth: Reaches to about 20 inches. Fingernails protrude beyond fingers. The head is large as compared to body. The arms and legs are in flexed position. Lungs become mature.

Placental and uterine changes: Uterus is back to height at 34th week. Placenta with one inch thickness have 6 to 8 inches diameter. Umbilical cord having length of approximately 20 to 22 inches has twisted or spiral appearance.

Common physical and emotional changes: Contractions, bloody show, progressive effacement and dilation, backache, ruptured membranes and loose bowel movements are some of the signs of labor.

Postpartum Care of Child and Mother

- Newborn needs 10 to 20 hours sleep.
- Touching, cuddling and skin contact required.
- Uterine is at the height of navel after the birth and returns to pre-pregnant location and size by 10 days postpartum.
- After-pains in uterus are common and there is no need to worry.
- Urination and perspirations increases.
- Lochia (vaginal flow) is present.
- Breasts enlarge in case of breastfeeding.
- Fatigue and excitement exist.

- Weight loss may be 6 to 8 kg in early postpartum.
- The menstruation generally does not return for months if breastfeeding, otherwise periods start in 4 to 8 weeks.
- Ovulation may be delayed, but is possible within weeks.
- Sexual relationship is readjusted and contraception.
- May feel left out at time.

20

IMPORTANT HEALTH TIPS DURING PREGNANCY

Leakage of Milk During Pregnancy

Breasts are felt hard, sore and soaked because of milk secretion from breasts in early or mid pregnancy often in the morning. Consult a gynecologist who will teach you how to take care of the breasts during pregnancy. Give a firm support to the breasts using a good quality and correct-sized brassier to match the cups, which should be loose and supportive, but not tight. Light exercises for the breast keep breast disorders at bay.

Sex During Pregnancy

Having sexual intercourse during pregnancy will not harm the fetus. One may continue sexual intercourse right up to the onset of labor. As the abdomen enlarges, a woman may find intercourse more comfortable in positions that put less or absolutely no pressure on abdomen like side-by-side or the female on the top. If you have complications like bleeding or pain in abdomen, avoid sexual activity and even nipple stimulation is to be avoided in such cases as it can induce pre-term labor.

Doctors often advise to avoid intercourse from 6th to 12th week of pregnancy as it can cause miscarriage. Sexual abstinence is recommended during the last two months of pregnancy too. At this time, there is risk of the essential amniotic fluid leakage during intercourse. However, the couple can and should engage in gentle love making, fondling and kissing. Intercourse during the first three months and the last two months of pregnancy is not advisable. During

4th to 7th month of pregnancy, intercourse is allowed unless there are medical reasons. Sexual act such as oral and anal sex should be strictly avoided throughout the pregnancy.

4-D Ultrasound

A 4-D Ultrasound is the latest addition. A 3-D ultrasound gives a 3-D dimensional view of the baby in womb. An ultrasound gives a 2D dimensional view, which makes the diagnosis of the malformations and the surface of the body of baby and internal malformations can be visualized clearly. A 3-D Ultrasound is like a still photograph whereas a 4-D Ultrasound is like taking video film of fetus malformation and the pregnancy, especially in case the mother is over the age of 35 years and has delivered a malformed baby in past.

Rashes or Pain in Breasts

Rashes on the breast can be due to various reasons. The most common cause is due to the allergy by wearing synthetic brassiere or due to bacterial viral or fungal infection. A mammogram or an ultrasound is done in case of lumpy, painful breasts. If there is cyst in the breasts, you can take any analgesic and wear tight bras to support them and relieve pain. 400 mg of vitamin E or B taken over a period of time may lessen the pain. If the pain is severe, danazol or hormone therapy is recommended. Periodic examination of breasts is also necessary.

Stretch Marks on Abdomen and Stomach

Stretch marks on abdomen and stomach are common in women generally during pregnancy and after delivery of child. Striae gravidarum or stretch marks appear on the lower abdomen in 50 to 90 percent of all pregnant women usually in the later half of pregnancy. These may also appear on thighs, hips, buttocks, breasts and upper arms of women, which appear as pinkish lines on fair complexioned women and lighter than the normal skin in dark complexioned women. The market is flushed with creams and ointments to cure these stretch marks. The stretch marks depend upon the family history, weight gain and nutritional status.

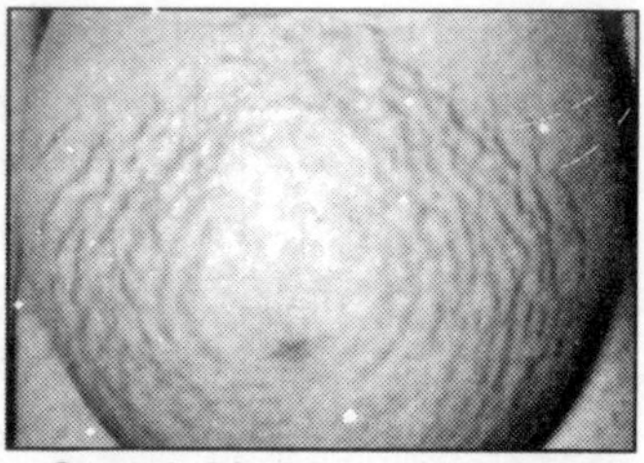

Stretch Marks on Abdomen

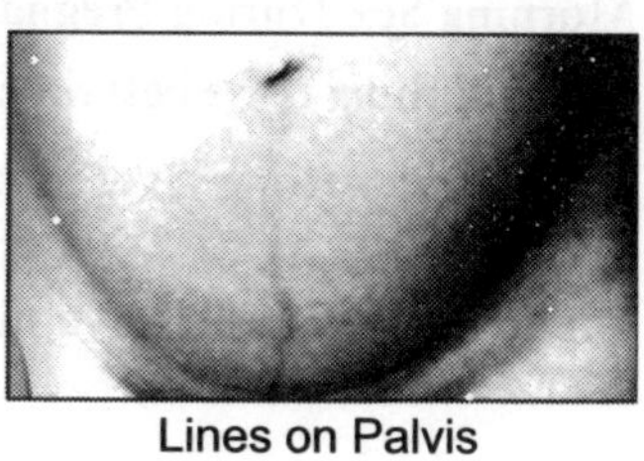

Lines on Palvis

Cramps and Pain in Abdomen During Pregnancy

Between 30 to 50% women suffer cramps pain during or before menses, which differs from woman to woman. Persistent night cramps are often caused by poor circulation.

The cramp felt in abdomen before menses are difficult to cope but doesn't show that there is any abnormality in the genitals of the woman. About 10% women pass through severe pain and cramps during menses and are even unable to walk due to stress and strain as in case of delivery of child. During menstruation the pain in the lower back and pelvis is common and is called as 'initial pain'. The main reason for such pain is due to hormonal changes generally as a result of the contraction of uterus when it discharges blood. Yogic exercises stimulating the nerves of affected part of legs relieve cramps.

There are several natural remedies to cure this painful disorder as below:

- Add 7 drops of essential oil of aromatic spicy herb cloves to a teaspoon of sunflower oil and massage the muscles of affected area.
- Tincture of myrrh rubbed directly into the affected muscle, gives quick relief.
- Mix two drops of each of the essential oils of lemon, pine and juniper, and shake with 1 tablespoon of sunflower oil. Massage with the oil prior to exercise.

A hot water bath of the lower part of the abdomen relieves pain. Consult a doctor if the pain is severe and doesn't stop for few days. This pain is different from menstruation pain or a pain experienced during and after intercourse. Smoking, sleeplessness and taking carbohydrates and fatty foods worsen conditions. Bad sitting posture, frequent headache, diarrhea, constipation, nausea or pain prior to menstruation further worsen the condition.

Morning Sex During Pregnancy

Early morning is the best time to have sex due to the following reasons:

- The testoterone level in male partner is higher in early morning hours.
- Men and women have higher levels of growth of the hormones due to increased energy after the restful night.

- Often a man awakes with a full bladder, which compresses the venous blood return and prevents blood escaping from the penis as a result the male partner experience spontaneous erections in the morning.
- Sex during the night when the blood flow to the digestive system is predominant lacks pleasure. Good sex act requires good blood flow towards sex organs and is achieved better in the morning with empty stomach.

Why Ovary Cancer is Common in Women Due to Frequent Childbirth?

It is due to rapid succession of childbirth resulting in wear and tear of the cervical tissue and natural genital secretions. The following symptoms are observed when patient suffers from cervical cancer:

- Abnormal blood stained vaginal discharge.
- Intermittent prolonged menstrual bleeding.
- Intercourse bringing on bleeding.
- Foul smelling vaginal secretion.
- Pain in the lower abdomen.
- Constant backache.
- Wear and tear of cervical tissues.

To treat cancer of cervix, measures such as surgical removal of affected part and destroying cancerous cells by radium or cobalt are adopted. If not treated at initial stage the cancerous cells may spread to liver and the brain.

Essential Blood Tests for a Woman During Pregnancy

A blood test could reveal various disorders in a woman's body. Every female from a pre-teen to a menopausal stage will at some time or the other have to undergo a blood test on the recommendation of doctor. The blood tests suggested for women are usually of six types:

- **CBC-ESR test:** is required to find out the presence of an infection or an inflammatory reaction. The test may count red cells in the blood. A high white blood count reveals the dreaded cancer of blood (Leukemia).
- **Follicular stimulating Hormones (FSH) Test:** This test is recommended to the teenage girls by the gynecologist in case of irregular periods.

- **Haemogram:** Women with excessive bleeding are required to go for Haemogram test, which highlights anemic condition and to check diabetes.
- **The Serum Beta (HCG Blood) Test:** The test is carried out to confirm pregnancy and is recommended when the woman has missed her periods.
- **HIV Test:** It is compulsory for every pregnant to examine sexually transmitted diseases such as Syphilis, Gonorrhea and Hepatitis-B, and to make a decision whether to continue the pregnancy.
- **RH factor:** The test is essential for pregnant women. If the mother is RH negative (RH-) the baby is usually delivered through a caesarean procedure.

Pre-elcamptic Toxemia in Women

Pre-elcamptic toxemia (PET) is a combination of oedema (e.g. swelling on the ankles and fingers followed by puffiness of the face and with increased blood pressure and presence of protein in the urine). Obese women and teenage girls are usually seen suffering from this disorder. Women with family history of high blood pressure are prone to the risk. In case it is not treated timely there may be serious conditions of fits and the birth of a retard child due to infra-uterine growth affecting the growth of the infant in womb. The disease is more common in anemic and malnourished women. For a healthy growth of unborn baby, it is important to part with smoking and alcohol. Certain conditions like high blood pressure, chronic kidney diseases, heart ailments and some infections also affect baby's growth.

Nausea and Vomiting

Nausea and vomiting are referred as 'morning sickness'. Pregnant women frequently feel nauseated and need to vomit when they have not eaten for several hours or when they smell some odors such as cigar smoke or certain foods being cooked. A woman may worry about her baby's health if she vomits frequently. A medical survey indicates that women healthy at the time of conception have sufficient reserves to supply the growing embryo and fetus even though they eat less. The following treatment is recommended:

- Try to modify eating habits.
- Include sufficient protein in each of the meals.
- Eat crackers or toast before getting up in the morning.
- Drink liquids between instead of during meals.

- Increase intake of vitamin B 6 (Pyridoxine).
- Have a sense of humor.
- Medications are available to help control nausea and vomiting. Better consult your doctor.

Heartburn

Heartburn – a feeling of fullness is a common complaint in late pregnancy caused by combination of hormonal effects that relax the muscular opening, cause the stomach to empty more slowly and increase pressure from the growing uterus. Fatty foods, foods that produce gas and large meals may contribute to the condition. The following treatment is recommended:

- Avoid fatty foods and foods that produce gas.
- Eat several small meals and eat slowly.
- Do not eat just before bedtime.
- Use anti-acid or other drugs to control heartburn.

Constipation

During pregnancy the movement of food through the intestines is slowed due to pressure from the growing uterus on the large intestine magnifies the problem. Drink plenty of fluids. Eat foods with high fiber content such as raw or dried fruits, vegetables, whole grains and prune juice. Exercise regularly. Preventing constipation also alleviates the discomfort of hemorrhoids during pregnancy.

Sudden Pain in the Back that Moves towards the Right Shoulder

It is common during pregnancy and generally starts in the night when pain suddenly starts in the back and radiates to the right shoulder. To get relief, press the stomach. Sometimes, this pain may be due to accumulation of acidity in gall bladder. In case the pain is due to liver or kidney a complete bed rest is advised.

RH Factor in Blood

There are hardly 10% women who have RH factor in blood. In case of RH negative female getting married to RH positive male, her children can be either RH negative or positive. If the fetus is RH positive, the mother's system produces antibodies to protect her infant's RH positive blood. This may lead to jaundice in the baby or a severe complication called erythroblastosis foetalis (severe anemia accompanied by jaundice). The pregnant woman's blood should be tested for RH negative antibodies.

Pain in Stomach and Lower Belly

Mild stomach or liver pain during pregnancy is not a matter of worry and is usually caused due to increased weight of the embryo and mother's nerves getting stained. Massage the stomach lightly with ghee to get relief. Constant pain in lower belly should be brought to the notice of doctor. A weak pregnant woman may have several abdominal discomforts during early pregnancy due to infection in pelvic organs or urinary tract.

When a Drop or Two of Blood Oozes from Uterus

This problem usually develops during 4th and 5th month from the date of conception and sometimes may lead to miscarriage. There is a small membrane in the uterus filled with amniotic fluid in which the fetus develops. In some cases the membrane gets swollen and the placenta orifice gets closed due to inflammation. This leads to the placenta puffing up and blood mixed with water accumulates in the region.

Severe Itching, Pain in Vagina After Intercourse

It could be either due to semen remaining in the vagina after intercourse or abrasion in the vaginal tract caused due to friction. It is suggested to avoid frequent sex during early stage of conception. If possible avoid frequent intercourse during the entire period of pregnancy as it may harm the child. The itching and the pain may spread to the anus also. Better have suggestion of a doctor.

Sudden Increase in Weight and Swelling of Body

Signs like sudden increase in weight, swelling of body, rise in blood pressure, appearance of albumin in urine, severe breathing trouble, constant thumping of heart and abrupt bleeding are warning signs that something is wrong with the pregnancy. Go for immediate medical advice. The pregnant woman must have a periodical check on weight, blood pressure and urine. A woman should not put more than 10 kg of weight during the entire period of pregnancy. There is often an increase of weight from the 3rd month onward, except the couple of weeks when there is hardly any increase in weight. Take a low salt but high protein diet.

Weakness, Insomnia and Exhaustion During Pregnancy

Feeling too week and exhausted, loss of sleep (insomnia) especially during night, a constant tension, loss of appetite and constant fever are common disorders among women during pregnancy because of growing embryo. The following home remedies can alleviate the problems:

- Mix 2 parts each of pumpkin oil and poppy seed oil to I part of camphor and massage the head daily in the morning and evening.
- Massage the head with 'Brahmi' or 'Narayan' or 'Mahanarayan' oil.
- Take 'Sarpagandatvaka Churan' (readily available at leading stores dealing in naturopathy goods) mixed in hot milk during night for a sound sleep.

Piles

Piles generally develop due to faulty food habits, irregular bowel routine, taking spicy foods and as a result of constipation, which irritate the stomach and intestines. In pregnant, piles usually develop due to abdominal pressure. It is better to maintain proper bowel habits. Early cases of piles are treated with local anesthetics and ointments. In severe cases pile masses are pricked with syringes to shrink them. In some cases, piles develop a couple of months after the delivery. If the problem develops immediately after childbirth an anti-hemorrhoid ointment is recommended.

How to Have a Pregnancy Test?

Most of the pregnancy tests are based on hormonal concentration of bHCG in urine. This test is sensitive and become positive as early as 2 to 3 days before missed period due to pregnancy. The accuracy is 98.5%. Collect the early morning urine sample in a clean bottle. Only a few drops of urine are sufficient for a pregnancy test. 14 days after a missed period is the usual time to have a pregnancy test. A few doctors suggest hormone pills. Sometimes, a woman may bleed even if she is pregnant and this delays the finding out sure pregnancy.

When a Woman is Willing for a Abortion

Women with unwanted pregnancies always resort to abortion. With restricted law imposed by the Government, an abortion is illegal. The pregnancy may be due to the following reasons:

- Contraceptive failure.
- Act of an intercourse when got drunk in late night parties in higher society and fairly liberal families, which sometimes end with sex.

- Strong mutual attraction towards opposite sex.
- Effect of sexy TV serials and movies.
- Too shy to discuss contraception with the male partner, when a female becomes pregnant.
- Urge to have sex with opposite sex in youth without thinking about its after-effect.
- Fulfill the desire of boss at the place of work.
- Desire to have more money.
- Bad society in youth.

Most abortions are carried out 12 weeks of pregnancy and by the common method called vacuum aspiration or suction. The cervix is dilated or widened carefully and the contents of the womb are sucked out using a suction apparatus.

Another method of abortion, instead of vacuum aspiration between 12 to 14 weeks of pregnancy is dilation and curettage by inserting prostaglandin pessaries (a thimble -like fine rubber cervical cap about 15 cm. long, which looks like a condom used by males, can be pushed into the vagina to cover the external genitalia and uterine mouth prior to coitus and should be slipped out 5 to 6 hours after the intercourse. The use of pessary combined with a spermicidal cream is more effective. Another substance called laminaria is also inserted into the vagina to avoid pregnancy.

The contents of the womb are removed by instrument called a curette made of soft wire rather than by section. It cleans the womb and most of the tissues removed during abortion look like a very heavy period. If the bleeding persist and is very heavy, consult a doctor immediately. Retained products in uterus lead to an infection. This sometimes happen about a week or ten days after the abortion.

Abortion after 12 Weeks

It becomes more difficult although it is still a safe technique. In this process instead, after dilating the cervix, the doctor may insert instruments into the womb. The technique is called dilation and evacuation and is carried out under general anesthesia. Late abortions are conducted by hysterectomy, a technique used very rarely, which involves removing contents of the womb in an operation very like a caesarean section. It is done under general anesthetic.

Any abortion conducted after 12 weeks is likely to cause pain and cramps, which may last several days and the womb shrinks back to its pre-pregnancy size. The bleeding will also go on for about a week. Avoid activities like swimming, soaking in a hot bath, wearing tampon or having sexual intercourse for six weeks.

A regular practice of exercises to strengthen the reproductive organs makes pregnancy strong and a healthy fetus. Premature delivery is common in women in which usually the infant is delivered in the eight month and doesn't survive in 75% cases. This is due to the weakness of cervical muscles, which support the uterus in expectant mother and suffer miscarriage.

Do's and don'ts about breast care and breastfeeding

- Keep breast nipples clean and dry to prevent them from becoming sore and infected. Do not apply soap to clean nipples and areola to avoid cracks.
- Wash breasts and nipples with water to remove traces of milk.
- Make sure to change bra frequently. The secretion of nipples causes infection.
- In case nipples are not soft and supple, apply some cream or oil. Avoid use of mustard oil, it irritates. Keep breasts exposed to air for sometime in a day.
- Prevent engorgement of breasts to ensure frequent emptying after a feed.
- Breasts sag if the infant suckles while sitting or reclining in a faulty posture. Always let the baby suckle in a sitting position with the child in the lap and mother's hands under the head.
- Remove the remaining milk with a couple of jerks after feeding the child.

Importance of Breast Milk

Breast-feeding is the most perfectly balanced food that a baby needs for growth during first 3-4 months. It prevents many illness, infections and allergies. Lactation helps in controlling the bleeding after the delivery, the womb returns to its normal position, sheds extra weight gained during the pregnancy, prevents cancer and helps in spacing children. Breastfeeding is very convenient for mother during travel and the milk is more digestible as compared to cow's milk.

21

WARNING SIGNS DURING PREGNANCY

During pregnancy, report any of the following warning signs to your doctor or midwife:

Warning Signs	Possible Problems
Vaginal bleeding	Miscarriage, Placenta previa, Abruptio placentae, Premature labor.
Abdominal pain	Ectopic pregnancy, Abruptio placentae, Early labor contractions.
Leaking or gushing of fluid from vagina	Rupture of the membranes.
Puffiness or swelling of hands, feet and face	Preeclampsia (toxemia).
Severe, persistent headache	Preeclampsia (toxemia).
Vision disturbance, blind spots and flashes	Preeclampsia (toxemia).
Dizziness, light headedness	Preeclampsia or supine hypotension.
Pain or burning on urination	Urinary tract infection, (STD) Sexually transmitted disease.
Irritating vaginal discharge, sores and itching	Vaginal infection and STD.
Fever (oral temperature)	Infection.
Persistent nausea or vomiting	Hyperemesis gravidarum and infection.
Noticeable reduction in fetal activity	Fetal distress.

Perineal Massage for Painless Delivery

Perineal massage has different purpose than most massage. It is used to soften the tissue around the vagina, relax pelvic floor muscles and increase the elasticity of the perineum by taking advantage of the hormonal changes that loosen connective tissue in the late pregnancy when there is pressure before and during birth. A regular perineal massage (at least 6 to 8 weeks before due date) helps avoiding an episiotomy or a serious tear during childbirth. Remember, if you have vaginitis, herpes or other vaginal problem, be sure to get checked before beginning perineal massage as it could worsen the condition. You can do self-massage or seek the help of your partner. Wash your hands before massaging. Be sure that your fingernails are short. If the skin of hands is rough, wear disposable rubber gloves. Sit in a comfortable semi-sitting position squatting against a wall or sitting on the toilet. The following procedure should be adopted while doing perineal massage:

- Lubricate your fingers with oil or water-soluble jelly (K-Y jelly). Wheat-germ oil is recommended as it contains high vitamin E content. Do not use mineral oil or petroleum jelly. Wash your hand every time before dipping into lubricant.
- Rub enough oil or jelly into the perineum to allow your fingers move smoothly over the tissue and lower vaginal wall.
- You may use your thumb during self-massage or your partner can use his index finger. Put the fingers or thumb well inside the vagina up to the second knuckle, move them upward along the sides of the vagina in a rhythmic U or sling-type movement to help stretching the vaginal tissue (mucosa), muscles around vagina and smoothen skin of the perineum by rubbing between the thumb and forefinger.
- Concentrate on relaxing your muscles as you apply pressure comfortably.
- Massage for about five minutes.

How to Strengthen Pelvic Floor Muscles?

The pelvic floor or perineal muscles act as a support for your abdominal and pelvic organs, which usually sag during pregnancy due to increased weight of your uterus and the relaxing effect of the hormones produced by your body. A regular exercise of the pelvic floor muscles (which forms a figure 8, circling around the urethra,

21

WARNING SIGNS DURING PREGNANCY

During pregnancy, report any of the following warning signs to your doctor or midwife:

Warning Signs	Possible Problems
Vaginal bleeding	Miscarriage, Placenta previa, Abruptio placentae, Premature labor.
Abdominal pain	Ectopic pregnancy, Abruptio placentae, Early labor contractions.
Leaking or gushing of fluid from vagina	Rupture of the membranes.
Puffiness or swelling of hands, feet and face	Preeclampsia (toxemia).
Severe, persistent headache	Preeclampsia (toxemia).
Vision disturbance, blind spots and flashes	Preeclampsia (toxemia).
Dizziness, light headedness	Preeclampsia or supine hypotension.
Pain or burning on urination	Urinary tract infection, (STD) Sexually transmitted disease.
Irritating vaginal discharge, sores and itching	Vaginal infection and STD.
Fever (oral temperature)	Infection.
Persistent nausea or vomiting	Hyperemesis gravidarum and infection.
Noticeable reduction in fetal activity	Fetal distress.

straightening both legs until you feel your low back come up.

- **Stretching:** helps increase flexibility and promotes comfort during pregnancy and childbirth. Sit on the floor with your knees bent and soles of your feet together. Lean forward from your hips, relaxing your legs. Allow the weight of your legs to stretch muscles of the inner thighs, outer thighs and buttocks gently pressing your knees toward the floor. Repeat this exercise for three to four times.
- **Hamstring stretch:** stretch the hamstring muscles (at the back of thighs) to help relieve backache. Sit on the floor extending your left leg straight out. Touch your left foot with both hands keeping your back straight. Repeat on the other leg.
- **Calf stretch:** stretch the tendons and muscles of the calf and ankle. Slowly and gently bend your front knee, putting your weight onto the front leg keeping back straight. Hold for 30-60 seconds. Then repeat on other leg. Repeat 3-4 times.

Why and When Miscarriage?

A miscarriage or spontaneous abortion is the unexpected and involuntary expulsion of the embryo or fetus before the 20th week of pregnancy. Occasionally, a miscarriage occurs because of an acute infection, a severe physical shock, an imbalance of hormones, a defective ovum or sperm and faulty intrauterine environment. The signs of a possible miscarriage are vaginal bleeding and intermittent pain, which usually begins in the lower back and is later felt as abdominal cramping.

Prenatal Examinations?

Prenatal examination or care helps assure the birth of a healthy baby. The following tests and examinations are performed at the prenatal visits:

- A complete medical history and physical examination of expectant mother.
- A pelvic (vaginal) examination to estimate the size and shape of your pelvis, to confirm pregnancy, to do a Pap smear to detect cervical cancer and to test for venereal disease such a syphilis and gonorrhea.
- A complete blood test to determine your blood type, Rh factor, to test for anemia, blood sugar, infection and German measles immunity.

- Weight check, blood pressure, urine tests for diabetes and to detect excess protein.
- Abdominal examination to measure the growth of the uterus (fundal height), growth of the fetus and estimate the size and position of the fetus.

Effect of Fever During/After Childbirth

Symptoms	What it might be
Fever in a hot place, no sweating, rapid heart beat, confusion, loss of consciousness:	Heatstroke.
Fever with severe headache, stiff neck, nausea:	Meningitis.
Fever with stiff jaw, muscle spasms, pain, sweating, trouble swallowing:	Tetanus, bacterial wound infection.
Sudden high temperature, vomiting, diarrhea, red rash, fatigue, headache, dizziness:	Toxic shock syndrome.
Rapid onset of fever, chills, pounding heart, confusion, sign of infection:	Blood poisoning.
Low fever, pain in lower right part of abdomen, nausea, vomiting:	Appendicitis.
Low fever at first, pain in lower pelvis, foul discharge from vagina, painful urination:	Pelvic inflammation.
Fever and cough with or without sputum, chest pain, shortness of breath:	Pneumonia.
Sudden onset of fever and sore throat, white coating on tonsils:	Scarlet fever.
Fever, night sweats, swollen lymph nodes, repeat infections, weight loss, fatigue, sores, diarrhea:	HIV infection or AIDS.
Low fever, nausea, loss of appetite, yellowish skin or eyes, dark urine, light colored stools, fatigue:	Hepatitis or jaundice.
Fever with fatigue lasting weeks or months, bad sore throat, swollen lymph glands:	Mononucleosis (viral illness).
Persistent low fever, coughing, blood sputum, chest pain, weight loss, heavy night sweats:	Tuberculosis.
Fever over 103 degree, weakness, headache, chills, raw throat, dry cough, running nose, aching muscles:	Flu

22

PLANNING A HEALTHY CHILD

Depression during Pregnancy

Depression is common among pregnant women as well as after the childbirth, which causes a woman not only to lose sexual and other interests, besides feeling irritability and fatigue most of the time. The depression is more likely to occur if a woman feels isolated and inadequate support from her husband and other members of her family. During the period of pregnancy, the mother should pay visits to the doctor for regular check up between six and eight weeks and also after delivery of the child, which gives the mother the opportunity to discuss any problem faced by her. The following natural remedies are suggested:

- **Sunlight:** Body needs sunlight. The lack of sunlight can disturb the production of key hormones and brain chemicals triggering depression.
- **Exercise:** It is must to reduce depression. An hour a day of exercise for a week is universal prescription for depressed people.
- **Light music:** Music lifts depression.

Overweight

If you have started gaining weight during pregnancy, your tummy has put on extra flesh because of your skin and muscles must have grown to hold the constant weight of baby in womb. Do not worry, the muscles gradually start tighten up again some time after the childbirth. Do not forget to undertake gentle exercises during pregnancy after consulting your doctor. Breastfeeding helps the stomach to get back to shape as it helps the uterus to contract and within two months after the delivery, the uterus takes non-pregnant size.

Plan a Healthy Child?

Remember, child's health does not start after the birth, even before the baby is conceived in the mother's womb. Planning of a child must be considered in three factors: before conception, during conception and after conception – the period of pregnancy. Oral contraceptives have harmful side effects and are not advised. Start treatment under acupressure therapy at least three months prior to conceiving in the following ways:

- The couple should take a glass of charged water (health drink) daily.
- The female partner must have three regular menses before conceiving to have a healthy fully developed uterus.
- A daily massage on both sides of wrists for five minutes by female partner proves beneficial for a healthy pregnancy.

To prepare charged water (health drink), mix 300 gm. of Amla powder to 100 gm. ginger powder. Swallow one teaspoonful of this powder with water in the morning and evening. Another way is to add two teaspoonful of above powder of Amla and ginger in four glasses of water. Use fresh Amla and ginger (if available). Boil the mixture, till it is reduced to three glasses. Filter the liquid and add to it salt or honey to your taste. Amla is concentrated form of vitamin C. It has 16 times more vitamin C than lemon and helps to provide protection to the body against cold and increases digestion power. Health drink is beneficial especially for the convalescing people, old, growing children and the expectant mothers.

Acupressure Therapy

It is exceptionally beneficial for pregnant women. Nature has provided the body with proper regulators and protectors. These are our endocrine glands, which secrete hormones directly into our blood. The proper functioning of these glands is very important and most vital for good health, for the development of our body, mind, our looks and even character. Malfunctioning of endocrine glands affect the reproductive organs in human body. Pineal gland, too, control sex system and water in the body, which leads to premature sex development. Malfunctioning of ovaries, testes and sex glands control heat of productive organs of body, which damage reproductive organs and cause problems of menstruation, self-abuse and lesser or more sex desire. Applying pressure on the palms plays an important role for healthy pregnancy. Here are few important tips to be kept in mind during, before and after conception, pregnancy and post-natal period:

- The couple must start treatment under acupressure therapy at least three months prior to conceiving.
- Ensure proper creation of hormones.
- Drink a glass of Health Drink (Gold/Silver/Copper/Iron charged water) every day.
- Ensure female partner must have three regular menses before conceiving.

How to Have a Healthy Child?

According to Naturopathy, if the intercourse is conducted during the dates 10th to15^{th} day on which the menses is seen, there is better possibility of conceiving and the child to be born, if conceived, will be healthy. During the period of menstruation flow, the couple should avoid intercourse and if the conception occurs during this period, there is possibility of the child being born with physical and mental defects. You should keep in mind the following tips, which are essential to have a healthy baby:

- In case of problems, such as early, irregular, scanty, painful or excessive menstruation, the treatment of pressing on both wrists will leave amazing results to regulate menstruation and cure leucorrhoea (white or yellow vaginal discharge accompanied by pus).
- During first pregnancy the expectant mother is usually much worried and have lot of tension, which adds to the labor pains vitally affecting both body and mind. Even in case of use of forceps or caesarean section (surgical operation) the child's body may get damaged and even the mother is hurt.
- To have a painless childbirth, roll grooved wooden roller vigorously on the back of both arms from nail to elbow for about 15 minutes. If roller is not available, rub palms and soles with two metal combs vigorously from nails to wrist for 5 to 10 minutes. For painless

childbirth, apply continuous pressure on the back part of the tongue beyond the teeth for a minute and repeat few times with an interval of three minutes.

- To avoid difficult labor, press hard on the inner side above the ankles for two minutes. Pause and press again and again till the child is born. There is often severe pain in breasts after the birth of infant due to accumulation of milk in the breasts, which should be expressed after breastfeeding. Press on the middle portion of the back of both palms. It relieves breast pain and inflammation.

Few Important Points

- After the delivery of the baby or operation for sterilization there is great possibility of the woman putting on fat because the sex glands are disturbed. Acupressure therapy helps a lot to relieve this problem. Press on the palms, which benefit in maintaining of good physique.
- Applying pressure on palms helps enough production of milk for the baby. This also cures impotency in males and frigidity in females.
- Men and women if disturbed by erotic dreams and get discharged (due to wet dreams) while in sleep, successfully try this natural treatment.
- In case of suffering from syphilis or other venereal diseases, massage ice on the affected part for two to four minutes a day according to the condition.

Have a Child of Desired Sex

The couple will be in a position to have a child of desired sex if the day on which the menses is seen is to be counted as the first day. The couple should avoid sexual intercourse during menses. Otherwise if there is conception in this period, there is possibility of child born with physical and mental defects. According to naturopaths, the following tips are advised for getting a child of desired sex:

- For getting a male child, on the even dates such as 4,6,8,10,12, 14 day, the husband should lie with his wife on the left side during sleep for 15 minutes to enable him to breathe with his right nostril before they indulge in sexual intercourse.
- For getting a female child, it is suggested that on odd dates such as 5,7,9,11,13,15 day the husband should lie with his wife on right

side for 15 minutes to enable him to breathe with his nostril before preparing for sexual intercourse.

- If the intercourse is made during the later dates between 10th to 15th day after the first day of last menses, there is possibility of conceiving immediately and the child to be born will be healthy.

After the baby is conceived, the mother should take proper care about her nourishment as described below:

- Eat plenty of seasonal fruits and drink enough milk to get maximum natural calcium.
- The expectant mother should have acupressure therapy treatment.
- Should undertake light exercises including walking throughout pregnancy period to ensure healthy growth of baby in womb.
- Remember, the child starts learning from the mother's womb. The husband should keep his wife happy during the vital period of pregnancy.

Marriage in Blood Relations

It should be avoided as far as possible. Such marriages are genetically unhealthy as both husband and wife carry the same type of genes, which could intensify the unhealthy manifestation in the newly born child.

Cleaning Genital Organs

Cleanliness of genital organs is very essential for men and women. For having genital bath, take off your clothes. Sit on a stool in a water tub filled with cold water in summer and lukewarm water in winter. The level of water should be 1-2 inches above the organ to be washed. Take a piece of cloth in water and gently rub your abdomen for two minutes.

In case of men, take hold of the foreskin of male organ in two fingers and rub in lightly with soft piece of cloth dipping in cold water followed by rubbing the entire spine with a wet towel.

In case of women, they should rub their abdomen first as above. Then pull the lips of the vagina and rub slowly with a wet piece of cloth. In the end rub the spine. Genital bath as well as Hip Bath should not be taken at the time during menstruation. If the tub is not available, genital bath can be taken in the sun in the same way.

Pregnancy Causes Cancer in Women?

In women two most likely places where cancer may develop includes breasts and the uterus. Both areas can easily be examined. Every young woman should be taught to examine her own breasts after each menstrual period. In case of detection of a tumor or anything unusual, a woman should seek advice of a doctor. Any kind of abnormality or feeling of the breast tissue outlining the curves within the breasts and up in the armpit should be examined thoroughly. Cancer of the cervix, breast or uterus is most common in women. Over 40% females suffer from cervical cancer, nearly 12% from breast cancer and the remaining cancer patients are seen suffering from vaginal or cancer of the other parts of body.

Breast Tumor and Cancer is very common in women of every age. If there is only one single nodule or lump in the breasts: painful or without pain, it should always be removed. In case the cancer appears to have extended into the neighboring lymph nodes, the patient should be given extensive radiation therapy. Majority of breast cancers occur in either the upper portion of the breast, towards the shoulder or close to the nipple. Breast cancer is more common in women between the age of 35 and 65 years. It may also occur in teenage girls.

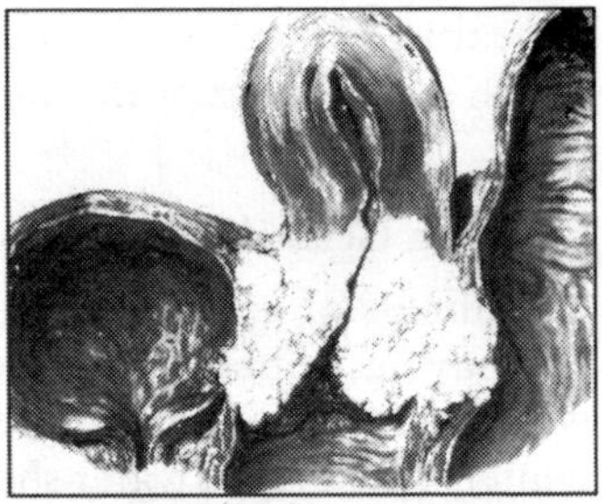
Cervical cancer

Cancer in Cervix is a vicious killer of woman today. Every female after the age 18 should have a pelvic examination and a Pap smear at least once a year or after six months. Any pain in the lower belly or a water discharge should be investigated, as it could be a cancer. Be careful, if the bleeding or spotting follows intercourse or douching. Modern treatment for the uterine cancer consists of implanting a small amount of radium within the cervical canal followed later by heavy dose of radiation therapy to the whole area. Performing a hysterectomy, removing the uterus, cervix, ovaries and tubes are the common treatments performed when suffering from a cervical cancer.

Cancer in uterus is less common type of cancer, known as fundal carcinoma. It may sometimes develop within the cavity of uterus itself. This is less malignant than cancer of the cervix and can be detected by Pap smear. If cancer is found, a hysterectomy should be done without delay. The cancer cells find their way into the abdominal cavities and may spread to the pelvis and eventually in the whole body.

Ovarian Cysts and Cancer is most frequent tumor in the body. Every woman has a small cyst on the ovary, which may disappear spontaneously. The ovarian cyst causes distension of the abdomen and pressure on the organs such as the bladder or rectum. It should be removed by surgery without delay. Cancer may develop in the wall of ovarian cyst, may spread to other nearby organs causing obstruction of the bowel.

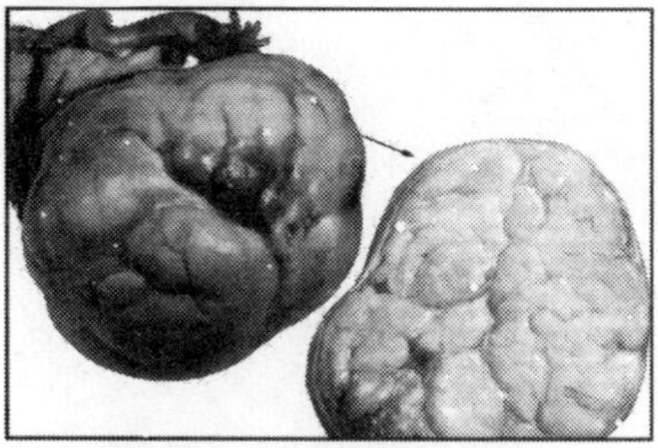

Ovary cancer and cyst

23

PROBLEMATIC DELIVERIES

Surgical Delivery

Usually if the fetal head is stuck up highe, a cesarean delivery is needed and surgery is required. Cesarean section should not be the last resort of the obstetrician after other methods of delivery have been attempted and have failed. Today, cesarean birth is a relatively safe, surgical operation in which the baby is born through the incision in the uterine and abdominal walls instead of through the vagina. An incision is made horizontally at the lower part of abdomen and the baby and placenta are removed through a cut in uterus and abdomen, closed by stitching. In an emergency delivery the baby is removed out by a long vertical cut. A cesarean birth may be indicated for the following reasons:

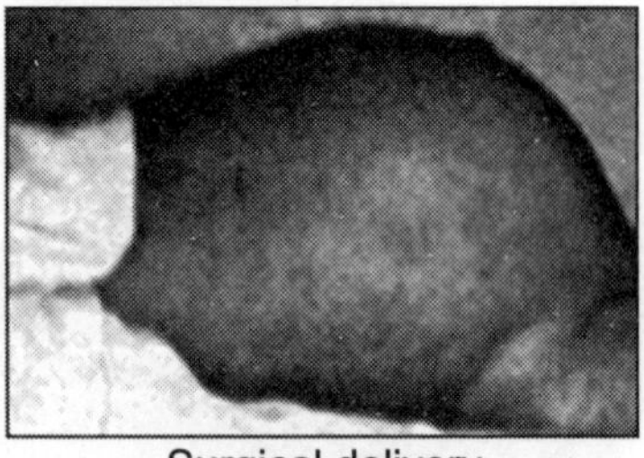

Surgical delivery

- **Pelvic disproportion**: A space problem resulting from a large baby or a small pelvic structure or a combination of the two.
- **Mal-presentation**: When the baby is situated unfavorably for a vaginal birth.
- **A prolonged labor**: Often, when the contractions are of poor quality or the dilation and descent are not progressing.
- **Fetal distress:** Due to changes in the fetal heart rate when the baby's oxygen supply has been reduced.

- **Prolapsed cord:** It occurs when the umbilical cord descends through the vagina before the baby is delivered resulting reduced oxygen supply.
- **Placenta previa:** When the placenta covers the cervix. As the cervix dilates, the placenta separates from the uterus depriving the fetus of oxygen.
- **Abruptio placenta:** When placenta prematurely separates from the uterine wall.
- **Maternal disease:** If the mother has toxemia, diabetes, high blood pressure, heart disease or other conditions, she or her baby may not be able to withstand the stress of labor and vaginal birth.
- **Repeat cesarean:** Sometimes, it is planned in advance because the original problem still exists or there may be risk of uterine rupture.
- **Heart disease in pregnancy:** Every attempt must be made to avoid cesarean section in these cases. A cardiac patient is not a suitable candidate for trial labor.

Complications: An incision is made in the middle line of the abdominal wall about six inches in length. Just before incising the uterus, it is desirable to give 0.25 mg. of methergine (strictly as advised by the doctor) intravenously directly into the uterine muscle to promote efficient uterine contraction and retraction. The suturing of the uterine incision immediately after the baby is delivered helps to control the hemorrhage. The placenta should be expressed by pressing the fundus and pushing out the placenta through incision in the uterine. Care should be taken before delivery of the head, to see that the incision is sufficiently long to allow the head to pass out comfortably.

Ectopic or Tubal Pregnancy

It is rare complication in which the fertilized ovum or embryo becomes blocked in its passage through the Fallopian tube. The embryo continues to grow as it normally would within the uterus. However, the space within the tube is too small to allow expansion, which may rupture causing a serious hemorrhage. Ectopic pregnancy is one of the leading causes of maternal death, with severe pain, abnormal vaginal bleeding and a palpable adnexal mass present in most of the patients. The factors increasing the risk of ectopic pregnancy include:

- Tubal abnormality resulting in delayed transit.
- Previous tubal pregnancy.

- Previous history of tubal reconstructive surgery.
- Intrauterine contraceptive devices and factors such as increased age and parity.

Induced Delivery

In this delivery, labor is brought on or induced artificially by rupturing the membranes and letting out a little amniotic fluid, which stimulates labor pains. When the pains are too feeble or the deliver y is overdue, labor is induced through medicines to contract the uterus.

Premature Delivery

The termination of pregnancy after the fetus become visible, such as capable of living independently is called premature birth. If the fetus is born dead, it is still-birth. Causes of abortion can also endanger the growth of the fetus resulting in a still-birth or premature delivery. Premature birth is usually the problem with the placenta to the faulty blood supply to the fetus, defective hormone production and effect of injurious toxins and chemicals through the blood to the fetus.

Precipitate Labor

A precipitate labor lasts less than three hours. A precipitate labor passes so quickly that a pregnant miss the early signs of labor. If a hospital birth is planned, leave home hurriedly, trying to cope with strong, late labor contractions. If the pregnant is unaware that her labor is progressing rapidly and thinks she is in early labor with very painful contractions, she may feel unprepared, discouraged, experience feelings of loneliness and lack of direction, panic and unsure of her ability to handle labor. Take deep, slow and relaxing breaths. Have a vaginal examination before making any decision about anesthesia. When the second stage begins, lie on your side rather than using a gravity-assisted position, which will give your birth canal and perineum more time to stretch, decrease the likelihood of tearing and protect baby's head from being pressed through the vagina.

Prolonged Labor

A labor that lasts longer than 24 hours is considered a prolonged labor. A labor with a long pre-labor or long latent phase can discourage, exhaust and emotionally drain the mother. On the other hand, a labor that slows or stops in the active phase or later may turn into a complication.

Emergency Delivery

You may find it very disturbing if you had arranged your delivery in a hospital, and you have to change your plans to have baby at home. Don't feel panic, it is better to stay home than to attempt to rush to the hospital. The following suggestions will help you maintain control of an emergency situation and ensure the best possible outcome. The following are the signs of an imminent birth:

- Feeling of a strong urge to bear down.
- Baby's head or a part is visible at the vagina.
- Feeling of the baby coming out.

Call for someone to help you at home- your partner, a relative, a neighbor or a friend. You should immediately follow the following routine:

- Remove your clothes from the lower half of your body.
- Lie on the side or in a semi-sitting position in a warm, comfortable place, preferably on the bed with a waterproof sheet and clean towels or folded linen under her buttocks.
- Stay as relaxed as possible. Let the uterus do the work. Try not to push or bear down with the contractions. Keep tissues, clean towels and blanket nearby.
- During the birth, when baby's scalp is seen at the vagina, it will be wet and somewhat wrinkled, and it may be streaked with blood in places. The pressure of baby's head bulges the perineum and anus. With the contractions, more and more baby's head is visible. As baby's head descends, the expectant mother should expel the contents of her lower bowel. She must keep her thighs and pelvic floor relaxed. If the baby's head is delivered slowly, it lessens the risk of tearing the perineum.
- Once the head is fully emerged from the vagina, the partner or attendant should use the clean handkerchief to wipe away excess mucus from around the baby's nose and mouth. Wipe baby's face thoroughly. With the next contractions, the expectant mother delivers shoulders and rest of the body smoothly. Your partner or attendant can support the baby's wet and slippery body as it emerges.

Childbirth in the 8th Month

Mostly an infant born in the 8th month doesn't survive. A 30 years old woman gave birth to a baby, which did not survive beyond 16 hours. Her second child too was born premature and died within 24 hours. Many natural salts including calcium are needed for the healthy growth of a child in the womb. If the diet of an expecting mother is deficient in these salts the fetus doesn't develop normally and the mother may suffer from weakness of muscles, which support the uterus and may have a miscarriage. Even if the delivery is normal, the child more often is sickly and too weak. Calcium is found in leafy vegetables and milk in abundant quantity and if an expecting mother takes a diet containing ample quantity of nutrients, she will deliver a healthy baby. She must seek advice of a doctor.

Pregnancy in Women Over 40 years Old

Advanced age is considered to increase the likelihood of pregnancy and labor complications, especially in the first-time mother. The chances of complications include Down's syndrome in the baby, pre-eclampsia and poor labor pattern during pregnancy in women over 40. A healthy expectant mother over 40 can, however, enjoy the pregnancy.

Symptoms Just before the Delivery

Every expecting mother should be familiar with the symptoms as the time of confinement nears. At the time of childbirth, a woman requires lots of love, affection and confidence from her husband and family members to overcome the pain barrier. The following symptoms are observed just before a delivery:

- The sudden onset of labor pains is brought on by drop in the level of progesterone hormone.
- There is urge for frequent urination.
- The low position of the fetal head makes walking and sitting difficult.
- There is backache and tiredness in the limbs.
- Vaginal secretion increases; it may be blood-stained.

The abdomen goes into regular, periodic tightness due to uterine contractions.

24

VENEREAL DISEASES

Sexually Transmitted Diseases

Symptoms	What it might be
Sore throat; fever; swollen glands in neck, underarms and groin, fatigue, frequent cold sores, fever, chills, night sweats, yeast infection, sudden weight loss, chronic diarrhea, dry cough, sores, breathing problems, vision loss and memory loss.	AIDS caused by HIV.
Watery mucus from penis or vagina, pelvic burning with urination and mild lower abdomen pain.	Chlamydia (bacterial disease).
Itching or burning pain in genital area, red bumps in or on genitals, blisters or open sores.	Genital herpes (viral infection spread through sex).
Small, round, red, flat itchy bumps on genitals (around anus or inside vagina).	Genital warts.
Thick yellowish discharge from vagina or penis, burning and itching while urinating, discharge from rectum, pain in abdomen, bleeding between periods.	Gonorrhea (bacterial infection).
Painless sores on or in genitals and rectal area or mouth, lymph nodes near sores. and nervous system.	Syphilis (highly contagious infection) In neglected can damage brain, heart.
Heavy greenish discharge in women, sometimes gray discharge from vagina, pain during intercourse, vaginal odor and painful urination.	Trichomoniasis (an infection caused by parasite).

Syphilis

A dangerous venereal disease caused by a small corkscrew-shaped germ. This tiny germ is transmitted from one person to another generally through sexual contact. In a few cases syphilis is acquired through contaminated material and even through injections or blood transfusions, if the germs are present in the blood. If a mother is infected with syphilis, the germs may find their way into the child's body before birth. Prominent signs and symptoms of disease in males is a painless sore on the penis lasting several weeks and in females there may be sore deep in the vagina. The early primary lesion is known as a Chancre. At first the germs are generally confined to these areas, and later they are carried to all parts of the body through the blood and spread causing mild rashes on the skin, which fade in a short time. Tumors or swellings may appear in various parts of the body and there may be severe inflammation and degeneration, which lead to headache, loss of memory, tremors of the lips, tongue, fingers, hands, change in the pupils of the eyes, loss of vision, vomiting, acute abdominal pain lasting for hours or even days and developing large ulcers on the toes, heels and soles.

Pregnant women suffering from syphilis may pass on the disease to their unborn child in growing fetus resulting in serious conditions. Soon after the birth the bones of the child sometimes appear deformed, the liver and spleen enlarged, damage to the brain and central nervous system causing the birth of a mentally and physically retarded child. A syphilitic pregnant expectant mother runs the risk of recurrent abortions and stillbirths due to the infection, damage to placenta and the growing embryo. Here is a naturopathic remedy to treat syphilis. Ground in water a tablespoon of Hirankhuri booti (corchorus fascicularis) and few grains of pepper. Strain and take for two to three weeks. The patient should take a salt-free diet and avoid taking bitter, sour and pungent substances.

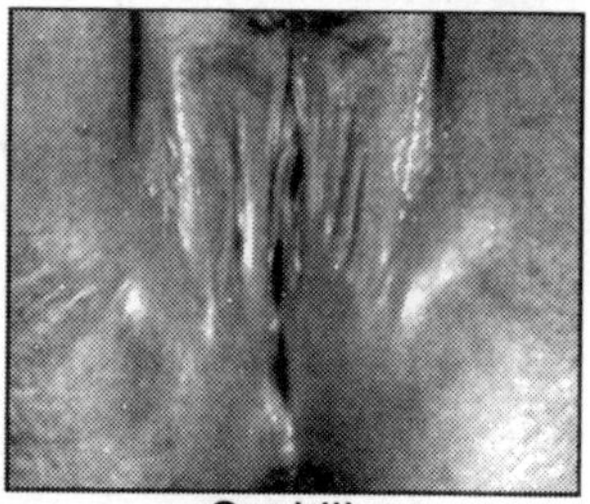
Syphilis

Gonorrhea

Persistent pus discharge from vagina, inflammation of entire genital passage, burning and discomfort are symptoms of Gonorrhea - a fatal venereal disease usually transmitted by sexual contact and caused

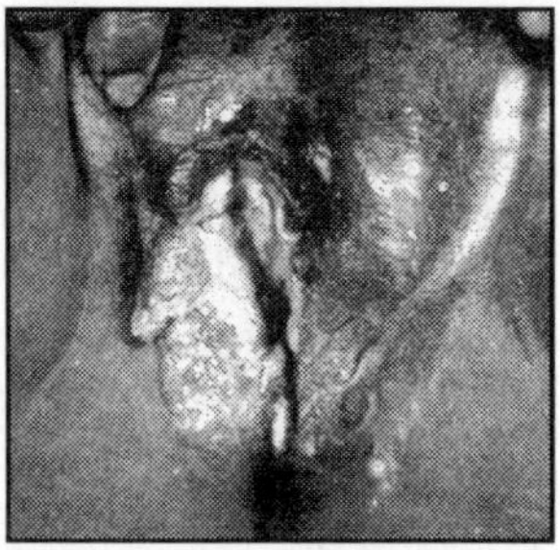

Gonorrhea

by a tiny bean-shaped germ called a 'gonococcus'. The disease may also be contracted from contaminated hands, instruments, clothing, toilet seats, and even bath water. Burning on urination, urge to frequent urination, a profuse greenish-yellow discharge, red and swollen end of the penis in males and hot swollen opening to the vagina along with thick yellow discharge are some of the symptoms of this disease. Adult men and women carry gonorrhea germs transmitted during sexual intercourse. If a mother happens to be infected with gonorrhea, there is great danger of newborn infant contracting the disease at the time of birth. In the males the prostate gland becomes infected resulting in slow urination. In females the fallopian tubes get closed as a result of formation of abscess and the inflammation in the pelvis.

Penicillin or Terramycin are the best drugs recommended for the treatment of this fatal disease (strictly under the guidance of an expert doctor as there may be a reaction due to these drugs). A Hip Bath in hot water is useful. Urethra should be flushed with a solution of potassium permanganate (1:3000) with the help of a syringe to be kept in urethra for five minutes. The patient should avoid constipation. Sex should be strictly forbidden.

Genital Herpes

Herpes simplex virus produces infection generally passed on through sexual contact. Appearance of blisters on genital areas, thighs, buttocks, fever, body ache, weakness, thick vaginal discharge, irritation, urinary burning and enlarged lymph nodes are some of the symptoms of this disease. Different sized vesicles and reddish ulcers appear in the vulvae region. Women who practice rectal sex

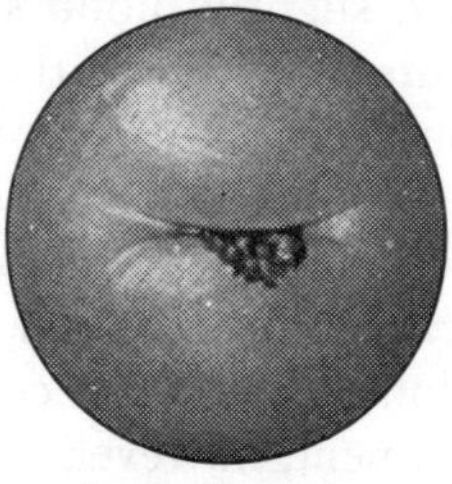

(Intial Stage)

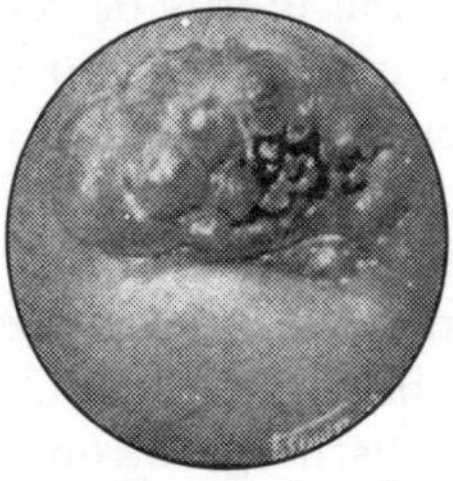

Genital herpes (Final stage)

also develop the lesions in the area around the anus and higher up in the rectum. This disease is treated by the application of anti-viral cream or a lotion. Use condoms during sexual intercourse. Take bath in warm water. Worry, depression and lack of sleep are biggest enemies during the attack of this disease. Soothe the affected skin with essential oil (diluted in a base oil) of lemon, geranium, chamomile or lavender. The oil should be gently rubbed on to the rashes.

Fungus Infection

Occasionally, the female genital organs of a pregnant woman get infected with fungus because of the increased sugar content in the blood. Women suffering from diabetes are more likely to have fungus infections resulting in intense itching around the genital area and a thick discharge from the vagina. Take a warm vinegar douche once or twice a day in consultation with your doctor.

Leucorrhoea (Vaginal discharge)

The secretion from the uterus and upper portion of the vagina flowing down and reabsorbed in the lower part of the vagina is a normal phenomena in a woman. The presence of infection in any of these tissues usually causes a whitish or pale discharge accompanied by pus is called leucorrhoea. Pelvic congestion, endocrine disturbances, lacerations, injuries, perhaps atrophy of the vaginal tissues, an irritation of the labia (external genital organs in females), soiled undergarments, dirt, intestinal worms and masturbation are some of the causes of this disease. Excess secretion is common when the girl reaches puberty due to over activity in sex glands and organs. Many young women have slight discharge at the time of ovulation, which is not abnormal nor indicate the presence of any disease.

A profuse, yellowish discharge associated with burning and intense itching while urinating may be due to infectious disease gonorrhea. A thin, watery discharge may be due to the presence of cancer in the uterus or cervix. A creamy, slightly blood stained discharge may be due to some severe infection. From the early pregnancy period to mid forties, infections may sometimes follow the birth of a child because of the cervix been damaged during delivery of the baby. Unless properly treated, infection may spread to other areas of the genital tract, even leading to cancer. A Pap smear, blood test and the skin test should always be done if there is a constant yellowish discharge. Strong antibiotic treatment, however, subsides infection. Take a regular vinegar douche. Mix two tablespoons of vinegar to ½ liter warm water. After douching a vaginal suppository or tablet should be inserted in the vagina. In case of severe itching, triple sulphonamide cream may be applied inside the genital organ (as prescribed by the doctor) to control infection. Cream containing the hormone estrogen when applied locally will benefit. In case of female infection the husband should be carefully examined and treated. A leucorrhoea patient should undertake regular exercise. Late nights and sexual intercourse are taboo during the course of disease. Avoid fried. Spicy foods and pickles.

Excessive bleeding

Menstrual bleeding occurs in all women from adolescence till the menopausal change of life. Women, sometimes also have slight signs of blood on the day of ovulation, which is normal. Heavy vaginal bleeding during the childbearing age may be due to the miscarriage of abortion, ectopic pregnancy and malignant tumors of the uterus or cervix. Women with irregular or very heavy bleeding should have a Pap test done at least every six months. Heavy bleeding may also be due to fibroid tumors and polyps in the uterus. In such cases either the tumor or perhaps the entire uterus have to be removed. Various other conditions, such as blood diseases, heart failure, alcoholism, cirrhosis of the liver, vitamin B deficiencies, and abnormality in either thyroid or pituitary, or adrenal glands may result in heavy bleeding. Heavy bleeding following abortion usually requires a surgical operation to clean uterus whereas bleeding arising from tumors of the uterus and other pelvic organs is controlled by surgery.

If the woman is in mid-pregnancy and suddenly begins to hemorrhage, she should be rushed to hospital at once otherwise it may be too late to save the baby as well as mother's life. All the products of conception should be expelled from the uterus, otherwise bleeding may not cease and there is danger of serious infection in the uterus.

Candida (white vaginal thrush)

Females during reproductive age sometimes suffer from candida. Factors like the state of pregnancy, diabetes, administration of antibiotics and steroids and use of contraceptive pills cause this disorder, which produces white vaginal discharge with intense irritation and burning sensation. To treat affected area, apply anti-fungal cream recommended for both men and women to eliminate the fungus and prevent re-infection from the sex partner. In case of females, doctors generally recommend tablets inserted intra-vaginally. Thrush is another infection of candida usually develops in the gastro-intestinal tract. Whitish curd-like deposits appear on the tongue. The thrush infection of vagina is known as **vulva vaginitis**, which cause itching, redness and discharge. The vaginal infection can be transmitted to the male partner and vice versa. Symptoms of vaginitis include:

- Pain, redness and itching into the vagina and vulva.
- Severe pain when urinating and involved in sexual intercourse.
- Foul smelling white or blood-streaked discharge.
- Pelvic inflammation resulting in infertility.

The following measures are taken for the treatment of viginitis (strictly as prescribed by your doctor):

- Avoid wearing nylon panties, tight jeans and a moist environment around genital area.
- Avoid sugar, refined carbohydrates and alcohol, which turn into glucose in the body.
- Eat 100 gm of unsweetened yogurt daily.
- Garlic is antibacterial, anti-fungal that fights both bacterial vaginitis and candidiasis. Take one capsule once or twice a day.
- Insert a 600 mg capsule of boric acid powder into vagina twice a day for a week. To prevent recurrence insert one capsule daily at bed time for four days during menstrual period. Do not insert capsule in case of pregnancy.
- Insert a vitamin E capsule into the vagina once or twice a day for seven days, which is soothing to vaginal tissue, decreases irritation, redness, swelling and congestion.
- Ayurvedic herb 'triphla' helps remove toxins from the body and helps in treating a yeast infection. Soak ½ teaspoon of dried herb in 1 cup of hot water for five minutes. Drink the liquid at night before sleep. Douching, too, dries the vagina.

Common Conditions of Genitalia

Scabies, warts, herpes, candidiasis, phimosis and AIDS virus are some of common conditions of Genitalia.

Lesions of scabies: may be seen on male genitals with intense itching. These lesions are observed as papules on the prepuce, glans, shaft of penis and scrotum in male organs. Female genitalia are rarely involved.

Surface warts: also do occur on genitalia. Genital warts are usually transmitted by sexual contact or through infection from the hands and nail, as such both the partners should keep hands clean when having sex. Warts can occur in both sexes and are usually located on the moist surface of genitalia. Initially, they appear as minute reddish swellings growing in groups of lesions. The genital warts should be treated with the consultation of a good doctor.

Genital herpes: are caused by a virus, in which groups of little blisters appear on the genital area, thighs and buttocks. The following natural remedies for genital herpes are recommended:

- Vitamins and minerals: A herpes outbreak is a sign that your body is under stress and needs more nutrients. The following nutrient program may help reduce the stress, shorten the herpes attack and reduce its severity:

Vitamin A: Daily dose of 20,000 international units (IU) twice for a week.

Vitamin B Complex: Daily dose 50 mg for a month.

Vitamin C: Daily dose 500 to 1000 mg three times a day for one to two weeks.

Vitamin E: 400 IU twice a day for two weeks.

Zinc: 10 mg twice a day for a week.

Calcium/Magnesium: 500 mg of calcium and 250 mg of magnesium twice a day for a month.

Selenium: 200 micrograms daily for two weeks.

- Drink water as much as you can, which helps flush toxins out of the body that weaken immune system and allow the virus to reactivate.
- Soothe group of little blisters appearing on genital area with essential oils (diluted in a base oil) of lemon, geranium, chamomile or lavender.
- Common warts are treated by electro-cautery, which excises the warts with electric current.

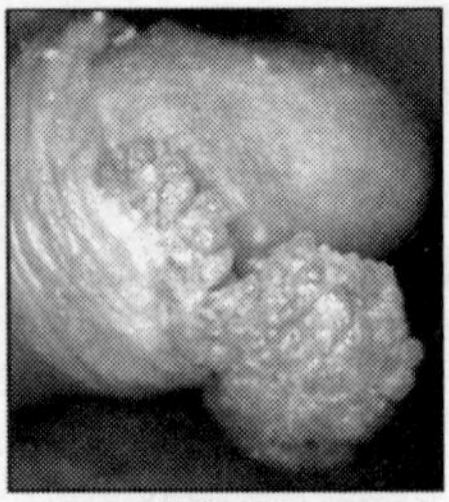

Warts

Remedies to cure warts: Warts should be diagnosed accurately and treated early rather than waiting until they spread and enlarge and are more difficult to eliminate. Genital warts can be sexually transmitted and may be a risk factor for cervical cancer in women. The following natural remedies are suggested:

- Garlic oil is a traditional remedy for warts. Swab the oil on the wart or on a bandage applied to the wart.
- Remove warts with cryosurgery or freezing with liquid nitrogen or carbon snow.

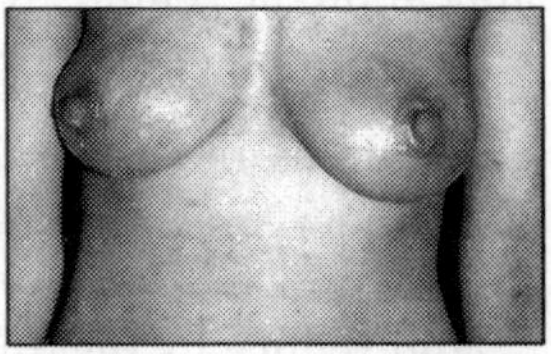

Scabies on breast-fold

Scabies: is a contagious disease caused by a mite, which lays eggs in burrows in the skin. The disease spreads through contact with infected individual. The commonly affected parts of the body are finger webs, wrist, arms, buttocks, lower abdomen, thighs, breast-folds, female genital area and penis (in men). There is severe itching on the affected area at night and sometimes a thin, slimy fluid oozes out of the scratched surface and scabs. To treat scabby following remedies are advised:

- Boil leaves of oleander (Karbir) till charred in 250 ml mustard oil and massage the affected skin.
- Mix juices of lemon and jasmine in equal quantity and rub on the itching skin.
- Grind poppy seeds in water. Mix to it lime juice. Massage affected skin with the paste.

25

SKIN DISEASES ASSOCIATED WITH PREGNANCY

In a study conducted on pregnant women most of them were found to have any lesion involving the skin. The following are the more important physiological changes, which affect the skin of the pregnant woman as described below:

Pigmentation

Present in about 75% of all pregnant women by the last trimester. It usually appear during pregnancy and after delivery, but it may persist for varying periods of time and occasionally until the menopause. The commonest and most characteristic site for pigmentation is the face and the forehead where it is known as 'chloasma'. The cause of pregnancy pigmentation is due to increased production of progesterone, which directly affects the melanocytes. Other pigment changes occurring during pregnancy are the following:

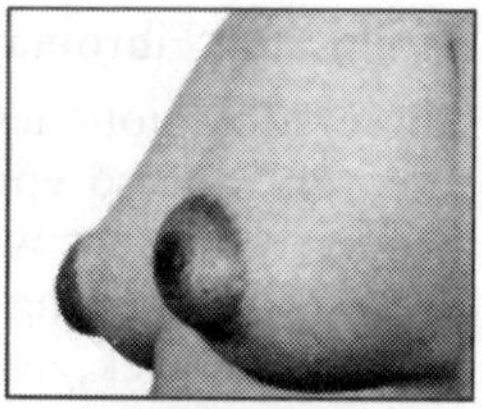

Pigmentation and breasts

- Hyper-pigmentation of pigmented areas especially of the vulva and labia, areola, nipples and umbilicus.
- Pigmentation of linear alba, usually developing in the 3rd month of pregnancy.
- The linea nigra fusca – pigmentation running to the umbilicus.
- Pigment marks on and around the areola on breasts.

Alteration in the Growth of Hair (Hypertrichosis)

Excess growth of hair on the face, which usually disappears after delivery but reappear in subsequent pregnancies.

Striae Gravidarum

Almost 75% women usually suffer from this disorder by the 6th month of pregnancy, which appear as thin, clear-cut lines of atrophy in parallel or in curves on abdomen, breasts, flanks, lumbar and sacral regions, hips and inner side of thighs. The lines become less visible with the passage of time after delivery.

Erythema of Palms

Present as mottled erythema distributed on entire surface of the palm, which increases with the advance of pregnancy. Erythema is found to be present in 60% of fair complexioned women and 40% of dark complexioned women. It fades in 90% of cases within 6 to 8 weeks after delivery.

Multiple Spider Naevi

Bright red lesions usually appear between second and fifth month of pregnancy and slowly increase in size mainly on the face, neck, upper arms and chest. About 75% of the lesions disappear completely within two months of delivery and sometimes remain un-curable even for years. The cause of spider naevi is due to hormonal reasons.

Molluscum Fibroma Gravidarum

These contagious lesions caused by virus is known as 'cutaneous tags' are due to epidermal hyperplasia and consist of a core of connective tissues without any elastic tissue covered by epidermis. They appear during second half of pregnancy on the front, sides, nape of the neck, in the axillae, on the breast and upper chest.

Skin Diseases Related to Pregnancy

These include pruigo gestationis, herpes gestationis, impetigo herpetiformus, papule dermatitis of pregnancy, lesions of prurigo, macules, papules, excoriations, lichenification, urticarial eruptions, eczematous eruptions, erythematos and scabies. Most of these eruptions develop in late pregnancy. Irritation and rashes disappear in 7 to 14 days with proper medication prescribed by the doctor.

Herpes Gestationis

Lesions develop in first pregnancy or during the successive pregnancies due to hormonal changes in which lesions develop during the second trimester of pregnancy and usually itching and burning between the age 30 to 35 years. It starts clearing within 30 days after the pregnancy. Recurrences occur on the resumption of menstruation and in rare occasions the disease has made first appearance in the puerperium. The patches may become pussy or haemorrhagia and the rashes spread. Eventually the whole body may be involved. The lesions heal leaving behind pigmentation. Constitutional symptoms such as pyrexia, rigors, constipation and vomiting appear.

Impetigo Herpetiformis

An inflammatory condition of the skin accompanied by severe constitutional disturbance with pyrexia, rigors, vomiting and delirium is conspicuous, which cannot be identified by the primary lesions, pustule in groups containing pus. The eruption having yellow crust spreads, oozes and resembles eczema. Most of the children born of mother suffering from this disease die soon after the birth.

Papule Dermatitis of Pregnancy

The symptoms include intense itching lesions widely scattered over the trunk, arms, legs, face and scalp throughout the pregnancy. The condition is associated with a high fetal morality. Consult a doctor for treatment.

Intertrigo (Intertriginous Dermatitis)

An highly inflammatory reaction of the epidermis, which occur in the region of the body folds or area on the skin surfaces in close contact. Such areas include the axillary folds, inguinal folds, inter-gluteal cleft and inter-digital cleft of toes. The causes of this disease are friction, sweating and heat, which lead inevitably to reddening, scales, soreness and irritation and maceration of the epidermis of skin followed by infection, erosions and fissures with skin organism, fungi or yeasts especially candida albicans. The diagnosis of this skin disorder during pregnancy must be made from flexural psoriasis, seborrhoeic dermatitis, eczema, fungal infection and monilial infection. The treatment includes soothing the inflammation, keeping affected skin clean with soap and water, sitz baths or foot baths of potassium permanganate solution for minimum 10 minutes or wet dressings of potassium permanganate, application of steroid lotions or creams and fungicidal ointment, control over obesity, diabetes and glycosuria.

Psoriasis

The skin disease is common during pregnancy on limbs and trunk usually due to friction, moisture and overweight. To cure psoriasis, warm bath, potassium permanganate bath and application of steroid lotion or cream. If untreated, it leads to the risk of irritant dermatitis or sensitization.

Eczema and Scabies

The areola and the nipple are common sites for eczema on the body of a pregnant woman having eczematous lesions on the breasts, wrists, anterior and posterior axillary folds usually appearing on skin creases.

Condyloma Acuminate

Oozing warts growing rapidly in pregnant women with offensive odor generally affecting external genitalia, pre-anal region and perineum. This contagious virus disease of the skin spreads in moist medium and become very infective in the presence of vaginal discharges due to presence of venereal diseases (especially gonorrhea) or other infections. To have a curb over disease scrupulous cleanliness of affected area is essential and all vaginal discharges should be investigated.

Pityriasis Versicolor

A fungus skin disease in pregnant women generally characterized by round macules. The color of lesions varies from light to deep brown giving an appearance of hyper-pigmentation accompanied by scales. It is difficult to cure this disease during pregnancy. To treat the disorder wash the affected areas thoroughly having daily hot bath, application of a 10% solution of sodium thiosulphate with a brush or applying ointment containing sulphur and salicylic acid.

Candidiasis (Cutaneous Moniliasis)

Nearly 25% of pregnant women suffer from this disease in the vaginal area and attribute to the increased amount of glycogen present in the vaginal cells. Candidiasis is classified into three groups: cutaneous and mucosal thrush, secondary eruptions due to yeasts and monilial granulomata.

Monilial Vulvo-vaginitis

There is chronic vaginal discharge in this disorder. Heavy leucorrhoea discharge during pregnancy causes fungus. The symptoms include pruritus vulvae and soreness of introitus, odema, excoriation and lichenification of the labia and perineal region, congestion and reddening of the vaginal mucosa, white patches accompanied by fungus on the labia and vaginal wall. Consult a doctor immediately. The remedial measures include daily sitz bath in the solution of potassium permanganate solution, insertion of nystatin pessaries into the vagina at night and in the morning. For 2 to 4 weeks apply nystatin ointment or powder (as recommended by the doctor).

Trichomoniasis

Infection is the common cause of vaginal discharge and vulvo-vaginitis occurring in pregnant and non-pregnant women; also found during the post-menopausal periods in virgins, which may be transmitted to the male during intercourse giving rise to urethritis, palano-posthitis and chronic prostatitis. The main symptoms of this disease are pruritus vulva, odema and redness of vulva with frothy vaginal discharge. To clear infection, oral therapy and insertion of pessaries have shown 80% curative effects. If repeated relapses occur in married women, it is advisable to treat the husband also.

Malignant Melanoma

High malignant, dangerous pigmented flat, brown moles on the head, neck, lower limbs and trunk appear. The irritating lesions rapidly increase in size developing dark pigmentation, ooze watery discharge on outer zone. The lesions are diagnosed by pigmented basal cell and squamous epithelioma, pigmented papilloma, seborrhoeic wart, haemangioma pigmented naevi and solar keratosis. Patients already suffering from malignant melanoma are warned that pregnancy carries the risk of activation and dissemination of any metastasis.

Pruritus in Pregnancy

Common skin disorder during 2nd and 3rd trimester of pregnancy, which interferes with sleep and exhaust the patient mentally and physically, localized to the vulva or perineal regions often associated with pain, itching, striae gravidarum, urticaria, scabies and varicosities of the vulva. The causes of generalized pruritus include dermatoses related to pregnancy, metabolic disorders (such as diabetes, jaundice and uraemia), leukemia (blood dyscrasiois), skin diseases (eczema, dermatitis, scabies, herpetiformis and herpes gestationis), malignant abdominal and pelvic diseases, lack of personal cleanliness, bacterial infection of inguinal folds, excessive vaginal discharge, pediculosis pubis, use of contraceptive pessaries and creams, contact dermatitis due to sanitary pads and nylon underclothes. To treat the disorder, remove the cause, if possible. Apply corticosteroid creams or lotions in consultation with the doctor. Tepid baths are helpful to treat this disorder.

26

STAGES OF LABOR

Labor is divided into four stages as below:

- **First Stage-the Dilating stage:** During which the cervix opens completely.
- **Second Stage-the Expulsion stage:** Also called actual birth, which begins when the cervix is fully dilated and ends when the baby is born.
- **Third Stage-the Placental stage:** Which begins with the birth of the baby and ends with the delivery of the placenta.
- **Fourth Stage-the Recovery stage:** Which begins after the placenta is born and ends one to several hours later when the mother's condition stabilizes.

Dilation and Signs of Labor

When the gestation period is over and the baby is about to be delivered, the mother starts getting severe labor pains. Following types of women feel less pain during delivery:

- Who are accustomed to domestic work.
- Who do regular morning and evening walk.
- Who do regular exercise.
- Who have sound health and well-developed pelvis.

Dilation refers to the opening of the cervix. It is usual for the cervix to dilate slightly before the onset of labor. The dilation is estimated during a vaginal examination and is measured in centimeters. When the cervix is opened only a fingertip, it is one centimeter dilated, at the halfway point, it is four to five centimeters and when fully dilated, it is eight to ten centimeters dilated. The prominent signs of labor are the following:

- Backache that come and go accompanied by uneasiness and restlessness.
- Frequent soft bowel movements often mistaken for an intestinal upset. Diarrhea-like symptoms on or near your due date may be a subtle sign of early labor.
- Passage of a thickened mucus plug tinged with blood from the rupture blood vessels in the cervix, which can appear days before any other sign of labor.
- Contractions of uterus become longer, stronger and closer together as labor advances. Contractions usually become painful near the delivery period. Uterine contractions shorten the muscle fibers in the body of the uterus, pull open the cervix and push the fetus down and out of the uterus.
- Rupture of the membranes or breaking of the bag of liquids begins labor usually immediately or within 24 hours. When the membranes break, followed by a gush of amniotic fluid (or a slow, uncontrollable leak of fluid may feel like urination). When rupture of membrane occurs and labor doesn't begin, the risk of infection increases as time passes. Seek medical advise and note the time, color, odor and amount of fluid. Do not insert anything into your vagina to control the flow. Avoid inserting fingers, and taking a tub bath. That can increase the possibility of infection.

Pain in Childbirth

There are several factors as below:

- Insufficient supply of oxygen to uterine muscles. The pain is more intense if the interval between contractions is short.
- Stretching of the cervix.
- Pressure by the baby on the nerves near the cervix and vagina.
- Tension on and stretching of the supporting ligaments of the uterus and surrounding structures.
- Pressure on the urethra, bladder and rectum.
- Distention of the pelvic floor muscles.
- Fear and anxiety, which release excessive stress hormones.

True Labor *vs.* False Labor

Before cervix begins to dilate, many women experience non-dilating contractions that may continue for hours or even days, sometimes called 'false labor' also called Pre-labor. The following comparison chart will help you decide if you are in true labor or a false labor.

	Labor or True Labor	Pre-labor or False labor
Uterine contractions	Become longer, stronger and closer together.	Tend to stay at about the same length, strength and frequency.
	Accompanied by abdomen discomfort or pain.	Usually are not painful.
	Rarely exceed one minute.	May last ½ to 4 minutes
	Accompanied by backache restlessness.	No effect.
	Never subside or reduced.	May subside as the mother becomes active.
Show	Slight blood discharge before or during early labor.	No blood discharge.
Intestinal symptoms	Frequent bowel movement.	None.
Changes in the cervix	Progressive dilatation.	Dilatation not Progressive.

Pelvic Examination Before Labor

The objects are twofold-to investigate the condition of the pelvic organs and to estimate the size and shape of the pelvic canal. It is necessary to measure the pelvis by your doctor by means of a bimanual examination. The diagnosis of pregnancy is confirmed and the presence or absence of pelvic swellings such as uterine fibroids or ovarian cysts can be determined. If the fundus (top of the uterus) can be palpated abdominally there is no need to carry out the pelvic examination at the first visit and can be postponed until need arises. There are three methods of pelvic examination as below:

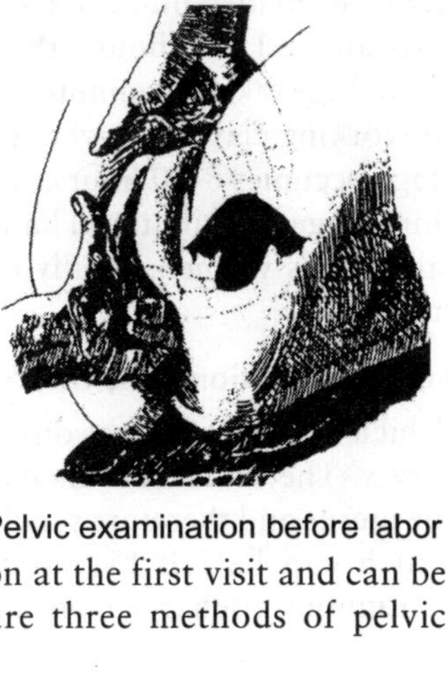

Pelvic examination before labor

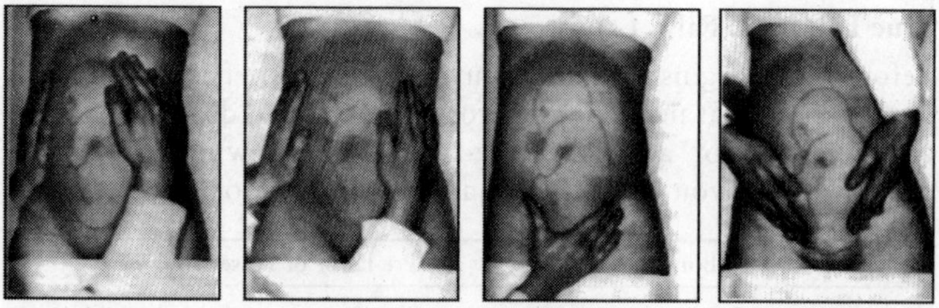

(a) (b) (c) (d)

Examination of pregnancy

Preparations before Delivery

The following things should be kept ready before delivery:

- A hard bed to avoid excess labor pains.
- Oily cloths for spreading on the bed.
- Two rolls of sterilized cotton wool.
- Few napkins duly rinsed in carbolic lotion and dried.
- Two basins, each for membranes and waste cotton.
- Enema pot, boric acid and anti-septic lotion.
- Four binders of size 36" long and 16" broad for stomach required immediately after the delivery.
- Four loin clothes to manage vagina.

Just before and after Delivery

Labor is divided into three stages as described below. The first stage lasts about 12-15 hours, the second stage about two hours and the third stage takes 20 minutes to half an hour. In the patients belonging to working class, the average time is considerably shorter. The first stage occupies 8-10 hours, the second stage one hour or less and the third stage 20 minutes to half an hour. These are average figures and labor class women usually complete their labor in a much shorter time.

Stage of Dilation (The first Stage of Labor)

Which extends from the onset of true pains to the full dilation of the cervix. The occurrence includes periodic pain due to contraction of the uterus and therefore synchronous with a hardening of that organ, which can be felt by hands are placed on abdomen. There is continuous discharge from vagina (cervical mucosa), also known as 'show'. As the pain becomes more frequent and severe, the patient begins to cry out and feels relief by sitting bent forward. A gentle massage on the back from shoulder to lower back is also helpful for the patient to relieve tension. It takes 12 to 15 hours to complete the first stage. At the end of it there is usually a sudden gush of fluid indicating that the fetal membranes have ruptured.

Birth Guide during 1st Stage

There are three phases in this stage such as lateral stage, active stage and transition stage as per the following detail:

- **Lateral phase:** The cervix dilation occurs from 1 to 4 cm. The breathing pattern should remain slow. Sometimes, there is bloody show during this stage. The contractions become longer, stronger and more frequent with small chance of rupture of membranes. The delivering woman may have backache and loose bowel movements. She should frequently empty bladder (every hour) and eat and drink sensibly according to desire. She must bathe or shower and feel relaxed as far as possible. It is suggested to call doctor or midwife. The husband/partner should help pass the time with walking, talking, music, TV and back rub.
- **Active phase:** The cervix dilation ranges from 5 to 7 cm. during this phase when contractions become more intense and there is possibility of rupture of membranes. Better shift the expectant mother to the nursing home. She must use positions of comfort, drink liquids, chew on ice chips or suck on damp cloth, apply cool cloth to her forehead, warm towel to the abdomen, have ice or liquid and move in bed or walk with the help of her husband or partner.
- **Transition phase:** The cervix dilation varies from 8 to 10 cm. with strong contractions and heavy pressure on vagina and rectum. The delivering woman feels nausea, vomiting (or vomiting sensation), drowsiness, hiccups, cold feet uncontrollable shaking and frequent leg cramps. There is always possibility of rupture of membranes. The expectant mother feels restless, irritable, forgetful, fearful, often control urge to push and have difficulty with breathing. She should not be left alone. Back rubbing provides her comfort.

Stage of Expulsion (The Second Stage of Labor)

This is a stage of expulsion and extends from the complete dilation of the cervix to the expulsion of the child. The pains often stop for few minutes after the rupture and then begin again with greater frequency, which gradually become more expulsive or 'down bearing' in character. The patient usually braces herself by holding on to some solid object or pressing her feet against the foot of the bed. The diaphragm is thus fixed and the intra-abdominal pressure brought to bear on the expulsion of the child. The patient perspires freely. The effect of these pains is to drive the head through the cavity of the pelvis. It presses upon the rectum and on the perineum, which begins to bulge a little during the pains. The vulva also begins to gape more. Gradually, the pains become longer and more frequent, the head recedes a little, but with each succeeding pain it is driven a little farther down. The perineum bulges more and more, the vulva too gapes more and more and the scalp of the baby is seen when the head is forced down during a pain. Larger and larger area of the head comes to lie in the vulva opening during successive pains. The opening becomes transformed from a slightly gaping slit to an oval and ultimately an almost circular opening. The perineum meantime has been so pressed that it becomes stretched out and thinned. After the head is born, there is a short pause during which the face of the child becomes congested. After the head, the shoulders, the trunk and lower limbs are pushed out, followed by a gush of the remainder of the liquor amnii. After the end of the second stage the retracted uterus may be felt as a firm tumor extending up to just below the umbilicus.

Birth Guide during 2nd Stage

The expectant mother have possible full contractions in this stage when urge to push becomes stronger due to pressure of stretching vagina and physical signs of birth of baby's head, then body. She must relax perineum, buttocks, legs and change position for comfort and as necessary. Remove the clothing from the lower half of the body. Lie on the side or in semi-sitting position in a warm comfortable place with clean towels or folded linen under the buttocks. A waterproof sheet will protect the mattress. Stay as relaxed as possible.

Stage of Delivery (The third Stage of Labor)

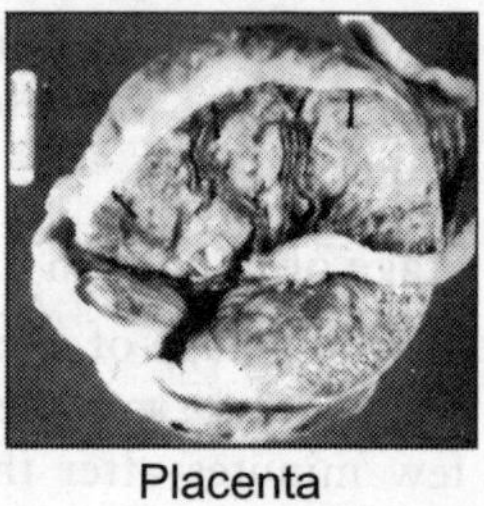

Placenta

This is stage of delivery of child and extends from the birth of the child to the birth of the placenta. There is usually a short cessation of pains with a corresponding relief to the patient. Ultimately, the uterus begins to contract again, and may be felt by the hand to grow more hard and solid. Sometimes, there are little gushes of blood during the pains, indicating the separation of the placenta. Many times there is no bleeding. In the end, the placenta is expelled out by strong pain in the vagina. The third stage may take a few minutes to an hour or even more. The average time is about 20 minutes.

Birth Guide during 3rd Stage

The breathing pattern should be slow or accelerated breathing. The delivery mother may try to push to expel placenta. There are mild to moderate contractions and uncontrollable shaking during this period. Excitement, fatigue and engrossment with baby are possible emotional signs an expectant mother may experience. The mother should push placenta out as directed and hold baby skin to skin. When you first see the baby's scalp at the vagina, it will be wet and wrinkled and may be streaked with blood. The pressure of the baby's head bulges perineum and anus. If the head is delivered slowly, it lessens the risk of tearing the perineum. Keep thighs and pelvic floor relaxed as the head emerges from the vagina. Once the head has fully emerged, the attendant should use the clean handkerchief to wipe away excess mucus from around the baby's nose and mouth. If the cord is around the baby's neck, the attendant should lift it gently over the baby's head.

Usually the baby begins breathing and crying immediately. Place the baby on the side on bare abdomen with head slightly lower than the body to drain any mucus remaining on the face. Wipe away any mucus and dry the baby completely. Keep baby warm. Remember, contractions will resume when the placenta separates from the uterine wall and slide down into the vagina. A mother can start breastfeeding right away, which will stimulate the uterus to contract and reduce bleeding. If the uterus is not firm, massage the fundus (top of the uterus) until it contracts. In case the newly born baby does not breath spontaneously, rub his/her back or chest briskly but gently. If not respond within 30 seconds, hold baby's feet together and smack the soles sharply. If still doesn't respond then mouth to mouth resuscitation is required by placing mouth over baby's nose and mouth and blowing gently air in the cheeks until the chest rises a little.

Separation of Placenta

The resumption of pains after the birth of child indicates still further contraction and retraction of the upper segment. This brings about such a disproportion between the placental site and the placenta when the attachment between the two separates. The placental site may be reduced in area 4-1/2 by 4 inches (11 by 10 cm.) without separation taking place. There are two methods of expulsion of placenta:

- **Schultze's method:** In which the placenta is expelled like an inverted umbrella when the fetal surface comes first and the membrane trailing behind.
- **Dubcan's mechanism:** Its also known as Matthews Duncan. In it the lower edge of the placenta is first extruded, and the whole organ slides down folded longitudinally upon itself. This method is more common.

4th stage (Recovery)

First hours after birth is known as the 4th stage in which the delivered mother must breathe slowly. This is the stage when she feels shaking, have after-pains (painful uterine contractions), perineal discomforts, fatigue, exhaustion, empty feeling, difficulty in urination, hunger and nausea. She has desire to see and hold baby. Rest and relaxation are important factors at this stage. She must drink or eat, urinate (sitting up helps), massage fundus and apply ice pack to perineum to decrease discomfort and swelling.

How to Control Hemorrhage?

As the placenta is separated from the wall of the uterus, the blood vessels passing from the one to the other are torn across, and many of the large sinuses in the uterine wall thus laid open. Bleeding from these is, however, prevented by the very retraction of the uterus, which causes the separation. If owing to exhaustion of the uterus, retraction fails to occur after the separation of the placenta, then free and alarming bleeding may take place – known as postpartum hemorrhage.

Some bleeding will occur after labor and delivery. If there is blood loss more than two cups, the mother may be hemorrhaging characterizing by a steady flow of blood and symptoms of shock with rapid pulse, paleness, trembling, cold and sweating. On suspecting hemorrhage firmly massage the uterus through the abdominal wall until it contracts. If the bleeding appears to ooze from tears at the vaginal opening, pad the perineum with an ice pack and towels.

Method of Cleaning Genitals after Labor

Nature follows the principles of antisepsis in labor. The birth canal can be divided into three parts:

- **The vulva (the entrance to vagina):** This area swarms with organism of various sorts. It may therefore be designated the Septic tract.
- **The vagina:** The portion containing the vaginal bacilli with their acid secretion, a few fungi, and some leucocytes. This is Antiseptic tract.
- **The cavity of the uterus:** Separated by the plug of mucus from the vagina, is entirely devoid of any form of organism. It is therefore the aseptic tract.

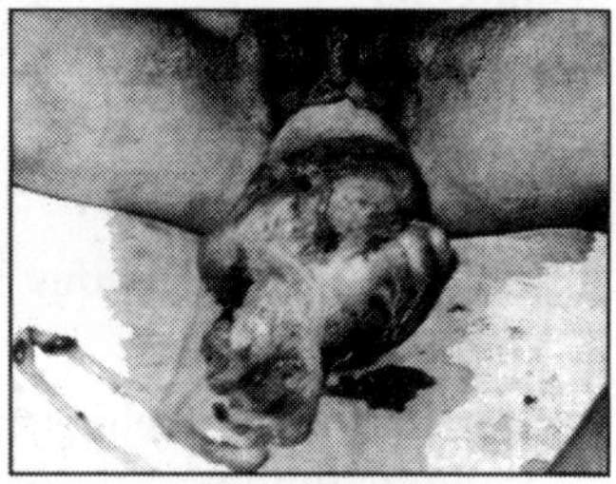
Vaginal secretion

Wherever possible the patient should have a complete bath at the very commencement of labor, and the nurse should see that the rectum and bladder are emptied. It is usually suggested that the patient should be given an enema in every case, irrespective of whether the bowels have acted naturally or not, unless the patient is in strong labor when the nurse arrives. The nurse should then pay special attention to the genitals. The hair should be shaved. Before a vaginal examination is made the vulva is swabbed with a antiseptic solution. The labia minora must be separated and wiped with pledget of wool soaked in an antiseptic solution. The pledget must always be drawn from being backwards to prevent carrying forward any septic matter from near the anus. No pledget must be used for more than one wipe.

Puerperal Infection

The term puerperal infection can be used to describe any infection during or after labor, it generally applies to infection of the uterus and surrounding tissues after delivery. This can vary from mild to life threatening in severity. Some of the most severe infections may appear within hours of the delivery and are often opportunistic and non-associated with reliable risk factors. Vigilance and aggressive diagnosis and treatment are required. The puerperal infection causes due to colonization and infection of the tissues of uterus, peritoneum or surrounding organs. Abscesses usually contain both aerobic and anaerobic bacteria. Nearly 50% of the ascending uterine infections involve harmful bacteria due to lack of cleanliness. The risk factors of this infection includes a cesarean delivery, invasive procedure during labor, prolonged rupture of the membranes, prolonged labor, multiple examinations, retained placental fragments, urinary catheter, intravenous line(s), low socioeconomic status and chronic diseases including diabetes.

The signs and symptoms of the infection are fever and tachycardia often developing rapidly after delivery, uterine tenderness, signs of septic or cardiovascular shock, hypertension, anxiety, disorientation, prostration, impaired renal function, hemolysis or hemoconcentration. The infection can be diagnosed by the following symptoms:

- Urinary tract infection with the presence of large number of white blood cells.
- Wound infection.
- Infection in intravenous line or site and contaminated fluids.
- Disturbed abscess.
- Septic thrombophlebitis, necrotizing fascistic, transfusion reaction, amniotic fluid or pulmonary embolism.
- Cardiogenic shock and toxic shock syndrome.
- Mastitis and afelectasis.
- Possible associated conditions such as septic shock, adult respiratory distress syndrome, acute renal failure and disseminated intra-vascular coagulation.

Perinatal Infections

Infections especially neonatal bacterial sepsis is the commonest cause of neonatal morality in which fetus may get infected in-utero and during passage through the birth canal during pregnancy and after birth. The following infections are common:

- **Intrauterine infection:** Occurs due to viruses and sometimes by bacteria causing diseases such as syphilis, tuberculosis, malaria, varicella, hepatitis B, HIV, rubella, herpes simplex etc.
- **Cytomegalic:** 60 to 70% patients due to this infection may suffer from bleeding, anemia, interstitial pneumonia and deafness.
- **Rubella:** About 60 to 70% patients suffer from bleeding, which may cause retardation, retinitis with pigmentation, congenital cardiac defects, vulva pulmonic stenosis, deafness and glaucoma.
- **Toxoplasmosis:** Causes severe anemia due to bleeding.

- **Congenital syphilis:** Causes rashes and snuffles, depressed nasal bridge periosteitis and chondrites.
- **Herpes virus:** Cause vesicles and pneumonia, herpes genitalia in mother.
- **Coxsackie B:** Causes respiratory distress due to carditis.
- **Congenital malaria:** Occurs due to administration of infected blood.
- **Bacterial infection:** Causes blood infection, umbilical cord and ear and throat swab.
- **Fungal infection (Candida):** Causes oral and perineal moniliasis pneumonia.
- **Protozal infection:** Causes congenital malaria.
- **Spirochetal infection:** Causes rashness, snuffles, hepatitis and periostesis.
- **Viral infection:** Includes cytomegalo virus, herpes virus, vericella-zostar (chicken pox herpes zoster) influenza and measles, which may cause vesicles, throat swab, hepatitis, anemia, deafness, cataract and cardiac malformations.

Medical Interventions in Labor

There are various interventions involved in labor and birth, which have benefits and risk and some of the important are described below:

- **Intravenous (IV) fluids:** The fluids are administered through plastic tube or needle inserted into the vein in the back of hand or in the arm when the patient is unable to drink liquids. Usually Pitocin is administered through IV for induce labor.
- **Prostaglandin:** A gel or tablet of prostaglandin is placed in the cervix for 24 hours or at least overnight to soften the cervix and start labor causing uterine contractions. Most of the times this intervention fails to induce labor.
- **Artificial rupture of membranes:** Before or during labor, a small hole is made in the membrane by a specially designed instrument during vaginal examination enabling to start labor, enhancing dilation and examine color of amniotic liquid in the fetus. Sometimes, it increases the risk of infection and may increase the discomfort of uterine contractions.
- **Induction of labor:** A finger is inserted between the membranes and cervix before labor begins as light bloody vaginal discharge is

often mistaken for bloody show. Labor may or may not start by this intervention. However, it may cause ruptured membranes.

- **Synthetic oxytocin (Pitocin):** Usually it is given in an IV to cause uterine contractions to induce labor when membranes have ruptured. Oxytocin increases the intensity and frequency of contractions. In some cases it may result in incidence of jaundice in newborn or cause premature birth.
- **Fetal stethoscope:** Used to monitor fetal heart rate (FHR) and listening baby's heartbeat through abdominal wall using a stethoscope. The FHR may be counted before, during and after a contraction about 15 to 30 minutes.
- **Episiotomy:** A surgical incision made into the perineum from the vagina towards rectum just before the birth of the baby's head to enlarge the birth canal, speed the delivery of the baby, to provide more space for application of forceps or vacuum extractor and reduce compression from vaginal tissues on the head of premature baby. Episiotomy causes certain disadvantages such as discomfort in the early postpartum period, infection, frequent bleeding after delivery and pain during intercourse for several months.
- **Forceps:** A stainless steel instrument inserted into the vagina applied to each side of baby's head to aid rotation at the time of birth of head and helps to bring the baby down, reduce prolonged pressure in the birth canal and allow rapid delivery. Sometimes, the process may bruise the soft tissues of baby's head or face and vaginal tissues.
- **Vacuum extractor:** A cap like device applied to the fetal head connected to vacuum pump through a rubber tube to create suction on the baby's head. It requires less space and operational time (5 to 10 minutes) in the vagina than forceps and can be applied when the fetus is at a higher place. It may cause bruising or swelling of soft scalp tissues.

Vaginal Examination when Labor-pain Starts

The use of abdominal palpation instead of this method of examination in normal cases has already been recommended. Where a vaginal examination is necessary it must be done with care. The patient should lie on her back rather than on her side, so as to diminish the risk of the hand coming into contact with the anus. Cleanse hands and vulva before conducting the examination. The labia minora is separated apart by the left hand fingers. The fingers of right hand are introduced in the vagina without coming into contact with vulva at all, or at least only the inner surfaces of the labia minora, which have also been cleansed. In case, the patient is passing through the stage of labor, it is well to introduce the fingers into the vagina during a pain and prolong the examination until it passes off. One can learn the state of matters both during and between pains. Ascertain the following points during vaginal examination:

1. State of labor; how far advanced it is?
2. Presentation and position?
3. Are the membranes ruptured? (if not, be careful not to rupture the same).
4. State of vagina and perineum to check rigidity, moistness or dryness.
5. Is pelvis normal?
6. Is cord prolapsed?

27

BREASTS DISORDERS AND BREASTFEEDING

In the early 1900, mostly the babies were breastfed or fed by the cow's milk. Solid foods were not offered till the age of 1 year. In 1920, people started offering solid foods. By 1975 a change had taken place, but still breast milk was more popular. Today, over 60% mothers breastfeed. Breast milk is recommended for many reasons:

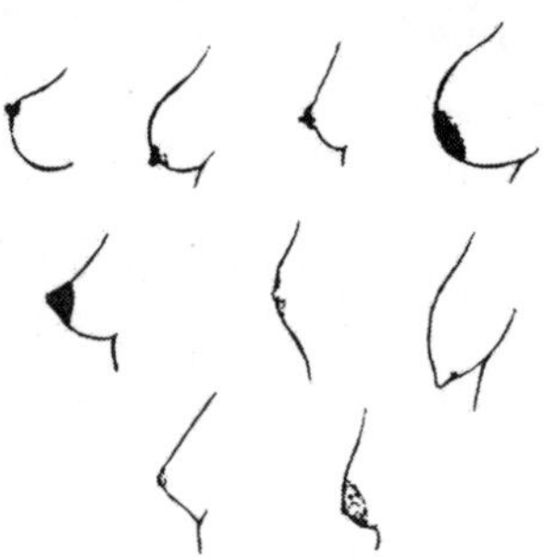

Shapes and sizes of breast nipples

- Is the ideal food for human babies.
- Is easily digested.
- Contains antibodies that protect the baby from infections.
- Reduces the possibility of allergic reactions.
- Aids involution and returns the uterus to its normal size.
- Makes special intimate relations between mother and baby.
- Is convenient and economical.

When Breast Milk is not Recommended?

- If the mother has had extensive breast reduction surgery.
- The mother has hepatitis.
- Mother's breasts are infected with beta streptococcus or active herpes.
- The mother is taking drugs for cancer, seizure preventing drugs and radioactive materials.

Wearing Bra during Pregnancy

Ensure to make a right choice for wearing bra during pregnancy as below:

- The bra should be made of cotton and not of synthetic material.
- The bra should be well fitting to support the extra weight of the breasts during pregnancy and at the time of lactation.
- The bra should not be too tight as to compress the breasts as the pressure on breasts can harm the glands besides causing pain and irritation.
- Remove bra during night. An ideal dress a pregnant woman should wear during night is a loose gown.
- Avoid washing nipples with soap or wipe away the greasy material as this may result in soreness of the nipples. Just splash plain water to keep nipples clean.

Caring Breasts during Lactation

Breasts are considered an important part of a woman's sex appeal. It is important to understand what is likely to happen to the breasts if the woman is breastfeeding her baby. The breasts enlarge because of the milk and the nipples enlarge and darken. The shape of breasts can be preserved if a woman take care of and wears well-fitting brassiere to support the breasts. The shape of breasts usually changes with age. Following care should be taken for breasts during lactation:

- Keep breasts and nipples clean and dry to prevent them from becoming sore and infected.
- Do not use soap to clean the nipples and areola; it will make them sore.
- Do not let the nipples remain moist for long; this will lead to cracking and infection.
- Keep a clean piece of cloth or a pad in your bra cup when breastfeeding to absorb leakage of milk. Make sure to change the cloth after feeding.
- Often breast nipples secrete oil. There is no need to clean the secretions from the nipples, since these protect the nipples from infection.
- If the nipples are not soft and supple, apply some cream or oil. Avoid using mustard oil as it irritates the sensitive skin. Wash the cream or oil before breastfeeding.

- Expose nipples and breasts to air daily for some time.
- Prevent engorgement of breasts by emptying them immediately after breastfeeding.
- Make sure to empty the breasts after breastfeeding to relieve tension. Press areola so that the milk comes out and remove the remaining milk with a couple of jerks.
- Do not feed the child when sleeping in incorrect posture; this may cause breast sagging. Always let the baby suckle in a sitting position with the child in the lap and your hand supporting the head.
- Wash the breasts with hot and cold baths simultaneously for 4 to 5 times daily to ensure proper blood circulation.
- Wear well fitting bra while exercising. Not wearing bra when exercising further spoils the shape of bust-line. Swimming is an ideal exercise to improve the shape of breasts.

Basics of Breastfeeding

- Nurse the baby soon after the birth, this will help enhance the flow of milk and the engorgement is less of a problem.
- Get into a comfortable position. Sit comfortably supported or lie on your side. If your perineum is sore, ask for an ice bag to ease the pain and help you relaxed while breastfeeding.
- If you have had a cesarean, sitting in the bed with the baby across your lap on a pillow may be comfortable.
- Nurse your newborn in calm atmosphere, which allow you and your baby to concentrate on feeding.
- Now grasp your breast with your free hand behind the areola and compress the nipple with thumb and forefinger aligning nipple with the baby's mouth.
- Stroke your baby's cheek with your nipple. Bring your baby to your breast rather than bringing your breast to your baby.
- Let your baby suckle at each breast for at least 10 minutes.
- Make sure as much of your areola as possible is in the baby's mouth to ensure a good latch.
- Arouse your baby's sense of taste by expressing a few drops of colostrums and rubbing nipples on baby's lips.
- Breastfeed on demand – every one to three hours or 10 to 15 times a day to establish an adequate milk supply.

In Case of heavy Breasts

There are no muscles in the breasts and they consist mainly of mammary glands and fat.

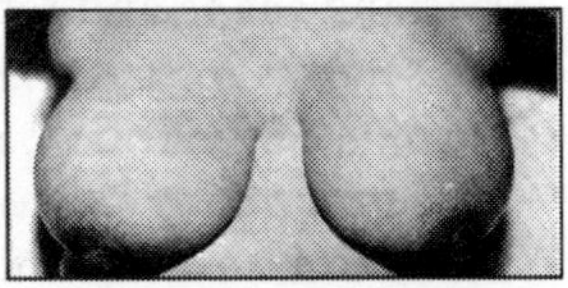

Heavy breast

Mammaplasty is a modern cosmetic surgery, in which surgery procedure for breast reduction is performed to desired size in case of over-developed breasts by reducing excess breast tissue and lifting the gland if the breast sag. Some people fear that breast reduction increases the chances of breast cancer. However, studies have given no evidence of it. The main cause of over-development of breasts is hyperactivity of female hormones during puberty. Sometimes, the breasts may grow to pathologically abnormal size. During pregnancy the breasts may become enlarged but regain their original shape and size after childbirth. Obese women generally have over-developed breasts, which is known as 'fatty macromastia'. Women with abnormally enlarged breasts feel the following symptoms:

- Strain on cervical and thoracic vertebrae resulting in pain in the neck and backache.
- The brassiere may become a painful embodiment during menstrual period.
- Sagging breasts creates problems between the lower part of the breasts and chest wall.
- Pressure on the neck or nerve plexus due to the weight of the heavy breasts.

Breast Cancer

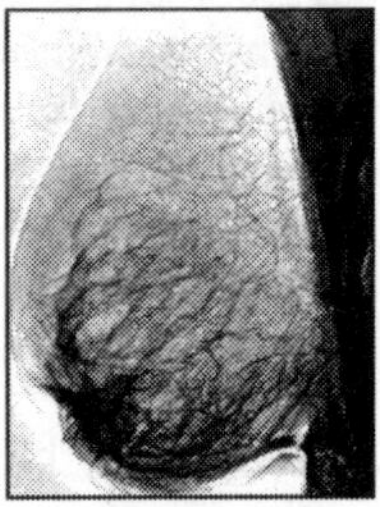

Leakage of milk

Cancer is a malignant condition caused by abnormal rapid multiplication of cells in a part of body in women more common in cervix, uterus or breasts. According to a medical survey, out of total numbers of cancers reported over 40% are cervical cancers, 12% breast cancers, nearly 10% uterus cancers, about 10% throat cancers and rest nearly 30%. The usual age to be afflicted by cancer is between 30 and 50.

Breast Self-examination?

The following steps are undertaken:

- Examine the breasts standing before a mirror for symmetry in size and shape and retraction of the nipples.
- Raise arms over the head and study the breasts for similar signs.
- Recline on bed with a pillow under the shoulder on the side of breast to be examined.
- Raise arms over the head to examine the inner half of the breast. Begin at the breastbone and palpate the inner half of the breast.
- Carefully palpate the area over the nipples with flats of fingers.
- Now examine the lower half of the breasts.
- With arm down the side, examine the breast by carefully feeling the tissues extending to the armpit.
- Examine the upper outer part of the breast with the flat part of fingers.
- Finally examine the lower outer part of the breast with the flat of the fingers in successive stages.

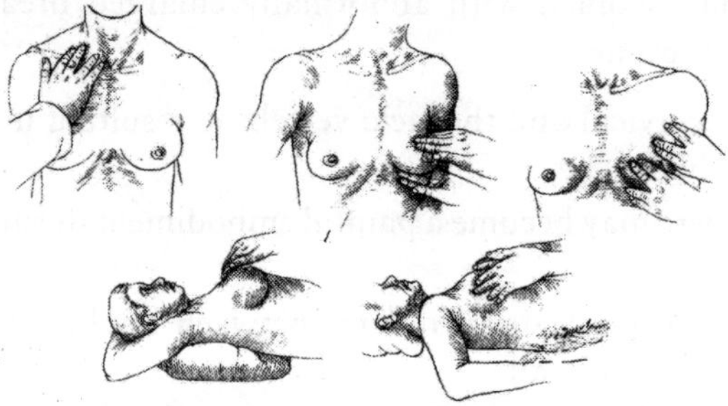

Steps of Breast Self-examination of Breast

If there is only a single nodule or lump in the breast, this is more likely to be malignant, if there is no pain. The tissue is removed by surgical procedure. In case of symptoms of cancer, immediate treatment is required. If the cancer appears to have spread to the neighboring lymph nodes, the patient should be given extensive radiation therapy to the whole affected area. Self-examination of breasts should be conducted once a month. When the cancer is present in the breast, the following symptoms are observed:

- There is usually one hard single lump with no pain.
- There may be a slight blood discharge from the nipple. Although the disease may occur at any time of life, it is much more common between the age of 35 and 60. After the age of 65, breast cancer is rare.

- Painful breasts.
- Formation of painful abscess.
- Excessive watery discharge from the nipples.

Breastfeeding Problems

Difficulty with let down reflex: Anxiety, fatigue, inadequate nipple stimulation, taking excessive amount of alcohol, caffeine and smoking, especially during the hour before feeding, may inhibit the let down reflex.

Reduced milk supply: Fatigue, insufficient intake of fluids and calories or poor diet may reduce milk supply.

Poor latch: If the baby has not positioned his mouth properly on the nipple, he will be unable to compress the areola properly, and will not stimulate a let down reflex. This may lead to the baby making a clicking sound during sucking.

Engorgement: There are two causes – increased blood supply and accumulation of milk in the breasts. In such condition the following symptoms are observed:

- Swelling in the breasts.
- Breasts become hard to the touch with severe pain.

The following treatment is suggested:

- Wear a well-fitting bra during day and night for support to the breasts.
- Make sure that no area of breast is compressed.
- Apply cold pack to reduce blood flow to the breasts.
- Express milk while standing in a warm shower. Cover your breasts with warm moist towel.
- Express milk before feeding to soften a hard, swollen areola.
- Breast massage stimulates the milk flow.
- Use an electric or mechanical breast pump to relieve the fullness in breasts.

Flat and inverted nipples: Poor shape of nipples interferes with feeding. If the nipples appear flat or inverted, it is advised to press the areola between the thumb and the finger to help nipple to stick out and the baby will not have any difficulty in suckling. Do not apply cream or ointment on your nipples nor it is necessary to wash them with soap.

Cracked and Sore Nipples

This condition occurs usually in the first week of nursing due to improper positioning of baby's mouth on the areola or poor latch.

There is difference between a crack and a fissure. A fissure is generally at the base of nipple and more painful and sometimes the blood may ooze out of it. To prevent crack or sore nipples the following remedies are suggested:

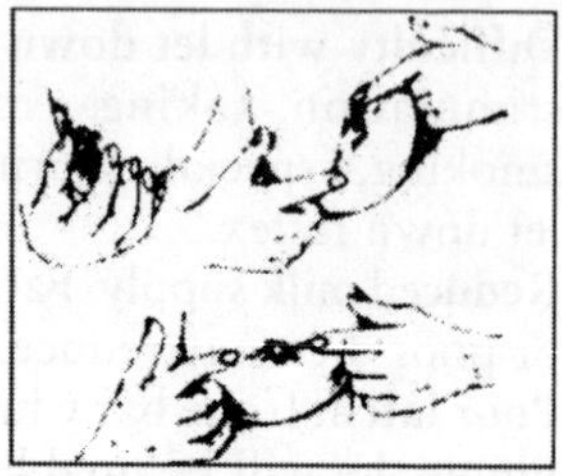
Cracked and sore nipples

- Wash your breasts with plain water and keep them dry in between the feeds as wet nipples tend to become sore.
- Do not apply soap to nipples.
- Make sure that the baby's mouth is correctly positioned on your nipple.
- Feed the baby more frequently and start feeding on the less sore nipple.
- Apply oil or cream to keep nipples soft and supple. Do not apply mustard oil.
- Clean nipples after feeding.
- Expose nipples and breast to air (sunshine or sun lamp) for some time daily.
- Apply oil or cream during pregnancy. During pregnancy a greasy material is usually produced, which keeps nipples supple.
- In case of leakage of milk, use a piece of clean cloth to absorb it. Keep the cloth in cups of your bra.
- Always wear a clean bra.
- Change the feeding position very frequently. Try sitting or lying so that the pressure from the baby's sucking will not be in the same place all the time.
- Dry the nipple air dry with your bra flaps or set a hair dryer.
- Apply an ice pack to the sore area before feeding at the breast.
- Express a small amount of breast milk and rub it over the sore area. Breast milk has the healing properties.
- Use a nipple shield readily available in the market in case of severe problem.

Blockage of Milk in Breast

The main reason for this disorder is milk of thick density unable to secrete through the blocked tube. It starts accumulating behind the blocked tube resulting in pain. Feeding mothers may also have symptoms of fever in such condition. At times, tubes get blocked because of wearing tight bras. Always wear bras, which doesn't exert pressure on the breasts. It is suggested that mothers suffering from this disorder should continue to breastfeed from the affected breast first so that the milk instead of accumulating and aggravating the problem drains, thus relieving the block. Massage the affected breast towards the nipple. After feeding the nipple express the breasts. You may consult a doctor if you are not getting relief. The pain and tension can be relieved by hot and cold compresses. If proper care is not taken, there are chances of mastitis suffering. In case of engorged nipple, the flow of milk in the tubes gets blocked and milk starts leaking into the infected part of the breast. In case of mastitis the infected part of the breast becomes red, painful, swollen and shiny because of stretching of the skin. However, you may continue feeding the child, because in spite of infection the germs do not pass into the milk and the baby will not suffer. A mother suffering from mastitis may develop an abscess if she discontinues breastfeeding

Epidemic Mastitis

Swelling of breasts with severe pain, a tender, reddened, hot breast, nausea, fatigue are the main symptoms of epidemic mastitis and you should consult a doctor for the treatment. and to find out whether to feed the baby or not. Drainage of milk is the only remedy for getting relief from the pain. Sometimes pus may also ooze along with the milk. The patient may also have fever. The following treatment unclog the ducts:

- Apply warm moist pack or a warm towel to the affected area.
- Massage the area towards the nipple. Perform wide circle exercise for quick relief. To do this exercise, rotate both arms five to eight times in circles without wearing a bra to strengthen the nerves and unclog ducts.

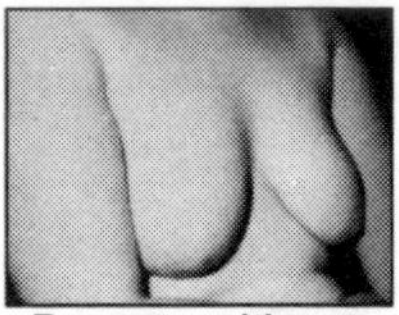

Breasts without nipple

- If you have an abscess in one of the breast, you should continue feeding the baby with the other breast.
- Express milk. Make sure the mastitis breast is as empty as possible after feeding.
- Take antibiotics as prescribed by the doctor only.
- Drink lot of water, juice and other fluids.
- Rest and stay in the bed as much as possible.

Expressing Breast Milk

There are many ways to express milk by hand or a breast pump:

- Express by hand conveniently. Once the breast is flowing, grasp your breast at the back of the areola and press towards your chest. As you compress the areola, milk may drip or spurt into a collecting bottle.
- Breast pump is a effective equipment designed to squeeze out milk.
- Never wear anything tight or uncomfortable during pregnancy. Avoid tight bands around the waist.

Breast Pain or Lumps

Breasts change with puberty, the menstrual cycle, age and pregnancy. Women should examine their breasts every month, especially after the childbirth so that they know the breast's structure and can detect any masses or lumps.

Symptoms	What it might be	What to do
Painless lump in breast	Non-cancerous cyst	Biopsy exam.
Lump in underarm	Non-cancerous tumor	
Change in contour, texture	Breast cancer, if painful	
Change in the size of breast		
Change in nipple (indrawn)		
Itching or burning feeling		
Dark or bloody discharge		
Pain and tenderness after delivery	Infection caused by bacteria	Drink water See a doctor
Hard or swollen breast	Abscess in the breast	
Redness and pain		
Fever		
Pain, tenderness and swelling	Pregnancy developed	Wear bra Pregnancy test
Missed period		
Fatigue and nausea		
Swelling, tenderness after birth	Swelling with milk	Nurse often Warm - compresses
Pain in nipple when feeding	Sore or cracked nipple. Common after delivery	Wash after nursing. Apply Vitamin E oil
Breast pain while taking estrogen	Drug side effect	Consult doctor
Lumpy or swollen breasts	Fibrocystic breasts Its harmless	Consult doctor
Pain or discomfort before periods		
Pain or tenderness in breasts	Premenstrual syndrome	See a doctor

Expressing Breast Milk

There are many ways to express milk by hand or a breast pump:

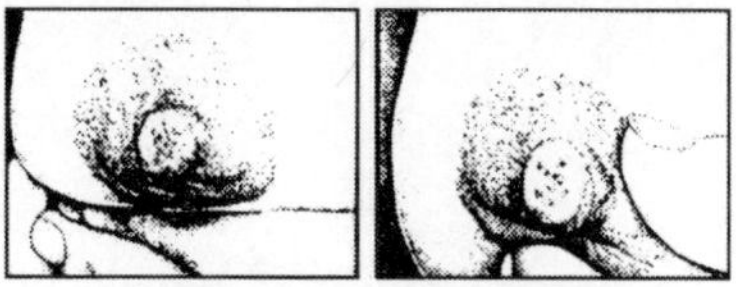

Expressing breast milk

- Express by hand conveniently. Once the breast is flowing, grasp your breast at the back of the areola and press towards your chest. As you compress the areola, milk may drip or spurt into a collecting bottle.
- Breast pump is a effective equipment designed to squeeze out milk.
- Never wear anything tight or uncomfortable during pregnancy. Avoid tight bands around the waist.

Breast Pain or Lumps

Breasts change with puberty, the menstrual cycle, age and pregnancy. Women should examine their breasts every month, especially after the childbirth so that they know the breast's structure and can detect any masses or lumps.

28

DIET CONTROL DURING AND AFTER PREGNANCY

Importance of Breast Milk

Breastfeeding a baby is one of the most valuable gifts. Breast milk is a natural, pure and unadulterated form of nourishment for the baby. It provides antibodies to the child which is why it is superior to formula feeds or cow's milk.

Why Breast Milk?

1. Breast feeding nurtures the emotional bonding between the mother and child.
2. It is a very convenient way to feed the baby at any place and time.
3. A breast fed baby does not require vitamin supplements as breast milk fulfils all the requirements. The nutritional quality of breast milk is much higher than that of cow's milk or buffalo's milk as it contains more lactose (milk sugar) and vitamins A,C and E. It also contains fat and iron.
4. Fat and protein in the breast milk are easily digested, thus the danger of gastro-intestinal problems is low in breast milk fed by newborn babies.
5. There is also a reduced likelihood of allergic reactions as breast milk contains protein which do not cause allergic reaction.

Food you Eat

Food is grouped into two parts:

- Nutritive, which provides energy, heat and nutrition.

- Non-nutritive provides only energy, vitamins and minerals. Vitamins and minerals do not supply energy, but play very important role in regulating metabolic activities. Minerals help in the formation of body structure and skeleton.

You must keep in view the following tips:

- Fasting two-three days during menstrual phase helps to provide physical, mental and psychological rest.
- A well-balanced food with restriction on salt are essential as water rotation, before, during and after periods is quite common.
- Drink plenty of water or warm milk to relieve fatigue and sleeplessness.

Digestive System of Food

The main function of the digestive system is to break down carbohydrates, proteins and fats into simpler substances for proper absorption of the same, to keep the body systems working and also to expel the residual waste. The process of digestion is two types: mechanical and chemical. Digestion includes chewing of food, swallowing of food, churning of food, contraction of the intestinal tract and acidity reaction. There are several kinds of acid present in the food and are utilized by the body. Citric acid is present in lemons, oranges, grape fruits and tomatoes. Italic acid is formed in grapes and in pineapple. Acetic acid is present in vinegar and in soy sauce. Oxalic acid is found in spinach, rhubarb, cocoa, tea and pepper. Benzoic acid is also used as preservative. Uric acid is one of the waste products of the body. Spinach, beans, peas, cauliflower and mushroom also produce uric acid. Folic acids are very useful for growth and maintenance of general health. These must be consumed by children and pregnant women as additional supplements of nutrition required by them.

Some of the important root vegetables are potato, carrot and beetroot. Jams are rich in carbohydrates and are important source of energy and contain vitamin C. Beans, lady's finger, tomato etc. are very low in calories and are easily digestible. Nuts and oil seeds are rich in proteins and contain high level of fat. Amla and Guava contain vitamin C. Yellow coloured fruits like Mango and Papaya contain carotene. Banana and sweet lime are rich in potassium. Dried fruits such as figs, dates, raisins are rich in iron. The seeds used for extracting oils include safflower, sunflower, groundnut, coconut, and mustard.

Diet During Pregnancy

The first three months of pregnancy are called the first trimester and the next three months as the second trimester. During the first trimester of pregnancy, a pregnant shows only a few outward signs of pregnancy, although she experiences tremendous physical and emotional changes. Throughout pregnancy, the baby in womb needs a regular supply of energy and a high quality of nutrients for its growth. It is during the first few weeks after conception that the fetus begins to form the organs and heartbeat can be detected by the second month. However, growth and maturation continues till the end of pregnancy period. The state of mind of the mother during the pregnancy affects too much over the child. Reading books, listening to music and rest makes an expectant mother happy and relaxed.

As the months roll by, the pregnant woman gets exhausted quickly. The best way to relieve tiredness and exhaustion, is to ask your husband to rub your back and shoulders. In case of severe nausea and vomiting, consult your doctor, who will prescribe an anti-vomiting drug. Intravenous glucose in a drip may be required if you are losing fluid every time you vomit. Have frequent small meals six to seven times in a day. Restrict your fluid intake in the evening to avoid frequent urination during the night. Eat hygienically cooked food. Relax for few minutes after meal. Avoid excess of tea, coffee and smoking.

The second trimester of pregnancy starts from the 13th week and continues up to the 28th week. The total weight gain during the pregnancy should not be more than 10 to 12 kg. During the first three months, there may be little or no increase in weight. At the end of this period there may be an increase ranging from 0.7 to 1.4 kg. or in the first 20 weeks a total of 4 kg. Make sure to watch your weight during each visit to your doctor for check up. If the weight is less than the normal gain, it indicates a poor growth of your baby in womb and you must improve your diet. If the weight is more than the normal gain, the reason could be that you are taking on excess or wrong kind of food.

Eat well balanced diet to avoid excessive weight gain. Include foods providing fibre in the diet to avoid constipation. Drink plenty of fluids and water, 7 to 8 glasses in a day. Take extra vegetables, pulses or fruits. Avoid excessive intake of sugar, salt and spices. Avoid canned and highly processed foods. Avoid eating at unhygienic places.

The average weight gain during pregnancy is 12 kg. Out of this, 80% is the womb and its contents. Remember, if you are overweight, there are chances of rise in your blood pressure and blood sugar.

During the 3rd trimester the appetite returns and mother as well as baby need a nourishing and well-balanced diet. Here is a daily diet chart recommended during this period:

Food	Non Vegetarian	Vegetarian
Milk	375-500 ml	500 ml
Meat/fish/chicken or grams/cheese	150 gm	200 gm
Egg	One	
Curd	125 gm	250 gm
Whole wheat or Rice	200 gm	200 gm
Bread or cereal	50 gm	50 gm
Pulses	25-50 gm	50-75 gm
Vegetables	475-500 gm	475-500 gm
Root vegetable	50 gm	50 gm
Cooking oil/ Butter/Ghee	30-40 gm	30-40 gm
Fruits	300 gm	300 gm

Diet after Delivery of Child

The period after delivery is called postpartum and lactation. The term lactation means the secretion of milk by mammary glands (breast). During the first few days after delivery, a cloudy fluid called colostrum is secreted in place of milk. This fluid is very beneficial for the newly born baby as it contains important antibodies to protect infant from infections and diseases. Colostrum provides adequate nutrition to the infant until the appearance of true milk after two to three days. Breast feeding is very important, it helps to build a strong bond between mother and the baby.

There is no need to panic if you do not produce a lot of milk to feed your child immediately after the delivery. It will gradually increase as you start feeding your baby more frequently. Your state of mind along with your diet influences the quantity of milk you produce. The quantity and quality of milk produced is not related to the size of breast but is dependent on the amount of diet and fluid you consume. The more often you feed your baby, the more milk will be produced. Drink plenty of juices, milk shake, buttermilk soups and water. Have minimum four litres of fluid per day while you are a feeding mother. Do not fix any rigid timing to feed your baby. Your baby will let you know when he is hungry by crying out.

Diet while Breastfeeding

While breast feeding, the feeding mother will require a lot more calories than during the pregnancy. This is because breastfeeding your baby will make you burn 3500 kcal per day. However you need to consume only 2400 to 2700 kcal per day during first six months of lactation if you are exclusively breastfeeding your baby. Most doctors recommend that you breastfeed for one year, out of this period your baby should exclusively be breastfed for 4 to 6 months, and then you can gradually start weaning by slowly introducing your baby to a variety of foods so that he is no longer fully dependent on your breast milk at the end of one year. Thus during the last six months of lactation, the energy requirement will decrease to about 2250 to 2550 kcal per day. Your diet requirement during lactation period will be as below:

- **Protein:** 75 gm/day during the initial six months of lactation period, which will reduce to 68 gm/day after six months.
- **Fat:** It is a concentrated source of energy and require 45 gm/day.
- **Calcium:** It is essential for the baby's development of bones as well as for the mother. The daily requirement will be 1000 mg/day. Breast milk draws calcium from the bones in human body.
- **Iron:** 30 mg/day requirement is necessary to maintain haemoglobin level in the body that supplies oxygen to each cell of the body. Iron deficiency leads to anaemia.
- **Folic acid:** 150 mcg/day is required for the growth and development of the brain and spine of the baby. The deficiency can also lead to anaemia in the mother.
- **Vitamin C:** 80 mg/day is required for the formation of collagen and also for immunity against infections and diseases. Vegetables like cabbage and lettuce taken in raw form are rich source of vitamin C. Vitamin A (Beta-carotene-3800 meg/day) is required for clear vision, skin and immunity. The requirement for vitamin A increases during lactation.
- **Vitamin D:** It aids the absorption of calcium in body and sunlight is an excellent source of vitamin D. Dietary supplements are not required.

- **Vitamin B-12:** The shortage is due to deficient vegetarian diets. Soya milk provides enough amount of vitamin B-12.
- During this period, your diet should include almonds, garlic, milk and fenugreek. These products increase and stimulate the production of breast milk.

How to Slim without Tears after Delivery of Baby?

A fat surplus of 10 to 15% over the normal weight must be taken as overweight. Beyond this, it is called as obesity. Over 30% it is extreme obesity. Overweight can be of three types: fatty overweight, watery overweight and cellulite.

Fatty Overweight

is really 'fat and muscle' hypertrophy, uniformly spread, accompanied by a large appetite and is common in men. The obesity often excessively noticeable over the upper half of the body, head, neck, arms and trunk.

Watery Overweight

is a matter of 'watery fat', which does not affect the muscles at all. The obesity is most usual over the lower half of the body, and is not accompanied by any marked appetite. It is more common in women. Cellulite is a form of inflammation rather than overweight. Heredity factor, habit of overeating, ageing factor, poor functioning of system, nervous factor, sedentary life causing constipation and glandular system causing over-secretion by part of the sub-renal glands are some of the prominent causes of overweight.

To maintain a perfect figure and self grooming after becoming a mother, the amount of energy you consume must be equal to the amount of energy you burn. This includes both tangible activity and your basic metabolic rate, that is, the rate of which your body carries out its vital functions, the involuntary actions of heart-beat, breathing, digestion, growth. repair etc. which are vital to life and carry two-third of our energy intake.

In case of obesity:

- The face becomes round and bulky.
- Shoulders get plump and hollow over the collar-bones disappears.
- Fat overhang the hips and the waist disappears.
- The buttocks enlarge.
- The girdle shrinks and the rolls of flesh swells out above or below the girdle.

- The neck thickens and lose its normal contour. A double chin under the nape of the neck appears.
- Breasts sag down to the stomach.
- The stomach droops over the pubis and the pubis hangs over the genital organs.
- The skirt belt or jean gets a little tight and there is strain on jacket buttons.

There are several causes of obesity, but the main are due to over-eating and lack of exercise. The logic way to lose weight is to cut down food intake by 100 per cent without affecting the nutritive value of the food consumed. Exercise regularly to burn the extra fat. One kilogram of body fat contains 7500 calories energy. By having a daily calorie reduction of 500 calories, the total weight reduction in a month would be 2 kg.

How Exercise Helps?

- Tone up the muscles.
- Improve digestion.
- Increase oxygen supply to the body.
- Help to keep your weight down.
- Retain calcium in the body which delays the ageing process.
- Keep heart in good condition.
- Help glowing skin and shining hair.

The Calories-controlled Diets

Calories are themselves energy units and all foods contain calories to a greater or lesser amount. A normal daily diet should contain 2000 to 2200 calories to fulfil the needs of a healthy female. The protein intake should account for about 50% of your daily calories consumption. Carbohydrates should be kept to minimum. Cut down starchy foods containing sugar in favour of protein-rich foods. Lower the number of calories taken daily to about 1300 to 1600 every 24 hours.

Normally a healthy food can be digested within 15 to 20 minutes. A young woman of average height, who is not a pregnant or involved in hard physical labour, requires an average 2300 calories a day. One gram protein or carbohydrate gives four calories whereas one gram of fat gives nine calories. Protein is found in excess in milk, eggs, meat, fish, soybeans, almond, coconut, groundut etc to give strength to body. Carbohydrate is found in vegetables, fruits, cereals etc. The deficiency of carbohydrates leads to weakness. Avoid taking drastic steps in reducing weight. You are fat-prone, if you:

- Like eating.
- Have rather sedentary habits or a sedentary job.
- Put on weight during holidays.
- Are emotionally upset and worry makes you lose weight.
- Have little effect of massage and douches.

Daily requirement of calories for women doing light work is 1900. A teenager female needs daily 2200 calories. Women doing moderate work require 2200, a pregnant women 2500, a mother during lactation 2900 and a belly dancer needs 3750 calories every 24 hours. Per hour calorie consumption required by a female is given below:

- Women engaged in light household work need 120 to 300 calories.
- Women doing hard household work need 400 to 600 calories.
- Floor sweeping women require 240 to 300 calories.
- Boating consumes 125 to 220 calories in an hour.
- Swimming consumes 395 to 475 calories per hour.
- For gardening 200 to 250 calories are needed in a hour.
- Dancing consume 250 to 350 calories per hour.
- For morning walk about 150, for jogging about 800, for cycling 315 to 350 and for skating350 to 375 calories are required in an hour.

Effect of Overweight on Body

Overweight not only affects the looks and figure, but damages the health too, and lead to circulation troubles (Heart ailments, high blood pressure and diabetes,), psychological and nervous troubles (irritation, tiredness, nervousness, apathetic and lethargicbehaviour), digestive troubles (dilation of stomach, inflammation and spasm of intestines and congestion of liver, fatty degeneration and digestive upsets) and genital disorders causing inflammation of fat into the nervous and glandular tissues which control sexual appetite, and can cause temporary impotence.

Important Do and Don'ts

1. Weigh yourself every 28 days
2. Cut down on your food intake especially bread, biscuits and cakes.

3. Use little salt and no sugar.
4. Have breakfast on one apple and tea.
5. Avoid drink while you are eating.
6. Reduce your appetite an hour before your meals.
7. Take foam bath, if possible or take a Turkish bath.
8. Exercise for 15 to 20 minutes every morning.
9. Energetic sports may keep you slim and trim.
10. Drink diuretic water.
11. Do not lose patience.
12. Do not let yourselfbecome constipated.
13. Do not take drugs without consulting a doctor.
14. Do not weigh yourself very frequently.

A balanced diet should include fruits and vegetables. These are not only rich sources of vitamins and mineral salts but are also fibre rich foods. The fibre rich diet helps our digestive system and makes heart strong. Diet should be low in saturated fats and rich in fruits, vegetables and fibres. Vegetables should form 15 to 25 per cent of daily intake, followed by fruits about 10 to 15 per cent. The dairy products and meats should not be more than 10 per cent each. Fats, oils and sweets should not be over 5 per cent in daily diet.

Have at least six to eight glasses of water every day, which flushes out toxins from the body, keeps the skin cells hydrated and helps in keeping youthful and cheerful lessening the signs of ageing. Keep strict watch on sugar and salt intake, excess of salt ends up in water retention and excess sugar is stored as reserve energy in the form of fat. Substituting sugar by 'gur' or honey is beneficial. The Calcium requirement in human body increases with the advancing age. At least two glasses of milk should be consumed daily after the age 40. Vitamin supplements should be taken under doctor's guidance as overdose of certain vitamins can lead to toxicity.

Don't Neglect your Body after Childbirth

Daily care can help to keep your body smooth, soft and healthy. Chin, neck, upper arms, stomach, breasts, back, waistline, hips, thighs and bottom are some of the areas of the body which require special care by every woman to maintain her personality and improve skin texture, colour and tone.

Ten Steps to Get Rid of Flab after Childbirth

Mind set: The success of your weight reduction fairly depends on your will power, keenness and attitude - without which nothing really works.

Right aim: Looking to lose immediately is an unrealistic and unreasonable goal. Aim to reduce weight gradually, not quickly.

Exercising: Make exercise an integral part of your daily routine. Brisk walking, cycling, playing tennis or badminton, swimming, aerobics and yoga exercising are some of the easy exercises, Start up with a 10-minute routine and gradually increase it to 30-40 minutes daily.

Change in lifestyle: Lifestyle changes are must. If you are having sedentary habits, you are likely to lose more than gain. Avoid making obesity, a way of life. Walk briskly, take to the stairs instead of riding the lift or a elevator are good habits.

Diet control: Exercise control over your diet to lose weight. Remember, crash dieting is unhealthy, though it works well initially but leaves worse effects. You put on whatever weight you had lost. Eat slowly, avoid going to a party on an empty stomach, Eating an low or no-fat diet and consuming more of fibre-rich and unrefined foods are some of the good habits.

Don't skip meals: Skipping a meal and ending up eating more at the next meal is rather harmful.

Avoid late dinner: Watch what you eat after 7 pm, as the food you eat late is stored in the body as pure lard. Food enters the blood stream as energy after four hours of taking dinner. Since the body does not need energy, so the food is stored in the fat cells as fat. As far as possible, have light dinner.

Release toxins: Water helps washing away the toxins from the body. Start the day with a glass of water.

Skip meal: If you feel hungry in the evening, snack up but skip dinner. If you had a heavy lunch, then just take a bowl of soup for dinner.

Maintain food diary: In spite of diet control, if you have not reduced at all although visiting a gym or a health club regularly, then maintain a food diary. Make a record of everything you eat or drink from you wake up early morning till night you go to bed for two weeks. You will find your wrongs.

Obesity

Obesity is not a disease in itself but it is at the roots of many diseases like high blood pressure, heart trouble, diabetes, kidney trouble, gout, joint pains and skin diseases. As stated earlier, many causes of obesity include overeating, lack of exercise, lethargy, an imbalance of hormones in the body, mental tension, frustration, loneliness and after-effect of childbirth.

Physical Adjustments during Postpartum

After the birth of baby, mother feel exhausted, fatigued and let down and her body undergoes rapid physical and hormonal changes. For early recovery very frequently check your temperature, pulse, respiratory rate, blood pressure and monitor the amount and character of lochia (red-coloured, fleshy-odour discharge from vagina flowing heavily for the first day after the birth of baby, which diminishes in a week's time changing its colour to pale pink in next 3 to 4 days and finally becomes yellowish white or brown with the presence of bloody clots for 6 to 8 weeks). Avoid infection or over-exertion, which cause excessive bleeding. In such case consult your doctor. There are few more problems faced by the mother during postpartum period as below:

After-pains: Painful contractions of the uterus occur. To cope with the pain relax and usethe slow-breathing pattern. After-pains may disappear after a week.

Cervix conditioning: The cervix shrinks to its pre-pregnant size but remains somewhat wider for few months.

Vaginal toning: The vagina gradually regains its tone, but the labia remain looser, larger and darker as compared to pre-pregnancy condition.

Breasts: Breasts secrete colostrums (a yellow fluid that precedes breast milk). The milk production starts between the 2nd and 5th day after the delivery. During this period the breasts may feel tense, hard to the touch and painful (engorged). Non-breastfeeding mothers still produce milk. To suppress lactation, breast binding, ice packs and avoidance of breast stimulation help diminish milk production. Express milk from breasts, this will stimulate the breasts to produce more milk.

Circulatory changes: Some blood loss is natural after childbirth. Average blood loss amounts to approximate one cup in normal delivery, but may be double in case of an episiotomy. Slight blood loss during the childbirth is not harmful, but if blood losses are more consult a doctor.

Stretch marks and pigmentation of abdominal skin: After the birth, the abdominal muscles remain softfor about six weeks and stretch marks appear. These marks fade with the passage of time but do not disappear completely. However, skin pigmentation will fade away after few months.

Hormonal changes: After childbirth the body undergoes sudden and dramatic changes in hormonal production. The hormonal producing level drops abruptly and remain low until ovaries begin producing these hormones again. If a woman breastfeed, she may not menstruate for several months, though ovulation can occur during this time. However, if a mother is not breastfeeding, she will begin menstruating within 4 to 6 weeks after the birth. First few menstrual periods following delivery may be heavier than usual, but will return to normal soon.

Rest and activities: Adequate rest is essential to recover after childbirth. Try to rest an extra two hours daily and go to bed early at night.

Exercise: Perform the pelvic floor contraction exercise (known as Kegel exercise) to heal episiotomy or any tear, reduce the swelling and restore the muscle tone in the pelvic floor. Try to begin postpartum exercises within a day or two in case of a normal delivery. Better consult your doctor in this regard. The conditioning exercises during pregnancy help you recover former contours and strength during the postpartum period. Two areas of the body: abdominal muscles and pelvic floor muscles (to reduce swelling, increase circulation and promote healing in the perineum and restore vaginal muscle tone) need special attention Here are few postpartum exercise:

- Gently tighten and then relax the muscles of perineum several times a day for pelvic floor contraction.
- Lie flat in bed with knees bent. Tighten abdominal muscles to tilt the pelvis pressing low back into the bed. Pelvic tilts can be performed while standing or sitting also.

Uterus examination: Fundus can be felt midway between the navel and the pubic bone. Massage the uterus, which helps to maintain the firmness of uterus, prevent heavy blood loss from the placental site and return to its previous size. By the end of 5 to 6 weeks, the uterus returns to its previous size.

Sexual adjustments: Some men and women want to resume sexual intercourse as soon as possible after the birth, though most of females feel constrained or afraid and lack enjoying making love due to a sore perineum and extreme fatigue. If you are not ready to resume intercourse early, you may resume pleasuring (touching and enjoying each other's bodies sensually with or without orgasm). It is suggestedrefrain from intercourse for at least six weeks after the birth. It is, however, safe to have intercourse when stitches heal, vaginal discharge stops and you feel like it. There is decrease in vaginal lubrication after childbirth because of hormonal changes. The problem can be alleviated by use of a sterile, water soluble lubricant such as K-Y jelly or contraceptive cream during intercourse. Remember, conception can occur whether or not menstruation has resumed. The condom along with spermicidal foam, cream or jelly is safe and effective method after childbirth.

29

ALL ABOUT MENSTRUATION

Although, we have described briefly about menstruation in previous chapters, but this subject is very important for the health of females, a detailed description is required.

Menstruation is a periodic change occurring in human consisting of discharge of blood from the cavity of the womb. It usually starts between 12 to 13 years in warm climates and later in cold regions with duration of each menstrual period varying from 2 to 8 days. There is an interval of 21 to 28 days between the two periods. The menstrual flow stops when a woman becomes pregnant. It stops completely at the age of about 50, when it is known as the menopause. The two main disorders of menstruation:

- Absence of periods or scanty and painful discharge known as amenorrhoea and dismenorrhoea.
- Profuse bleeding during periods known as menorrhagia or irregular menstruation called as metrorrhagia.

Amenorrhoea

Scanty discharge of menstrual blood or absence of menses flow may be due to

- Anemia.
- Ill health.
- Disturbed nervous system.
- Imperfect development or functioning of ovaries.
- Inflammation of various internal organs (womb, ovaries or fallopian tubes).

- Serious or prolonged diseases like tuberculosis, aggravated dyspepsia malaria etc.
- Sudden fright or great grief, which may cause stoppage of the menstrual flow for months. Steep 1 tablespoon each sesame seeds and small Caltrops (gokhru) in 200 ml water. Sweeten with sugar or honey and drink.
- Do not over-strain yourself mentally or physically.
- Hot and cold hip bath and sunbathing will be beneficial.
- Fasting for 2 to 3 days during menstruation is advisable to provide physical, mental and psychological rest.
- A well-balanced food with restriction on salt is essential as water retention before, during and after menstruation is quite common.
- Drink plenty of coconut water, barley water, 'dhania' water or butter milk, which have diuretic effect. Drink a glass of warm water with honey before going to bed , which relieves fatigue and induces sleep.

Dismenorrhoea

The symptoms include:

- Pain during menstruation flow.
- Vomiting sensation during periods.
- Feeling of weakness generally due to inflammation of internal organs e.g. the womb, ovary defects or malfunctioning of fallopian tube. The following herbal remedies are helpful to treat this menstruation disorder:

1. The leaves of the herbs Indian wild pepper (sambhalu), horse radish, (sahinjana), Indian lilac (bakayan), wild chicory (kasni), black night-shade (mako), marsh-mallow (khatmi), cotton plant (narma kapas) and dill (soy) are boiled in water.
2. The leaves are cooked in sesame oil, dried and tied on the lower abdomen like a poultice.

Menorrhagia

It is the excessive discharge of blood from the womb during periods usually due to faulty functioning of ovaries. The following remedies help:

- Amla should be soaked in juice of green amla for three days and then ground into powder. Take this powder with milk.

- An hot and cold hip bath is very beneficial for menorrhagia patients.

Some Facts about Heavy Bleeding during Menstruation

- Heavy bleeding during the childbearing age may be due to miscarriage or abortion or as a result of an ectopic pregnancy. Tumor of uterus and cervix may result in vaginal bleeding. Women with irregular or very heavy bleeding should consult a doctor and have a Pap test every six months.
- A careful examination for the presence of cancer should be conducted by scrapping the inner lining of the uterus. Intermittent spotting may be due to cervical polyp – a common condition in women over 40. Heavy bleeding may be due to fibroid tumors and polyp within the uterus. In some cases either the tumor or perhaps the entire uterus may have to be removed.
- If a woman is in mid-pregnancy and starts bleeding, she should be rushed to the doctor. It may be too late to save the child in the womb. Severe blood loss may cause a danger to the life of woman.
- Heavy or painful bleeding is common in younger women due to various conditions such as blood diseases, alcoholism, cirrhosis of the liver, vitamin B deficiency and abnormalities either in thyroid, pituitary or adrenal glands causing heavy bleeding. A complete medical examination including a careful evaluation of pelvic organs have to undergo. In such case a complete bed rest, a high protein diet and multi-vitamin capsules are recommended. If the woman has lost excess quantity of blood, a transfusion may be needed. Heavy bleeding following abortion usually requires a surgical operation to clean out from the uterus any fragments of the placenta still present in the uterus.
- During teenage girls become depressed at the thought of painful periods, which is not abnormal and such girls should indulge in normal activities and there is no reason for them to go to bed for two to three days every month due to this indisposition
- During teenage young people suddenly become conscious of sex and striking changes take place within the body. Bad company and lack of proper guidance may lead to a life of sorrow and tragedy. A female should understand that her monthly cycle has a beneficial effect on her body. Menses may be irregular at first, but there is nothing to worry about. Some teenage girls have periods

as early as 11 years of age, others do not begin until their 16 year, yet all are perfectly normal.

Menstrual Irregularities at a Glance

Symptoms	What it might be and immediate steps to take
Missed or heavy, painful periods with cramps, pressure on lower abdomen. Sometimes, vaginal spotting or bleeding occur.	Ectopic pregnancy (pregnancy outside the uterus, usually in fallopian tube). If bleeding or abdomen pain, see a doctor immediately.
Bleeding or spotting during pregnancy.	Common, but may signal a serious problem. Prompt medical advice should be sought.
Very heavy or painful periods with pain in lower abdomen, vaginal or lower back before periods. Heavy pain during the intercourse. Blood in urine or stool while menstruating. Vomiting just before periods start.	Endometriosis (disorder in which tissue that lines uterus grow outside the uterus and become attached to other organs). See a doctor immediately.
Very heavy, irregular or missed menstrual periods. Foul smelling discharge. Nausea and vomiting just before periods start.	Pelvic inflammatory disease. Infection of reproductive organs caused by STD. See a doctor immediately.
Changes in heaviness of menses flow. Lengthy periods with aches or pain in abdomen.	Non-cancerous ovarian cyst or a ovary tumor. An early diagnose is helpful.
Heavy or painful menstrual period.	Early pregnancy and miscarriage. Seek doctor's advice.
No menses for several months.	Amenorrhea, lactation or menopause (if age above 45 years). Use of some drugs and stopping use of birth control pills are the basis cause.
Very heavy bleeding. in	Uterine fibroid tumors or cancerous masses uterus. Consult a doctor.
Heavy menstrual flow for periods lasting over a week	Usually, due to anemic conditions. See a doctor if you use more than one pad or tampon in an hour.

Leucorrhoea

Leucorrhoea or whites is a symptom of many diseases peculiar to women. It consists of white watery discharge from the uterus, which may be thick consisting mainly of pus if the patient is suffering from a serious disorder of the genital organs. Leucorrhoea discharge may be of several types as below:

- In most cases the discharge is catarrhal and chronic in nature.
- In few cases the discharge follows or precedes the menstrual flow.
- In sever cases the discharge continues throughout the intervening period.

The patients suffering from leucorrhoea have the following symptoms:

- Look pale and unhealthy.
- Feel tired at slight exertion.
- Have constant pain in lower back.
- During early adolescence and teen years, increased white discharge combined with itching is common due to infection immediately before and after the periods.
- During the mid-cycle, white discharge increases when ovulation occurs.
- The discharge increases during pregnancy.
- During sexual excitement, there is excessive vaginal wetness.
- In anemia and other general rundown states of health, the white discharge increases.
- Vaginal discharge and irritation increases because of bacterial or fungal infection due to vaginitis.
- There is always excessive vaginal discharge in ease-loving women, neither do household work or exercise their body. Manual workers are less susceptible to leucorrhoea.

Remedies

- Avoid wearing tight synthetic undergarments.
- Avoid use of strong antiseptics.
- Clean the genital parts once or twice a day to prevent vaginal infection.
- In case of husband has urinary infection or suffering from trichomonasis or candidiasis, he will have to be treated along with the wife, otherwise she would get re-infected repeatedly.
- Avoid highly spiced foods.
- Exercise the body by running, playing or getting involved in household work.

- Have sunbath daily for 15 to 20 minutes.
- Cold compress applied to the vagina helps a lot. A cold compress may be worn like a sanitary towel for an hour or may be worn during sleep.
- In young girls the discharge may be due to irritation of the labia or external genital organs, over-activity of sex glands and organs, due to soiled under garments, dirt and intestinal worms and masturbation.

In mature women, sometimes profuse yellowish discharge associated with urination may be due to venereal diseases (usually gonorrhea) or presence of creamy, slightly blood-stained discharge due to cancer in the uterus or cervix.

30

MENOPAUSE

A female becomes reproductive in early teens and can bear a child till her mid or late-forties. After passing through various stages of her sex life, a woman enters menopause, which marks the end of her fertile period and beginning of a new phase. When periods finally stop and fertility ceases, menopause sets in. At the beginning of menopause, the usual complaints include the following:

- Hot flushes.
- Dizziness and fainting.
- Lack of energy and depression.
- Fainting, burning feet and hands.
- Vaginal dryness.
- Loss of sleep.
- Severe itching.
- Facial hair growth.
- Sudden increase in weight.
- Mental tension.
- High blood pressure.
- Complete loss of interest in sex.
- Palpitations, chilly feeling and constant backache arising from low levels of estrogen in the blood stream.
- Imbalanced hormonal levels.

Gout and Leg Cramps during Menopause

Gout is a type of arthritis causing throbbing pain that often strikes quite often at night in pregnant women during the last trimester of pregnancy as well as during menopause. The skin turns red and hot, leaving the affected joint swollen and tender. Gout is caused by uric acid crystals, which settle in joints. Often the big toe is the prime target of its effect. Doctors usually inject very toxic drug to stop pain by dissolving uric acid crystals or prescribe ibuprofen (800-milligram) for relieving pain. The following curative measures are suggested to treat gout:

- If the affected joint is not too tender, try applying a crushed ice pack placing on the painful joint for about ten minutes.
- Avoid taking high-protein foods (include high protein animal products and sweet bread, dry beans, whole-grain cereals and yeast) that contribute to higher levels of uric acid.
- Drink lot of water to flush out excess uric acid from body system.
- Avoid taking alcohol if you have a history of gout. Alcohol increases uric acid production in the body, which get deposited on joints.
- Eating cherries prevents production of uric acid.
- Vitamin B 6 helps distribute water in the body to keep its all tissues hydrated, which helps prevent uric acid from turning into crystals.
- Taking a tablespoon of apple cider vinegar in the morning daily is very effective to prevent gout attacks.
- Mix charcoal into a bath and soak affected foot in it for 30 to 60 minutes. Mix ½ cup of charcoal powder in water.
- Persons with high blood pressure should control the blood pressure when they suffer from gout.

Leg cramps in the calves or feet commonly occur in women, especially in late pregnancy when she is resting or asleep. Cramps are usually caused by the factors, such as fatigue in calf muscles, pressure on the nerves to the legs, impaired circulation and calcium-phosphorus imbalance in the blood. Cramps are relieved by the following measures:

- The muscle is slowly and gently stretched.
- Gently stretch calf muscles. Keep knee straight, ankles bent and heels resting on the floor. When the leg cramp is severe you may need help.
- A foot cramp, which usually tightens the muscles of the arch and curls the toes can be relieved by stretching out toes. To prevent cramping do not curl your toes.

What is Menopause?

Menopause-usually around the age of 50 is called 'The Change' when functioning of ovaries to produce eggs, the swelling and bursting of the egg sac, release of the hormones (estrogen secretion), monthly menstrual shedding of uterine cells and blood becomes irregular and slowly comes to a halt. The prominent symptoms during menopause include hot flashes and sudden chills, lowered sexual desire, emotionally upset, insomnia, depression, memory loss and sudden change in the mood and night sweating. Sometimes, the sweating is so high you may have to change the bed sheet.

The following measures make better outlook of life during menopause:

- Make life an adventure. Find a new hobby and change in the career.
- Daily exercise should be a part of your daily life. Walking, jogging, bicycling, jumping rope, dancing, swimming or any other daily exercise can relieve menopausal disorders. Yoga aids relaxation and reduces stress.
- Hot flashes are body's response to lower estrogen levels and more than 75% women usually have hot flashes lasting between two to three minutes. During excretion of hot flashes, heat is produced in the body, the face reddens and there is excessive sweating.
- Nutrients can help control or completely eliminate hot flashes. Vitamin A is as effective as estrogen (recommended daily dose 400 to 1200 international units as recommended by your doctor). In case of night sweats, have two doses during the night as per suggestions of your doctor.
- Vitamin E helps in case of vaginal dryness.
- Learn meditation or yoga or sit quietly, eyes closed to relax your mind.
- Alcohol triggers hot flashes. Similarly cut down caffeine containing beverages that stimulate production of the stress hormones and trigger hot flashes.
- Wear fiber clothes. Synthetic fiber trap heat and produce perspiration during a hot flash.
- Drink lot of water or juice, especially after exercising to check body temperature.
- Eat small meals-minimum three meals a day. Even five to six small meals a day will help your body regulate temperature more easily.

- Vitamin B complex helps to reduce stress in menopausal women.
- The herb sage works very well if menopausal woman have hot flashes throughout the day and sweat during night. Drink a sage tea.
- Hydrotherapy treatment is very helpful for menopausal women. The body expels toxins during menstruation. When menstrual cycle decreases or stops the body requires another outlet for the toxins, so it starts sweating or has hot flashes. It is advised to have sauna (steam) bath to release toxins from the body. In case a sauna or steam room is not possible, take a hot bath for 10-20 minutes a day.
- Valerian and lavender herbs help better sleep. Take 300 to 500 milligrams valerian extract one hour before retiring to bed at night. Dabbing a few drops of lavender essential oil on your pillow before sleep can help you a sound sleep.
- Acupressure therapy relieves insomnia and anxiety in menopausal women. Stimulate two pressure points on the feet for 1 to 3 minutes each with your middle and index fingers.
- Women passing through their menopausal period if stay sexy and have regular intercourse once a week or once a fortnight have few or no hot flashes or night sweating as compared to those women who doesn't indulge in sexual intercourse at all. Having frequent sex helps moderate drop in estrogen levels, which reduce hot flashes. A study reveals that regular sexual activity stimulates the functioning of ovaries.
- Vaginal dryness from a lack of estrogen decreases interest in sexual intercourse among menopausal women. Lubricants suitable for vaginal dryness include vaginal jelly, vegetable oil and unscented cream or oil.

Vitamin E can be used to massage as a lubricant. Break open vitamin E capsules and mix to the lubricant.

31

ANEMIA

Anemia-an iron deficiency in the body is a problem that affects every one out of five women. Anemia is a condition in which the blood has too few red cells, which results in a lessened ability of the blood to supply oxygen to the tissues resulting in weakness, lassitude and pallor. Iron-deficiency anemia may cause symptoms such as dizziness, loss of appetite, diarrhea, abdominal pain, pale complexion, palpitation of the heart, shortness of breathe, feeling of weakness and frequent headache. The blood needs iron to produce red blood cells. Women who don't get enough iron in their diets or who have heavy menstrual periods may have insufficient levels of either red blood cells or hemoglobin and oxygen carrying protein in red blood cells. Women whose hemoglobin level decline feel tired and weak. If you have excessively heavy or lengthy menstrual flow or your menstrual period lasts for more than seven days, you should consult a doctor. If you are having rectal bleeding, you need to see a doctor. Improve your diet and lifestyle in order to have a healthy baby and trouble-free delivery of child.

How to Find that you are Anemic?

Press your unpolished fingernail against the nail bed for few seconds. The area will turn white. Then stop pressing, if the nail area turns pink very slowly and takes time, you have anemia. By having a complete blood count performed by a competent laboratory, it can be observed that a man or a woman is anemic. Skin color cannot confirm that he or she is anemic. Many people who seem to be pale have normal red blood cells and are not anemic at all. However, it is common for females in the age group that menstruate. The loss of blood during periods must be replaced by new blood produced in the bone marrow. This requires that the woman have enough iron in her diet. In case of un-sufficient iron contents in diet she may become anemic.

What is Blood?

Blood is the fluid circulating through blood vessels. It contains red blood cells, platelets and a pale yellowish liquid known as plasma. Plasma acts as a fluid medium for the suspension of blood cells, transports dissolved nutrients to the tissues, carries waste products from tissues to the organs. The red blood cells contain hemoglobin and red pigment of the blood. The oxygen is thus carried to all the tissues of the body. The white blood cells known as leukocytes, which act as body's defense again infection and combat fighting against bacteria and viruses. They also produce proteins called antibodies, which fights infection. Platelets are circulating cells that prevent and stop bleeding.

Few Remedies for Anemic Women

- Have iron-rich food. Good sources of iron include whole grains such as barley and oats, beans and peas, seeds and nuts, fruits and vegetables.
- Calcium rich foods put more iron in your body. Dairy products decrease iron absorption in women with anemia, whereas increase with intake of beans, peas, soybeans, sesame seeds, soups and leafy green vegetables. Inadequate diet is one of the most common causes of anemia.
- Vitamin C is acidic and helps the body to absorb iron contents. Squeeze the juice of a lemon into a glass of water and drink before meals. Alternatively, take vitamin C (1,000 to 2,000 milligrams a day with each meal).
- Remember, alcoholic beverages (wine and beer) deplete the body of vitamin B complex and minerals, which can worsen anemia. Reduce your sugar intake, which also depletes the body of vitamin B complex.
- Delete caffeine (products such as coffee, black tea, soda, chocolate etc.) from your daily diet, which depletes the body of vitamin B complex.
- If the anemia results from iron deficiency, iron pills are suggested. But if the anemia is associated with vitamin B-12 deficiency, the vitamin must be administered by injection.

Types of Anemia

Sickle-cell anemia: Usually characterized by a chemical abnormality of the hemoglobin, which results in the sickle-cell shape of the cells. The cells do not survive and circulate and the patient becomes anemic. In this case a severe anemia is present and children (including older children) with this condition are usually jaundiced, may have long, thin arms and legs and a protruding abdomens as a result of blood not circulating thoroughly in the body. To treat sickle-cell anemia, blood transfusions are given to restore red cells. Doctors recommend antibiotics to protect against infection. Good nutrition, plenty of fluids and vitamins help to improve condition. A female or a male suffering from sickle-cell anemia may get marry but they need genetic counseling before having a child.

Deficiency anemia: Usually caused by lack of a substance necessary for the formation of blood.

Pernicious anemia: It results from vitamin B-12 deficiency. Such women should take vitamin B-12 throughout the life.

Iron-deficiency anemia: It is caused by acute or chronic loss of blood. Such anemia can be treated by blood replacement by giving iron pills, which produce red blood cells.

Congenital anemia: This type of anemia occurs in women born with defective blood in the body. Blood cells usually are destroyed in the body.

32

WARNING SIGNALS DURING PREGNANCY

Effect of Position during Labor and Birth

According to the physiologic changes labor in divided into four distinct stages as stated earlier:

- First Stage (the dilation stage) in which the cervix opens completely.
- Second Stage (the expulsion stage), which begins when the cervix is fully dilated and ends when the baby is born.
- Third Stage (the placental stage) which begins with the birth of the baby and ends with the delivery of the placenta.
- Fourth Stage (the recovery stage), which begins after the placenta is born and ends in half or several hours later when mothers condition stabilizes.

The first stage of labor in pregnancy usually develops within two weeks before or after the due date. The process starts gradually and the early signs are subtle. Following are the signs generally recognized during labor, which may or may not experienced by a mother:

- Backache that comes and goes accompanied by a feeling of uneasiness and restlessness.
- Frequent soft bowel movements as in case of an intestinal upset usually occurring due to the lower digestive tract while making more room for the baby. There are often diarrhea-like symptoms on or near the due date.

- Flow of thick mucus accompanied with blood from ruptured blood vessels in the cervix. This bloody show appears days before the signs of labor.
- Brownish bloody discharge mixed with mucus.
- Contractions of the uterus few hours before the delivery, which become longer, stronger and closer as the time of delivery approaches nearer.
- There is feeling of tightening with backache and the contractions become painful due to fetus been pushed down and out of the uterus.

How to Find Difference in True or False Labor?

The following chart will help you to decide if you are having true labor or false labor and to call your caregiver or shifting to a nursing home:

Symptom	True Labor	False Labor
Uterine contractions	Become long, strong and closer.	Stay at same length.
	Abdominal discomfort and pain	No pain
	rarely exceeds one minute.	May last ½ - 4 min.
	Increase in backache and restless	No change
	not reduced by mother's activity	Activity lessen pain.
Show Intestinal	Bloody show.	None
symptoms	Frequent soft bowel movement.	None
Change in cervix	Progressive dilation.	None

What is Rupture of Membranes (Breaking of the Bag of Water)?

Contractions usually begin immediately or within 24 hours from the time of delivery. When the membranes break, there may be a sudden gush of amniotic fluid secretion from vagina and the leakage of fluid becomes uncontrollable and may be felt like urination. When rupture of membranes occurs the risk of infection increases. Observe the following at this stage:

- Note the time, color, odor and amount of fluid.
- Notify your doctor or midwife.
- Start or stimulate labor. Do not insert tampon or finger into your vagina to control the flow, which could increase the possibility of infection.

- Limit the number of vaginal examination done to determine whether or not the cervix is opening, and to reduce the chances of infection.
- Do not have intercourse or take a tub bath that may prove very harmful.

Ways to Start or Stimulate Labor?

The best way to handle a late pregnancy is to start labor. Some of the most common reasons for starting labor are:

- Prolonged pregnancy.
- Prolonged rupture of the membranes.
- Pre-eclampsia.
- Fetus which is small for gestational age.
- Illness in the mother, such as diabetes, heart disease and so on.

In such a situation, try some ways to start your labor. As far as possible avoid a medical induction of labor. Pitocin has been found most suitable (as recommended by a doctor) for inducing labor. Try the following measures to start or stimulate labor when these are too slow:

- Nipple stimulation causes the release of your own oxytocin, which contracts the uterus and helps starting labor. Repeat these measures after a few hours. Self-stimulation may be done by lightly stroking or brushing the nipples with fingertips causing contractions immediately.
- Massage your breasts gently with warm, moist towel three times a day. An electric or manual breast pump may be used for 10 to 15 minutes.
- Oral stimulation by your partner is effective and pleasant.
- Start nursing a borrowed baby. Suckling by a six to twelve week old baby for at least 10 minutes on each breast is very effective form of nipple stimulation.
- Walking may help start labor.
- Sexual excitement, particularly orgasm, causes contractions of the uterus. Manual or oral stimulation of the clitoris may be very effective. Intercourse or manual stimulation can be done as long as the membranes are intact. But if they have ruptured, avoid this practice. Blowing into the vagina is dangerous.
- You can sometimes start labor by causing enough bowel action to initiate uterine activity. Give yourself the enema at home or in the

hospital. Castor oil causes powerful contractions of the bowel making it a strong laxative. Take two tablespoons castor oil and mix it to three to four tablespoons orange juice and a teaspoon of baking soda. Stir and quickly swallow. Repeat after every 30 minutes.

- Teas help to induce labor.

What is Emergency Delivery?

Usually babies born without much warning are in excellent condition. The following suggestions help to control an emergency delivery and some of the signs of an imminent birth are as below:

- Feeling a strong urge to bear down.
- Baby's head is visible at the vagina outlet.
- When you feel the baby coming out, in such conditions call for someone – your partner, a relative, a neighbor or a friend to help you in shifting you at the hospital or call a doctor in case your partner is not available.

Before the birth, the following care should be taken:

- Remove the clothing from the lower half of the body.
- Lie on the side or in semi-sitting position in a warm, comfortable place in bed.
- Keep clean, folded towel or linen under the buttocks A waterproof sheet will protect the mattress.
- Stay as relaxed as possible. Try no to push or bear down with contractions.
- The partner or the attendant should scrub his/her hands and arms up to the elbows.
- When you first see the baby's scalp at the vagina, it will be wet, wrinkled and streaked with blood and mucus. The pressure of the baby's head bulges perineum and anus.
- Keep thighs and pelvic floor relaxed when the head emerges from the vagina. If the head is delivered slowly there is less risk of tearing the perineum.
- When the head has fully emerged, the partner or attendant should use a clean handkerchief to wipe away mucus from around the baby's face (nose and mouth).
- If the cord is around the baby's neck, lift it gently over the baby's head.

- Baby begins breathing and crying immediately after delivery. Place the baby on the side on the bare abdomen with head slightly lower than the body to drain any mucus accumulating in the nose and mouth.
- Keep the baby warm.
- Do not cut the cord immediately after delivery of baby. You will know when the flow stops and the cord stops pulsating.
- The contractions will resume and the placenta separates from the uterine wall and slide down into the vagina.
- Start breastfeeding right away after delivery of baby, which stimulates the uterus to contract and reduce bleeding. At this stage the uterus will be at the level of navel and feel firm. If the uterus is not firm, massage the fundus (top of the uterus) until it contracts. Do not continue massage for the long if uterus is still hard. Massage again after some time if necessary.
- If the baby does not breathe spontaneously, place baby's head lower than the body and rub back or chest briskly but gently. If the baby doesn't respond within 30 seconds, hold baby's feet together and smack the soles sharply.

What is Prolonged Labor?

A labor that lasts longer than 24 hours is considered a prolonged labor. Do not become discouraged or depressed. Nurture yourself with food or drink, baths and showers, walks and backrubs. Apply various methods as described in this chapter to stimulate labor.

How to get Rid of Severe back Pain during Labor?

- Change position every 20 to 30 minutes.
- Stand or walk and try to enhance pelvic mobility.
- Ask your partner or attendant to use counter pressure on the painful area.
- Ask your partner for a back massage.
- Use cold or hot packs on your low back during or between contractions.
- Stand or sit in the shower and let the water spray on the painful area.
- Continue using relaxation and breathing techniques.
- Use pain medications, if necessary.

When a Cesarean birth?

A cesarean birth may be indicated for the following reasons:

- **Cephalo-pelvic disproportion:** It usually results from a large sized baby in womb, when there is a small pelvic structure to accommodate.
- **Mal-presentation:** When the baby is situated unfavorably in transverse lie position (horizontally with bottom or feet first) for a vaginal birth.
- Failure to progress or prolonged labor.
- **Fetal distress:** When baby's oxygen supply has been reduced.
- **Prolapsed cord:** When the umbilical cord descends through the vagina before the baby resulting in reduction of oxygen supply.
- **Placenta previa:** When the placenta fully or partially covers the cervix. As the cervix dilates, the placenta separates from the uterus depriving the fetus of oxygen or causing painless bleeding.
- **Abruptio placenta:** When the placenta prematurely separates from the uterine wall causing reduced oxygen supply, vaginal bleeding and abdominal pain.
- **Maternal disease:** If the expectant mother suffers from toxemia, diabetes, high blood pressure, heart disease, herpes in genitalia or any other condition, the baby or mother will not be able to withstand the stress of labor and vaginal birth.
- **Repeat cesarean:** There is a risk in vaginal delivery during subsequent births due to ruptured uterine. If you had a cesarean birth and plan to have more children, discuss this option as well as plans with your doctor for a repeated cesarean birth.

Anesthesia is necessary for the surgery to be conducted in cesarean birth. During surgery, the mother lies on back, possibly with a wedge under one hip to reduce the likelihood of supine hypotension. Usually a cesarean birth takes about one hour and the baby is born 10 to 15 minutes after surgery begins. During cesarean birth, the doctor makes two incisions (vertical and horizontal) – one through the abdominal wall (the skin, muscle, fat and connective tissues) and other through the uterus.

33

DISORDERS OF DIGESTIVE SYSTEM CHANGE FOOD INTO SOLUBLE FORM

Digestive System

Digestion–the process by which the body breaks down food into smaller pieces that can be absorbed by the blood and is sent to each cell of the body. The digestive system is the group of organs that work together to break down the food into substances. It is the process of converting food into a form that can be assimilated by the body. The digestive system changes food into soluble form, suitable for use by the cells of the body. Digestion starts in the mouth and is completed in the intestine passing through the food pipe (esophagus) and the stomach. The complete digestive process of food takes about nine hours. The digestive system transports nutrients around the body and roots out the part of food and fluid that are not needed by the cells.

The digestive system is known as the alimentary canal and consists of the following:

1. **Mouth:** comprises of the hard and soft palate, lips, muscles, teeth, salivary glands and tongue.
2. **Pharynx:** has links with respiratory and digestive systems. It protects the body against infection entering the body via food, fluid and air.
3. **Oesophagus:** is a long tube of approximately 25 cm. length, which extends from the pharynx to stomach located behind the wind

pipe and in front of the spine, which helps to move the food down into the stomach.

4. **Stomach:** is a J-shaped sac, which lies under the diaphragm on the left side of the body. The layer of stomach has lots of folds that allows it to stretch out when full and contract when empty.
5. **Small intestine:** has approximately six metres long pipe coiled around it self, which secrete intestinal juices to help the digestion of the food.
6. **Large intestine:** are also known as bowel or colon; is 1.5 meter long and divided into five sections *i.e.* the caecum, the colon, the rectum, the anal and the anus.

The digestive system is assisted by organs, which include:

1. Gall bladder
2. Pancreas
3. Liver

Functions of Digestive System

There are four main functions of the digestive system:

1. **Ingestion:** involves the taking in, chewing and breaking down of food in the mouth.
2. **Digestion:** is the breaking down of food from the pieces we put into our mouth. It can be divided into two processes—mechanical digestion, which involves chewing and chemical digestion, which involves in breaking down of food by digestive juices containing enzymes. An adult body produces approximately five liter of digestive juices a day.
3. **Absorption:** is the process of passing nutrients from the alimentary into the circulatory system, which takes place in stomach, small intestine and large intestine.
4. **Elimination:** involves the release of indigestible food from the body as waste.

Conditions affecting the digestive system

- **Anorexia:** a psychological disorder; avoidance of eating resulting in extreme deficiency.
- **Appendicitis:** inflammation of the appendix. Chronic appendicitis can continue for several months.
- **Bowl cancer:** cancer affecting the large intestine.

- **Bulimia**: a disorder associated with over-eating, followed by vomiting and/or the use of laxatives.
- **Cirrhosis of liver**: hardening of liver generally caused by consumption of excess alcohol.
- **Colitis**: an inflammation of the large intestine resulting in diarrhea, sometimes combined with blood and mucus.
- **Constipation**: infrequent, dry passing of waste from the anus.
- **Diarrhea**: abnormally frequent elimination resulting in dehydration and weakness due to loss of too many nutrients from the body.
- **Dysentery**: an infection of the large intestine causing severe diarrhea.
- **Flatulence**: air in the stomach or intestines causing indigestion.
- **Gallstones**: solid mass formation of particles in the gall bladder.
- **Gastritis**: irritation or inflammation of stomach.
- **Gastroenteritis**: inflammation of the stomach and intestines resulting in vomiting and diarrhea.
- **Indigestion**: pain due to eating certain foods, which are more difficult to digest.
- **Ileitis (Crohn's disease)**: an inflammation of small intestine.
- **Jaundice**: a yellow discoloration of the skin which signifies serious disease as a result of the breaking down of old blood cells in the spleen.
- **Obesity**: excessive weight gain.
- **Oesophagitis**: a burning sensation of the chest.
- **Piles**: swollen veins in the anus causing pain and discomfort. Bleeding from these veins can result in anemia due to the excessive loss of iron in the blood.
- **Proetitis**: inflammation of the lining of the rectum resulting in pain while passing faeces with the urge to pass more.
- **Prolapse**: the displacement of a part of the body e.g. rectum.
- **Ulcers**: a break in the surface of any part of the body associated with digestive system, usually caused by over production of acid in the gastric and intestinal juices.

Care of Digestive System

The efficient functioning of the digestive system ensures that the cells, tissues, organs and systems of the body are provided with the nutrients and water necessary for their survival. The body loses about 1.5 liter of water a day through the kidneys as urine, through the lungs as we breathe out, as sweat through the skin and in feces. The body makes about a liter of water a day through the processes of energy production in the cells. Therefore the body needs the remaining quantity of water in order to maintain its fluid balance and avoid the problems associated with dehydration. Absorption of the nutrient food is essential to keep the body alive. The food we eat can be classified as Carbohydrates Proteins, Fats, Vitamins, Minerals and insoluble fiber e.g. wheat, bran, fruits and vegetables.

Care of the digestive system should involve in:

- Regular meals to provide sufficient energy to sustain activity.
- A balanced diet to maintain the healthy functioning of the whole body.
- At least one liter of water per day to avoid dehydration.
- Fresh, unprocessed feed for maximum nutritional value.
- Avoiding intense activity during and after eating.
- Eating when hungry not out of habit.
- Taking time out to eat to avoid indigestion.
- Taking time out to visit the toilet for efficient, regular elimination.
- Chewing food well to assist the mechanical digestion.
- Avoiding excessive stressful situations.
- Avoiding fried or browned food, which contribute to premature ageing.

Digestive Enzymes

An enzyme is a substance that aids in the body's chemical reaction. Responsible for the chemical changes in food are the enzymes present in the digestive secretions. Digestive enzymes are chemicals that change certain kinds of food into a form capable of being used by the body. Intense emotions, excitement, and fatigue seriously disturb digestion. On the other hand, happiness and relaxation promote good digestion.

Diseases of Digestive System

Some of the common disorders include indigestion, constipation, diarrhea, dysentery, dyspepsia, ulcer of the stomach, Jaundice, colic gastralgia, intestinal parasites, ageusia (loss of sense of taste), anorexia (loss of appetite), excessive thirst, nausea and vomiting, bad teeth and halitosis, difficulty in swallowing, gastritis, Peptic ulcer, hepatitis, cirrhosis of the liver, chronic passive congestion, cancer of the liver, gall-bladder disease, pancreatitis, food poisoning, botulism, regional enteritis, appendicitis, peritonitis, intestinal obstruction, mucous colitis, diverticulitis, ulcerative colitis, sprue, celiac disease, adhesions, tumor and cancer of stomach and bowel and several rectal troubles.

Constipation

It may be defined as infrequent bowel evacuation or decreased frequency of the usual bowel movements. If the stool is unusually hard, dry and difficult to expel, the patient is said to be constipated. The main causes include habitual or due to a disease. Some of the causes are:

1. Addiction to tea, coffee and smoking.
2. Excessive use of laxatives and purgatives.
3. Stress.
4. Sluggish peristalsis in old age.
5. Change of place of evacuation (known as psycho-genic).
6. Lack of exercise.
7. Erratic and poor diet; insufficient food and water intake.
8. Use of drugs are habitual causes whereas obstructive colon dis-orders (carcinoma of rectum, colon and congenital mega-colon).
9. Intestinal obstruction due to round worms (common in children).
10. Weakness of the intestinal system and abdominal muscles.

Symptoms

- Cracked tongue.
- Loss of appetite.
- Headache and discomfort.
- Abdominal pain.
- Flatulence in abdomen.
- Piles and ulcer.

Treatment

- A correct diet therapy.
- Adequate food intake.

- Consumption of food having high fiber content (bran, raw fruits and vegetables).
- Adequate fluid. Drink at least eight to ten glasses of water a day.
- Regular exercise relieves constipation and improves digestive system.
- A Hip Bath should be given regularly followed by abdominal massage.
- Have sleep at least eight hours a night.
- Enema with the advice of a doctor may prove beneficial, as far as possible. Do not use an enema on a child unless absolutely necessary. Laxatives and enemas are only for unusual conditions.

Enema Therapy?

It is also known as rectal irrigation. An enema involves the injection of fluid into the rectum. A hot water enema is beneficial in relieving irritation due to inflammation of the rectum and painful hemorrhoids. An enema with warm water 1 to 1.5 liters should be taken when you are on a diet of fruits. Lukewarm water with or without limejuice is used for cleaning the bowels. An enema can be taken lying on the back or in standing position. It also benefits women suffering from leucorrhoea (white discharge from the vaginal. To take enema, lie down on a hard floor or hard bed, the foot of the bed must be four inches higher than the head and buttocks should be higher than the rest of the body. The nozzle should be introduced in the rectum to allow the water to go in, retain water inside the rectum for two to three minutes before going to the toilet. Do not stain at the stools after an enema. When taking enema in standing position, lie on the floor after enema so that the water should remain in the rectum for some time for proper results. The vessel containing water for the enema should be suspended at a height of three feet from the body.

Home Remedies for Constipation

1. Eat 2 teaspoons 'gulkand' (confection of rose petals) with milk, preferably before going to bed in the night.
2. 'ajmoda' seeds (two parts) mixed to one part aniseed (saunf) and sugar taken twice daily is a beneficial remedy.
3. The powder of ginger, black pepper, mint (pudina) and celery seeds (ajamoda) mixed and taken in the morning and evening daily leave a curative effect.

4. Rose petal jelly is a useful naturopathic remedy for constipation. To make it mix 1 tablespoon lemon juice, 2 tablespoons orange juice, 2 tablespoons clear honey, 400 gm white cane sugar and 150 ml water. Stir until the sugar dissolves. Add to it 100 gm white rose petal and heat gently until the petals appear to dissolve. Allow the mixture to cool stirring constantly. You will have syrup with transparent pieces of petal floating in it.
5. In case of a child, dilute a few drops of any essential oil (rosemary, hyssop, fennel, majoram or camomile) with sunflower or olive oil and soothe wretched tummy giving a gentle rubbing to relieve tension and encourage bowel movement.

Fasting

Many of the ailments such as acne, rheumatism, asthma, ulcers, heart disease and alcoholism just seem to dissolve while fasting. It is used to cleanse the body of all the imbedded waster matter. Remove deep-rooted toxins and give rest to the different organs of the body. In order to prepare the body for fasting begin with eating only raw vegetables for 4-5 days, for the next four days take only liquid diet including the juice of raw vegetables or fruits. Have over 4-5 glasses of liquid a day you are ready for complete fasting. Just like you cannot begin fasting suddenly, you cannot end it suddenly. So for the next 4-5 days, take only raw or boiled vegetables. And slowly, over a period of a week or so, you can come back to your original cereal diet.

INDIGESTION

Symptoms

- Pain in the stomach.
- Heartburn.
- Tenderness over the stomach.
- Badly coated tongue.
- Acidity or belching of gas.
- Frequent headache.
- Nausea and vomiting.
- Pain in the lower back.

Causes

- Eating too fast.
- Having partially cooked foods habit.

- Use of intoxicant liquors.
- Indulging much in deskwork.
- Having untimely meals.
- Eating between meals.
- Late hour eating.
- Emotional upsets.
- Severe mental strain.
- Constipation.

Treatment

- Eating well balanced, well cooked, well chewed food.
- Do not overeat. Eat only when you are hungry.
- Never eat when you are tired, emotionally upset and anxious.
- Enema should be given only at the time of commencement of the treatment to clean bowels.
- Hot fomentation, mud pack on abdomen daily, cold hip bath twice a day, oil massage and mud bath are beneficial treatments in curing indigestion.
- Avoid taking seeds, fried foods, spiced foods, processed foods and sour things.

DYSPEPSIA

Common Symptoms

- Nausea and vomiting.
- Heartburn and gastric problem.
- Upper abdominal pain.
- Pain in stomach flatulence.
- Belching, sour taste in the mouth.
- Sense of fullness in the abdomen after eating food.

Heartburn is mainly due to deficiency of digestive fire and enzymes of the body. Take rock salt with 20 gm ginger after the meals. Alternately, 'Narayana churna' 2 gm. with sugar should be given at bedtime. 'Hing vashtaka churna' is another useful remedy for dyspepsia.

Causes

- Poorly cooked foods may cause trouble.
- Some people react unfavorably to beans, cabbage, onions, cucumbers, radishes, strawberries and various sea foods.

- Fried foods often cause gas and abdominal discomfort.
- Excessive smoking is another cause of trouble.
- Carbonated drinks release a lot of carbon dioxide, which produces a sense of fullness in the stomach.
- Gas within the intestines may be due to fermentation and actual decay of food within the intestines. It is advisable to have a complete X-ray of the stomach and bowel.

Treatment

- Choose a well-balanced diet.
- Chew thoroughly.
- Eat slowly. Avoid haste while eating.
- Constipation should be corrected. Use some suitable laxative such as milk of magnesia or a small quantity of cascara.

Diarrhea

It is a condition where stools are passed loosely through the anus. The stool may contain water, formed or semi-formed or solid digested or undigested food in small or large quantity. These may contain virulent bacteria like typhoid fever, cholera, intestinal tuberculosis, lung infection, kidney disorders, liver trouble.

Causes

- Diarrhea is caused by the vitiation of Vata, Pitta and Kapha.
- Sometimes, it is caused due to sudden fright, shock, worry, sudden change of climate or a change of diet.

Treatment

Here are few home-recipes to cure diarrhea:

1. Collect the following ingredients:

1 Liter	freshly boiled mineral water
2 tablespoons	honey
¼ teaspoon	sea salt
¼ teaspoon	bicarbonate of soda
1 teaspoon	lime juice (fresh)

An adult should take a little quantity of this liquid every five minutes and consume at least three liters within 24 hours. The children need to drink at least one liter in 24 hours.

2. Drink Barley water preferably with lemon. Rice water, too, relieves diarrhea. Boil 25 gm. of rice gently in one liter water for 60 to 90 minutes. Strain and drink to soothe the irritated bowel.
3. The juice of fresh potatoes mixed with carrot juice and honey clears infection.
4. In case of an allergic reaction to a food or drug, causing diarrhea, drink two glasses of grape juice and water.
5. Certain foods, such as figs, bananas and prunes have a strong laxative effect on the bowel. One should eliminate these until the loose stool is brought under control.
6. Severe cases of diarrhea, if the stools contain mucus or blood should be referred to the doctor.

Dysentery

In Ayurveda, it is known as Raktatisara. Dysentery is a condition wherein the patient notices passing of blood in stool along with mucus or with or without faeces. It is due to inflammation of the lower part of the large intestine. The patient experiences pain in the abdomen. There is heaviness in the stomach and intestines.

Treatment

1. Bael fruit is most beneficial in the treatment of dysentery. The pulp of the fruit mixed with 'gur' may be taken a few times in a day.
2. Castor oil should be administered with milk to help to eject hard lumps of stools.
3. 2 teaspoons of Isphagula (flea seed) mixed with 100 gm. of curd should be taken three to four times in a day.
4. Boil 50 gm. seeds of basil (tulsi) in ½ liter water till half of the water is left. The infusion cooled and is taken thrice a day cures dysentery.
5. The inner bark of the mango tree is another good remedy. The bark should be steeped in water overnight. It should be expressed in the morning and the water drunk during the day in small doses.

Sprue Syndrome

Sprue or Psilosis also called 'Sangrahini', is characterized by diarrhea with passage of large fatty stools. An inborn error of metabolism is another prominent cause of disease leading to weakness.

Symptoms: include a sore tongue, anemia and loss of weight.

Treatment

1. Ground together in powder equal weights kernel of old mango and kernel of 'jamun' fruit, taken thrice daily with buttermilk.
2. Pulp of Bael fruit taken few times in a day is another remedy.

CHOLERA

Symptoms

The condition is characterized by vomiting, diarrhea and severe pain in abdomen. It is also called 'vishoochika' in Ayurveda.

Causes

It is spread through flies, fomites, feces, water and open foods and vegetables.

Treatment

The disease can be prevented by the administration of liquid extract of 'ajwain' mixed with coriander water in small doses. Cholera can be treated by administering onion juice and bitter gourd.

Thirst

Thirst is a desire for water, which occurs whenever there is a great demand for water in the body in which the patient has dryness in the throat. The patient is given buttermilk with a little quantity of sugar, honey and ghee.

Colic Pain

Produced due to indigestion and stomach disorders. It is called 'amayshaya shoola' in Ayurveda. Ginger juice mixed with castor oil relieves the pain.

Gastritis

It is an inflammation of the lining of the stomach. The patient usually complains of pain, loss of appetite, nausea, vomiting, head-ache and dizziness. Gastritis is usually caused by the use of alcohol, spices, certain drugs, strong acids or caustic substances. Prolonged nervous tension may be the result in gastritis. The patient usually complains of heartburn, nausea and vomiting, and may suffer from hemorrhage from the stomach. Patients who have too much acid are likely to have ulcers. Avoid anything that irritates the stomach (above mentioned eatables that cause trouble) and harsh laxatives. Extra vitamins are recommended, especially B-12. In case of massive bleeding with black tarry stools should have early treatment.

Peptic Ulcer

It is most common condition affecting human race. Even young children may suffer from it. In adult women ulcer of the stomach are common. In men, ulcers of the bowel are more common. Peptic ulcer is an ulcerated, or eroded area of the mucous membrane that lines all the digestive organs. It occurs mostly in the lower end of the stomach. Emotional tensions seem to play a large part in the development of ulcers. The following precautions should be taken:

- Do not smoke. Tobacco—an irritant and always aggravates the digestive organs.
- Avoid taking tea, coffee or alcohol.
- Do not eat fried foods, chillies, spices and all hot seasonings.
- For beverages, it is best to use milk, water and fruit juices.
- Take sufficient rest.
- Avoid all nervous tension as far as possible.

Bad Breath

Nothing is more objectionable than bad breath. Bad teeth are the common cause of bad breath. Dental decay at the roots of teeth results foul-smelling pus. You may easily prepare homemade mouthwash yourself. Here are the following recipes:

1. Collect the following ingredients:

Vinegar	¼ cup
Wine	½ cup
Powdered cloves	1 teaspoon

   Boil above ingredients together and use as a mouthwash when it cools.

2. Collect the following ingredients and mix together to make a recipe of tooth powder and also to avoid bad breath:

Soda bicarbonate	3 tablespoons
Sodium Chloride (Salt)	2 tablespoons

   When powder is mixed with warm water, it makes an effective mouthwash.

3. One teaspoon hydrogen peroxide added to a cup of warm water and a teaspoon sea salt is very cleansing for teeth. It may be used as a mouthwash. Avoid swallowing.
4. Mix the following ingredients together:

Eucalyptus oil	6 drops
Cloves oil	2 drops
Tincture of myrrh	2 drops
Hot water	600 ml

Shake well and bottle to make a refreshing mouthwash to be used first thing in the morning.

Appendicitis

Appendicitis is a common of all serious intestinal conditions. The Appendix is a small tube about 4 inches long located at the end of the first part of the large bowel attached to the caecum. The small pencil-sized tube may become inflamed, followed by further inflammation and infection from certain germs present in the intestinal tract. This causes severe pain usually on the right side in the abdomen. If the inflammation continues to increase, the appendix may rupture. Consult a doctor immediately.

Appendicitis usually begins with pain in the middle of abdomen, followed by nausea, vomiting and diarrhea. Then this pain shifts to the lower right side of abdomen. Coughing and sneezing make the pain worse. Surgery is the only method to cure appendix. Meanwhile, keep an ice bag over the abdomen. An early surgery is advised to remove appendix, before it ruptures.

Peritonitis

It is an extremely serious condition due to infection within the abdomen. It may come from acute appendicitis, a ruptured appendix or a perforated peptic ulcer. It may also follow ulcerative colitis, pancreatitis and typhoid fever. Gonorrhea (VD) involving the female genital tract may also produce peritonitis. It is very painful. All patients with peritonitis should be treated in a hospital. Surgery may be needed to drain an abscess or to relieve intestinal obstruction.

Mucous Colitis

It is also known as an irritable colon, and is a disorder of the large bowel, producing discomfort and irregular bowel habits. Most patients suffering from Mucous colitis are tense, anxious and hurried. The main symptoms of patients suffer from hemorrhoids have streaks of blood appearing in the stools. Enema should rarely be used. The patient must give up the use of strong Laxatives. Rest and relaxation are important.

34

DISORDERS OF CIRCULATORY SYSTEM

The Circulatory System—for Maintenance of Good Health

The circulatory or vascular system is vitally related to the maintenance of good health. The system controls the steady circulation of the blood through the body by means of the heart and the blood vessels *i.e.* the arteries, veins and capillaries. The blood-vascular system consists of the heart and blood vessels for the circulation of blood. The other division—the lymphatic system consists of lymph glands and vessels through which the lymph circulates. Both the systems are intimately linked with each other. Lymph is derived from the blood and is gradually shifted back into the bloodstream. The blood circulation is a two-way system:

1. Transporting substances such as oxygen, water and nutrients necessary for survival to every cell in the body.
2. Transporting unwanted substances such as carbon dioxide and waste products away from every cell to be released out of the body.

How does System Function?

1. Oxygen enters the lungs as we inhale.
2. Blood picks up oxygen in the lungs.
3. Blood carries oxygen to the heart.
4. Heart pumps blood to the cells.
5. Blood vessels carry oxygen to the cells.

6. Oxygen is given to the cells.
7. Cells give carbon dioxide to the blood.
8. Blood vessels carry carbon dioxide to the heart.
9. Heart pumps carbon dioxide to the lungs.
10. Blood carries carbon dioxide to the lungs.
11. Blood gives carbon dioxide to the lungs.
12. Carbon dioxide leaves the lungs as we exhale.

The Heart

The heart is a muscular, conical-shaped organ, about the size of a closed fist. It is located in the chest cavity, and is enclosed in a membrane. The heart is made up of three layers of tissue:

1. Endocardium or inner layer forming the lining of the heart.
2. Myocardium or middle layer made up of cardiac tissue, and controls producing contractions in the form of the heartbeat.
3. Pericardium or outer layer forming a double layer. The space between the layers is filled with a fluid which prevents friction and allows the layers to move freely as the heart beats. At the normal resting rate, the heart beats about 72 to 80 times in a minute. The heart beats approximately 130 times per minute in a new born baby. The heart is divided up into four sections or chambers and four valves:
   - (*i*) Right atrium—the upper thin-walled chamber.
   - (*ii*) Left atrium—makes up the upper chamber of heart.
   - (*iii*) Right and left ventricles making up two lower chambers of heart.
   - (*iv*) A muscular wall called the septum separates the left and right chamber to prevent blood mixing. The pericardium acts as an efficient pump that keeps the blood moving within the circulatory system.

The Blood

Blood is the nutritive fluid circulating through the circulatory system. It is sticky, salty fluid with a normal temperature of 98.6 degree Fahrenheit (37 degree Celsius), and it makes up about one-twentieth of the weight of the body. Blood is bright red in colour in the arteries and dark red in veins. The change of colour is due to the exchange of carbon dioxide for oxygen as the blood passes through the lungs and exchange oxygen for carbon dioxide as the blood circulates through out the body.

The blood is composed of red and white corpuscles, platelets, plasma. The function of red corpuscles (red blood cells) is to carry oxygen to the cells, White corpuscles (white blood cells) or leucocytes perform the function of destroying diseases causing germs. Blood platelets are much smaller than the red blood cells. They play an important part in the clotting of the blood. Plasma is the fluid part of the blood in which the red and white blood cells and blood platelets flow. About nine-tenth of plasma is water. It carries food and secretion to the cells and carbon dioxide from the cells.

Functions of the Blood

The following are the primary functions of the blood:

1. Carries water, oxygen, food and secretions to all cells of the body.
2. Carries away carbon dioxide and waste products to be eliminated through the lungs, skin, kidneys and large intestine.
3. Helps to equalize the body temperature, thus protecting the body from extreme heat and cold.
4. Aids in protecting the body from harmful bacteria and infections.
5. Clots the blood, thereby closing injured minute blood vessels and preventing the loss of blood.

There are three main types of blood cells:

1. Erythrocytes or red blood cells are formed in red bone marrow and do not contain a nucleus as this disappears as the cells develop. These cells live for about 120 days, are removed from the body by the liver or the spleen and are replaced by new cells. Erythrocytes contain hemoglobin *i.e.* 'haemo' means iron and 'globin' means proteins, which contribute to the red colour of the blood.
2. Leucocytes or white blood cells are colourless, irregular in shape and contain a nucleus. They have a life span of between just a few hours and a few years depending upon their activity.
3. Thrombocytes or platelets are much smaller than red blood cells, are fragile, do not contain a nucleus and are associated with the formation of blood clots due to an injury. They have a life span of 5-9 days.

The Lymph-vascular System (Lymphatic System)

The lymph-vascular system also called lymphatic system, acts as an aid to the blood system. Lymph is a colourless, watery fluid that is derived from the plasma of the blood. Following are the primary functions of lymph:

- It reaches the part of the body, not reached by blood and carries on an interchange with the blood.
- It carries nourishment from the blood to the body cells.
- Acts as a defense against invading bacteria and toxins.
- Removes waste material from the body cells to the blood.
- It provides a suitable fluid environment for the cells.

Blood Pressure

It refers to the pumping action of the heart caused by the relaxation and contraction of the ventricles and can be treasured with a sphygmomanometer. (The maximum pressure associated with the contraction of the ventricles = systolic pressure. Whereas the minimum pressure associated with the relaxation of the ventricles = diastolic pressure). The normal blood pressure in an adult is approximately 120 systolic over 80 diastolic and is maintained by the force of the heartbeat, the volume of blood in the system and the resistance of blood flow in the arteries. High Blood Pressure (hypertension) occurs when the heart has to work harder to force the blood. Low Blood Pressure (hypo-tension) occurs when the heart is unable to exert enough force on the blood as it leaves the heart resulting in insufficient blood to the brain and causing the person to feel faint. Shock is another reason for low blood pressure.

Common conditions affecting the circulatory systems

- **Anemia:** a decrease in the production of red blood cells or hemoglobin. This may be caused by excessive blood loss and lack of iron.
- **Angina:** reduction of blood supply to the heart by excessive exertion.
- **Aneurysm:** localized swelling of an artery, especially when blood pressure is high.
- **Arteritis:** inflammation of an artery.
- **Atrial fibrillation:** irregular heart beat.
- **Blue baby:** heart disorder present at birth resulting some of the blood not passing through the lungs to receive oxygen.

- **Coronary thrombosis**: a common cause of heart attacks.
- **Diabetes**: a condition whereby the body cannot use the sugar and carbohydrates from the diet.
- **Gangrene**: lack of blood supply to fingers and toes results in decay and eventual death of the part.
- **Hemorrhoid**: varicose veins in the rectum or anus. Also known piles.
- **Heart failure**: the heart weakens as a result of weak pumping action.
- **Hepatitis B or C**: inflammation of the liver due to viruses that are transmitted by infected blood.
- **Hodgkin's disease**: cancer of the lymphatic tissue.
- **Leukemia**: over-production of white blood cells resulting in blood cancer.
- **Pulmonary embolism**: blockage of blood vessels in the lungs.
- **Rheumatic fever**: inflammation of heart, which often follows stonsillitis.
- **Septicemia**: blood poisoning.
- **Stress**: causes the heart to beat faster raising blood pressure.
- **Thrombus**: a blood clot in the blood vessels or the heart.

How to take care of Circulatory System?

- Include useful nutrients like iron, folic acid and Vitamin B-12 in your diet.
- Lack of fluid in the body and lack of rest affects the circulatory system slows down.

Diseases of circulatory system: These include

Liver and Heart Diseases

The cardio-vascular system comprises of organs of the body concerned with the manufacture, storage and circulation of the blood, namely, the liver, the heart and the arteries. Blood is the most vital fluid in the body and any interruption in its supply or lack of balance. Anemic conditions give rise to many diseases.

Heart Attack

In a heart attack the defective oxygen supply is caused by a decreased flow of blood due to narrowing of the blood vessels supplying blood to the heart. The most important causes of narrowing of the blood vessels are loss of elasticity and deposition of fat in their walls. This condition is called atherosclerosis. The heart attack has been differentiated into two forms. The first form, in which the patient experiences heaviness, pressure, tightness or a squeezing type of pain in the chest lasting for a few minutes. It is called angina pectoris. In the second form, the chest pain is of extremely severe squeezing and crushing type, which lasts for long periods and is associated with nausea, vomiting and giddiness.

Chest Pain

All chest pains are not due to heart diseases. Several other conditions, such as gastro-intestinal disorders associated with indigestion and gas formation, diseases of the gall bladder, liver, spleen, lungs and muscles of the chest wall may also cause chest pain. On the other hand, a patient of heart attack needs prompt care and treatment.

Precautions

1. The patient should take absolute bed rest as soon as the attack comes.
2. The drug should be chewed by keeping it under the tongue. It should not be swallowed.
3. The patient should not be allowed to leave the bed as there may be sudden fall in blood pressure resulting in fainting.
4. Avoid alcoholic drinks, these may cause faintness and vasodilation.

Hypertension (High Blood Pressure)

If the pressure of the blood flowing in the arteries is more than normal because of loss of elasticity, certain hormone changes in kidneys and the nervous tension—a condition known as high blood pressure or hypertension. A certain tumor (known as a pheoch-romocytoma) may raise the blood pressure. The normal blood pressure is 120/70 but may go up to 140/90. If the pressure goes up to 180/120, it is a matter of concern and need immediate medical attention. Take rest and avoid intoxicating substances and exercises.

Hypo-tension (Low Blood Pressure)

If the blood being pumped by the heart into the arteries fails to maintain the normal pressure the condition is known as hypo-tension.

The main causes are hemorrhage due to injury or bursting of an ulcer of stomach or nose bleeding. Food poisoning and anaemia may also lead to low blood pressure. Some of the symptoms of a low blood pressure are weakness, nausea and coma (when the pressure falls too much).

A person suffering from low blood pressure should be given a balanced nutritious diet full of proteins and carbohydrates. A vigorous exercise and excessive sex should be avoided. Intoxicant products e.g. alcohol and tobacco may be permitted in medium quantities.

Congenital Heart Disease

Some babies are born with damaged heart. This is known as congenital heart disease. The defect arises from infection or injury to the baby's heart during the first three months after conception. The disease is not common, but when it occurs, it can cause plenty of trouble. There are many varieties of this disease:

Atrial septal defect: It is an abnormal opening or shunt between the two upper chambers of the heart: the right and left atria or auricles causing part of blood to flow from left atrium into the right atrium and then through lungs. This forces right side of the heart to work hard thus raising blood pressure on the right side of the heart. Sometimes, the blood starts flowing in reverse direction, from the right to left side causing patient turn blue, a condition known as Cyanosis. When the patient turns blue, the risk increases. Surgery on the heart is the only treatment. The chest is opened and the defect repaired.

Venticular septal defect: It is an abnormal opening or shunt between the right and left ventricles or pumping chambers of the heart. Because of the higher pressure on left, the bright red blood coming from the lungs is forced through the dividing wall to flood the right side of the heart. This excess blood thus starts to re-circulate through the lungs and the pressure on the right side of heart is increased. Sometimes, the patient develops a very serious condition known as subacute bacterial endocarditis causing severe inflammation involving the heart muscles. Surgery of the heart is the only remedy.

Patent ductus arteriosus: In this condition, certain vessels called the ductus, which normally closed at birth remain open, allowing blood to pass from the aorta to the pulmonary artery. This produces a effect similar to the atrial and ventricular septal defects described above. Surgery is the best treatment for this condition. The abnormal channel should be closed.

Coarctation of the arota: It is a localized constriction or narrowing of the aorta near the point where that vessel crosses behind the pulnary artery. This narrowing of the arota causes low blood pressure on the lower part of body than that found in the head and neck. There is very slow flow of blood in the lower portion of body and the patient complain of numbness and weakness in the legs and severe headache due to pressure of the blood stream going to head. Surgery of the narrow portion of the aorta is the only treatment.

Tetralogy of fallot: It is a serious malformation in which there is defect in the ventricular septum, which allows the aorta to receive blood from both right and left ventricles. A child with this deformity have to squat down to get his breath after vigorous attempt depriving the child of a normal supply of oxygen. This disorder may cause clubbing of the fingers and toes besides the child's growth may be retarded. Most of the children suffering from this disease die in their early teens. A good surgery is the only remedy.

Pulmonic stenosis: A narrowing of the outflow tract from the right venticle, either directly at the valve or in the muscle tissue. Child with fulmonary stenosis often suffers from shortness of breath when playing. A harsh murmur is heard all over the chest. As a result of this disorder, the liver becomes enlarged and tender. The legs and ankles swell.

Rheumatic Heart Disease

Rheumatic fever or inflammatory rheumatism is a serious disease that mainly affects children and teenagers. It attacks connective tissues of the body causing joint pain. The child suffers from the sore throat or cold, followed by an attack of tonsillitis. Nose bleeding is common in this condition. The symptoms among children include a sore throat in the beginning, later he may have a fever with aching in joints, a lack of appetite, profuse sweating and rashes.

The first attack of rheumatic fever usually comes on at seven or eight years of age, followed by severe infection of the throat with beta hemolytic streptococcus germs. Rheumatic fever affects the heart and most serious damage occurs in the valves. It is observed, out of 100 children with some form of heart disease, nearly 98% have rheumatic disease. The aortic valve has three doors that open and close simultaneously with the motions of the heart. The edges of doors may stick together and prevent the valve from opening properly. This causes the serious condition known as aortic steno-sis—a type of obstruction that raises the blood pressure inside the venticle and puts a heavy strain on the heart muscle. In some cases the valve cups fail to close properly, which result in another serious condition known as aortic insufficiency. The leakage of blood lowers the pressure in the aorta, causing dizziness and weakness. The narrowing or stenosis of the aortic valve may be corrected by the surgery, but the risk is higher.

Coronary Artery Disease

It is the most common of all forms of heart disease. Coronary thrombosis is a dreaded disease even than infections, accidents and cancer. Coronary vessels supply the heart muscle itself with blood. This type of heart disease is four times more common in males than in females, which occurs most commonly in the age group forties and fifties. In some cases it begin in the thirties or in late twenties. The true cause of coronary artery disease is somewhat mysterious. However, people who live on a high-fat diet supplemented with highly refined food products are not likely to develop coronary artery disease. Those who take plain diet, low in fats seem less likely to develop this disease. Cholesterol is also an important factor, because many victims of heart disease have a high cholesterol level in the blood. Patients with heart disease should learn to live on a plain, sensible diet and avoid the use of tobacco.

Angina Pectoris

It comprises of a sharp, stabbing or crushing pain felt mainly in the chest. Sometimes the pain is felt in other areas in the body, such as the left shoulder, arm or jaw, which are brought on either by exercise or by emotional stress. These are the pains of coronary insufficiency when coronary arteries are unable to supply enough blood to the heart muscles for the amount of work to be done. Many times the angina comes on when climbing stairs, walking against the direction of wind and passing through some period of excitement. Pains may also be felt after having heavy meal. These are often associated with gall-bladder disease. These pains may last from 20 to 60 seconds.

To treat Angina pectoris, avoid over work, take Nitro-glycerin tablet to dissolve placing under the tongue. These are life-saving tablets. Patients with angina should not smoke, avoid coffee and alcohol, use blood thinning medicines, should have mild sedative to reduce nervous tension and try to relieve the heart of heavy strain, worry and mental tension.

Coronary Thrombosis

It is a serious conditions affecting heart. The patient faces severe pain and often a state of shock. It is more serious than angina. In this condition the blood supply to the heart is completely cut off to some area of the heart wall. In few cases a large clot of blood forms over the part of the inner surface of heart. The blood clot itself is known as a thrombus. A fragment broken off is called an embolus. In this condition, the patient complains of severe pain in the chest. The pain continues for hours or sometimes for days with nausea, vomiting and hiccups, followed by extreme weakness and fear of death. The pulse usually remains weak. The color of the skin turns pale, cold and moist.

A correct diagnose is essential. The following treatment is advised:

- Pain and shock must be relieved immediately with powerful pain-killing medicine or with morphine (with the consultation of doctor).
- Combat shock.
- Keep blood in circulation.
- Have bed rest.
- Take easily digestible diet.
- Avoid over-exertion.

Heart Failure

Heart attack is a serious condition that develops when the heart is no longer able to carry on its normal work. It occurs in patients with a serious heart disease. The heart has one function: to pump the blood stream and keep it circulating in the body. When the heart is tired or weekend, the blood stream tends to slow down and the lungs may begin to fill up with fluid making breathing difficult.

High blood pressure, coronary thrombosis, kidney disease, rheumatic fever, diphtheria and low thyroid activity are some of the conditions causing heart failure. Delayed circulation reduces the flow of blood to the kidneys. This failure to excrete fluid produces oedema or swelling of the tissues. The lungs may then begin to fill up with fluid, and this reduces the exchange of oxygen and carbon dioxide. A good nursing care is most essential in severe case. After a severe bout of heart failure, the patient should rest as much as possible having well-balanced living.

Fainting

A temporary loss of consciousness due to lack of oxygenated blood in the brain. The victim suddenly becomes pale and has a feeling of weakness and nausea, then falls unconscious. The recovery is usually rapid. The main causes of this disorder are fatigue due to over work or a sudden emotional shock. This results in a rapid drop in blood pressure. To treat fainting, keep the patient lying flat with the head low and feet slightly elevated until he regains consciousness.

Palpitation

A common problem causes discomfort in the heart and chest. It is a bumping feeling in the chest. This is not a true heart attack. The increased workload on the heart may bring on the feelings of discomfort.

Sinus Tachycardis

Also known as Racing Heart, is an annoying condition. The heart rate may increase because of severe emotional strain, heavy exercise, lack of oxygen, fever, hemorrhage and various infections. The best way to treat this disorder is to control an irritable heart.

Pericarditis

An inflammation of the pericardium-the tough, fibrous bag which surrounds the heart and protect it from injury. Pericarditis may sometime follow a severe throat infection or an attack of rheumatic fever. It is frequently seen prior to tuberculosis. The disease is often associated with coronary thrombosis when the muscles and the surface of the heart get injured.

Aneurysm

It is a localized enlargement of a blood vessel, such as aorta. It may be due to inflammation. Swellings of aorta usually occur due to weakness in the arterial wall caused by arterios-clerosis and hypertension.

Phlebitis

Inflammation of a vein that occur in the lower extremities. The trouble usually begins with the formation of a clot in one of the vein of the calf or foot. The clot may completely block off the vein, preventing any flow of blood from that area. The following treatment is recommended:

- Good nursing care is most important.
- A complete bed rest for over a week with hot water bottles or warm moist packs will relieve pain.
- Do not massage the legs as this may force more clots out of the vein to develop in the lungs.
- Doctor recommends blood-thinning (Anticoagulants) medicines in treating this condition.
- An elastic bandage provides support to inflamed area.
- Surgery may save the patient's life. The vein in the area of infection should be divided preferably up near the groin.
- Patients with congestive heart failure should move their legs while on the bed and should take gentle exercise or walking to maintain circulation of blood in the lower limbs of body and avoid varicose veins.

Varicose Veins

As the blood returns to heart it passes through thin walled channels called veins. These veins swell when pressing on a vein with fingers. Blood flows from the head and upper chest downwards towards the heart. On the other hand, blood coming from the lower extremities must flow upward.

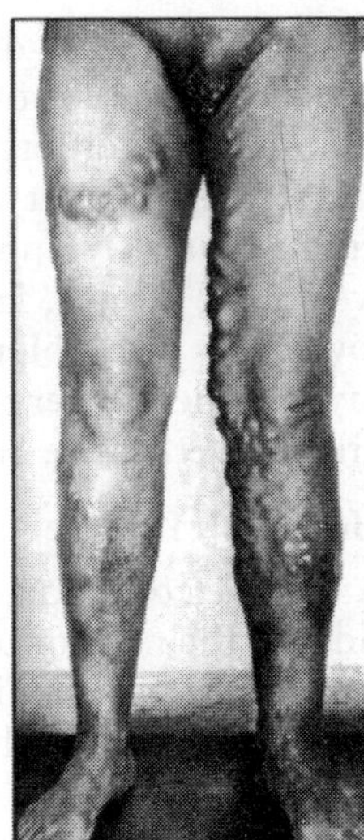

Varicose veins

There are two types of veins. The deeper veins are located within the muscles having good support, whereas the veins near the surface of skin lack proper support and are easily damaged and often inflamed. Sometimes, the veins in the legs become weak and swell easily. One frequent cause of varicose veins is pregnancy and another obesity. During pregnancy, the pressure increases on pelvis or abdomen causing the flow of blood to slow. The pressure of extra weight in the veins of the legs and thighs may weaken or break down the little valves and the veins become enlarged, the blood does not find way back to the heart. Varicose veins are ugly, dangerous and the blood clots within dilated veins. This condition is known as pulmonary embolism and may cause serious hemorrhage followed by the muscle cramps. Surgery is the best treatment, especially when the larger veins of the legs and thighs are involved.

Buerger's Disease

A painful disorder of toes and feet, seen in younger adult males. Excess smoking is the most frequent cause of this disease. The patient usually complains of coldness and tingling or burning in the feet or toes, and sometimes also in fingers and hands. Other symptoms include the toes and feet appear red or dark and the skin looks pale, gangrene and ulceration may develop. To treat this disease the following measures are taken:

- Avoid use of tobacco.
- Avoid extremes in temperature.
- Fungus infections of the feet.
- Carry out leg exercise while lying down.

Leukemia

A serious disorder of the blood forming tissues due to some virus. Leukemia is a type of cancer of the blood forming organs. There are a number of different varieties of Leukemia, which produce an excessive number of white blood cells. They may be either granulocytes, lymphocytes or monocytes. The symptoms include weakness, fatigue, lack of appetite and weight loss. Anything that lowers the white blood cells in the body helps to treat leukemia. X-ray treatments over the spleen, bones, lymph nodes and other tissues are often effective. Seek medical assistance for the treatment.

Hodgkin's Disease

A chronic condition causing swellings in the lymph nodes along the sides of the neck or under the armpits may be the first indication of trouble. In this condition the spleen and liver enlarged and become tender. It also causes high fever and pigmentation of skin and shingles. Good nursing care, a balanced diet of proteins and vitamins, avoiding excessive fatigue and respiratory infections are the best mode of treatment.

Lymphosarcoma

A malignant disease, similar to leukemia resembling Hodgkin's disease. It affects the lymphoid tissues and lymph nodes. Enlarged lymph nodes (like lumps) may be seen on the side of neck, which can be removed surgically.

Septicemia (Blood Poisoning)

A most serious condition in which toxic or poisonous materials find their way directly into the blood stream and the poisons spread to all parts of body. This is an inflammatory disease, which include skin problems, subcutaneous tissues, white blood cells and anti-bodies. The toxic materials are absorbed directly into the blood stream, causing localized inflammation, or cellulite all over the body. The spread of infection may be rapid if the body is weak.

Symptoms of this disease include fever with chills, weakness, headache and the skin becomes red, swollen, painful and hot. To treat the disorder, the patient should be kept in the bed and applied hot moist dressings over the inflamed area. Antibiotics are advised strictly as per the advice of a doctor.

Lymphadenitis

Inflammations of the lymph nodes in any part of body generally seen on groin and under the arms. Apply hot moist packs to the inflamed areas two or three times a day. Penicillin is recommended strictly as per advice of a doctor as it may react sometimes.

35

DISORDERS OF NERVOUS SYSTEMS

Neutrons are Cells that Make up the Nervous System

The nervous system responsible for external communication and control the body with electrical impulses is known as the nervous system. It allows the body to detect external and internal changes through the sensory organs such as skin, eyes, ears, nose and tongue. The nervous system can be divided into three parts. It is made up of nervous tissue, which consists of nerve cells.

The Central Nervous System (CNS)

It consists of brain and spinal cord, which are protected by skin, muscles and bones. The brain stem is made up of three parts:

(a) The mid brain, which transmits impulses linking together the spinal cord.

(b) The second part, which forms a bridge between the two hemi-spheres transmitting impulses to and from the spinal cord.

(c) The medulla oblongata, which controls the involuntary actions of respiratory and circulatory systems and some related reflex actions e.g. sneezing, coughing, swallowing and vomiting.

The muscles of the scalp include Epicranius or occipito-frontalis (which covers the top of the skull from eyebrows to the base of occipital bone), Occipitalis (posterior part of epicranius) and Frontalis (anterior part of epicranius).

The Peripheral Nervous System (PNS)

It consists of nerves, which link the various part of the body with central nervous system. The peripheral system can be further divided into two parts:

(a) Sensory (afferent nerves), which take message from the sensory organs to central nervous system.

(b) Motor (efferent nerves), which relay message from central nervous system to the muscles and organs.

The Automatic Nervous System (ANS)

It consists of the following:

(a) Sympathetic system, which prepares the body for action.

(b) Parasympathetic system, which prepares the body to relax.

Common Conditions Affecting the Nervous System

- **Alzheimer's disease:** gradual shrinking of the brain resulting in a decline in mental activities.
- **Bell's palsy:** inflammation of the facial nerve resulting in sudden paralysis on one side of the face.
- **Cataplexy:** a sudden collapse of posture.
- **Cerebral palsy:** a permanent disorder of the brain affecting the control of muscles.
- **Cluster headache:** severe headache that starts three to four hours after falling asleep.
- **Dementia:** gradual death of brain cells through normal ageing.
- **Epilepsy:** temporary loss of consciousness.
- **Extradural haematoma:** a complication of an injury to the head whereby one of the bones of the skull is fractured.
- **Meningitis:** a severe infection of the membrane surrounding the brain and spinal cord.
- **Migraine:** recurrent severe headache. Nausea and vomiting may occur.
- **Motor neurone disease:** a condition, which affects the motor neurons causing progressive weakness in the muscles.
- **Multiple sclerosis (MS):** degeneration of nervous tissue in the central nervous tissue. This disease starts in adults between the age 20 to 50 years.

- **Myalgic encephalomelitis (ME):** also referred to as post-viral fatigue that follow many viral infections including muscle pain, fatigue, exhaustion, depression etc.
- **Neuralgia:** pressure on a nerve caused by irritation.
- **Neuritis:** inflammation of nerves resulting in muscle weakness.
- **Noctural myoclonus:** a sudden jerking of muscles.
- **Sciatica:** abnormal pressure on sciatic nerve.
- **Parkinson's disease:** a condition in which muscular stiffness and tremors develop on the brain.
- **Spinal bifida:** a condition that is present at birth. Spinal nerves are affected due to malformation of bones and tissue surrounding the spine resulting in mental and/or physical handicap.
- **Stroke:** a sudden loss of function on one side of the body caused by an interruption of the blood supply to the brain.
- **Tension headache:** pain resulting from overworked muscles.
- **Vertigo:** feeling of dizziness.

Since nervous system is responsible for the control of the whole body and needs lot of care. Food plays an important role in maintaining the well being of nervous system. Toxins damage nervous tissues and affects all aspects of the system including intelligence, memory and concentration. Diet and good sleep is necessary for nervous system.

Disorders of Nervous System

The nervous system is a very delicate and complicated set of nerves spread throughout the body. A direct examination is very difficult to diagnose and treat disorders in case of the spine and the brain. Some of the more common nervous disorders are as below:

1. **Vertigo or giddiness:** a condition of body in which the patient suffers loss of power to balance himself. Giddiness may be caused by several factors like disturbance in the balance of the fluids in the body, resulting disorders of blood pressure, digestion, mild attack of epilepsy and often migraine. The condition is dealt by the administration of a mild laxative and a nutritious diet. Increase the quantity of milk, eggs and butter in your diet.
2. **Faintness:** arise from a number of causes, such as hunger, fatigue, anxiety or even emotional shock (hearing a bad news). When a

person faints, there is temporary lack of strength, muscles become limp, failure in breathing and the pulse may be very weak. To relieve this disorder, the victim should bend forward placing the head between the knees or lie flat on the back with head a little lower than the body. If there is no recovery, seek the help of a doctor.

3. **Unconsciousness:** An unconscious person may appear to be asleep, but this sleep is different from the actual sleep. If a patient is found to be unconscious lying on the ground, look around quickly for the cause to find if there is an injury on the head. Check, does the pupil of one eye appear wider than the other? If so, the victim may have had a stroke or a head injury. Find out any evidences of poisoning, drinking, electric shock or asphyxia from gas. Call the doctor at once and meanwhile keep the patient lying down. If the face is red, raise the head a little, but give no stimulants. For vomiting, turn head sideways to prevent choking. If the face is white and the pulse is weak, lower the head just a little below the level of body and apply gentle heat. If the face is blue, the victim is in shock. Give artificial respiration till the arrival of doctor, if required.

How to give Mouth-to-mouth Breathing?

Lay the victim on back, bringing the chin forward and up. Hold the nose firmly and breathe gently into his mouth for about 15 to 20 times a minute. This will inflate the lungs and help restore the circulation (if the breathing stops). If preferred and possible, use a tube, firmly holding the victim's lips around the tube while inflating the lungs.

If the heart has stopped beating, continue mouth-to-mouth breathing and a cardiac massage by pressing firmly with the heel of the hand over the middle of breastbone about 60 times a minute. Make sure to lift the hand off after each pressure.

Insomnia

Sleeplessness or insomnia is an annoying condition, which interferes one's activities because of lacking natural sleep. Nervous weakness leads to loss of sleep. An insomniac must avoid worry and tension. He or she should keep bowels clear. 'brahmi booti', 'vacha' and 'amla' are beneficial for insomnia. These can be taken individually or in combination mixed (one teaspoon each) to water or milk and taken thrice a day. Have vigorous exercise to tire for a good sleep. Alcohol helps produce sleep. Sleeping without a pillow also helps. A teaspoonful of dried powder of cumin seeds should be mixed with the pulp of a ripe banana and taken the last thing to night.

Coma

A profound state of unconsciousness when the breathing of the patient may be indifferent and heart beats strongly, is termed as coma. It may be caused by apoplexy, high fever, diabetes, consuming excess liquor, epilepsy, cerebral tumors, meningitis, head injury, an overdose of insulin, carbon monoxide poisoning, consuming opium or other narcotic drugs. If this state continues for more than 24 hours it should be treated as a serious condition and should be referred to a doctor.

Persons subject to fits of coma should observe the following precautions:

- Lead a worry and tension-free life.
- Tough exercise should be shunned.
- Remember, constipation complicates matter.

Epilepsy

Nervous disorder in which there is sudden loss of consciousness and convulsions. The attack comes on suddenly, but a person subject to attacks of epilepsy starts having a strong smell. The pulse becomes rapid and pupils dilated. Epilepsy is the result of a sudden discharge of electrical energy by the brain. Sudden fright, prolonged worry, overwork and alcoholism can increase the possibility of attacks.

It is not an easy malady to cure and the patient must be kept under a close watch because he may fall while walking. The only remedies of this condition are to:

- Strengthen the heart and nervous system.
- 'Brahm booti' is an Ayurvedic medicine to treat epilepsy.
- One teaspoonful of the juice of this herbal plant should be sweetened with honey and given to the patient thrice a day.
- Various factors such as changes in the blood gases, decrease in blood sugar and calcium, stress and strain may precipitate an attack of epilepsy.

Hysteria

If some part of nervous system becomes hyperactive, it usually shows in the form of what is known as hysteria. Hysteria generally strikes suddenly and a precipitating factor may induce sudden laughter or weeping. A paralysis is found with hysteria. An epileptic falls into unconsciousness regardless of the place where he is standing, but the hysterical patient is conscious about the surroundings, he or she may moan, move and even roll eyes, exhibit emotions of fear, ecstasy or joy. The fits can be cured by the remedies recommended for epilepsy as above. Here is a naturopathic treatment. Almonds (almond oil) and Amla are helpful in strengthening the brain. 10 gm. of the powder of 'Sarpgandha' should be administered with milk twice a day.

Paralysis

Paralysis or palsy, means loss of muscular power due to interference with the nervous system. When nerve affections lead to loss of tone or power of the muscles, paralysis is the result.

- Hemiplegia is the term applied to the paralysis of one side of the face and the corresponding arm and leg.
- Diplegia is used to denote total paralysis.
- Monoplegia is a term for the paralysis of a single limb.
- Paraplegia is a term used to signify paralysis of both sides of the body (usually below waist).

But the most common form of paralysis due to brain disease is hemiplegia. In this condition, the hemi-sphere of the brain opposite to the side of the body subjected to paralysis is affected. It may be caused by hemorrhage in the brain resulting from high blood pressure or by the formation of a clot in the blood. An expert medical assistance should be sought.

Mental Depression

A patient of mental depression suffers from a slowing down of his/her physical and mental process. The patient lacks interest in surroundings, suffer from complete or partial loss of memory, lacks energy and loss of weight, suffer from insomnia and the sexual desire diminishes. There are various causes of mental depression, such as reactive depression (reaction to particular event), endogenous depression (not due to any obvious external reason but comes from within the patient) and manic depression (associated with violent symptoms in the form of excitation, agitation, hyperactivity, aggression and panic).

36

DISORDERS OF ENDOCRINE SYSTEM

Hormones are chemicals substances produced in certain glands in the body that help to regulate the way your body functions. They are produced by the organs of the endocrine system. The **endocrine system** is the system of glands throughout the body that regulate body functions. The endocrine system closely linked with the nervous system acts as the main communication centre of human body. The nervous system communication with electrical messengers or impulses via nerves and the endocrine system communicates with chemical messengers and hormones. The chemical messengers are produced by endocrine glands and pass directly into the blood stream to be transported to the body. The nervous system is involved with the rapid action within the body whereas endocrine system is involved with slower adjustments to the growth in the body.

The endocrine system consists of a set of endocrine glands. Each gland is responsible for the production of hormones. A hormone is a chemical substance which has the ability to effect changes in other cells. They are secreted directly into blood stream and transported to various systems of the body. The main endocrine glands of the body are the following:

1. **One pituitary gland**: located in the brain, which controls other glands.
2. **One pineal gland**: located in the brain referred as third eye of the brain.
3. **One thyroid gland**: located in the neck having shape of butterfly.

4. **Four parathyroid glands:** located on the sides of the thyroid glands into the neck, which help to regulate the calcium and phosphorus levels in the body.
5. **One thymus gland:** located in the thorax, which protect the body against antigens.
6. **Two adrenal glands:** located on the top of each kidney, and composed of an outer cortex and an inner medulla.
7. **Two ovaries:** located in the lower abdomen in women. They are situated within pelvic girdle.
8. **Two testes:** located in the groin in men, which hang externally under the penis.
9. **Pituitary glands:** They control ACTH and TSH
10. **Thyroid hormones.**
11. **Gonadotrophins:** control ovaries in women and testes in men. There ate two main gonadotrophins: FSH follicle stimulating hormone, which stimulates the ovaries in women (to produce female sex hormone oestrogen) and also stimulates the testes in men (to produce sperm). LH luteinising hormone, which stimulates the ovaries (to produce female sex hormone progesterone) and the testes (to produce the male sex hormone testosterone).

The hormones produced in the anterior pituitary that control other system include:

1. GH growth hormone (which promotes the growth of skeletal and muscular systems).
2. PRL prolactin (which promotes the growth of the ovaries, testes and mammary glands besides stimulating lactation e.g. milk production in the breasts.
3. MSH melanocyte stimulating hormone, which promotes the production of melanin in the epidermis of the skin.

The hormones produced in posterior pituitary gland are responsible for the production of two hormones.

1. ADH antidiuretic hormone, which regulates the fluid balance of the body by decreasing urine production in the kidneys.
2. OT oxytocin stimulates the contraction of mammary glands to force the milk from and uterine contraction in the womb during childbirth.

Pineal Gland

Tiny gland situated deep in the brain is often referred to as the third eye of the brain. They produce hormones melatonin, which are responsible for regulating monthly menstrual cycle among women.

Thyroid Gland

Consists of two lobes having shape of a butterfly situated just below the larynx in the neck are responsible for producing following hormones in the pituitary gland:

- Thyroxine.
- Tri-odo-thyronine.
- Calcitonin.

These glands regulate metabolism (the rate at which the body cells use oxygen), the calcium and phosphorus levels in the body.

Parathyroid Gland

There are four glands arranged in pairs embedded on either side of thyroid gland. They help to regulate the calcium and phosphorus levels in the blood.

Thymus Gland

They lie behind the sternum in between the lungs. They help in the protection of the body against antigens.

Adrenal Glands

Two adrenal glands each situated on the top of each kidney and are composed of an outer cortex and an inner medulla.

Islets of Langerhans

They are small clusters of cells within the pancreas.

Ovaries

There are two ovaries those form part of the female reproductive system. The almond-shaped ovaries situated within the pelvic girdle on either side of the uterus.

Testes

There are two testes, which form the male reproductive system. They are situated in a sac known as the scrotum, which hangs externally from the body under the penis.

Control of Hormonal Secretion and Imbalance

The secretion of hormones is controlled in three ways—the hypothalamus, the nervous system and the internal environment of the body. Hormones are circulated in the body by blood stream. They are broken down and excreted from the body in urine.

Hormone imbalance is created when the endocrine glands produce either too much or too little of the hormones needed to maintain homeostasis, which result malfunction and conditions. Sex corticoids, which include androgens, promote the sexual development in males and females growth of pubic and underarm hair. It is also responsible for sexual drive.

Sex Hormones

Sex hormones are responsible for the development of secondary sex characteristics.

In female these include:

- The development of breasts.
- The start of the menstrual cycle.
- The reproductive organs becoming functional.
- The widening of hips and increase in fat in this area.
- Pubic and underarm hair growth.

In males, these include:

- The reproductive organs become functional.
- The production of sperm and semen.
- The breaking of the voice.
- Increased growth of muscles and bones.
- Facial, pubic, underarm, abdominal and chest hair growth.

Sexual Development

The human body goes through various stages of sexual development. These include puberty, menstrual cycle, pregnancy and menopause in a female and puberty in a male.

1. **Puberty**: marks the onset of sexual development. The ovaries in female and testes in male stimulate sex hormones and sexual characteristics, such as production of sperm in a male and ova (eggs) in a female. Every month the uterus in a female is prepared for the fertilization of an egg. This is known as the menstrual cycle. The menstrual cycle lasts for approximately 28 days.

2. **Pregnancy:** occurs when fertilization is successful and the ovum becomes embedded in the walls of uterus and produces the hormone. The placenta develops during the first 3-4 months of pregnancy, which forms a direct link between the circulation of the baby and mother.
3. **Menopause:** marks the end of childbearing years in a woman and usually starts between the ages of 45-55. The breasts and ovaries decrease in size and become less responsive. The hormone levels change and the menstrual cycle becomes irregular and eventually stops altogether. The other symptoms include short term flushing and sweating, loss of bone mass, loss of pubic and underarm hair and thinning of skin.

Common Conditions Affecting the System

- **Acromegaly:** an over-secretion of hormone in the anterior pituitary gland resulting in thickening of skin and an enlargement of the hands, feet and face, particularly the lower jaw.
- **Addison disease:** disorder of the adrenal glands, this is an under-production of the hormones causing muscle weakness, irregular menstrual cycle and dehydration.
- **Amenorrhoea:** over-production of the male sex hormone testosterone in females resulting in loss of normal menstrual cycle.
- **Chloasma:** dark patches of skin appearing as a result of a hyper-secretion.
- **Conn's syndrome:** results from the over-secretion of aldosterone in adrenal cortex, usually causing high blood pressure and kidney failure.
- **Cranial diabetes insipidus:** an inability of the body to conserve water due to hypo-secretion in the pituitary gland.
- **Cushing's sydrome:** disorder of the adrenal glands due to over-production of the hormones.
- **Dwarfism:** under-secretion of hormone from pituitary gland resulting in the failure of bones and organs to grow.
- **Endometriosis:** an imbalance in the production of the female sex hormones.
- **Fibroids:** the development of non-cancerous tumors in the wall of uterus as a result of imbalance of female sex hormones.
- **Galactorrhoea:** an excess of milk flow caused by an over-secretion of prolactin in the anterior pituitary gland.

- **Goitre**: enlargement of the thyroid gland caused by lack of iodine.
- **Gynaecomastia:** over-production of estrogen in males causing the development of breasts.
- **Hirsutism:** an over-production of testosterone in females leading to the development to the male pattern hair growth during puberty, pregnancy and menopause.
- **Hypercalcaemia:** excess calcium in the blood caused by the over-secretion of parathormone.
- **Hyperglycaeaia:** under-secretion of insulin and/or over-secretion of glucagaon causing high blood sugar levels.
- **Hypetalcaemia:** lack of calcium in the blood caused by under-secretion of parathormone in parathyroid glands.
- **Hypoglycaemia:** an over-production of insulin causes low blood sugar levels.
- **Polycystic ovarian syndrome:** under-production of LH in females resulting in the development of ovarian cysts. This is accompanied by an irregular menstrual cycle and sometimes infertility.
- **Pre-menstrual syndrome (PMS)**: generally swollen, tender breasts accompanied to menstruation in women.
- **SAD (seasonal affective disorder)**: an over-production of the hormone melanonin produced in the pineal gland.
- **Tetany**: abnormally low levels of calcium in the blood causing muscle spasms mainly in hands, feet and face.
- **Virilism**: an over-production of testosterone in females causing increased body and facial hair, the deepening of voice and affected menstrual cycle.
- **Vitiligo**: white patches of skin that may be caused by an under-secretion of MSH in the anterior pituitary gland.

Care must be taken to ensure that this system gets the balance it needs in the form of fluid (water) intake, nutrition, rest and regular exercise.

ENDOCRINE DISORDERS

Simple or Adolescent Goitre

A simple colloid goitre usually arises from deficiency of iodine in diet and usually develops in young girls during early adolescence as well as during pregnancy.

Symptoms

- Usually appears as a soft, symmetrical enlargement of the thyroid gland.
- Soft swelling in the neck is not due to a malignant tumour, nor does it have to be removed by surgery, except for cosmetic reasons.

Treatment

- Iodine should be given in some form (Hydriodic Acid syrup 1/3 teaspoon daily diluted in water should be taken for three weeks).
- Use iodized salt.

Hyperthriodism (Graves Disease or Thyrotoxicosis):

A serious condition of body, arising from too much activity in thyroid gland. The excess amount of thyroid hormones produced by the overactive gland raise the metabolic rate of the body. True cause of this disease is not known, but it run in families and likely to develop during emotional or physical stress.

Symptoms

Patient is usually nervous, week, sensitive to heat, sweat frequently, is overactive and often underweight apart from increased appetite. A tremor in fingers and the patient complains of palpitation in the heart, bulging of the eyes and rapid pulse rate.

Treatment

May be given a trial of iodine. Five drops of saturated solution of potassium per day is an idle treatment. Another treat-ment is a dose of 10 drops of Lugol's solution twice daily.

Addison's disease (Adrenal insufficiency)

True cause of this disease is not known.

Symptoms

(*i*) Weakness and easy fatigue

(*ii*) Increased pigmentation in the skin.

(*iii*) Scars and folds of the skin.

(*iv*) Marked weight loss due to dehydration of loss of fluid from the body.

(*v*) Fall in blood pressure.

(*vi*) Loss in appetite.

Treatment

(*i*) Adequate fluids must be given along with sodium to bring the blood level back to the normal.

(*ii*) Hydrocortisone or one of the steroids must be given to increase the appetite.

(*iii*) Restore weight.

(*iv*) In case of a tumour, remove by surgery.

Diabetes

Insufficient production of insulin to meet needs. Insulin is the powerful hormone that aids the body in storing nutrients, instead to allow it to drain away in the urine. Lacking sufficient insulin, the blood sugar or glucose rises to a high level. The cells of body do not receive their normal supply of nutrient. The excess glucose then spills over into the urine. This condition is known as diabetes. Not only the pancreas, the other organs including the adrenals, pituitary, thyroid and the liver are involved. If continued for a long time, the patient becomes weaker and may eventually die from malnutrition.

Symptoms

(*i*) Extreme thirst.

(*ii*) Loss in weight.

(*iii*) Excretes large quantity of urine and drains away nutrients.

(*iv*) Suffering from chronic skin troubles.

(*v*) Fatigue.

(*vi*) Cuts and bruises heal slowly.

Treatment

Provide body with sufficient insulin and affects the body in the following ways.

- **Effect during pregnancy**: During pregnancy diabetes can be serious. Diabetic babies weigh more than normal. Pregnant women should have a blood sugar test taken two hours after a meal. If the sugar shows higher than normal, start treatment at once.
- **Effect on older people:** Older people often tend to gain weight and develop mild form of diabetes because of a strain on pancrease. It is important for older people to keep the weight down to the normal.

- **Heredity factors:** A family history of diabetes cause the disease develops in children. Have urine test for sugar/blood sugar two to three times a year.
- **Infection:** Diabetics are susceptible to infections of skin e.g. boil, carbuncles and generalized itching.
- **Arteriosclerosis:** Hardening of the arteries occurs frequently in diabetic patients.
- **Deep ulcers:** These may form in the legs and gangrene may result from secondary infection.
- **Heart attacks:** are common in diabetics.
- **Cataracts:** It occurs more frequently in older diabetics or those patients who have had diabetes for five years or more than that.
- **Diabetic retinitis:** is a most serious condition involving eyes (frequently seen in children).
- **One of the most serious complications of diabetes is known as the Kimmelstiel - Wilson syndrome:** a condition, in which kidneys are damaged because of uncontrolled diabetes. The patient loses albumin, suffers from high blood pressure, swelling or oedema of various parts of body. Younger diabetics are more likely to develop these serious kidney complications.

Precautions

- Guard against all types of infection.
- Test the urine every day in the morning and also occasionally at mid day as well.
- Diabetics who are overweight should bring their weight down to normal by gradually reducing dietary intake. The daily intake of foods should not be more than 1500 to 2000 calories.
- Skin complications: These are common in patients with uncontrolled diabetes.
- Wounds tend to heal slowly.
- Boils and carbuncles may appear.
- Often there is severe itching in the skin under the breasts, armpits, in the groins and around the genitals and rectal area.
- If the gangrene develops in the feet, amputation may be necessary. Treat all foot infections seriously.

Glucose Tolerance Test

The simplest test to detect diabetes is to test the urine for sugar or glucose. Blood sugar test is a more accurate method. Generally diabetics show little or no sugar in the urine, but the blood sugar level may be very high. The normal blood sugar level lies between 80 to 120 mg. whereas after a regular meal the level rises to 150 mg. If the level figure goes above 170 mg. within an hour or two after a meal, the glucose tolerance test should be run and several samples of blood are drawn at frequent intervals after a meal to find out the actual level.

Low Blood Sugar (Hypoglycemia)

This disorder usually occurs in those who do not take enough protein in their diet. This is more or less opposite of diabetes where the blood sugar becomes lower than the normal instead of being high. The lack of balance causes due to excess production of insulin by the islet cells of the pancreas or due to a tumour or faulty function of the liver, pituitary, thyroid or adrenal glands. Fall of glucose level in the blood also causes sweating, trembling, feeling of weakness, headache and disturbed vision.

Symptoms: Include complain of numbness, dizziness, palpitation of heart, feeling hungry and to eat too frequently to combat the hypoglycemia and emotional instability.

Treatment: The patient is advised to take a low-protein diet, avoid taking sweets, carbohydrates and sugars. If overweight, cut down on meals.

Poly-cystic Diseases of Kidney

A serious condition, which begins before birth. In this disease some of the tiny tubules fail to join up with the normal drainage system of kidney. The urine collects in the little pockets or cysts that grow larger and may eventually burst. The first sign of trouble may be appearance of blood in urine and pain on affected side. Poor drainage of urine encourages infection.

Bright's Disease (nephritis or glomerulonephritis)

Shortly after the infection begins, the patient may suffer from puffiness in the face and swelling of feet and ankles. Often there is blood in urine and also albumin and casts consisting of clumps of red and white cells from the damaged kidneys. This also gives rise to the swelling or oedema in the tissues. Unfortunately, the damaged kidneys cannot be restored.

Kidney Stones

Kidney stones of various forms and sizes are formed in any part of urinary tract but most frequently in kidneys. It causes considerable pain as they attempt to pass down the muscular tube or ureter on their way to the bladder. The stones are formed from the chemicals found in urine e.g. uric acid, phosphate, calcium, oxalic acid and many more. Patients suffering from kidney stone should avoid taking too much milk (because it has high calcium contents). To detect stone in the urine, strain all the urine through fine cloth for several days and watch carefully.

Cancer of Urinary Tract

It is rare in kidneys, the more common type being a hypernephroma, which spread to the bones. Cancer is more common in bladder. Blood in the urine is the first sign, followed by fever and pain. Kidneys and bladder cancer should be examined by ultrasound or X-ray for the presence of tumors. There is no successful home remedy for this.

37

DISORDERS OF SKELETAL AND MUSCULAR SYSTEMS

The Skeletal System—Framework of the Body and Bones

Personal appearance in height and body shape is determined by general body structure, which depends upon the skeleton. The scientific study of bones, their structure and functions is called the anatomy of bones (osteology), which is the technical term for bones. The skeleton system is the physical foundation or framework of the body. It is composed of differently shaped bones united by movable and immovable joints.

The function of skeleton system is to serve as a means of protection, of support and of locomotion. Bones vary according to race, sex and age from person to person. Individual variations are due to many causes such as differences in size and weight of bones. Such differences are related to the height and muscular development of individuals.

The skeleton is divided into three main regions:

The Skull

Several bones unite together to form the skull, which protects the brain. The skull rotates on the spine. The position of the skull makes more acute the senses of seeing, smelling and hearing.

The Spine

Spine (backbone) is made up of many irregular shaped bones having elastic tissues, which permit flexibility of the spine. The spinal column helps to keep the body and head erect. The ribs are attached to the spine. They run circulatory around the body and meet in front at the breastbone. The ribs aid in respiration and form the chest cavity, which holds the heart and lungs.

The Limbs

Each of the two upper limbs terminates in hand with five fingers. Each of the two lower limbs terminates in with the five toes. The lower limbs help the body to stand erect and move about. The upper limbs permit easy movement.

Bones

Bone is the hardest structure of the body and is composed of about one-third organic or animal matter and two-third inorganic or mineral matter. The animal matter (organic) consists bone cells, blood vessels, connective tissue and marrow. The mineral matter (inorganic) consists mainly of phosphate and carbonate of lime. In human body, bones are found in several forms such as flat bones (the skull), long bones (legs and arms) and irregular bones (spine).

Externally, bones appear to be light pink in color, internally deep red. There are two type of bone tissue:

(a) **The Cancellous (spongy tissue):** They form the interior of bones, the end of bone shafts and very thin bones. It consists of a mesh work of bony arches through which blood vessels and nerves pass.

(b) **The compact tissues (dense tissue):** They form the hard bone found in the shafts of long bones; and on the outside of flat bones. The compact bony tissues have small channels containing minute blood vessels.

Marrow is a soft fatty substance filling the cavities and nourishment of bones, whose function is largely concerned with the formation of red blood cells. Periosteum fiber membrane is the covering of the bone, the function of which is to protect the bone and also serve as an attachment for tendons, ligaments, blood vessels and nerves. Bone receives its nourishment through blood vessels (capillaries), which make their way through Periosteum into the interior of bones. The functions of the bones are:

- To give shape and strength to the body.
- To protect organs from injury.

- To serve as an attachment for muscles.
- To act as levers for all bodily movements.

The point of junction of two or more bones is called a joint, having classification as movable (as in fingers), immovable (as in the cranium) and slightly movable (as in the spine). Following are the various types of joints found in the human body:

- **Pivot joint:** in which one bone turns on another with a rotation movement as in case of neck.
- **Hinge joint:** in which two or more bones are connected like the hinge of a door as in case of elbow and knee.
- **Ball and socket joint:** in which one bone is rounded and fits into a socket as in case of hips and shoulders.
- **Gliding or sliding joint:** in which two bones glide over each other as in case of spine, ankle and wrist.

The Skull

Skull is the skeleton of the head in oval bony shape, which protects the brain and forms the contour of the head. The skull is divided into two parts:

1. **The cranium:** consists of six major parts as below:
   - Occipital bone, situated at back and lower part of the cranium.
   - Two parietal bone, are formed at the union of sides and top (crown) of the cranium.
   - Frontal bone forms the forehead.
   - Two temporal bones form the sides of the head in the ear region.
   - The ethmoid bone forms part of the nasal cavities.
   - Sphenoid bone joins together all the bones of the cranium.
2. **Facial bones**: consists of eight types of bones as under:
   - Two nasal bones placed side by side in upper middle part of the face forming the bridge of nose.
   - Two turbinol bones having thin layers of spongy bone curled upon them like a scroll.
   - Vomer, a single bone at the back of the nasal fossae.
   - Two lacrimol bones, which are the smallest and most fragile bone of the face situated at the front of the inner wall of the orbits.

- Two zygomatic or malar bones forming the prominence of cheeks, part of the outer wall and floor of the orbits and part of the temporal.
- Two palatine bones situated at the back part of the nasal fossae forming the floor and outer wall of the nose, the roof of the mouth and the floor of the orbits.
- Two maxillae (upper jawbone) are the largest bones of the face.
- Mandible bone (lower jawbone) is the largest and strongest bone of the face containing the lower teeth.

Bones of the neck: are usually two types:

- Hyoid bone is a 'U' shaped bone in front of throat, which supports the tongue.
- Cervical vertebrae is located in the neck region and forms the top part of the vertebral column.

Bones of the chest: an elastic bony cage made up of the breast bone, the spine, the ribs (12 ribs on each side) and their connective cartilage. It serves as a protective covering for the heart, lungs and other internal organs.

Bones of the arms and hands: are divided in six parts:

- **Humerus:** the largest and longest bone of the upper arm.
- ***Ulna:*** the large bone on little finger side of forearm.
- **Radius:** the small bone on thumb side of forearm.
- **Wrist:** a flexible joint composed of eight small bones held together by ligaments.
- **Palm (metacarpus):** consists of five long slender bones.
- **Fingers (the digits):** consists of three bones in each finger and two in the thumb totaling 14 bones.

Common conditions Affecting Skeletal System

- **Ankylosing spondylitis:** disease of the joints affects spine resulting in back pain.
- **Arthritis:** inflammation of joints, sometimes may be chronic.
- **Bunion:** a swelling of the joint of toe due to excessive pressure.
- **Bursitis:** affects knee, which becomes inflamed.
- **Cartilage:** a knee injury resulting from sudden twisting movement.

- **Coccydynia:** pain in the base of the spine occurs after injury.
- **Flat feet:** lack of arching in the feet causing foot strain and pain.
- **Fracture:** a break or crack in a bone due to injury or stress to bone.
- **Ganglion:** a harmless swelling near a joint on hands/feet.
- **Gout:** a pain in the joints, it affects knees, ankles, wrists and elbows.
- **Kyphosis:** a concave curve of the spine creating a 'hump back'.
- **Lordosis:** a convex curve of the spine in lumbar region creating a 'hollow back'.
- **Mallet finger:** a finger that cannot be straightened due to damage.
- **Metatarsalgia:** pain along the ball of the foot due to overweight.
- **Osteoarthritis:** a degenerative disease of joints usually affects hip.
- **Osteogenesis:** defect of bone cells causing brittle bones.
- **Osteomclacia:** softening of bone due to lack of Vitamin D.
- **Osteomyelitis:** inflammation of the bone caused by bacterial infection.
- **Osteoporosis:** weakening of bones caused by changing level of hormones.
- **Osteosarcoma:** a rapidly growing tumor of the bones.
- **Rheumatoid arthritis:** a destructive swelling of joints initially affecting the fingers and feet, then spreading to wrist, knees, ankles.
- **Scoliosis:** a lateral curve in the spine.
- **Slipped disc:** disc that separates the vertebrae causing pain.
- **Sprain:** a sudden stretching or tearing of a ligament resulting pain.
- **Synovitis:** inflammation of a joint after injury.

Muscular System—for the Movements of Body Organs

Muscle is a contractible, elastic, fibrous tissue by which movements of every part of the body are produced. The fibrous tissues have the ability to stretch and contract according to the movements such as stretching and bending. Muscles are attached to bones, cartilage, ligaments, tendons, skin and to each other. Each muscle contains its own nerve and blood supply. The muscular system consists of over 500 muscles, large and small, comprising of 40 to 50 per cent of the weight of the human body. There are three kinds of muscular tissue:

1. Striated (Striped) or Voluntary, which include facial, arms and leg muscles.

2. Non-striated (smooth) or involuntary muscles, which function automatically in the stomach and intestines.
3. Cardiac (heart muscles), which is the heart itself.

Muscles have three parts: the origin, the insertion, and the belly. Origin is the part that does not move. It is attached to the skeleton, and is usually part of a skeleton muscle. The insertion is the part that moves. Muscular tissue can be stimulated by any of the following method:

- Massage with the help of electric vibrator or hand massage.
- **Electric current:** high frequency and faradic current.
- **Heat rays:** heating lamps and heating caps.
- **Light rays:** infrared rays and ultraviolet rays.
- **Moist heat:** steamer or moderately warm steam towel.
- **Nerve impulses:** through nervous system.
- **Chemicals:** acids and salts.

It is essential to know where these muscles of head, face, neck, arms and hands are located and what they control. Muscles need nutrients and oxygen, which are brought to them via the blood to 'fuel' the action of movement. The muscles are mainly of four types:

1. **Agonists or prime movers:**These are the muscles where the action (contraction) takes place.
2. **Antagonists:** These are the muscles, which lie opposite to the agonist muscles and work in an opposing manner.
3. **Synergists:**These are small muscles, which help the agonist to ensure more controlled action.
4. **Fixator:** These are large muscles responsible for maintaining posture.

Muscles of the Head and Face

These include

1. **Muscles of the scalp:** which are generally of three types. Epicranius a broad muscle that covers the top of the skull and consists of two parts: the occipitalis (back part) or posterior and frontalia front part. Both parts are connected. The frontalis raises the eyebrows, draws the scalp forward and causes wrinkles across the forehead.
2. **Muscles of the eyebrow:** are of two types. Orbicularis oculi- completely surrounds the margin of the eye socket and enables

to close eyes. Corrugater muscle is beneath the frontalis and orbicularis oculi, and draws the eyebrow down. It produces vertical lines, and is the muscle used for frowning.

3. **Muscles of the nose**: are the procerus, which cover the bridge of the nose, depresses the eyebrow and cause wrinkles across the bridge of the nose. There are few other muscles smaller in size around the nasal openings that contract and expand the openings of the nostrils.

Muscles of the mouth: are of various types:

- Quadratus labii superioris: consists of three parts and surrounds the upper part of the lip, raises and draws back the upper lip, and elevates the nostrils.
- Quadratus labii inferioris, surrounds the lower part of the lip.
- Buccinator, is the muscle between the upper and the lower jaws. It compresses the cheeks and expels air between the lips.
- Caninus, lies under the quadratus labii superioris. It raises the angle of the mouth.
- Mentalis, is situated at the tip of the chin. It raises the lower lip, causing wrinkles of the chin.
- Orbicularis oris, forms a flat band around the upper and lower lips. It compresses, contracts and wrinkles the lips, as in case of kissing or whistling.
- Risorius, extends from the masseter muscle to the angle of the mouth and back, as in grinning.
- Zygo maticus, extends from the zygomatic bone to the angle of the mouth. It elevates the lip, as in laughing.
- Triangularis, extends along the side of chin and draws down the corner of the mouth.

Muscles of the ear: are practically functionless. They are:

- Auricularis superior located above the ear and draw ear slightly upward.
- Auricularis posterior is located behind the ear and draws the ear slightly backward.
- Auricularis anterior is located in front of the ear. It draws the ear slightly forward.

Muscles of Mastication: are the muscles that coordinate in opening and closing the mouth and is functioning to close jaws, as in chewing.

Muscles of the neck and back: are of several types:

- Platysma is a broad muscle that extends from the chest and shoulder muscles to the side of the chin. It depresses the lower jaw and lip, as in the expression of sadness.
- Sterno-cleido-mastoid extends from the collar and chest bones to the temporal bone in back of the ear. It rotates and bends head, as in nodding.
- Trapezius is a large muscle covering the back of the neck and upper part of the back. It draws the head backwards or to one side and rotates the shoulder blade.
- Latissimus dorsi is a muscle attached to lower ribs of the body and covers middle region of the back. It draws the arm downward and backward and rotates it inward.

Muscles of the chest: **are three types:**

- Pectoralis major muscle covers the chest and rotates it inward, as in swinging movement of the arm.
- Pectoralis minor muscle situated underneath, and is covered by pectoralis major. It rotates the scapula downward.
- Serratus anterior is attached to upper ribs. The muscle assists in breathing and in raising the arm.

Muscles of the shoulder, arm and hand: are given below:

- ***Deltoid***: is the large, thick, triangular-shaped muscle, which handle the shoulder and control the movement of arms.
- ***Biceps***: is the two-headed muscle in the front of upper arm. It lifts the forearm, flexes the elbow, and turns the palm outward.
- ***Triceps***: is the three-headed muscle of the arm that covers the entire back of the upper arm and extends the forearm.
- ***Pronators***: are the most important muscles of forearm, which turn the hand inward, so that the palm faces downward.
- ***Supinators***: are muscles, which turn the hand outward, and the palm upward.
- ***Flexors***: are muscles, which bend the wrist and draw the hand and close fingers towards the forearm.
- ***Extensors***: are the muscles, which straighten the wrist, hand and fingers.

The hand has many small muscles overlapping from joint to joint and imparting flexibility and strength. The Abductor muscles located in the thumb and fingers separates the fingers and draw them together.

Common disorders of muscles affecting muscular system

- **Atrophy:** wasting of muscle tissue.
- **Cramp:** sudden involuntary contraction of a muscle causing acute pain.
- **Fatigue:** build up of lactic acid in the muscle.
- **Fibrositis:** inflammation of the muscle fiber.
- **Muscular dystrophies:** diseases resulting in the collapse of muscle.
- **Myalgia:** muscle pain.
- **Myasthenia Gravis:** chronic disease of muscles in which they are weak.
- **Myoma:** tumor composed of muscular tissue.
- **Myotonia:** prolonged muscular contraction.
- **Myokymia:** persistent trembling of muscle.
- **Myositis:** inflammation of skeletal muscle.
- **Paralysis:** loss of ability to move a part of the body due to muscles failure.
- **Paresis:** slight paralysis of muscles.
- **Rupture:** tearing of muscle from bone joint.
- **Spasm:** sudden muscle contraction.
- **Strain:** over-use of muscles.
- **Stress:** excessive muscular tension causing tight, painful muscles.
- **Tendinitis:** inflammation of muscle attachments.
- **Torticollis:** contraction of the muscles of the neck.

Care of the Muscular System

- Drinking water during, before and after exercise as well as at regular intervals throughout the day.
- Nutrient foods containing carbohydrates, fats and vitamins.
- Adequate rest and a balance of varied activity keep muscles healthy.

38

REPRODUCTIVE AND GENITOURINARY SYSTEM

DISEASES OF REPRODUCTIVE ORGANS

Bartholin's Glands

A vulva disease with an infection in one or both Bartholin's glands resulting in swelling and or abscess formation with pain, which usually occur during the reproductive years (about 85% cases happen during reproductive time).

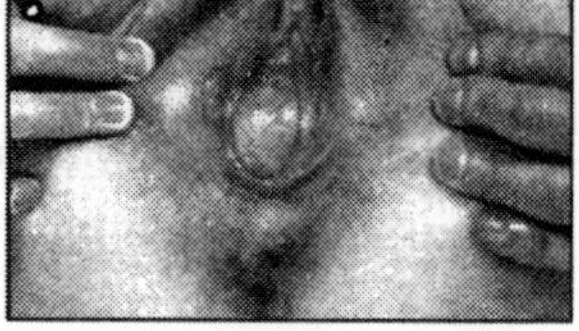

Bartholin gland

Symptoms: Cystic, painful swelling of the labia. Cysts can range to 8 cm followed by fever.

Diagnostic approach: cellulitis, necrotizing fascitis, mesonephric cysts of vagina, lipomas, fibromas, hernias, hydrocele, neuro fibroma and sebaceous cyst.

How to prevent?: Avoid/reduce exposure to sexually transmitted diseases (STD) and vulva trauma.

Bartholin's Cysts

Cystic dilation of Bartholin's gland and duct, generally it is stage secondary to past infection. 80% gland cysts occur during reproductive years whereas 20% of adult women develop infection or enlargement of (one or both) glands.

Symptoms: Small, yellow or bluish color, chronic cysts at the base of labia majora, which has smooth finish.

Diagnostic approach: Similar to the disease of Bartholin's glands.

Prevention: Avoid exposure to STD. However, there is no effect on pregnancy.

Contact Vulvitis

Vulva irritation caused by contact with an irritant or allergen most common in reproductive and menopausal years.

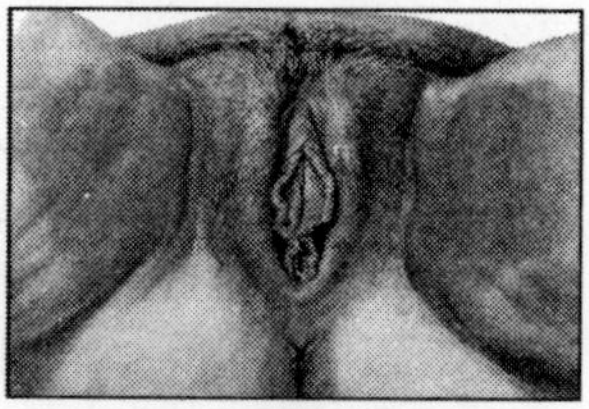

Contact vulvitis

Symptoms

- Diffuse reddening of vulva skin accompanied by itching or burning.
- Symmetric, red, edemous change in the tissue.
- Ulceration with weeping sores and secondary infection.

Diagnostic approach: include vaginal infection, local candida infection, vulva dermatosis, atrophic vulvitis, vulva dystrophic, pinworms, psoriasis , seborrhoeic dermatitis, Neuro-dermatitis, Impetigo, Hidradenitis suppurative, vaginal secretions, dysuria and dyspareunia.

How to prevent?:

- Apply wet compresses or soaks using burow's solution followed by drying.
- Application of Steroid creams 2-3 times a day.
- Eucerine cream reduces itching and rehydrate the skin.

Dysareeunia Insertional

Pain occurs with sexual penetration and in many cases it leads to severe vaginal spasms that interfere with vaginismus. The disease occurs during reproductive and beyond age and generally causes due to congenital factors such as duplication of vagina, vaginal agenesis and vaginal septum, cystitis (frequent urination), hemorrhoid, inadequate vaginal lubrication, insufficient foreplay (love-making before sex), phobias, arousal disorders, medication, pelvic muscle spasm, pelvic scarring mostly due to episiotomy, surgical repairs, proctitis trauma, urethral syndrome, urethritis, vaginismus, vulvitis, chemical irritation (due to deodorants and lubricants), lichen sclerosis, herpes vulvitis, venereum and vestibolitis.

Symptoms: Burning and pinching felt externally during attempts at vaginal penetration. It is generally localized to the vulva, perineum or outer portion of vagina.

Diagnostic approach: Vulvitis, vestibulitis, vaginitis, bartholin's gland infection, hymenal stenosis, abscess and cysts, atrophic change, anxiety, depression, phobia, sexual abuse.

How to prevent?

The following methods to cure this disease are required:

(i) Proper vaginal lubrication.

(ii) Pelvic exercises.

(iii) Modifying the sexual techniques to help Reducing pain during intercourse.

(iv) Correct sexual position during sex.

(v) Vaginal apex expansion.

Female Circumcision

Removal of the part or complete external genitalia including labia major, labia minora and/or clitoris. Female circumcision is generally performed as a ritual process under anesthesia or under un-sterile conditions. The resulting scars may be of several types as below usually occurs during early teens or many times younger than 18 years:

1. Excision of the prepuce with or without excision of the part or entire clitoris.
2. Excision of clitoris with partial or complete labia minora.
3. Excision of part or all of external genitalia and stitching or narrowing of vaginal opening.
4. Pricking, piercing or incision of clitoris and/or labia, stretching of clitoris and/or labia and cauterization to burn the clitoris and surrounding tissues.
5. Genitalia mutilation *e.g.* scraping of tissues surrounding the vaginal orifice, surgery of vagina, introduction of herbs or corrosive substances into vagina to cause bleeding or tightening or narrowing it.

Diagnostic approach: Scarring and deformity of the external genitalia structures, amenorrhoea or dymenorrhoea and dyspareunia/ orgasmic dysfunction.

Causes: Childhood burn injuries, inter-sex condition and imperforate hymen, which cause deformed external genital tissues.

How to cure?

- Surgical opening of fused/scarred genital tissues.
- Menstrual hygiene and hygienic sexual function.
- Episiotomy required at the time of childbirth.
- Bleeding, infection, tetanus, urinary retention, pain, sexual dysfunction, difficulty with menstrual hygiene, retrograde menses, urinary-tract infections, pelvic inflammatory diseases and increased bleeding at the time of delivery are some of prominent causes.

Hidradenitis Suppurative

Infection of the skin and subcutaneous tissues cause inflammation of aprocrine glands with formation of sinus and abscess, which involve axilla, vulva and perineum generally during reproductive period. It doesn't occur before puberty.

Symptoms: Recurrent and chronic inflammation on the portion of labia with pain and foul smell in vaginal discharge. Sometimes, an abscess is formed.

Diagnostic approach: Causes STD, crohn's and fox-fordyca disease.
Causes: Dyspareunia and vulcodynia, inflammation of the apocrine glands, cystic dilation and formation of abscesses.

How to prevent?:

- Perineal hygiene.
- Having a sitz bath.
- Wearing loose-fitting clothing.
- Wide excision of affected area.
- Topical therapy with administering antibiotics in consultation with a doctor only.
- Topical steroids and oral contraceptives.
- Avoiding formation of scarring and abscess.
- Sexual dysfunction.

Hymenal Stenosis

Thickening or narrowing of hymenal opening, resulting difficulty in playing intercourse usually in early reproductive years. It is caused due to congenital narrowing of hymen or scarring after surgery or trauma.

Diagnostic approach: Vulvar vestibulatis, vaginismus, vulvitis and diseased hymen examined by physical examination.

How to prevent?: Gentle digital dilation and surgical excision.

Usual complications: Sexual dysfunction. Hyper plastic vulva dystrophy causes thickening of the vulva skin over the labia majora and inflammation over clitorial areas. It is seen in 40-50% females during middle to late reproductive and beyond.

Symptoms: Vulva itching, white appearance of vulva, fissuring and excoriations.

Diagnostic approach: Vulva cancer, chronic mycotic vulvitis, contact vulvitis, psoriasis, lichen sclerosus leading to conditions e.g. vulvodynia, vulvar pruritus and dyspareunia.

How to prevent?:

- Perineal hygiene.
- Stress reduction.
- Having sitz's baths.
- Reduction of candidiasis or contact allergy. (The patient should wear gloves during night to avoid tissue damage due to scratching).
- Avoid itch/rash scratch.
- Tropical steroids help to reduce itching. Consult your doctor before having treatment.
- Avoid local irritants.

Possible complications: include vulva cancer.

Imperforate Hymen

It results from abnormalities in the development of canalization of mullerian ducts.

Symptoms: Vaginal obstruction, primary amenorrhoea, abdominal pain and hematocolpos.

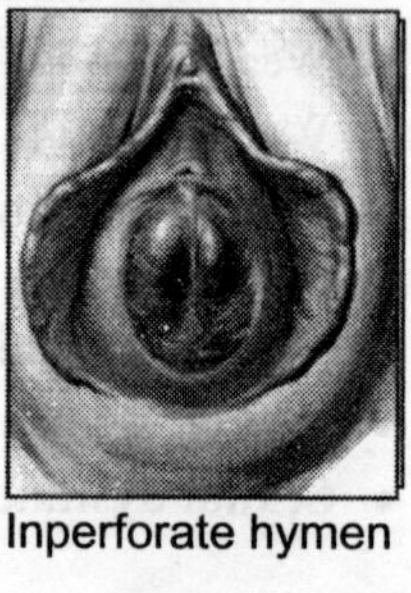

Inperforate hymen

Diagnostic approach: It is diagnosed by vaginal agenesis. The conditions include endometriosis, vaginal adenosis, infertility, chronic pelvic pain and sexual dysfunction. (It can be detected by ultrasonography to upper genital tract).

How to Prevent?: Incision of hymenal membrane and drainage of vaginal canal. (Hymenal scarring and narrowing occur usually after surgical excision).

Labial Adhesions

This disorder is found in children of age 2 to 6 years and up to puberty caused by local inflammation, resulting in labial infections or irritation.

Symptoms

(i) Fusion of the labia majora just below the clitoris.
(ii) Retention of urine in the vestibule or vagina resulting in irritation, discharge and odor.

Diagnostic approach: Inter-sex, female circumcision, sexual abuse, urinary tract infection and vaginal bleeding.

Prevention

- Perineal hygiene.
- Sitz's baths.
- Tropical estrogen cream applied to vulva for seven days.
- Gentle traction to separate the labia. (Surgical treatment not required in this case).

Complications: include vaginitis, urinal-tract infection, urinary retention and formation of vaginal cyst.

Lichen Planus

An epithermal disorder that affects skin, hair-loss, scalp, nails, mucous membranes and the vulva generally between the age 30 to 60. The exact cause of this disorder is not known.

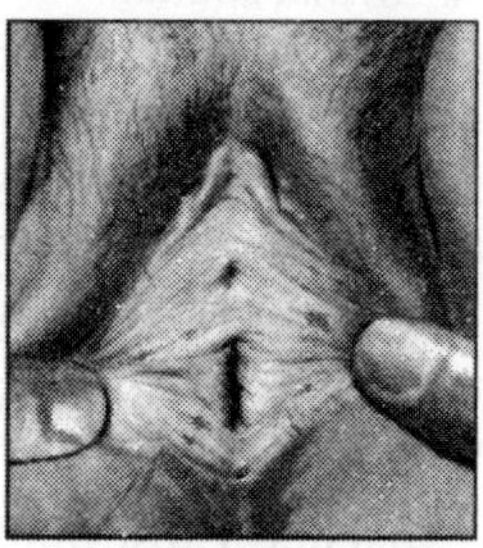

Lichen planus

Symptoms

- Red erosion and ulceration of vulva.
- Loss of labia minora with scarring.
- Complete obiteration of the vagina.

- Dyspareunia and post-coital bleeding.
- Oral lesions.

Diagnostic approach: Amebiasis, Behcet's syndrome, candidiasis, dermatophyte infection, lichen sclerosus, neuro-dermatitis, plasma cell, vulvitis and psoriasis.

How to prevent?

- Local cleansing.
- Treatment by anti-pruritics therapies e.g. steroids, retinoids, griseofulvin, dapsone, cyclosporine and surgery.
- Vaginal dilators may be necessary to maintain vaginal caliber.

Complications: May cause vulva cancer or vulva lesion. (No treatment should be given during pregnancy).

Lichen Sclerosus

A chronic condition of the vulva skin, which cause inflammation generally in the late reproductive to early menopausal caused by epidermal growth factor deficiency.

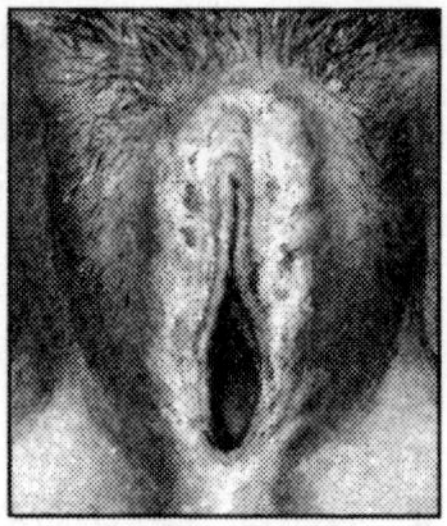

Lichen sclerosis

Symptoms: include intense itching, scratch marks or fissures extending around the anus. Fissures and scarring cause marked pain.

Diagnostic approach: Hyper-plastic vulva dystrophy, sclero-derma, vitiligo, paget's disease, vulva candidiasis and carcinoma.

Prevention

- Perineal hygiene.
- Cool sitz's bath.
- Moist soaks.
- Application of soothing solution (Burow's solution).
- Wear loose fitting clothes.
- Keep area dry and well ventilated.
- Apply petroleum jelly.
- Tropical steroid therapy.
- Surgical excision is occasionally required.

Complications: Vulva cancer, scarring and narrowing of the vaginal canal may cause hindrance to preclude intercourse. Excoriation with infection may occur.

Vulva Cancer

Cancer of the vulva generally presents an ulcer, mostly in the age group 65-70 years.

Symptoms: Itching, irritation, cracking, bleeding of the vulva on the posterior two-third of labia majus. Ulcerated lesions usually appear (known as carcinoma of the clitoris, carcinoma on leukoplakia, sarcoma of the labium and metastatic hypernephroma). Special test include biopsy of lesions or vulva and careful follow up for recurrence or additional new lesions.

Vulvar Hematoma

Swelling of one or both labia because of interstitial bleeding after blunt trauma. The disorder is caused by straddle injury, sexual abuse, rape, vaginal surgery, delivery of baby, varicose-vein of vulva, uncommonly consensual intercourse and excessive sports activities.

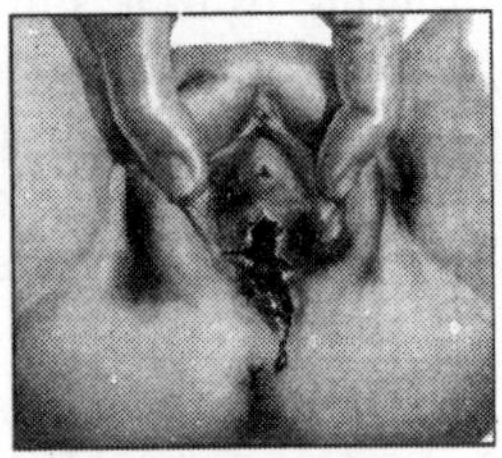

Vulvar hematoma

Symptoms: Painful swelling of one or both labia, dark blue or black discoloration of vulva and bleeding.

Diagnostic approach: Bartholin's gland, cysts or abscess, varicose veins of vulva and lympho-granuloma.

Complications: It may complicate delivery and chronic presentation before or during labor.

Vulvar Lesions and Cysts

The skin of the vulva varies similar to the skin elsewhere in the body. The tissues of vulva have close interactions with the fluids, hormones and microbes in the body. The skin of vulva contains hair follicles, sebaceous, sweat and apocrine glands. The vulva is affected by inflammatory and dermatological skin diseases, such as atopic dermatitis, intertrigo, hidradenitis suppurative, psoriasis, seborrheic dermatitis, fox-fordyce disease, fifth disease, Crohn's disease, viral infections and parasites.

Symptoms: Irritation, vaginal secretions, fleshy tumor of vulva, recurrent urinary loss, irritation when in contact with soaps, perfumes, fabric softeners and infestation by pinworms.

Diagnostic approach: Folliculitis and furunculosis, herpes genitalia, psoriasis, senile atrophy, leukoplakia, varicose veins, elephantiasis, diabetic vulvitis, trichomoniasis, bartholin's disease, sebaceous cysts and canal disorders. There are as many as 18 types of vulva lesions and cysts usually seen in women.

Cystocele/Urethrocele

Loss of support for the anterior vagina rupture, prolapse of urethra (urethrocele) or bladder (cystocele) are the usual cause of this vaginal disease. About 10-15% women are usually seen suffering from it, out of which 30-40% cases pertain to after menopause. The possible complications found are ureteral drainage, urinary-tract infections, vaginal ulceration, bleeding, frequent infection and pain.

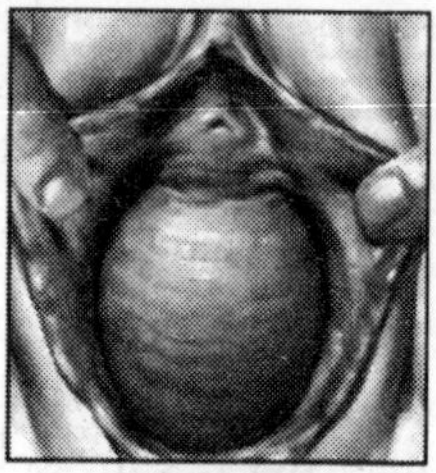

Cystocele

Causes

- Loss of normal tissue integrity or tissue disruption as a result of childbirth.
- Obstetric injury, surgery etc.

Risk factors: include obesity, chronic cough, smoking, intrinsic tissue weakness or atrophic changes caused by estrogen loss.

Diagnostic approach: include the following:

- Pelvic pressure or heaviness.
- Stress.
- Urinary recurrent infections.
- Bulging of tissue at vaginal opening.
- Formation of cyst, tumor or abscess.
- Garner's duct cyst, anterior enterocele, uterine prolapse and hernias.

How to prevent?: When urethrocele or cystocele is present, a downward movement of the vaginal wall towards the introitus is felt. Weight reduction, treatment of cough if present, topical estrogen replacement therapy, pessary therapy, pelvic muscle exercises and surgical repairs are recommended. Avoid heavy lifting. Have a periodical check on vaginal bleeding and breast cancer.

Enterocele

This disorder occurs due to deep loss of support for the apex of the vagina and rupture or prolapse of the vaginal wall or vaginal hysterectomy.

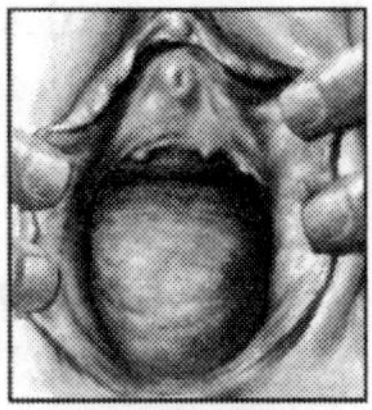

Entrocele

Diagnostic approach: The disease is diagnosed by urethral diverticulum, cystocele, rectocele, vaginal prolapse and gartner's duct cyst.

How to prevent?: It can be prevented by weight reduction and surgical repair.

Rectocele

Failure of the normal support mechanism between the rectum and the vagina results in this disorder usually in post-menopausal period.

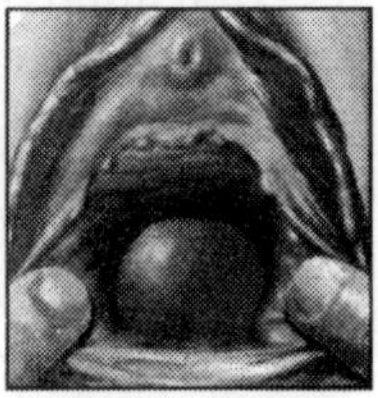

Rectocele

Causes: It is generally caused by the:

- Loss of normal tissue integrity as a result of childbirth.
- Obstetric injury and surgical repair.

Symptoms: Bulging of the posterior vaginal wall and difficulty in passing stool.

Diagnostic approach: Enterocele, rectovaginal hematoma, rectal cancer and vaginal cyst after episiotomy.

How to prevent?: Weight reduction, treatment of chronic cough (if present), systemic estrogen replacement, pessary therapy, pelvic muscle exercises and surgical repair are some of measures to relieve this disorder. Avoid lifting weight and straining. Vaginal delivery and pregnancy may cause or contribute to worsening of pelvic support problems.

Sarcoma Botryoides

A form of sarcoma is generally seen in the vagina among teenage girls. These tumors may arise from the cervix and cause bleeding and vaginal mass, which resemble a cluster of grapes, urethral prolapse, vaginal polyp and endo-dermal sinus tumor. The treatment may be done by surgical excision combined with multi-agent chemotherapy.

Vaginal Cysts

Cystic masses in the vaginal wall may arise from either congenital or acquired processes generally from adolescence to middle reproductive years.

Causes: Factors like episiotomy or obstetric laceration and gynecological surgery are usually responsible for this disorder. Difficulty with tampon insertion or retention and cystic mass lesion (ranging from 1 to 5 cm.) are generally found in the lateral vaginal wall.

Diagnostic approach: include urethal diverticulum, cystocele, rectocele, bartholin's gland, cysts, vaginal adenosis, vaginal endometriosis, vaginal fibromyoma and perirectal abscess.

How to prevent?: Surgical excision, vaginal dryness, loss of normal vaginal moisture resulting in irritation, itching or pain when indulged in sexual intercourse are some of the reasons caused by this disorder due to infection or loss of estrogen stimulation.

Symptoms: include the following:

- Inadequate or inappropriate sexual stimulation.
- Sexual phobia or pain commonly in menopausal women.
- Vaginal dryness, itching or irritation.
- Dry, inflamed vaginal tissues are usually seen on pelvic examination.

Prevention:

- Topical moisturizing and lubrication of vagina.
- Estrogen replacement therapy.
- Counseling regarding sexuality (fore-play).
- Application of water-soluble lubricants and coital techniques.

Complications: include vaginal lacerations, vaginal infections, vulva excoriations and sexual dysfunction.

Vaginal Lacerations

Lacerations of vaginal wall are often the result of sexual trauma generally in reproductive age caused by sexual intercourse, injury, sexual assault, penetration by foreign objects which cause virginity, vaginisus, postpartum, postmenopausal vaginal atrophy, hysterectomy and use of alcohol and drugs.

Symptoms: include vaginal bleeding, acute pain during intercourse and persistent pain after intercourse.

Diagnostic approach: include cervical polyp, menstrual bleeding, threatened abortion, episiotomy and vaginal surgery.

How to preven?: Have pelvic rest and avoid sex until healing occurs.

Vaginal Prolapse

Loss of normal support mechanism resulting in vaginal walls pour down in vaginal canal. In extreme cases, vagina becomes everted beyond the vulva outside the body.

Causes: Causes because of childbirth, surgery, intra-abdominal pressure, chronic cough, heavy lifting, intrinsic tissue weakness and atrophic changes resulting from estrogen loss which cause conditions such as urinary incontinence, pelvic pain, damage to the rectum dyspareunia, inter-menstrual or post menopausal bleeding, cystocele, urethrocele, rectocele, bartholin cyst, vaginal cyst or tumor.

How to treat?: The treatment includes pessary therapy, surgical repair and estrogen replacement therapy. Avoid estrogen therapy if undiagnosed vaginal bleeding exists.

Vaginitis Atrophy

Caused by the loss of ovarian steroids which grips post-meno pausal women (age above 50), caused as a result of surgery, chemotherapy, radiation and natural cessation of ovarian function.

Symptoms: include vaginal dryness, burning and itching, pain or bleeding during sexual intercourse.

Diagnostic approach: Vaginal infection, vulvitis, vaginitis, hot flushes and sleep disturbance.

How to prevent?: Use of vaginal moisturizer and lubricant (when involved in intercourse) is recommended. Oral or injectable estrogens are the effective treatment for this disorder.

Bacterial Vaginitis

A vaginal infection caused by an overgrowth of normal or pathogenic bacteria, which cause irritation and inflammation in females between the age 15 to 50 years.

Symptoms: include vulva burning or irritation, increased vaginal discharge, white blood cells, dysuria, dyspareunia, edema or erythema of the vulva.

Risk factors: include suffering from diabetes, pregnancy, smoking, excess number of sex partners, use of vaginal contraceptives, oral sex, faulty menstruation and lack of hygiene.

How to prevent?

- Perineal hygiene.
- Medical therapy (oral and topical). Tetracycline 250-500 mg and topical triple sulpha cream is recommended strictly on the advice of a doctor.

Complications: Cystitis (frequent urination), pelvic pain, infertility, cervicitis, infection of Bartholin's glands, increased risk of upper genital tract infections, risk of premature delivery and premature rupture of the membranes are possible complications.

Vaginitis Monitial

A vaginal infection caused by fungi found in the air or common inhabitants of the vagina, rectum and mouth usually occur in females between 15 to 50 years. Various risk factors are stress, use of antibiotics, pregnancy, diabetes, mental depression, warm and moist environment.

Diagnostiv approach: include bacterial vaginitis, bacterial vaginosis, vaginal infection, allergic vulvitis, atrophic vulvitis, vulva dermatosis and pinworms.

How to prevent?:

- Perineal hygiene to keep clean and dry.
- Avoiding tight or synthetic undergarment.
- Avoiding topical steroid preparations.

Vaginal Infection

Common in females between age 15 to 50 caused by several factors such as multiple sexual partners, vaginal pH (less acid in blood and semen).

Symptoms

- Vulva itching or burning.
- Thin yellow and green odor vaginal discharge.
- Infection of the cervix and upper vagina.
- Dysuria, dyspareunia and edema of the vulva.

Complications: include sexually transmitted infections, pelvic inflammation, cystitis, infertility and pelvic pain.

How to prevent?: An immediate medical treatment is must.

Abnormal Pap Smear Intra Epithelia Lesion

Causes carcinoma in cervical generally in reproductive age. The main risk factors are exposure to HPV and STD.

Symptoms: include vaginitis, cervicitis, cervical dysplasia and invasive carcinoma of cervix.

How to prevent?: The specific measures to meet this disease may be followed by serial Pap smears at 4 to 6 month intervals for two years. However, avoid HPV infection.

Carcinoma in Cervix

Usually, it occurs in the age early 30s. Risk factors causing carcinoma include infection by EPV, herpes virus, early sexual activity, multiple sexual partners, smoking, oral contraception and early childbearing.

Symptoms: Asymptomatic, abnormal cervical cytology and abnormal colposcopy are some of prominent signs and symptoms.

How to prevent?: Standard hysterectomy, ablative therapy, cryosurgery (Co_2 laser therapy) and radical electro-cautery. However, there is no effect on pregnancy, but the presence of pregnancy complicates both the diagnosis and treatment.

Cervical Cancer and Carcinoma

Almost all cancers of cervix are carcinoma. The disease is common in women between the age of 40 to 60. The prominent causes include early sexual activity, multiple sex partners and presence of sexually transmitted viral infections.

Symptoms

- Abnormal Pap smear.
- Vaginal bleeding.
- Dark vaginal discharge.
- Post-coital bleeding.
- Back pain.
- Loss of appetite.
- Weight loss.
- Bleeding lesion.
- Inguinal lymph nodes.
- Swelling of legs.
- Pleural effusion.

Diagnostic approach: Cervical eversion, cervical erosion, cervi-cal polyp and cysts.

How to prevent?: Chemotherapy treatment is usually given. 90% of recurrences usually occur in the first five years. There are generally three stages of this disease.

Cervical Erosion

Loss of the epithelial surface on the vaginal portion of the cervix, usually caused by traumatic reasons such as fingernails, sexual appliances, diaphragm, pessary or other instrumentation.

Symptoms

- Irregularly shaped lesions.
- Bleeding tissue.
- Post-coital spotting.
- Increased discharge.

Diagnostic approach: include ectopy (cervical eversion), herpes simplex, cervicitis, syphilis (VD), cervical polyp, carcinoma under the epithelium surface and chronic cervicitis.

Cervical Polyps

Fleshy tumors arising from the cells of the cervix (endo-cervical canal or the ecto-cervix) generally in the age group of 40 to 50 in women having history of cervical infections and use of oral contraceptives, resulting in frequent inflammation.

Symptoms: Asymptomatic, inter-menstrual spotting, post-coital spotting and a smooth, soft, reddish purple to cherry red friable mass up to 4 cm size at the cervix, which bleed on slight touch.

Diagnostic approach: Cervical cancer, cervical eversion, cervical erosion, intra-menstrual bleed-ing, post-coital bleeding and leucorrhoea (white vaginal discharge).

How to prevent?: Consult a doctor immediately. A Pap smear test is essential.

Cervical Stenosis

This may occur in the region of internal cervical between the age of 30 to 70 years. It comprises of narrowing of the cervical canal, which may result in complete or partial obstruction. The damage is caused by cone-biopsy, electro-cautery, cryo-cautery, radiation, infection, neoplasia, atrophy and sometimes due to congenital reasons.

Symptoms: include pre-menopausal dysmenorrhea, abnormal bleeding, amenorrhoea, infertility, uterine enlargement, post-menopausal asymptomatic.

Risk factors: This may result in endo-cervical cancer, endometrial cancer, uterine leiomyometa, endometriosis, chronic pelvic pain and infertility. The disorders can be diagnosed by physical examination surrounding the endo-cervical canal and ultra-sonography.

How to treat?:

- Symptomatic therapy. Use of non-steroidal anti-inflammatory drugs and dilation of the cervix under ultrasound guidance.

Cervicitis

Acute or chronic inflammation of the endo-cervical glands or ecto-cervix, usually during reproductive age and sometimes in adolescents (early 20s). It is sometimes caused by exposure to sexually transmissible infections, multiple sexual partners, postpartum period, herpes simplex and trichomones vaginalis.

Symptoms: include asymptomatic, a yellow discharge with white blood cells, cervical erythema or edema, vaginitis, cervical neoplasia, cervical metaplasia, cervical erosion, cervical eversion, post-coital bleeding, premature rupture of membrane in pregnancy, pelvic inflammation, dyspareunia, premature labor and pre-maturity.

Diagnostic approach: Monoclonal antibody testing and colposcopy.

Prevention: Avoid doxycycline drug. Treatment should be strictly as per doctor's advice.

Nabothian Cysts

Retention cysts, which include white to blue to yellow bumps of size ranging from 3 mm. to 3 cm., usually occur close to a gland opening sometimes during reproductive age and cause chronic inflammations of the cervix, followed by mucus-filled cysts and sometimes may cause cervical cancer. Get pelvic examination immediately as soon as distortion or enlargement of the cervix is observed.

The Reproductive Organs in Human Body

The reproductive system of body-a combined genito-urinary system is severely affected. However, the reproductive organs are different in a male and female although their prime functions are similar. The organs of the urinary system are also similar in the male and female and their functions contribute to the balance of water level within the body. There are five functions of the urinary system, which include filtration, re-absorption, production, excretion and regulation. The genito-urinary system consists of the male and female genitalia, the kidneys, bladder, ureter tubes (leading from the kidneys to the bladder) and a urethra tube (leading from the bladder to the outside of body). Female genitalia include the ovaries, the fallopian tubes, the uterus and the vagina. The urethra is approximately 4 cm. in length in a woman and about 20 cm. long in a man. Ureter tubes are two long, narrow muscular tubes having approximately 25 cm. length and 3 mm. width. There are bean shaped two kidneys situated either side of the spine at waistline. The bladder is a pear shaped oval organ as it fills with urine.

The testes in males and ovaries in females (known as the sex glands) are responsible for producing male and female sex hormones. The testes produce male hormones known as androgens and testosterone, whereas ovaries produce the female hormones oestrogen and progesterone. In male and female these hormones are responsible for producing the sexual characteristics with the onset of puberty *i.e.* the development of spasm, the change of voice and growth of facial hair etc. In females, they are responsible for the start of menstrual cycle, the pregnancy and eventually the menopause (when the ovaries stop developments). The blood enters the kidneys and passes some substances, which include water, minerals, glucose, amino acid and vitamins absorbed into the blood from the digestive system. Urea and uric acid are formed in the liver. The other substances include hormones, drugs and toxins. The production of the urine depends upon the consumption of water and loss of water through sweating.

Role of Kidneys

There are two, narrow muscular tubes leading from kidney to the bladder having 25 cm. length and 3 mm width. There are two been-shaped kidneys situated either side of the spine. The bladder is pear shaped, which becomes oval in shape when it fills with urine. The blood enters the kidneys via renal artery. Common conditions affecting the genito-urinary system are amenorrhoea (absence or abnormal menstruation) caused by hormonal imbalance, cancer (in breast, ovary, bladder & Uterus), cystitis (inflammation of the bladder accompanied by pain in lower abdomen), dysmenorrhoea (painful period caused by hormone imbalance), fibroids (developing in the uterus), mastitis (tender lumps present in the breasts), thrush (an infection of vagina causing itchiness and urethritis (inflammation of the urethra).

Common condition affecting the genito-urinary system are briefly described as below:

Amenorrhoea: absence or abnormal stoppage of menstruation.

Cancer: the development of malignant cells. The common cancers include the breast, ovarian, bladder and uterus.

Cervical erosion: disorder at the lining of neck of the womb accompanied by a slightly discharge.

Cystitis: inflammation of the bladder resulting in frequent urge to pass urine.

Dysmenorrhoea: painful period caused by hormone imbalance.

Ectopic pregnancy: occurs when the fertilized ovum develops outside of the uterus usually in the fallopian tubes.

Endometriosis: cells from the uterus formed in fallopian tubes or ovaries causing pain during menstruation.

Fibroids: non-cancerous growth developing in the uterus.

Mastitis: tender lumps present in the breasts.

Nephritis: inflammation of glomerulus inside the kidneys.

Prostatitis: inflammation of the prostate gland.

Pyelonephritis: inflammation of the kidneys due to an infection.

Sexually transmitted diseases (STD): acquired through sexual contact.

Thrush: an infection of vagina causing itchiness and discharge.

Urethritis: inflammation of the urethra.

NATURE CURE FOR THE GENITO-URINARY AND REPRODUCTION ORGANS

Kidney Disorder

Disorder, symptoms, causes and cure include renal colic, pain in the kidneys and inflammation. Collect two parts black cumin seeds, one part 'ajwain' and a pinch of black salt. Ground together and mix with a little vinegar taken in a little quantity every hour till relief is obtained. Alternatively, as for local applications, two egg yolks should be beaten in a copper vessel. Add to it turmeric and little quantity of water. It should be warmed and applied as a poultice to the region of kidneys.

Dysurea

It includes scanty discharge, pain while urinating, pain in the penis (in men) and ovaries (in women), blood while urinating, heaviness in kidneys and urge for frequent urination.

Cystitis

An inflammation of the bladder and urethra, and enlargement of the prostate gland within the pelvis.

Hyperacidity (**excessive amount of acid present in urine**):

Desist from eating beans and pulses. Avoid eating green vegetable e.g. spinach, tomatoes and ladyfinger. Constipation should be avoided. Most important drug used for this condition is 'shilajit', followed by the compounded preparations 'chandraprabha vati.'

Kidney Stones

Severe pain in kidneys and the bladder due to infection. Drink every morning and evening radish juice mixed with pearl ash (jawakhar) for few days to break the stones and expel out with urine.

Scalding Urine

A burning sensation when urination usually due to hyperacidity or malfunctioning of kidneys. Boil 250 gm. milk with an equal quantity of water and drink. Alternatively, grind 50 gm. of 'rattanjot booti' with 5 grains of pepper in water. Strain and drink it after mixing to it sugar candy.

Polyuria

Excess of urine (amount increases in winter and decreases in summer) due to excessive intake of liquids or failure of sweat glands to function. Eat any confection. A confection from black sesame seeds can be prepared by mixing 4 parts seeds, 2 parts 'ajwain' and 6 parts of jaggery taken twice daily in the morning and evening. Alternatively, the kernel of tamarind seeds and leaves of horseradish should be ground together in water and apply lukewarm mixture to the pelvic region.

Haematuria

Presence of blood in urine. The symptoms include smoky or brownish color urine

Stone in Kidneys, Scratched Urethra:

Mix a pinch of turmeric (haldi) in 100 gm. dried 'amla'. Crush and steep overnight in water. The water should be given to the patient in the morning.

Urinary Calculi Pain

Formation of stone in kidneys or ureter. Consult doctor for the treatment.

Infection or chronic inflammation of the womb following child bearing and a venereal disease:

Exercise the body by running, playing and household work. Take every morning a dose of dried and powdered bark of the Mulsari (Minusops Elengi) tree and mix an equal quantity of brown sugar with water (consult a doctor also). Avoid fried, spicy food and pickles. Late nights and sexual intercourse are taboo during the course of disease.

Nacturnal Seminal Discharge

Mental tension is the main cause of this trouble. A hot and cold Hip Bath is recommended.

Emission During Sleep

Sexy TV programmes/adult movies usually cause this problem. Avoid these.

Threatened Spotting

A drop or two of blood ooze from the uterus, usually in the morning. Avoid heavy physical exercise or work load. Take 'amla' wrapped in silver foil daily during pregnancy to save pregnancy. Have bed rest as far as possible.

Phospaturia

A whitish liquid follows urination. Sexual weakness or disorder is the prominent cause of this trouble. Defective digestion can give rise to emission of phosphates. Tone up the digestive processes the naturopathic way.

Apprehension of Miscarriage

Symptoms include pain or the slightest bleeding. Excess burden or mental tension by the expectant mothers is one of the prominent cause. The foot of the bed should be kept raised a couple of inches for a few hours in the day when the patient is on bed rest. A wet pack should be placed on the pubes for an hour in the morning and evening. The process should be repeated on the dates the pregnant woman would have had her period. After the third month the apprehension of a miscarriage will recede.

Vaginitis

Blood stained discharge, local infection, burning, itching, heavy yellowish discharge are the symptoms of this disorder. Take bed rest and have consultation with a doctor.

Tumor or Sore in Uterus

Lesions in uterus, heavy pain, infection are main symptoms. A vaginal douche with water in which leaves of 'neem' plant are boiled. Fomentation of lower abdomen and the pubes by cloth pad is an natural treatment.

Dysmenorrhoea

Weakness and pain in groin proceeding menses due to irritation and malfunctioning of ovaries. Consult your doctor.

Metritis: Inflammation of uterus and internal Inflammation. Consult your doctor for suitable treatment.

Sterility: Unable to conceive due to malfunctioning of reproductive organs. Have treatment of anemia and nutritious diet.

Method of Family Planning

After marriage a woman should know how to plan an ideal family. She should also be familiar with the various methods of family planning.

- **Condom for men:** Made of latex rubber, the condom is used by the male partner, in which the semen collects and does not discharge freely into the vagina. It can be removed from the male organ after ejaculation with the semen inside.
- **Condom for women:** Loose fitting polyurethane sheath about 15 cm. long, which covers the vagina and external genitalia and should be used prior to coitus.
- **Diaphragm:** Rubber lid with a spring margin that closes the cervix. Diaphragm is pushed into the vagina and rotated in a place to cover the uterine mouth. The diaphragm is slipped out 5 to 6 hours after intercourse. Diaphragm combined with a spermicidal cream is more effective.

- **Cervical cap:** Thimble like fine rubber cap to be pushed into the vagina to cover the cervix, and can be left inside for three months at a time. This is not a foolproof method and sometimes fails.
- **Sponges and pessaries:** Old method of family planning in which the sponge covers the uterine mouth. Sometimes, it may fail.
- **Vaginal tablets and creams:** Contain medicines that are lethal to the sperms. They are used half an hour before sexual relationship, but the failure rate is high and sometimes before chemical action a few sperms may enter the uterus.
- **Intra-uterine devices:** Synthetic spiral or T shaped tiny gadget that is fitted into the uterus. The device retards passage of sperms into the uterus and prevents pregnancy. There are various types like the spiral loop, copper T and nova T with silver. Sometimes, there is chance when the device slips and the woman become pregnant. Frequent bleeding, heavy periods and infection are some of the common problems in women fitted with this device.
- **Intra-cervical device:** Similar to intra-uterine device but have many modifications. They lie in the cervical canal and not inside the uterus.
- **Vaginal rings:** These have chemical lethal to the sperms or contain various hormones that suppress ovulation and thus stop conception.
- **Oral contraceptives:** The pills containing the female sex hormones known as progesterone and estrogen in a specific proportion. When taken regularly prevents conception by stopping ovulation.
- **Natural contraceptive methods:** Coitus interruptus, rhythm method and fully lactating the baby as long as possible are the natural methods for the family planning. Coitus interruptus is an unreliable method when the sex act is interrupted at the time of male ejaculation when the organ is withdrawn out of vagina and, the semen is discharged out. This is not a totally safe method. In Rhythm method, the ovum is capable of getting fertilized for 2 or 3 days after its liberation. The best natural method is to avoid sex during ovulation.

Common Disorders During Pregnancy

- Piles
  1. Develop due to faulty eating and poor bowel habits.
  2. Cause as a result of constipation.
  3. Taking highly spiced food.

- Blood Pressure
  1. Due to salt and water retention in the body.
  2. As a result of hormonal load in the body.
  3. Kidneys disorders.
- Pain in lower belly
  1. Causes due to infection in pelvic organs.
- White vaginal discharge
  1. Discharge with itching, burning due to infection.
  2. Erosion of the cervix.
- Skin problems
  1. Due to the action of sex hormones.
  2. Dark spots on the face and the neck and pigmented lines appear on abdomen and thighs.
- Pregnancy Toxemia
  1. Causes sudden increase in weight, swelling of the body.
  2. Rise in blood pressure.
  3. Appearance of albumin in urine.
- Rh Factor in blood
  1. Affects the baby, which could be born jaundiced.
- Breast inflammation
  1. Common disorder in which woman loses the taste of her mouth.
  2. Inflammation passes towards the throat.
- Stomach pain
  1. Due to increased weight of the embryo.
- Morning sickness
  1. Causes vomiting sensation, which subsides by afternoon and in some cases continue till evening.
- Constipation
  1. Due to bowels not working properly.
- Gastritis
  1. Woman starts feeling inflammation in breast and throat.
  2. Frequent vomiting.
- Premature separation of placenta
  1. The worst disease during pregnancy.
  2. The vaginal orifice starts widening and placenta gets burst.
  3. Sometimes hemorrhage.

- Anemia
  1. The pregnant women suffer from the shortage of blood from 12th to 32nd week.
  2. The embryo extracts iron and blood from the body.
- Dyspepsia—or indigestion
  1. A fundamental digestive disorder in which a woman does not feel hungry and food taken is not digested properly.
  2. Cause belching.
- Liver pain
  1. Causes due to accumulation of acidity in gallbladder.
- Diarrhea
  1. Due to careless digestive system.
- Cramps
  1. The trouble starts usually in the fourth month and the pain shoots up in the night.
  2. It develops due to deficiency of minerals and vitamins in the body.
- Obstruction in urine
  1. Causes due to shifting of uterus from its place.
  2. Another reason which also obstruct the normal flow of urine due to puffing of air in urinary bladder or in urethra.
  3. Due to accumulation of blood or pus or swelling in the urethra.
- Itching, pain in vagina
  1. Causes due to some scratch or friction in vagina.
  2. Due to semen remaining in the vagina after the sex.
- Hydramnios
  1. Develops in the fifth or sixth month of pregnancy in which swelling develops in the membranes.
  2. The placenta orifice gets closed due to inflammation.
- Insomnia
  1. Women, generally exhaust their strength and energy in feeding the embryo.
  2. Cause severe weakness and loss of sleep.
  3. Constant fever and loss of appetite appear.
- Heart trouble

  In case the heart is too weak, it is better to have abortion after consulting the doctor.

- Threatened abortion
  1. A drop or two of blood comes out of uterus.
  2. Take complete bed rest and immediately consult a doctor.
- Pain in breasts
  1. Causes due to the veins in the breast become engorged.
  2. Avoid pain killers in such conditions.
- Headache

  Often due to constipation. A milk laxative would relieve the trouble.
- Frequent Urination
  1. No medication is required if the condition is found near the time of labor.
  2. In case of tendency in the beginning of the pregnancy, equal part of milk and water may be drunk.
- Retention of urine

  Due to the weight of fetus in the uterus presses upon the urethra.
- Vulvular pruritis
  1. Causes intense itching in the genital tract.
  2. Avoid spices and condiments.
  3. A warm water douche should be given in the genital tract.
- Jaundice

  Common among pregnant women. It is an ailment of liver. All fats, condiments and acidic substances should be banned.

Feeding mothers

In order to breast feed your baby successfully, you should be prepared for it mentally as well as physically. It is also useful to seek the guidance of an experienced mother who has successfully breast-fed baby, as practical knowledge is the best guide.

- Eat more than the normal diet during pregnancy. The rough rule is to eat equal to one extra meal in a day, this will help you build enough stores to be used when you start breastfeeding your baby.
- Pregnant women should eat things, which are rich in iron and help in producing blood to prevent anemia.
- A pregnant woman should avoid physical tiredness, especially during last three months of pregnancy and a nap or rest in the afternoon is also advisable during the last three months of pregnancy.

- Lot of care is required for the breasts during pregnancy, these become heavy during this period due to hormones in preparation for feeding the baby to be born. There is no need to worry about this change.
- Support the breasts with appropriate bras. There should be right selection of bras as during this period of pregnancy breast tend to grow and the bras should allow for breast enlargement. This would help prevent the breasts from being compressed during sleep and they would not hurt.
- Also learn to 'express' the breasts as it is a regular practice to release tension in the breasts caused by excess milk.
- Prevent engorgement of the breasts to ensure their complete and frequent emptying. Make sure to empty the breasts after a feed. If you feel too full and experience tension, it is advisable to press your areola so that the milk comes out.
- Another way of draining your milk is to splash some water on your breast so that milk comes out due to stimulus. In case of engorgement of breasts, it causes pain and these are hot to touch. As a result of engorgement, breastfeeding becomes very painful. Because of swelling caused by the accumulation of milk, the milk production may be reduced. If not treated immediately, this can lead to failure of breast-feeding. It is always advisable to express some breast milk before feeding the baby.
- Hot and cold compresses are very useful for the relief of engorgement. For the relief of engorgement of breasts, use breast pump.
- Taking care of nipples during pregnancy and feeding the baby is equally important as poor shape of nipple would interfere with feeding. There is no need to worry if the nipples stick out. However, if the nipples appear flat or inverted then it is advised to press the areola between the thumb and the finger to encourage the nipple to out. If the nipples stick out it is unlikely that the baby will have any difficulty in suckling.
- There is no need to apply cream or any ointment to your nipples nor is it necessary to wash them with soap. Do not remove secretions since they protect the nipples.
- Many ladies usually ask that their husband like to suck at their breasts. It is to advise them that there is no need to discourage,

this is a natural and helpful exercise for the nipples and will not harm the shape of nipples or breasts.

Selection of Bra and Clothes

Selection of clothes during pregnancy as well as soon after the delivery is also very important. The figure and the shape of breasts as well as body depend a lot on the clothes you wear during pregnancy and lactation. Avoid wearing bras of synthetic material. It is advisable to wear cotton bras, which should be well fitting to be able to support the extra weight of breasts during pregnancy and lactation. Remember, the bra should not be so tight as to squash or compress your breasts. The pressure on breasts can produce a collapse of milk besides causing pain in breasts. The bra should always be open at the front and should be easily fastened or undone by a clip from front rather than having to struggle with them at the back. Do not try to expose the breasts for feeding by pulling a bra up and down. Some women do not prefer to wear a bra and this is alright if the breasts are small and do not need support. During lactation period, a woman needs several bras, since they are likely to be soiled often by leakage of milk. If you experience leakage of milk it is wise to keep a cotton cloth or a piece of clean diaper to soak the leakage of milk.

You wear a well supporting firm bra for at least six months after weaning to maintain good shape of your breasts. You should prefer to wear clothes, which can be undone on the front. Among several queries as regard breastfeeding from women who are going to be mothers first time, a young pregnant lady asked that breastfeeding will stop her from socializing. These feelings are not correct. If one does not worry and feels at ease to socialize and continues to breast-feed, there should be no problem. It all depends on whether a woman feels embarrassed feeding the baby in the presence of others and whether she feels awkward when the baby weeps. In case these things do not bother a woman, then she may take the baby wherever she goes and put the baby to breast anywhere. It would not even be necessary to bare the breasts in public. One can feed the baby without even getting noticed covering herself with a shawl, a towel, a sheet, saree or 'dupatta' is all that is required. Such women should wear a blouse and a bra that can be easily undone and breast-feeding is easy. If a feeding mother has to leave her baby at home then she should express her milk before going out.

Many women are shy of breastfeeding in public. This problem can be solved partly by overcoming the shyness and partly by feeding the baby discreetly in a public place. Many of working women or those who have social obligations may feel that it 'ties them down.' This is more a problem of attitude than a real one. Many women feel worried that breastfeeding say spoil the shape of their breasts and may be less acceptable by their husbands. It is untrue. Think of many women who breastfeed their babies and have a successful married life.

In some cultures, breasts are considered as an important part of a woman's sex appeal. Obviously there is much concern about losing sex appeal, should their shape change following breastfeeding. It is therefore very important to understand what is likely to happen to the breasts if the woman breastfeed her baby. The breasts enlarge because of the effect of hormones during pregnancy, in preparation for secretion of milk. The nipples also enlarge and darken during pregnancy period. They never lose this pigment subsequently. Because the milk is secreted and stored in the breasts, they may enlarge further during lactation.

Breasts do change their shape as a result of breastfeeding and in some women they may become somewhat pendulous. However, the shape of breasts can be preserved, if a woman wears well fitting bra, which support the breasts and their shape can be retained. In fact, the looks and appearance change with the passage of time and it has been observed that a better understanding and a harmonious relationship prove very helpful to be as attractive and acceptable to a husband after breastfeeding the baby as without it. It is untrue that sex appeal reduces due to breastfeeding.

Following care should be taken for breast during lactation:

- Keep your breasts and breast nipples clean and dry, this will prevent them from becoming sore and infected.
- Do not use soap to clean the nipples and areola since this may make sore and cracked.
- Do not soak the nipples in water or let them remain moist as this will lead to cracking and infection. Just wash the breasts and the nipples with water during daily bath.
- The breast may be cleaned with water to remove the traces of milk that might be sticking to them after a feed. If the milk leaks

in between the feed, then keep a clean piece of cloth or a pad in your bra cup to absorb it. Make sure that this is changed frequently. There is no need to clean other secretions from the nipples since these protect the nipples from infection. In case nipples are not soft and supple, apply some cream or oil. Remember, not to use mustard oil since it is irritating. Before starting to feed wash the cream or oil thoroughly.

- Keep your nipples and breasts dry. Exposing the nipples to the air for some time every day, is a good way to keep them clean and dry.
- Prevent the engorgement of the breasts to ensure their complete and frequent emptying specially immediately after the delivery for a few days.
- Make sure to empty the breasts after a feed. If you feel too full and experience tension, it is advisable to press your areola so that some milk comes out.
- Breast care is very important especially for feeding mothers. Breasts sag if the infant suckles while sitting or reclining in a faulty posture. For example suckling with the infant in the lap or suckling lying down is harmful for the breasts. Always let the baby suckle in a sitting position with the child in the lap and your hand under its head so as to lift it and keep its head steady.
- Press breast nipples immediately after suckling and remove the remove the remaining milk with a couple of jerks. This gives lightness, freshness and correct shape to the breasts.
- Bath the breasts with hot and cold baths simultaneously to ensure rapid blood circulation. Sprinkle hot water and then cold, four to five minutes daily for four to five times alternatively.
- Remember, to wear a well-fitting bra while exercising. Some women do not wear any bra at all. Mind, this will further spoil the shape of the bust line.
- Swimming is an ideal exercise for improving the shape of the bust, especially breaststroke or backstroke.

What to do during the first trimester of pregnancy?

- Consult your doctor every month.
- Hospitalization and intravenous glucose in a drip may be required if you are losing fluid every time you vomit after consulting doctor.

- Have frequent meals in small quantity.
- Breathe in fresh air deeply.
- Brush your teeth twice daily.
- Get 8 to 10 hours sleep during night and at least two hours rest during daytime. Due to hormonal changes one feels dizziness. Sit down with your head between knees.
- Lovemaking and sex can be continued except when there is pain in the abdomen, bleeding from the vagina or any history of miscarriage in past.
- Do not wear tight clothes.
- Avoid standing for long periods of time.
- Excess tea or coffee is harmful.
- Smoking affects the unborn child adversely.
- Avoid overexertion and long journeys.
- Avoid jerky movements.
- X-rays are very harmful especially in the first trimester.

39

DISORDERS OF RESPIRATORY SYSTEM

Respiratory System—Vital to Maintaining Life

The respiratory system is situated within the chest cavity, which is protected by the ribs. The diaphragm, a muscular partition that controls breathing, separates the chest from the abdominal region. The main input vital to maintaining life is oxygen. As a result of using this oxygen, the body produces carbon dioxide, which is released from the body as output when we breathe out. This process is known as respiration, and the system responsible for ensuring that this process works efficiently is the respiratory system. Remember, oxygen is more essential than either food or water. A man or woman may live more than 60 days without food and a few days without water, if they are deprived of oxygen, they will die in a few minutes.

Nose breathing is healthier than mouth breathing because the air is warmed by the surface capillaries, and bacteria in the air are caught by the hairs that line the mucous membrane of the nasal passages. The rate of breathing depends on the activity of the individual. Muscular activity and energy expenditure increase the body's requirement for oxygen, as a result of increased rate of breathing. A person needs about three times more oxygen when walking than when standing.

Lungs are the spongy tissues composed of microscopic cells that take in air. These tiny air cells are enclosed in a skin-like tissue. Behind this, the fine capillaries of the vascular system are found. During inhalation, oxygen is absorbed into the blood. The cycle of breathing *i.e.* an exchange of gases is repeated many thousands of times, a day and night and is vital to the life of every individual cell, tissue, organ and system of the body. The respiratory system can be divided up into two main groups:

Upper Respiratory Tract Consisting of:

Nose—made up of the nasal bone and turbinate bones.
Sinuses—the air spaces in the nasal bones.
Pharynx—nasal cavity leads to back of the throat.
Larynx—passageway leads to upper throat.

Lower Respiratory Tract Consisting of:

Trachea—known as windpipe.
Bronchi—which provide a passageway for air to both lungs.
Lungs—soft, spongy, balloon-like structures on either side of the heart within the thorax. The thorax protects the lower respiratory tract and consists of:

- 12 pairs of ribs creating a cage like structure.
- 12 thoracic vertebrae providing connection at the back.
- The sternum providing connection at the front.

Breathing Process

Breathing can be defined as the movement of air in and out of the lungs by inspiration or inhalation and expiration or exhalation.

Inspiration (breathing in)

- Diaphragm contracts pushing abdominal cavity down.
- Inter-costal muscles contract.
- Ribs are pulled up and out.
- Thoracic cavity enlarges.
- The pressure in the lungs decreases.
- The pressure of the incoming air increases.
- Air rushes into the lungs.
- Lungs expand as they fill with air.

Expiration (breathing out)

- Diaphragm relaxes and returns to dome shape.
- Inter-costal muscles relax.
- Ribs return to normal position.

- Thoracic cavity returns to original shape.
- The pressure in the lungs increases.
- The pressure of the air outside decreases.
- The air is able to flow out of lungs.
- Elastic recoil of lungs helps to force air out.
- Contraction of the abdominal muscles will aid forced expiration by pushing the organs of the lower trunk up so increasing the force of the air out of the body.

Common Conditions affecting the Respiratory System

- **Asthma**: difficulty in breathing.
- **Adenoid enlarged**: obstruction in airflow from the nose to throat.
- **Bronchitis**: inflammation of the lining of the bronchi.
- **Common cold**: contagious viral infection resulting in a sore throat and runny nose.
- **Croup**: viral infection that effect children. It is known as barking cough.
- **Emphysema**: inflammation in the lungs causing blood flow through the lungs generally in old age.
- **Glandular fever**: a viral infection, which is most common in the 15 to 22 year old age group characterized by a persistent sore throat and tonsillitis.
- **Hay-fever**: caused by an allergy to pollen. It commonly affects the nose, eyes and sinuses causing excessive sneezing, watery eyes and build-up of mucus.
- **Hyper-ventilation**: rapid deep breathing.
- **Laryngitis**—inflammation of the larynx producing loss of voice.
- **Lung cancer**—a life threatening tumors in lungs.
- **Nasal polyp**—harmless extensions of the mucous lining within the nasal cavity containing fluid.
- **Pharyngitis**—inflammation of the pharynx resulting in a sore throat.
- **Pleurisy**—inflammation of the pleura surrounding the lungs.
- **Pneumonia**—inflammation of lungs resulting in chest pain, dry cough, fever etc. May cause from either a bacterial or viral infec-tion.
- **Pneumothorax**—collapsed lung.
- **Rhinitis**—inflammation of tine mucous lining of the nasal cavity causing a blocked, runny and stuffy nose.